Unfiltered

Conflicts over Tobacco Policy and Public Health

Edited by
Eric A. Feldman
and Ronald Bayer

HARVARD UNIVERSITY PRESS

Cambridge, Massachusetts

London, England

Library of Congress Cataloging-in-Publication Data

Unfiltered : conflicts over tobacco policy and public health/ edited by Eric A. Feldman and
  Ronald Bayer.
    p. cm.
  Includes bibliographical references and index.
  ISBN 0-674-01334-4 (hardcover : alk. paper)
    1. Tobacco industry--Government policy. 2. Tobacco habit--Health aspects--Government
policy. 3. Advertising--Tobacco--Government policy. 4. Tobacco--Taxation. I. Feldman,
Eric A. II. Bayer, Ronald.

HD9130.6.U54 2004
362.29'6561--dc22

                                                              2004040621

To
Gloria and Saul
Jane and Stephanie
Alessandra, Julian, and Stephanie
for their wisdom and love

Acknowledgments

We wish to acknowledge the Robert Wood Johnson Foundation's Substance Abuse Policy Research Program for generously supporting the collaborative project that is the basis of this volume. The American Legacy Foundation provided additional support for Ronald Bayer's work. Eric Feldman received funding from the Center for Global Partnership's Abe Fellowship Program, the Japan Society for the Promotion of Science, and the University of Pennsylvania Law School. We are grateful to John Arras, Marc Galanter, Thomas Murray, Robert Rabin, and Victor Rodwin, who attended numerous project meetings and shared insights that greatly improved the quality of this book. New York University's Institute for Law and Society helped to administer the project in its early stages, the National Academy of Sciences' J. Erik Jonsson Center in Woods Hole, Massachusetts, welcomed us to its superb facility for one project meeting, and Ariane Chebel d'Appollonia, along with the staff at the American Centre of Sciences Po in Paris, generously and graciously hosted our final gathering. James Colgrove made innumerable and invaluable contributions to the research project and to this book. Harold Pollack's thoughtful comments helped us to strengthen the final manuscript, as did feedback from several anonymous reviewers. Finally, we have greatly benefited from Stephen Scher's careful and extended editorial work.

Contents

UNFILTERED

Introduction:
Liberal States, Public Health, and
the Tobacco Question

In the 1950s, scientists began to demonstrate that smoking caused cancer, heart disease, and other health problems and was responsible for millions of premature deaths. Although these findings have become orthodoxy, their policy implications have been relentlessly challenged. Powerful corporate entities have fought aggressively against regulations that would limit the tobacco industry's freedom to market its products. Governments have protected domestic tobacco cultivation and production because of their fiscal and political importance. The industry's key constituency, hundreds of millions of cigarette smokers for whom smoking was a pleasure, a habit, an addiction, and a health hazard, has defended the right to smoke. Nevertheless, by the close of the twentieth century, anti-tobacco advocates, public health officials, physicians' groups, and international organizations, separately and in concert, had succeeded in putting tobacco control on the policy agenda of every industrialized democracy. In place of political timidity there emerged a commitment to policies that affect the conduct of the tobacco industry and individual tobacco consumption, and that have major consequences for society, politics, and public health.

The essays in this volume provide a context for understanding tobacco policy in the United States and other industrialized nations. Unfiltered by preconceived assumptions, ideology, or preordained conclusions, we explore the roots and implications of the new international enthusiasm for increasingly restrictive tobacco regulation. Eight national case studies—the United States, Japan, Canada, Australia, Great Britain, France, Germany, and Denmark—plus three cross-national essays, provide rich descriptions

1

and analyses of the political, economic, and legal forces that have informed tobacco policy. Together, the essays illuminate a number of pressing questions:

- How can one explain the deep similarities and important differences in tobacco policy among countries in the industrialized world?
- Do they illustrate the triumph of public health over vested economic and political interests?
- Are they an example of the globalization of health policy?
- In those nations where the tobacco industry is primarily owned or controlled by the state, have the industry and its allies more successfully resisted tobacco-control measures than in other nations?
- How deeply do tobacco-related policies and proposals reflect cultural traditions of temperance, where they exist?
- Have the recent turbulent legal and political battles over tobacco control in the United States been foreshadowed or echoed in other places?

Beginning in the twentieth century, modern, industrializing states began to take responsibility for protecting citizens from toxic assault, often as the result of political conflict that pitted the aggrieved against powerful economic forces. In most nations, tobacco succeeded in sidestepping regulatory control by agencies charged with protecting the public from harmful products. Those who initiated the fight against tobacco sought to end that situation. Not surprisingly, the industry's effort to resist regulation and its capacity to deploy enormous resources in its own defense are the subject of a large (and growing) literature.

The tobacco industry's actions, arguments, and dissimulations are critical elements fueling the international move toward a new regime of tobacco control; they shape and shadow every chapter in this book. Yet the harms caused by tobacco are more complex than those of many other toxic threats, so the focus of this book is significantly broader than an analysis of corporate behavior. At the root of the dilemma over tobacco policy is the fact that those most harmed by tobacco are those who (because of desire, addiction, the force of convention, or social circumstances) smoke. The challenge of tobacco control is that it compels us to address a set of questions at the heart of public health policy in liberal democracies—the relationship between personal preference, individual benefit, and the common good.

Democratic governments are undoubtedly obligated to inform and educate their citizens about significant health risks, enabling them to make informed choices. Tobacco-related addiction and disease, however, raise multiple issues about the complex relationship between individual choice, individual compulsion, and public health policy. Should governments regulate individual risk-taking in the name of public health? How far can and should the state go in seeking to modify the behavior of its citizens? When should it persuade? When should it pressure? When should it prohibit?

Some see the discussion of paternalism in the context of tobacco policy as illegitimate, a tactic and subterfuge that deflects the focus from corporate malfeasance to individual behavior. We share their concern about how discussing such a controversial issue could, with the best of intentions, inadvertently serve the interest of those who market a toxic product. But their conclusion that one should abandon this conceptual challenge because the tobacco industry has sought to manipulate the debate would represent yet another triumph of corporate power over legitimate scholarly engagement, an outcome that is neither desirable nor defensible.

For Australian philosopher Robert Goodin, smoking provides a clear example of why public health policy should be grounded on paternalism.

> The first and most obvious reason we may have for wanting to restrict smoking is to prevent harms that would be done to smokers themselves by their smoking . . . We do not leave it to the discretion of consumers, however well informed, whether or not to drink grossly polluted water, ingest grossly contaminated food, or ingest grossly dangerous drugs. We simply prohibit such things on grounds of public health . . . The fundamental point is to promote the well-being of people who might otherwise be inclined to court certain sorts of diseases.[1]

Libertarian critic Jacob Sullum, in contrast, sees in American tobacco policy a dangerous paternalism that threatens individual freedom. The crusade for a smoke-free society is, he argues, "an attempt by one group of people to impose their taste and preference on another . . . Given this country's tradition of limited government . . . most Americans are not prepared to accept 'public health' as an adequate reason for joining the march."[2]

In the United States, as in the rest of the industrialized world, public health policy on smoking has moved from a weak strategy of persuasion to an increasingly robust set of restrictions. At times such policies have taken on what Kenneth Warner has described as "Puritanical" features.[3] Writing a decade ago, Robert Kagan and David Vogel noticed the international trajectory of tobacco policy. "Despite the objections of economically powerful tobacco industries and of millions of smokers . . . virtually every democratic industrialized nation has enacted laws that curtail cigarette advertising, impose new taxes on cigarettes, and prevent smoking in public places where citizens have long been accustomed to light up at will."[4] In a striking and extreme expression of this shift *The Lancet* (a British medical journal) embraced a prohibitionist position late in 2003. "If tobacco were an illegal substance, possession of cigarettes would become a crime and the number of smokers would drastically fall. Cigarette smoking is a dangerous addiction ... We call on Tony Blair's government to ban tobacco."[5]

The turn toward more forceful forms of regulation has been motivated by the perceived inadequacies of a voluntaristic approach to the single most important preventable source of morbidity and mortality in advanced industrial societies. In part, public health advocates of stricter tobacco-control strategies have justified their position with (sometimes contested) evidence of the third-party dangers of passive smoking.[6] In addition, claims about the social costs of smoking, such as health care expenditures and lost productivity, are sometimes asserted as a wedge for more restrictive policies. Equally important has been the view that the state has a duty to protect the public's health by reducing individual tobacco-related illness.

Ironically, the increasingly vigorous approach to tobacco control has become more pronounced in the past two decades, at the same time as the AIDS epidemic appeared to be making voluntarism the core of an international public health paradigm. The new paradigm rejected the idea that effective public health policy could require the infringement of individual liberty, and instead was premised on respect for individual rights as the cornerstone of public health. In the context of AIDS, it counseled that those at risk for HIV infection would be driven underground if the public health system's approach to managing the disease entailed the compromise of individual freedom. There are, of course, important differences between smoking and AIDS. AIDS is the result of a viral infection typically transmitted during sexual relations between consenting adults or by the sharing of injection equipment by drug users. The regulation of intimate sexual relations is particularly vulnerable to charges that it violates privacy and autonomy. Tobacco-related disease and death are the result of the sale of a toxic product. But AIDS and tobacco morbidity share a common feature; each is the outcome of individual behavior that balances the taking of risks with a desire for pleasure. It is that shared quality that makes the challenge posed by the voluntaristic public health perspective so relevant.

The policies and ideological justifications put forth in the campaign against tobacco, particularly those that privilege public health over "smokers' rights," rest uncomfortably with the global movement linking health and human rights that emerged in the 1990s. Recognizing that public health could provide a justification for the "derogation" of rights, the human rights movement nonetheless emphasized the protection of the individual from the state. In one of the boldest formulations of this outlook, Jonathan Mann, director of the World Health Organization's Global Program on AIDS from 1986 to 1990, asserted: "All public health policies and programs should be considered discriminatory (or otherwise burdensome on rights) until proven otherwise."[7]

It was against this broad set of tensions and considerations that we undertook a comparative study of how eight economically advanced democratic nations addressed the public health threat posed by tobacco. Over the course of eighteen months and three meetings, an international group of political scientists, sociologists, historians, legal scholars, public health experts, and ethicists considered the comparative challenges of tobacco policy in the United States, Japan, Canada, Australia, Great Britain, France, Germany, and Denmark. Each of these nations shares a broad commitment to liberal political values. Yet each has approached questions of tobacco regulation from an interestingly different perspective. We wanted to know, for example, whether the legacy of the Nazi campaign against cigarettes would temper responses in contemporary Germany; if Denmark, which rejected moralism in its AIDS polices, would be more tolerant of smoking and smokers than the United States; and whether nations such as Great Britain (with its National Health Service) and Canada (with its single-payer system of health insurance) would treat the costs of health care for smokers as a collective burden justifying intervention in individual behavior.

The countries brought together in this volume can be grouped in a number of ways. In terms of legal traditions, four are common-law states (Australia, Canada, Great Britain, and the United States), and three are civil-law states (Denmark, France, and Germany). One—Japan—is a "mixed" system. From the perspective of politics, our study covers countries with strong (France, Japan) and weak (Australia, Canada) traditions of bureaucratic control, as well as federal (Australia, Canada, Germany, the United States) and unitary (Denmark, France, Great Britain, Japan) systems. With regard to welfare-state policy, the nations range from those with grand traditions of generous state-provided health and welfare (Denmark), to those that depend upon market mechanisms for health insurance (the United States). From the viewpoint of political philosophy and ethics, there is an interesting range of beliefs and practices in these eight nations with respect to privacy, autonomy, and paternalism.

All of the countries included in this volume have confronted three key policy questions: (1) How far should controls over advertising reach? (2) Should there be extensive restrictions on smoking in public settings? (3) How might taxes on tobacco serve the public health? The way that each of these questions has been approached and answered has given shape to the national encounters with tobacco.

Controls over Advertising

Public health interventions involving warnings to those who might engage in health- or life-endangering behaviors enhance autonomy because they permit individuals to make fully informed choices. Warnings alone, however, may be insufficient to counteract the impact of advertising. It is thus not surprising that public health advocates assumed early on in the campaign against tobacco that limits or bans on advertising and promotion by tobacco companies were crucial. In considering such restrictions, it was necessary to draw distinctions between commercial "speech" and political, social, and artistic expression. In fact, every nation that we studied chose to restrict or prohibit advertising in some way. What evidence about the effectiveness of advertising was relied upon to justify restrictions? Were such restrictions aimed at the vulnerability of children, or were they more broadly focused? Did they raise concern about infringement on the freedom of expression? If so, how were such limits on freedom to be balanced against the potential health benefits of advertising restrictions?

As governments imposed restrictions or prohibitions on advertising, those seeking to transform the culture of smoking pursued counter-advertising, sometimes informed by the insights of social marketing. Their goal was to change the preferences and desires of smokers and nonsmokers alike. Although some anti-tobacco activists believed that counter-advertising efforts were a necessary antidote to decades of cigarette advertising that glamorized a deadly habit—and the evidence for the efficacy of such efforts was stronger than that for advertising restrictions[9]—others feared that the manipulative foundations of social marketing could represent a dangerous practice.[5] When and how such anti-tobacco campaigns were undertaken, and how they evolved, are questions that are addressed in each of the national studies.

Restrictions on Smoking in Public Settings

The growing restrictions on tobacco advertising and promotion were echoed in the steady expansion of places where cigarette smoking was prohibited. Long considered acceptable public behavior, smoking was with ever greater frequency viewed as an antisocial act most appropriately enjoyed in private. This transformation was rooted in the reconceptualization of smoking as an environmental health issue, which emphasized that sidestream smoke could harm nonsmoking bystanders. Zoning restrictions were initially justified in terms of protecting third parties from the threat of illness—first cancer and then heart disease. As these efforts intensified, other justifications emerged: protections against irritation, discomfort, and annoyance. Were venues for the young and ill viewed differently than bars and restaurants? Were parks and stadiums to be treated like the enclosed spaces of trains and planes? Were efforts made to restrict smoking in settings that had been conventionally viewed as part of the private domain—offices and apartments, for example? Was the delegitimation of smoking the implicit, if not explicit, goal of advocates who pressed for zoning restrictions? Did the aggressive zoning efforts of some nations serve as models for others, or were such measures viewed as negative examples of public health moralism designed to foster a prohibitionist ethos?

Taxing Cigarettes

Tobacco has long been the object of taxation. Both for reasons of morals and revenue enhancement, governments have seen such levies as appropriate. A fundamental transformation occurred when it became clear to public health officials in some nations that taxes on cigarettes, by raising prices, could affect consumption. The extent to which the elasticity of demand was affected by the addictive nature of nicotine was a matter of some dispute. But that prices could affect consumption, particularly by adolescents and others with limited disposable income, was beyond question. By the 1980s some economists began to argue that certain costs of smoking—health care expenditures and lost productivity, for example—represented negative externalities. Those costs could be internalized, they claimed, through the imposition of taxes.

The relationship between tobacco taxes, prices, and smoking presents a number of fundamental questions: Did the potential health benefits of raising cigarette prices supplement, eclipse, or supercede the issues posed by negative externalities? Were taxes collected from tobacco sales used to finance smoking prevention and treatment programs or for general revenue enhancement? Were government health officials able to take on this issue, or did the formulation of tobacco tax policy remain lodged within ministries concerned with revenue? Did the arguably regressive nature of tobacco taxes raise troubling questions of equity or confer a laudable health benefit on the disadvantaged?

* * *

Each of these issues could be the subject of an individual, cross-national comparative analysis. In this book, they emerge in the context of the peculiarities of national histories, politics, and culture, revealing a complex interplay of forces that is neither uniform nor predictable.

Children and Bystanders First: The Ethics and Politics of Tobacco Control in the United States

Ronald Bayer and James Colgrove

Among liberal democracies, the United States stands out in terms of the extent to which anti-paternalism suffuses popular and elite values and the extent to which antagonism to government regulation of the economy dominates political ideologies. These central and defining features of American political culture would have a profound influence on how America would confront the public health threat posed by tobacco. In the course of the nearly four decades that followed the publication of the first surgeon general's report on the dangers of smoking in 1964, policy making was dominated by efforts to identify innocent parties in need of protection, on whose behalf government could interfere without setting off alarms of unwarranted paternalism. This was true as attempts were made to restrict advertising, limit smoking in public settings, and impose burdensome taxes on cigarette sales.

An analysis of the public health strategies against tobacco consumption must be understood in the context of the great political and economic influence of the industry. In 1994, a study funded by the tobacco industry calculated that some 1.8 million people were employed in tobacco-related jobs, and that state and federal tax revenues from the industry totaled some $36 billion nationwide. These estimates have been disputed—subsequent studies have arrived at more modest figures—but there is no doubt that the financial impact of the industry remains substantial. In 1998, American growers produced some 1.5 billion pounds of tobacco, valued at about $2.7 billion. Both the total number of farms producing tobacco and the total number of acres devoted to tobacco cultivation have declined since the 1960s, falling in the 1990s to about 644,000 acres on 124,000 farms. Although the importance of the tobacco industry to the U.S. economy in terms of employment and tax revenue declined during the twentieth century, the industry remains a significant factor, especially in certain regions. The industry is highly concentrated geographically; fully two-thirds of all U.S.-grown tobacco comes from just two states, North Carolina and Kentucky, while another one-quarter is produced in four others, Georgia, South Carolina, Tennessee, and Virginia.[1]

The overall structure of the U.S. tobacco industry has changed little over the past fifty years, during which time six cigarette companies—American Brands, Brown & Williamson, Liggett & Myers, Lorillard, Philip Morris, and R. J. Reynolds—have controlled virtually the entire domestic cigarette market (Brown & Williamson and American Brands merged in the early 1990s). Philip Morris (which in early 2003 changed its name to Altria) is the largest player, commanding just under half the domestic market in 1996. Because of the gap between cigarette prices and production costs, the tobacco industry has historically been one of the most profitable in the country. In the 1960s all of the major cigarette companies began to diversify, acquiring or merging with businesses that produced a variety of consumer goods, and by the early 1970s none of these companies was completely dependent on tobacco revenue.[2]

First Encounters: Public Health and Smoking

The early 1950s marked a pronounced shift in the way the medical community and the general public viewed the health risks associated with tobacco products. Although physicians and researchers had conjectured since the early part of the twentieth century about possible relationships between smoking and various cancers, the tools of epidemiology were not sufficiently developed to provide conclusive scientific support for these hypotheses; in the absence of solid proof, some of the more forceful opponents of smoking were dismissed as zealots.[3] During the 1950s, however, a series of pioneering studies on the dangers of smoking were published, offering powerful evidence of a link between smoking and lung cancer, as well as other respiratory diseases. The weight of the evidence was sufficient to lead the Royal College of Physicians of London to declare in 1962 that "cigarette smoking is a cause of lung cancer and bronchitis, and probably contributes to the development of coronary heart disease."[4]

In that same year Luther Terry, U.S. Surgeon General, moved to establish a commission to examine the scientific evidence on tobacco and cancer.[5] Two years later the commission issued its landmark report. After summarizing the vast body of evidence that had accumulated in the form of animal experiments, clinical and autopsy studies, and epidemiologic data, the report outlined in terse scientific language the now-familiar list of conditions with which smoking is associated: cancer of the lung, mouth, lip, larynx, esophagus, bladder, and stomach; noncancerous respiratory diseases, especially chronic bronchitis and pulmonary emphysema; cardiovascular disease; and a miscellany of other conditions, such as peptic ulcer, amblyopia, cirrhosis of the liver, low neonatal weight, and accidental death from fire. Addressing the contentious issue of causality, the authors claimed, "The array of information from the prospective and retrospective studies of smokers and non-smokers clearly establishes an association between cigarette smoking and substantially higher death rates. . . . When coupled with the other [clinical and experimental] data, results from the epidemiologic studies can provide the basis upon which judgments of causality may be made."[6] While the report did not include specific policy recommendations, it declared that smoking was a hazard of sufficient magnitude to warrant remedial action.

In spite of more than a decade of mounting scientific evidence about the dangers of cigarettes, about half of the men and almost a third of the women in the United States smoked in 1964. How they might respond to the surgeon general's warning was far from certain. What was clear was that the tobacco industry and the political forces that it could call upon would resist efforts to bring closure to the scientific question of the dangers of tobacco. They would also seek to thwart all measures that might challenge the status of smoking in American society.

Free Speech, Commercial Speech, and the Protection of Youth

Fully prepared for the release of the surgeon general's report, the Federal Trade Commission (FTC) moved within one week to propose regulations for the labeling of cigarette packs and for the inclusion of health warnings on all tobacco advertising. Such action was required, the commission asserted, because it believed "that many current advertisements falsely state or give the false impression that smoking promotes health or physical well-being or is not a health hazard."[7]

While public opinion supported such a move—45 percent would have approved a total ban on advertising[8]—the opposition from industry was formidable. With no support from the White House, the FTC was outflanked, and when Congress passed the Cigarette Labeling and Advertising Act of 1965—which mandated the weak statement "Caution: Cigarette Smoking May Be Hazardous to Your Health"—it was widely viewed as a victory for the tobacco industry.[9] The FTC, the Federal Communications

Commission (FCC), and the states were barred for three years from act-ing to implement measures that would have sounded a greater alarm.[10]

Two years later the FTC found that the warning label had had no impact on cigarette smoking. That judgment, in turn, set the stage for the FCC to declare that efforts to counteract the malign influence of advertising might necessitate "either termination or drastic alteration of cigarette advertis-ing on radio or television and will certainly also require a vast educa-tional campaign to negate the image of cigarette smoking as harmless and satisfying."[11]

That fundamental shift was to occur as the result of the first successful expression of antismoking activism. In early 1967 John Banzhaf, who would go on to form Action on Smoking and Health (ASH), petitioned the FCC to require that the public airwaves carry antismoking statements to balance the messages conveyed by cigarette advertising.[12] In his unusual request, Banzhaf relied on the Fairness Doctrine, which the FCC had developed to require publicly licensed television and radio stations to carry responses when they had taken positions on matters of public controversy. The radical nature of Banzhaf's request is underscored by the fact that $227 million of the $312 million spent on advertising by cigarette companies in 1967 was spent on television and radio, dwarfing the $41 million spent on newspa-pers and magazines.[13]

In explaining his effort, Banzhaf—who was unable to garner support from very powerful institutions such as the American Cancer Society, the American Heart Association, and the National Tuberculosis Association—struck on a theme that would, over time, come to define the strategy of those seeking to radically limit tobacco advertising. "I was con-cerned about the use of the public airwaves to seduce young people into taking up smoking without any attempt to tell the other side of the story on television and radio."[14]

Six months after Banzhaf's application, the FCC declared that it would require FCC-licensed television and radio stations to provide, free of charge, a "significant amount of time"—not equal time—to those who sought to present the case against cigarette smoking. In so doing, the com-mission relied not only on the Fairness Doctrine, but also on the obligation of stations to serve the "public interest."[15] In making its determination, the FCC stressed that its holding was limited to cigarettes, a product that it held to be uniquely dangerous. Its decision opened the way for a remarkable series of antismoking advertisements on the airwaves.[16]

When the requirement to accept antismoking advertisements was chal-lenged in the U.S. Circuit Court of Appeals for the District of Columbia, a powerful decision by its chief judge, David Bazelon, sustained the FCC's authority. Writing in 1968 against a constitutional backdrop that accorded advertising no First Amendment protection, and taking into account the emerging understanding of the unique risks posed by cigarettes, the famously liberal Bazelon held that the antismoking advertisements would contribute to fostering the values inherent in the First Amendment. "Where, as here, one party to a debate has a financial clout and a compelling economic interest in the presentation of one side unmatched by its opponent, and where the public stake in the argument is no less than life itself, we think the purpose of rugged debate is served, not hindered, by an attempt to redress the balance."[17]

The wisdom of both the FCC decision and the court's embrace of "rugged debate" appeared to have been borne out. Although total donated time for antismoking advertisements never exceeded one-third the time devoted to cigarette advertisements, it represented approximately a $75 million subsidy to the emergent antismoking movement.[18] Most importantly, cigarette consumption dropped perceptibly.

This, then, was the context in which federal agencies began to press for more aggressive antismoking efforts. Just three months after the court of appeals had so forcefully endorsed the value of rugged debate, the FCC called for a total ban on cigarette advertisements on television and radio. The commission declared, "It would . . . appear wholly at odds with the public interest for broadcasters to present advertising promoting the consumption of the product posing this unique danger—a danger measured in terms of an epidemic of deaths and disabilities."[19] Gone were any claims about the importance of presenting both sides of an issue of public importance.

The commission's proposed rule provoked a furious controversy. Not only did political figures aligned with the tobacco industry denounce the proposed ban—a Democratic senator from North Carolina, Sam J. Ervin, Jr., called the proposal "a supreme example of bureaucratic tyranny"[20]—so, too, did the American Civil Liberties Union. But in the end, in a remarkable and revealing turn of events, the tobacco industry supported congressional action that would ban all broadcast advertising for cigarettes. That decision was certainly driven by the recognition that the mandated presence of effective anti-tobacco ads—which would disappear with the end of advertising—undermined the industry's position. Broadcasters, who stood to lose more than $200 million a year,[21] remained adamantly opposed to the move. Along with an obvious self-interest, broadcasters were motivated by a principled opposition to government intrusion on the substance of what they chose to broadcast.

In 1971 the U.S. District Court for the District of Columbia, which only three years earlier it had promoted the virtues of permitting viewers and listeners to decide about smoking in light of fierce debate, considered the constitutionality of a complete ban that would largely remove that very debate from the airways. The court not only upheld the Public Health Cigarette Smoking Act of 1969, but went one step further. "Congress," it said, "has the power to prohibit advertising of cigarettes in any media."[22] It was the lone dissent by Justice J. Skelly Wright that gave expression to the virtues of robust and unfettered debate. "The First Amendment does not protect only speech that is healthy or harmless," wrote the liberal Wright.[23]

With the end of cigarette advertising on radio and television, the tobacco industry shifted its spending to newspapers and magazines. For newspapers, the increase was 400 percent, from $14.7 million to $59.3 million, the next year. For magazines, spending doubled from $49.5 million to $98.3 million.[24] And what were the consequences? In retrospect, the judgment of the tobacco industry about its own best interests proved correct. The years of compelled antismoking advertisements had resulted in a decrease in cigarette consumption. One analysis found decreases in consumption totaling 7.2 percent during those "equal time" years, whereas the three years following the ban witnessed the largest upward trend in smoking since the surgeon general's report, with per-capita consumption rising 4.5 percent.[25] Writing in 1979, Kenneth Warner concluded that the new policy "rated high in principle but low, even negatively, in its net effect . . . The weight of the evidence seems to favor the conclusion that the ad ban was myopic policy."[26] But such conclusions appeared to have little bearing on how antismoking advocates would confront the question of advertising as they intensified their struggle against tobacco in the next years.

With cigarette consumption declining slowly—per-capita sales had dropped by 16 percent in the twenty years since the surgeon general's report[27]—and in the belief that package warnings were no match for the more than $2 billion spent annually on the promotion of cigarettes, those committed to a "smoke-free America" began in the mid-1980s to press for a total ban on cigarette advertisements.

Efforts to impose radical restrictions—perhaps even total bans—on cigarette advertising had to confront an evolving constitutional debate over the extent to which commercial speech should be afforded protection under the First Amendment. During the 1980s the Supreme Court itself pursued an uncertain path. In some cases it handed down rulings that sought to find a balance between the government's authority to regulate the sale of goods and the right to speak about such goods.[28] In a 1986 case, however, the Court also held that total prohibitions on advertising might be permissible. In a case involving restrictions on advertising for gambling, the Court declared: "It is precisely because the government could have enacted a wholesale prohibition on [casino gambling] that it is permissible . . . to take the less intrusive step of allowing the conduct but reducing the demand through restrictions on advertising."[29]

It was this very formulation—one that the Court itself would later reject—that advocates of civil liberties found so appalling. Because of the uniquely important status of speech and communication, these critics of the Court's decision asserted that while the government might prohibit some activities, including the sale of some products, it could not permit such activities and at the same time suppress the speech that would make their availability and value known.

At the end of 1985, the American Medical Association called for a total ban on cigarette advertising and promotion,[30] and in so doing joined the American Heart Association and the American Lung Association.[31] Surgeon General C. Everett Koop publicly agreed.[32]

In response to industry claims that tobacco advertising had no aggregate impact on cigarette consumption, and that the vast expenditures on advertising and promotion served only to draw smokers to particular brands or to solidify brand loyalty, opponents were scornful and incredulous. Cigarette advertising was, argued a broad coalition of health professionals and advocates, a direct contributing factor in the decisions to begin and to continue smoking. Furthermore, advertising appeared to have a profound negative impact on the willingness of newspapers and magazines to publish articles detailing the ways in which cigarette smoking affected health.[33] From this perspective, it was advertising itself that represented a threat to "true freedom of the press."[34] As such, whatever constitutional protection was afforded to commercial speech, the protection of cigarette advertising warranted no such insulation from total prohibition.[35]

Strong advocates of civil liberties were drawn to the defense of the tobacco industry when it was confronted with proposals for bans or radical restrictions on advertising, and the industry sought out such advocates to defend its position. Thus, Burt Neuborne of the New York Civil Liberties Union testified before a congressional committee on behalf of the tobacco industry. For Neuborne the issue was simple: the ban represented an unwarranted exercise of "paternalistic manipulation": "In place of faith in the individual, the proposed ban is premised on mistrust of the individual. Starkly put, the proposed ban is a vote of 'no confidence' in the capacity of ordinary Americans to judge for themselves how to react to tobacco advertising."[36]

During this time period—the mid-1980s—as anti-tobacco activists and leading health associations pressed their case against the industry, just what was understood about the role of advertising and promotion, and about the potential impact of banning these activities? In a review of the available literature—a review that was clearly sympathetic to the goal of radically transforming the patterns of smoking in the United States—the conclusions were striking in their modesty.[37] Overall, the evidence of a direct impact of advertising on consumption was termed "far from definitive," and insofar as there were positive findings, the association was "typically relatively small."[38] The authors were quick to add, however, that even small percentages could represent substantial numbers in a nation where 50 million individuals smoked. On the important and controversial question of the impact of advertising on youth, there was scant evidence. The one econometric study identified in the report suggested that the ban on television and radio advertising reduced teenage smoking by .67 percent, a figure termed "not a substantial effect."[39] While embracing the idea that all forms of advertising or promotion "may well perpetuate the use of tobacco in our country,"[40] the report was compelled to conclude that despite the position of the public health community, "the body of formal research on the question [of the relationship between advertising and promotion, and smoking by children] is not definitive."[41]

While support for an outright ban on advertising had thus gained strength in the 1980s—involving a coalition of antismoking activists, leading health associations, and legal commentators[42]—there was little evidence that such a move had the necessary political support. But it was neither the compelling logic of those committed to civil liberties nor the absence of definitive evidence about the potential public health benefits that might follow from such a prohibition that explains the failure to impose such a ban. What rendered the movement for a total ban or radical restrictions politically impotent was, instead, the combined influence of the tobacco industry, the media, and those cultural and popular institutions that benefited from tobacco promotion and support. A reframing of the issue would be required to make the call for restricting or prohibiting advertising and promotion more powerful.

That reframing gradually took shape in the 1990s as the argument for restricting advertising and promotion increasingly focused on the protection of children. Concern for tobacco's effects on the young—portrayed as innocents—was, of course, not new. But now it was to be given new salience. In particular, what fueled this shift in focus was the R. J. Reynolds tobacco company's 1988 Joe Camel campaign, whose attempt to appeal to the young was hard to ignore.

At the heart of this reorientation of the debate was a pair of linked claims, one fundamentally moral and the other empirical. Children and young adolescents, incapable of making determinations on their own behalf, needed protection from manipulation by those who sought to stimulate their desires for harmful goods. Whatever the limits of paternalism in a liberal society, the exercise of protective authority was certainly appropriate in situations involving persons below the age of consent. Since cigarette smoking, once commenced, was driven by the addictive power of nicotine, the exercise of restrictive and protective authority to prevent smoking among youth was morally justified. No one objected to laws that prohibited the purchase of cigarettes by those defined as underage. By the same token, restrictions on advertising that could stimulate this age group's desire for tobacco products were also appropriate. That such measures would indirectly impose limits on advertising and promotion viewed by adults was a price worth paying in view of the toll imposed by tobacco consumption.

Informing this moral perspective was the empirical judgment that advertising and promotion played a central role in the initiation of smoking by the young. The evidence available to support such a claim was no stronger in the early 1990s, however, than it had been in the mid-1980s. In addressing this issue, Michael Schudson, who was sympathetic to radical restrictions on the advertising of tobacco products, was compelled to acknowledge the marginal impact such measures might have. In general, he concluded, "The available econometric evidence [on the relationship between advertising and cigarette smoking] is equivocal and the kinds of materials available to produce the evidence leave much to be desired."[43]

The groundwork for the shift toward a youth-centered prevention policy was provided by the first surgeon general's report to focus on youth. The 1994 report, *Preventing Tobacco Use among Young People,* boldly asserted, "When young people no longer want to smoke, the epidemic itself will die." Among the critical tasks of public health was to counteract the "indoctrination" of the young at a moment when they were most susceptible. In this regard the report dismissed as "misguided" the debate over whether cigarette promotion "caused" young people to smoke; the report concluded, "Whether causal or not, [promotion] fosters the uptake of smoking, initiating for many a dismal and relentless chain of events."[44]

Also in 1994 the Institute of Medicine (IOM) issued its report *Growing Up Tobacco Free.*[45] Its central assumption was that "in the long run tobacco use can be most efficiently reduced through a . . . policy aimed at preventing children and adolescents from initiating tobacco use."[46] Among the IOM's recommendations was a call for severe restrictions on tobacco advertising, including the possible imposition of a total ban. With a striking absence of attention to the constitutional requirements for restricting commercial speech, the report concluded:

> Portraying a deadly addiction as a healthful and sensual experience tugs against the nation's efforts to promote a tobacco-free norm and to discourage tobacco use by children and youths. This warrants legislation restricting the features of advertising and promotion that make

tobacco use attractive to youths. The question is not "Are advertising and promotion *the* causes of youth initiation?" but rather "Does the preponderance of evidence suggest that features of advertising and promotion tend to encourage youths to smoke?" The answer is yes and this is a sufficient basis for action in the absence of a precise or definitive causal chain.[47]

In 1995 the Food and Drug Administration (FDA) embraced the strategy proposed by the IOM a year earlier. Having determined that it had the authority to regulate tobacco—a finding ultimately rejected by the U.S. Supreme Court—the agency focused its attention on protecting children. Like the IOM, the FDA saw its new, youth-centered initiative as the most promising approach to the problem of tobacco consumption. "With some 40 million smokers in this country addicted to nicotine, a ban on tobacco is not feasible . . . A more reasonable approach is to focus on the problem of smoking where it begins—in young people."[48] Nicotine addiction, asserted the FDA's director, was a "pediatric disease."

To prevent this newly diagnosed pediatric illness, the FDA's final rule,[49] issued in 1996, would have made it a federal offense to sell cigarettes to those under eighteen years of age; ended the practice of distributing free cigarettes; restricted the placement of vending machines; and imposed far-reaching restrictions on promotion and advertising. Tobacco advertisements and billboards within one thousand feet of elementary or secondary schools and public playgrounds were to be banned. With the exception of publications whose readership was primarily adult (85 percent age eighteen or over) or whose non-adult readership was, by mass media standards, comparatively small (2 million or fewer readers under eighteen), all tobacco advertising was to be restricted to the tombstone format of black text on a white background. Aware of the constitutional challenge that such proposed measures would confront, the FDA asserted that its rules would "preserve the components of advertising and labelling which can provide product information to adult smokers."[50]

For newspapers that had an institutional interest in, and principled commitment to, First Amendment values, the proposed restrictions were troublesome. The conservative *Wall Street Journal,* which was antagonistic to the regulatory state, simply asserted that "as long as tobacco remains a legal product there's no reason to make its advertising practically impossible."[51] The *Washington Post* found the proposals a "worrisome" step toward "second-guessing commercial speech."[52] The *New York Times* noted that in a city like New York, the prohibition on outdoor advertising within one thousand feet of schools would apply to about 90 percent of the city.[53]

The Supreme Court never addressed the constitutionality of the restrictions on advertising. In reviewing the FDA's proposed regulations, the Court ruled—without needing to decide any constitutional questions— that the agency had overstepped its statutory authority by attempting to regulate tobacco.

A clash over the desirability of radical restrictions on advertising took place before Congress in 1998. At that point, Congress was considering legislation to create the legal structure necessary to permit a proposed settlement between the state attorneys general and the tobacco industry (involving a payment of $368 billion in exchange for immunity from class action lawsuits) to move forward. Stepping beyond the FDA-proposed regulations, the settlement would have prohibited the use of all human images and cartoon characters in tobacco advertising, and would have banned all advertising outdoors, in enclosed stadiums, and on the Internet. Once again, a number of First Amendment advocates responded critically. While acknowledging the importance of protecting children, they challenged the imposition of restrictions that would affect adults. Whereas the First Amendment required the use of a "scalpel" when speech restrictions were to be imposed, federal authorities had employed "a hatchet."[54] Like the FDA's proposed advertising regulations, the settlement's limitations were never to be subject to constitutional review. Acrimonious political maneuvering led to the collapse both of the settlement agreement itself and of the broad legislative package being considered by Congress.

When the tobacco industry and the state attorneys general subsequently reached a Master Settlement Agreement later that same year, the bold proposals contained in the 1996 FDA regulations and the previous settlement were reduced to a more modest series of limitations. The final settlement prohibited cartoon advertising but allowed the use of human characters; it banned tobacco product billboards, ads on public transportation, and signs and placards in arenas, stadiums, and shopping malls, but permitted retailers to post signs measuring up to fourteen feet square.[55] Beyond what any of the public health advocates might have thought possible, powerful political forces, bolstered and given cover by constitutional concerns, had succeeded in undercutting the antismoking strategy of radically limiting advertising and promotion in the name of children.

The Supreme Court itself finally spoke on the issue in 2001. In *Lorillard Tobacco Company v. Reilly*,[56] the Court struck down severe restrictions, imposed by the state of Massachusetts, on billboard, storefront, and in-shop displays of tobacco products. While it rejected the argument by the tobacco industry and its allies that the protections afforded to political and expressive speech be fully extended to commercial speech, the Court did underscore its own growing discontent with government restrictions on the freedom of advertisers. Not even the unassailable goal of protecting children could serve as justification for abrogating fundamental constitutional rights.

Protecting Bystanders

At the dawn of the public health movement against tobacco, smoking was ubiquitous. Public spaces and sociability were defined by the presence of cigarettes. In public transportation, in factories and offices, in restaurants and sports stadiums, in lounges and lobbies, in university classrooms and in hospitals, people smoked. For nonsmokers the presence of smoke was a part of the social environment. While for many there was little or no annoyance, some found it irritating, and others, discomforting. For those who found tobacco smoke difficult to endure, the only solution was to withdraw from the public space into the protection afforded by privacy. Over the next three decades, a profound social transformation was to occur. What had been the mark of sociability would become the antisocial, and smoking would increasingly be restricted to private settings. Such changes in social attitudes toward, and policies regarding, public smoking were seeded in the early 1970s, propelled by public health officials and antismoking activists who drew on the first hints and suggestive evidence about the hazards that smoking posed for nonsmokers. It was a challenge shaped by the broader and emergent environmental movement, a new health consciousness, and the array of rights-based assaults on the status quo. Although the focus of attention centered on the needs of the nonsmoking bystander, the most dramatic impact would be on smokers themselves.

In an address to a coalition of organizations concerned about smoking and health in 1971, Surgeon General Jesse L. Steinfeld underscored his concern for those placed at risk by smokers—innocents who could not protect themselves. "The mother who smokes," he said, "is subjecting the unborn child to the adverse effects of tobacco[;] as a result we are losing babies and possibly handicapping babies." Just as he raised alarm about the dangers of fetal exposure, the surgeon general expressed his concern for those compelled to breathe air filled with smoke. "Nonsmokers have as much right to clean air and wholesome air as smokers have to their so-called right to smoke, which I would redefine as a 'right to pollute.'" The surgeon general then went on to propose a policy agenda that would define the goals of the antismoking movement over the next three decades. It called for a ban on smoking in all confined public spaces, such as restaurants, theaters, airplanes, trains, and buses. "It is time that we interpret the Bill of Rights for the nonsmokers as well as the smoker."[57] In 1972 the surgeon general's report on smoking identified for the first time the exposure of nonsmokers to cigarette smoke as a health hazard.[58]

The newly apprehended hazard served as a catalyst for the development of the nonsmokers' rights movement in the 1970s. Among the most prominent organizations was the evocatively named GASP—Group against Smokers' Pollution. In its first newsletter—*The Ventilator*—the call went out to nonsmokers, "the innocent victims of tobacco smoke," to assert the "right to breathe clean air." That was a right that took precedence over "the right of the smoker to enjoy a harmful habit."[59] A grassroots organization with loosely affiliated chapters that coalesced in a number of states, GASP, together with ASH (Action on Smoking and Health), the organization founded by John Banzhaf in 1967, would begin to press for policies to restrict public smoking.

The two organizations did so against the backdrop of considerable public support for such measures. As early as 1970—before the surgeon general had spoken out about harm to smokers—58 percent of the men who had never smoked and 72 percent of the women who had never smoked agreed that lighting up should be allowed in fewer public spaces. More than three-quarters of those who had never smoked felt it was "annoying to be near" someone who was smoking.[60]

Some initial successes revealed how potentially effective the nonsmokers' rights movement could be; in particular, by focusing on how smokers placed others at risk, the movement could surmount a long-standing obstacle—the accusation of paternalism. In 1973 the Civil Aeronautics Board ordered domestic airlines to provide separate seating for smokers and nonsmokers. In 1974 the Interstate Commerce Commission ruled that smoking would be restricted to the back 20 percent of seats on interstate buses.[61] Restrictions also began to be imposed at the state and local level. In 1977 Berkeley, California, became the first local community to limit smoking in restaurants and other public settings.[62]

These initial successes occurred against a backdrop of skepticism about the precise nature of the physical harm, if any, incurred by exposure to secondhand tobacco smoke. It was such skepticism that informed a 1975 editorial in the *New England Journal of Medicine*. Gary Huber, who in later years would emerge as a sharp critic of the developing public health consensus on the risks of tobacco smoke to nonsmokers, concluded that beyond the "psychogenic" impact of exposure to environmental tobacco smoke (ETS), the questions centering on the potential biological impact "remain unanswered."[63] Writing five years later, Claude L'Enfant and Barbara Liu of the National Heart, Lung and Blood Institute stated, "Generally speaking, the evidence that passive smoking in a general environment has health effects remains sparse, incomplete, and sometimes unconvincing . . . The case against smoking in the environment has often been anecdotal, based on annoyances, feelings and sometimes more objective physical reactions such as eye and nose irritation."[64]

Nevertheless, for the tobacco industry the early impact of the nonsmokers' rights movement was viewed as potentially ominous. Most dramatic was a report prepared in the late 1970s by the Roper Organization for the Tobacco Institute.[65] The report reached what were, for the industry, some very troubling conclusions. Just less than 60 percent of those surveyed believed that smoking was probably hazardous to nonsmokers. Strikingly, however, 40 percent of smokers agreed that they themselves posed a danger to bystanders. Given these data, Roper concluded that the issue was no longer "what the smoker does to himself, but what he does to others." Writing to the industry that had commissioned the study, Roper painted a stark picture. "We believe it would be difficult to overemphasize the importance of [these] finding[s], indicating as [they do] that the battle to convince the public of the dangers of passive smoking is in the process of being lost, if indeed it is not already over." This trend in public opinion posed a hazard to the very viability of the tobacco industry, concluded Roper. The industry had no alternative. It had to confront the proponents of restrictions on public smoking head-on by "developing and widely publicizing clear-cut, credible medical evidence that passive smoking is not harmful to the nonsmoker's health."

That effort was to become more difficult in the early 1980s. In 1980 a scientific paper in the New England Journal of Medicine reported that the exposure of nonsmokers to tobacco smoke reduced breathing capacity.[66] It was that study that led L'Enfant and Liu, who had characterized earlier assumptions about the risk of passive smoking as uncertain, to conclude, "Now for the first time we have a quantitative measurement of a physical change—a fact that may tip the scales in favor of the nonsmoker."[67] In 1981 two studies (one from Greece[68] and one from Japan[69]) demonstrated that nonsmoking wives exposed to smoke by their husbands' cigarette smoking were at an increased risk for lung cancer. Whatever their methodological limitations, these studies had a profound impact on shaping public perceptions and concerns.

An editorial in the New York Times captured the new mood. Writing in response to the studies of wives exposed to smoke, the Times, with obvious allusions to violent spousal abuse, titled its editorial "Smoking Your Wife to Death." The newspaper claimed that the new data "adds to the growing evidence that second-hand smoke kills. The result strengthens the case for banning smoking in public places, especially where abstainers are exposed to smoke for long periods."[70]

When the National Academy of Sciences addressed the issue of ETS in its 1981 report *Indoor Pollutants,* it provided an imprimatur to the goals set a decade earlier by the nonsmokers' rights movement. "Public policy should clearly articulate that involuntary exposure to tobacco smoke has adverse health effects and ought to be minimized or avoided where possible."[71]

The emerging scientific consensus provided antismoking forces with a weapon that they skillfully used to mobilize public opinion for greater restrictions, even in the face of fierce opposition by the tobacco industry. In 1983 a Gallup poll found that 82 percent of nonsmokers believed that smokers should refrain from smoking in their presence, and that 84 percent of nonsmokers believed smoking posed a health hazard for them—a position with which 64 percent of smokers agreed. While there was little interest in a total prohibition on smoking in the workplace and in restaurants, airplanes, trains, and hotels, there was significant support among both smokers and nonsmokers for limiting the activity to designated areas.[72]

Reflecting the shifting climate, the former secretary of the Department of Health, Education and Welfare, Joseph Califano, testified before a Senate subcommittee that cigarette smoke was "America's top contagious killer," accountable for more deaths than all of the emissions regulated by the Environmental Protection Agency (EPA). Drawing the moral lesson, he concluded, "Cigarette smoking is slow-motion suicide. It is tragic when people do it to themselves, but it is inexcusable to allow smokers to commit slow-motion murder."[73]

By 1986, forty-one states and the District of Columbia had enacted statutes that imposed restrictions on public smoking. While only 8 percent of the U.S. population resided in states with some restrictions in 1971, 80 percent lived in such states by the mid-1980s. Although the laws varied in their scope, the trend over the fifteen years since the surgeon general's 1971 call for such enactments was for progressively more stringent regulation.[74] In addition to state laws, local jurisdictions began to enact prohibitions or limitations on public smoking. By the end of 1985, eighty-nine cities and counties had done so, approximately 75 percent of which were in California—a measure of the impact of the Berkeley-based Americans for Nonsmokers' Rights.[75]

The year 1986 represented a watershed in the then fifteen-year-old struggle to impose ever stricter controls on public smoking. Both the National Academy of Sciences and the surgeon general issued critically important reports that underscored the dangers of exposing nonsmokers to tobacco smoke—and that thereby propelled the movement for broader and more restrictive public-smoking measures.

In the years following the publication of the National Academy's and surgeon general's reports, efforts to further restrict smoking intensified, as did resistance on the part of the tobacco industry. In 1987 the Department of Health and Human Services established a smoke-free environment in all of its buildings nationwide, extending protection to more than one hundred thousand federal employees. In 1988 Congress imposed a smoking ban on all U.S. domestic flights of two hours or less. Two years later the ban was extended to flights of six hours or less—in effect banning smoking on all domestic flights. Finally, by 1988, four hundred local ordinances restricting smoking had been enacted in the United States.[76]

Confronted with a movement that had widespread support, the tobacco industry sought to thwart the imposition of smoking restrictions through a number of strategies. Preeminent was the perpetuation of controversy to preclude closure of the scientific discussion. In 1988 the industry created the Center for Indoor Air Research to fund studies that would attempt to undercut the claims that ETS threatened the health of nonsmokers.[77] A second element of the industry's strategy was to transform the issue of restrictive smoking policies from one centered on potential hazards to one focused on liberty and choice. The industry thus sought to underwrite activities and publications for smokers' rights.[78] Characterizing regulatory efforts to restrict smoking and smokers as intrusive and unnecessary, the industry put forth the virtues of common sense, courtesy, and mutual respect by smokers and nonsmokers. Finally, as the industry discovered that it could not match grassroots efforts in cities and counties to restrict smoking, it supported the enactment of state statutes that preempted more restrictive legislation and regulation at the local level. "Over time," said an industry executive, "we can lose the battle over smoking restrictions as decisively in bits and pieces—at the local level—as with state or federal measures."[79]

Reflecting on the significance of what had been achieved and what still needed to be done, antismoking activists recognized that the shift to an environmental perspective had been extraordinarily effective, permitting the movement to avoid the taint of an intrusive paternalism. The executive director of Americans for Nonsmokers' Rights thus said in 1986, "We're just telling smokers to step outside, not how to save their lives."[80] And in addressing himself to other activists, Stanton Glantz—who, more than any other individual, had defined the ETS issue as crucial—underscored the strategic importance of the focus on protecting innocents. "Activists should state that they are not 'antismoker' but rather environmentalists concerned with clean air for everyone. The issue should be framed in the rhetoric of the environment, toxic chemicals and public health rather than the rhetoric of saving smokers from themselves or the cigarette companies."[81] But despite that strategic posture, Glantz's vision was broader, concerned with the toll of smoking on American society. "Although the nonsmokers' rights movement concentrates on protecting the nonsmokers rather than on urging the smoker to quit for his or her own benefit, clean indoor air legislation reduces smoking because it undercuts the social support network for smoking by implicitly defining smoking as an anti-social act."[82]

However politically astute and effective the nonsmokers' rights movement had become, it was, in the end, remarkably dependent on the evolving scientific understanding of the burden that ETS imposed on nonsmokers. Just as the first accounts of lung cancer deaths among the wives of nonsmoking men had galvanized concern in the early 1980s, the 1986 reports by the surgeon general and National Academy of Sciences propelled the movement in the late 1980s. The relationship between antismoking activists, scientific research, and those public health institutions able to attach a powerful imprimatur to findings on the harms associated with ETS was not, however, a simple matter. The growing sentiment against cigarettes shaped both the interpretation of the data and the willingness to make necessary extrapolations and propose policy solutions. Thus, as late as 1991, legal scholar Robert Rabin, who was sympathetic to the antismoking campaign, wrote: "Since the evidence presently fails to demonstrate across a broad range of settings that sidestream smoke causes lung cancer and other diseases, the data serve only as a starting point. The question, like so many current issues of environmental risk assessment, is whether government intervention is warranted in extrapolating from the clear case to contexts where considerable scientific uncertainty exists."[83]

The precautionary principle, which provided the justification for interventions to protect public health even in the absence of definitive data, entailed a weighting of how the risks and benefits of uncertainty should be borne. It was that perspective and the political values it reflected that informed the struggle against ETS.

In the 1990s the singular moment for those seeking to rid the public space of smokers came with the publication of the EPA's *Respiratory Health Effects of Passive Smoking: Lung Cancer and Other Disorders.* What the agency did was to place numbers on burdens that had only been vaguely apprehended, and it did so with an apparent precision that made the toll politically electric. Children and infants in large numbers were placed at risk. Each year, between 150,000 and 300,000 cases of lower-respiratory tract infections such as bronchitis and pneumonia were linked to ETS in those less than eighteen months of age. Between 200,000 and 1 million asthmatic children had their conditions exacerbated by exposure to tobacco. More damaging still, the EPA declared that ETS was a Class A carcinogen, placing it in the same category as asbestos, benzene, and radon. Approximately 3,000 lung cancer deaths were attributed to ETS.[84]

Newspapers across the country responded to the report with a sense of urgency. In an editorial titled "No Right to Cause Death," the *New York Times* spoke of "toxic fumes" and "lethal clouds" generated by smokers. Drawing an analogy between secondhand smoke and other hazards regulated by the EPA, the *Times* stated: "No one would grant his neighbor the right to blow tiny amounts of asbestos into a room or sprinkle traces of pesticide onto food."[85] The *Wall Street Journal* remained a contrarian voice, openly questioning the antismoking science even after the government reports of 1986 and 1993. In a 1994 editorial, the paper claimed that "the anti-smoking brigade relies on proving that second-hand smoke is a dangerous threat to the health of others. 'Science' is invoked in ways likely to give science a bad name ... [T]he health effects of secondhand smoke are a stretch."[86]

Armed with science, activists joined forces with their public health allies and with sympathetic political figures to press for more far-reaching restrictions in the early and mid-1990s. In 1992 the national Accrediting Association of Health Care Facilities required providers to develop policies that would prohibit smoking by patients, visitors, employees, volunteers, and medical staffs. In 1993 the U.S. Postal Service banned smoking in all of its facilities; Vermont prohibited smoking in all government buildings and many others open to the public; Los Angeles banned smoking in all restaurants. The year 1994 witnessed further efforts. The Department of Defense prohibited smoking in all indoor military facilities; San Francisco banned smoking in all restaurants and workplaces.

At the end of 1999, forty-five states and the District of Columbia had enacted some legislation to protect indoor air. Forty-three states and the District of Columbia restricted smoking at government work sites, with twenty-nine limiting smoking to designated areas, and eleven imposing total bans. Twenty-one states restricted smoking in private work sites. Twenty-one states regulated smoking in restaurants.[87] The number of local ordinances restricting smoking had also grown dramatically from the mid-1980s, when there had been some four hundred such measures, to 1998, when there were more than eight hundred.[88] Seeking to capture the transformation that had occurred, the historian Allan Brandt said of smokers in the United States that they "literally had no place to hide."[89]

For almost four decades public health officials had underscored the enormous toll exacted by cigarette smoking, generally estimated at close to 400,000 lives a year. The consensus concerning the impact of ETS on lung cancer suggested that 3,000 to 4,000 deaths a year could be traced to exposure of nonsmokers to tobacco smoke. There was no such consensus, however, concerning the link between heart disease and passive smoking. Some researchers had proposed as early as 1991 that 37,000 deaths each year from heart disease were linked to ETS.[90] Those estimates served as a rallying cry for antismoking activists, who argued that with 53,000 deaths a year attributable to ETS, passive smoking was the "third leading preventable cause of death in the United States, behind active smoking and alcohol."[91] But by decade's end, uncertainty prevailed. When a meta-analysis of epidemiologic studies published in the *New England Journal of Medicine* in 1999 concluded that "passive smoking [was] associated with a small increase in the risk of heart disease,"[92] the accompanying editorial noted, "We still do not know, with accuracy, how much or even whether exposure to environmental tobacco smoke increases the risk of coronary heart disease."[93] To such doubts, the advocates of strict controls over public smoking responded with characteristic certitude that was a central feature of their political strategy.[94]

Given the controversy surrounding ETS and heart disease, and the *comparatively* small number of lung cancer deaths associated with exposure to others' smoke, why had the plight of the bystander become such a focal issue?

It was clear to anti-tobacco activists from the start that a focus on bystanders could further the ultimate goal of rooting out tobacco consumption. An analysis made in the early 1990s vividly captured the underlying goal. "Increasing restrictions on smoking in public places to protect nonsmokers from the toxins in ETS undermines the social acceptability of smoking. Decreasing the social acceptability and mandating restrictions on where and when one can smoke in turn discourages children from starting to smoke and facilitates adults' decisions to cut down or stop smoking. While generating significant health benefits for smokers and nonsmokers, this drop in cigarette consumption translates into fewer sales and lower profits for the tobacco industry."[95]

Some antismoking activists have exulted in the ever more stringent limitations on public tobacco consumption, pressing to extend such restrictions because of their social impact; in 2000, one community—Friendship Heights, Maryland—sought to impose a ban on smoking in virtually all outdoor settings. Nevertheless, other activists have begun to worry that their movement may have begun to take on the taint of moralism and authoritarianism. The debate over how far to press flared in the journal *Tobacco Control* in 2000, centering on the question of the legitimacy of imposing bans on outdoor smoking. Two officials at the National Cancer Institute's tobacco program noted approvingly that some communities had chosen to restrict outdoor smoking for reasons other than health—including the reduction of fire risks, litter control, and the elimination of nuisances.[96] Antismoking activist James Repace, who was among the first to quantify the burdens of ETS, asserted, "Even if outdoor environmental tobacco smoke were no more hazardous than dog excrement stuck to the bottom of a shoe, in many places laws require dog owners to avoid fouling public areas. Is this too much to ask of smokers?"[97] The response of the journal's editor, Simon Chapman, was one of dismay: "We need to ask whether efforts to prevent people smoking outdoors risk besmirching tobacco control advocates as the embodiment of intolerant, paternalistic busybodies, who not content at protecting their own health want to force smokers not to smoke, even in circumstances where the effects of their smoking on others are immeasurably small."[98]

The Power to Tax Is the Power . . .

Efforts to impose restrictions on advertising and smoking in public settings defined the campaign against tobacco in the first two decades following the release of the 1964 surgeon general's report. It was not until the 1980s that using the power to tax would emerge as a potentially critical tool in the effort to alter the public context within which the decision to begin or continue smoking would be made. By the early 1990s public health advocates would be asserting that "a substantial increase in tobacco excise taxes may be the single most effective measure at the state and local levels for decreasing tobacco consumption."[99] Once the issue was joined, it would become necessary to address a host of both technical and moral issues. How would price increases affect consumption of an addictive product? What was the elasticity of demand for cigarettes among those who might be poised to begin smoking, among young smokers, and among those who had smoked for years? Would such excise taxes be inherently regressive and therefore inequitable? Did smokers impose collective burdens on nonsmokers because of the medical costs they incurred, and did equity justify or require the internalization of such negative externalities? Was the imposition of excise taxes on cigarettes, at least in some part, an act of paternalism designed to place economic burdens on smokers in order to enhance the prospect of quitting? And if so, was such paternalism morally justified?

In the years immediately *preceding* the release of the first surgeon general's report, state governments had demonstrated an increasing interest in raising the level of tobacco taxes—but primarily for the purpose of revenue enhancement, not to modify the behavior of smokers and potential smokers. According to some interpretations, the willingness to impose new taxes reflected the emergence of anti-tobacco sentiments following the first medical and epidemiologic studies linking smoking and cancer.[100] Indeed, following the release of the surgeon general's report, there was a surge of excise tax activity[101]—a trend that the tobacco industry found alarming. A former president of the Tobacco Institute thus said in 1967, "Prohibition by taxation is still prohibition."[102] Whatever the motivations for such taxes, state tax increases slowed in the early 1970s, primarily because of concerns about cross-state smuggling.[103]

It would be another decade before adjustments in federal cigarette taxes would occur. In 1982, in response to the federal budget deficits, Congress increased the federal cigarette excise tax for the first time in three decades. As a temporary move, the tax was doubled from 8 cents to 16 cents per pack. But at this juncture the anti-tobacco movement would be poised to take on the issue of the role that excise taxes could play in reducing the demand for cigarettes. A critically important review of the economic literature, published in 1982, concluded that "excise tax increases [would] discourage smoking to the extent [they] were passed on to smokers in higher retail cigarette taxes."[104] Noting that the short-term impact of an increase in the federal excise tax would be small, the article nevertheless concluded that the long-term consequences could be substantial, the result of the effect of increased prices on young male smokers.

But the signal indication of the shifting perspective of antismoking activists—in a history of its own record of activity between 1964 and the early 1980s prepared by ASH, the issue of taxes never appears—was to come in the form of an analysis by the economist Kenneth Warner. In "Cigarette Taxation: Doing Good by Doing Well," published in 1984, Warner provided a virtual manifesto.[105] Noting that the just-enacted excise tax increase was a temporary measure designed to lapse in three years, he urged, "It is not too early for the public health community to begin developing political strategies to seek continuation of the tax and even larger and/or regular increases in it."[106]

Warner put forth two broad justifications for such a tax. The first was that increased prices translated into reduced consumption. Warner noted that domestic consumption of cigarettes had fallen in the first half of 1983 by 4 percent over the same time period in the prior year—by 14 billion cigarettes.[107] Second, he noted that because of tobacco-related illnesses, cigarette consumption was responsible for between 5 percent and 8 percent of national health care expenditures. Smoking-associated health care thus cost the average adult almost $100 annually in medical insurance premiums, taxes, and out-of-pocket expenditures for medical services, and it was time to transfer these costs back to those who created them.[108] Warner was acutely aware that such arguments carried with them the whiff of victim blaming—a phenomenon to which public health advocates confronting the ethos of the early Reagan years might be especially alert. But given the ways in which excise taxes could benefit those who would be dissuaded from smoking or who might be encouraged to give up smoking, Warner asserted, such measures could be thought of as "help[ing] the victim."[109]

Finally, Warner had to attend to the charge that a tobacco excise tax, like all sales taxes, would be regressive, unfairly burdening those with fewer resources. To this concern he responded by noting that the prevalence of smoking among the poorest was lower than among middle-income groups (a fact that would not hold true in later years); that a significant proportion of low-income smokers were relatively poor only because they were teen-agers; that because the poor were more responsive to price increases, they would spend less on cigarettes; and that although the poor would be dis-proportionately burdened by cigarette excise taxes, they would ultimately pay less out of pocket because of such levies. In all, "a cigarette tax is not clearly regressive; and it is not highly regressive."[110]

As Congress considered the issue of whether to make permanent the 16 cent excise tax on cigarettes—which it did in 1986—elements of Warner's argument would be reflected in the arguments seen in the popular media. In supporting the move to make the 16 cent tax permanent, the *New York Times* wrote that the increase would represent "a small payback . . . for what the cigarette habit costs government each year . . . Even if smokers end up having to pay 8 cents more, society will keep on paying a higher price for their pleasure."[111]

With the passage of the higher federal cigarette tax and the obvious enthusiasm of antismoking activists for further increases at the federal and state level, the tobacco industry began to press its case. Central to its strategy was the claim that such taxes were unfair; like other "sin taxes," they entailed an effort to burden consumers in ways that inevitably forced the most vulnerable to pay a greater share of the tax load. In a video prepared by the Tobacco Institute, two unlikely allies of the industry underscored this theme. The executive director of the League of United Latin American Citizens—the oldest and largest Hispanic membership organization in the nation—declared, "Smokers tend to be concentrated among lower-income households and minorities . . . so when you impose a tax on tobacco prod-ucts, lower-income people—blacks and Hispanics—will pay a dispropor-tionately greater percentage of that tax." His comments were echoed by a representative of a labor union-affiliated group, Citizens for Tax Justice, who remarked, "Excise taxes are taxes on the politically inarticulate."[112]

These issues would come into play as the tobacco industry launched a ferocious but unsuccessful campaign to thwart a 1988 citizens' initiative in California that sought to impose an additional 25 cent tax on cigarettes (bringing the tax to 35 cents). The state would use the funds generated by the tax—approximately $600 million—in large part to pay for health care for the poor. But 20 percent would also be earmarked for antismoking programs.

The conflict was joined again four years later in Massachusetts. A referendum sought to impose a 25 cent increase in the tax on each pack of cigarettes, and the proceeds were to be devoted to antismoking projects for children and pregnant women. The Coalition for a Healthy Future, which had placed Question 1 on the ballot, claimed that the additional cost of cigarettes would encourage fifty thousand adults to give up cigarettes and deter twenty-eight thousand young people from beginning to smoke.[113] Nevertheless, leaders of the coalition repeatedly stressed that their primary concern was for children and adolescents. "We are not after an adult habit—we're after keeping kids from smoking . . . Once kids are addicted, they're trapped for life."[114] Indeed, "The entire tobacco industry effort is based on addicting kids."[115]

The industry-backed Committee against Unfair Taxes sought to paint a very different picture. Not only was the tax regressive, but it represented an expression of an unseemly intolerance. Stressing the notion of freedom of choice and the virtues of living in a community that respected difference, the industry aired a thirty-second television advertisement that featured pictures of abortion rights advocates, racial minorities struggling for their rights, union workers, gay rights demonstrators, and antiwar activists. The voiceover declaimed, "Is there a personal choice you've made for yourself that a majority wouldn't agree with? And if you have, do the rest of us have a right to tax you just because we don't like what you've decided for yourself? Because that's what Question 1 is really about." The advertisement concluded, "Question 1: It raises questions of tolerance. And that shouldn't happen in Massachusetts."[116] On November 3, 1992, despite a $5 million campaign by the tobacco industry, Massachusetts voters approved Question 1, thus giving it the highest cigarette tax in the nation—51 cents.

By 1993 anti-tobacco activists had come to believe that excise taxes had enormous potential in the campaign against cigarette companies—that in the power to tax was to be found the power to destroy both the hold of the tobacco industry and the threat that it posed to the nation's youth. Emboldened by their victories in California and Massachusetts, a coalition to press for state tax increases (supported by the Robert Wood Johnson Foundation) met in mid-1993 to chart a course for the future.[117]

Between 1983 (when the first federal increase on taxes took effect) and 1993, federal taxes almost tripled to 22 cents per pack; state taxes had risen from an average of about 15 cents, to 28 cents per pack. Over that decade the price of cigarettes (adjusted for inflation) had risen by 55 percent, while taxes had risen by 29 percent. As a consequence, taxes as a proportion of the price of cigarettes had actually declined in the decade to just less than 25 percent; in 1964, the year of the first surgeon general's report, taxes represented almost half of the price of cigarettes.[118] Those who saw increased cigarette prices as a critically important tool in the struggle against tobacco companies thus had much work to do. The gravity of the challenge that they faced was made clear when the tobacco companies demonstrated how they might respond to the tax battles. On "Marlboro Friday" in April 1993, they slashed wholesale cigarette prices by 25 percent.[119]

At the state level the path blazed by California and Massachusetts was taken by others, including Arizona and Michigan, sometimes with the explicit goal of affecting tobacco consumption, on other occasions for purposes of revenue enhancement. The tax increases ranged from the modest to the steep. But whatever the justification for the increases, they reflected, in an extraordinary way, the growing political vulnerability of the tobacco industry and smokers.

For anti-tobacco activists, it was of little importance why a particular state sought to increase taxes on cigarettes, thus raising the cost of smoking. In a climate suffused with outrage at increasing revelations of how the industry had targeted youth, and in light of evidence of growing prevalence of smoking among young people, taxes were viewed as a powerful weapon. As an official of the American Cancer Society declared, "Raising tobacco taxes is our Number 1 strategy to damage the tobacco industry . . . The tobacco industry has found ways around everything else we have done to reduce smoking by teenagers, but they can't repeal the laws of economics."[120] It was the "laws of economics" that were to be in play when, at the end of the 1990s, an agreement was ultimately struck in the multistate tobacco settlement between the attorneys general and the tobacco industry, imposing $206 billion in costs on the industry.

Over the years of struggle leading up to the settlement in 1998, evidence had accumulated on three elements central to the justification of imposing taxes on cigarettes: the precise nature of the impact of price increases on tobacco consumption; the regressivity of cigarette excise taxes; and the social cost imposed by smoking. How that evidence was understood and used in the political controversy at decade's end would underscore the complexity of the task faced by the anti-tobacco movement as it sought to justify its strategy against an enemy that it viewed as treacherous.

During the 1990s, studies of the relationship between smoking and cigarette prices—the question of the elasticity of demand—tended to confirm assumptions about the potential impact of taxes. Yet the impact was not uniform. In a 1995 review of the literature released by the National Bureau of Economic Research, the authors concluded that cigarette smoking among youths and young adults was relatively more responsive to price than was smoking among adults. Increases in cigarette excise taxes were thus termed "a very effective means of reducing cigarette smoking among youth and young adults."[121]

But advocates for cigarette taxes had to address the argument that no matter what the social utility of such taxes, they were profoundly unfair, placing the largest burden on the poorest. An analysis published by the U.S. Centers for Disease Control and Prevention readily acknowledged the impact of cigarette taxes. "Lower income populations," said the CDC, "were more likely to reduce or quit smoking than those with higher incomes."[122] In an editorial note, the federal agency went on to balance the burdens of taxes against the benefits that would accrue to the socially most vulnerable. Low-income and minority individuals "would be more likely than other smokers to be encouraged to quit in response to a price increase and thus would obtain health benefits attributable to quitting."[123]

This line of argument had become a leitmotif of anti-tobacco activists and public health officials who stressed the potential benefits of higher cigarette taxes. Thus, in addressing this matter, Kenneth Warner asserted that while a typical cigarette tax would be "distributed regressively," a tax increase might not be regressive because the poor were more responsive to price increases than those who were wealthier. The poor would therefore benefit most from the health protection that would follow from giving up cigarettes. "In this regard, increasing the price of the cigarette tax is clearly a 'progressive' public health policy."[124] In making this claim Warner, like others, elided the issue of regressivity and public health progressivity, thus avoiding the question of whether unfair taxes that served the public good were justifiable.

The debate over the social costs of smoking has been much more complex, with a trajectory that had profound implications for a central feature of the claims of the anti-tobacco movement. In the early 1990s, Thomas Hodgson, in a widely cited study, concluded that the lifetime expenditures on medical care for smokers exceeded those of people who had never smoked.[125] Hodgson concluded that over a five-year period, smokers generated excess medical expenditures of $187 billion, or $2,324 per smoker. These additional costs—18 percent of the country's total expenditures for hospital care, physicians services, and nursing care—could, Hodgson argued, be considered a "premium being paid every five years to provide medical care for the excess disease suffered by smokers."[126]

While most studies of the economic burden imposed by smokers focused on the excess medical costs borne by society because of smoking-related disease, other research had made clear that the premature deaths of smokers could also create significant savings for pension systems, especially Social Security.[127] Some researchers concluded that, on balance, smokers probably paid their way.[128] To the extent that the justification for increased taxes rested at least in part on the claims that smokers imposed costs on society and that fairness dictated that they bear those burdens, these data had profound implications.[129]

By decade's end, popular assumptions regarding the social costs of smoking had thus suffered considerable empirical challenge. Indeed, Kenneth Warner, who had played such a crucial role in pressing the case for increased cigarette taxes, would assert that the assumption that smoking imposed an enormous financial burden on the country was a "myth." To ground the attack on tobacco on the cost of health care was therefore, he said, "disingenuous. Even if smoking imposed economic burdens on health care budgets, its net impact is likely modest."[130]

It is thus remarkable that the claims of the net social costs to the health care system provided a central element for the most significant development in tobacco policy in the United States. In mid-1997 a preliminary settlement was reached on issues involving the liability of the tobacco industry for health costs incurred by the states; it would have required the companies to pay $368 billion over a period of twenty-five years.[131] Annual payments under the agreement were to reflect, in part, the value of cigarette sales. Most strikingly, these payments were to be passed on, in full, to consumers in the form of increased prices. In effect, the agreement, which because of its extensive elements involving control over the tobacco industry and protection against class action lawsuits required congressional action, entailed the imposition of a significant excise tax.[132] Because pressure to increase the severity of the settlement's terms provoked the tobacco industry to withdraw from its earlier agreement, and because the political alliance that had sought to punish the industry was quite fragile, the dramatic policy initiative ended in failure. That failure did set the stage, however, for a more modest, but nevertheless significant, development.

Suits brought by the Florida, Minnesota, Mississippi, and Texas attorneys general came to successful conclusions between July 1997 and May 1998. And then in November 1998, a settlement was reached in the suits brought by the other states. The multistate settlement—based on claims that the industry was responsible for the costs to state Medicaid programs for treating tobacco-associated disease—involved an agreement to pay the states $206 billion.

As a consequence of the settlement, the price of cigarettes rose sharply. From early 1997 to early 1998, prices rose 12 percent, an increase that could be traced to the settlements with Mississippi, Florida, Texas, and Minnesota. And then in November 1998, on the very day that the multistate agreement was agreed to, prices increased 45 cents per pack. In all, while federal taxes rose by 5 cents and state taxes rose by 8 cents from 1996 to 2000, the average price of cigarettes rose by $1.13 over the same period. Between 1964 and 2000 the price of cigarettes, adjusted for inflation, had risen by 85 percent. All of that increase had occurred since 1985, and more than 60 percent since 1997.[133] The states' lawsuits thus achieved more by way of altering the national price structure for cigarettes than had more than two decades of efforts to increase cigarette prices through campaigns to raise state and federal sales taxes. This achievement had become possible because of the focus on the economic burden generated by smoking. It was, however, the burden and growing sense of outrage regarding tobacco-associated illness and death that gave moral force to the data on cost.

The Policy that Dare Not Speak Its Name

In the forty years since the release of the first surgeon general's report, the status of cigarette smoking and the tobacco industry has undergone a significant transformation. In 1964 more than 50 percent of men and 35 percent of women smoked cigarettes. Recent data suggests that the adult smoking population has subsequently declined by 40 percent.[134] Reflecting these changes, per-capita domestic sales of cigarettes declined by 50 percent, from 4,286 in 1964 to 2,287 in 1998.[135] Perhaps the most striking feature of the transformation in the epidemiologic profile of smoking has been its concentration among those of lower socioeconomic status. In the quarter-century between 1975 and 1998, overall smoking prevalence declined in the United States from 37 percent to 23 percent, but the drop was not distributed uniformly throughout the population. Among those with less than a high school education, smoking prevalence fell from 43 percent to 34 percent, a decline of only 21 percent. In contrast, among those with a bachelor's degree or higher, smoking declined from 27 percent to 11 percent, a decrease of 59 percent. Similar patterns of a gradient according to educational attainment (a proxy for socioeconomic status) can be found across lines of gender and race.[136]

The transformation in the status of smoking represents a hard-won achievement of public health institutions and anti-tobacco activists. But among those who see in tobacco use a continuing threat to well-being, and especially among those who see an issue of equity in the socioeconomic differences between those who have stopped smoking and those who have not, much still needs to be done.

At the end of the 1990s, the central thrusts of America's anti-tobacco movement were clear: protection of young people, of nonsmokers who might be exposed to ETS, and of the nonsmoking public compelled to bear the cost of tobacco-related disease. That the anti-tobacco campaign had adopted this strategy was largely a function of Americans' uneasy relationship to paternalism. In the 1970s, when public health officials pressed the states to enact mandatory motorcycle-helmet laws, and when the courts upheld those laws as a legitimate exercise of the "police powers" that provided government with the authority to act to protect the public health, the claim was *not* that motorcyclists needed to be protected from their own risky choices. It was asserted, instead, that the state had a right to protect itself from the financial burdens that unhelmeted driving could impose. Helmet restrictions were not an exercise of paternalistic authority. They represented a response to potential fiscal injury. In a similar way, by focusing on youth, bystanders, and the public purse, anti-tobacco activists have been able to frame a set of policies that could avoid the appearance of seeking to impose rectitude in the name of public health. Without the overt appearance of paternalism, which would have been anathema, public policy nevertheless succeeded in imposing increasingly heavy burdens on smokers—burdens that fostered the decline in cigarette consumption. It was an effective, but limiting, strategy.

In commenting on the centrality that had been accorded to the issue of ETS by the nonsmokers' rights movement and those connected with the public health, Richard Kluger—in *Ashes to Ashes*, his Pulitzer Prize-winning history of tobacco in America—questioned that strategy, despite its obvious success. "By stressing the risks of ETS exposure, the smoking control movement was effectively trivializing the risk from direct smoking which was thirty to forty times greater. It was an incendiary, effective and questionable tactic from those on the side of the angels."[137]

The anti-tobacco movement was, of course, moved by the degree to which ETS unfairly burdened nonsmokers and by the preventable deaths for which it was responsible. But more was involved. Having moved the bystander to center stage, it was possible to press for changes that, if pursued directly, would have been politically unpalatable. Just as restrictions on advertising could most easily be justified in the name of protecting children from manipulation, restrictions on smoking could be justified by the claims of the bystanders. In a public health equivalent of the Catholic doctrine of double effect—which holds that an effect that would be morally wrong if caused intentionally would be permissible if unintended, even if foreseen—it was possible to pursue the goal of a smoke-free society without adopting the paternalistic posture that would have been necessitated by expressly seeking to burden the choices adults made on their own behalf.

At the end of 1998, the Multistate Master Settlement Agreement imposed enormous financial costs on the tobacco industry. The scheduled payments to the states might have, in principle, made possible the funding of aggressive education campaigns to control cigarette smoking, although fiscally pressed states have increasingly chosen to use their payments to meet budgetary exigencies. The settlement did, in addition, impose some modest restrictions on advertising and promotion.[138] Potentially more critical for the fate of the tobacco industry would have been the FDA's final rule, "Regulations Restricting the Sale and Distribution of Cigarettes and Smokeless Tobacco to Protect Children and Adolescents," which a sharply divided Supreme Court overturned on March 21, 2000.[139]

In light of both the settlement and the Supreme Court decision, the question for public health officials and anti-tobacco activists was whether a strategy that sought to avoid a more overt embrace of paternalism for tobacco control could, in the long run, serve the goal of moving toward a "smokeless society." The rhetoric of protecting third parties continues to play a central role in justifying restrictive anti-smoking measures; when New York City banned smoking in all but a handful of bars and restaurants in early 2003, the move was put forth as an environmental health measure that would protect thousands of bar and restaurant employees from the dangers of secondhand smoke.[140] At the same time, however, there were signs that the social delegitimation of smoking—its denormalization—had progressed to the point that explicit paternalism was becoming more politically feasible. In a 1998 report, California's tobacco-control program openly advocated "social norm change" and acknowledged that its goal was not simply protecting youth and bystanders, but "changing the generations who have already reached adulthood."[141] When New York City Mayor Michael Bloomberg announced at the end of June 2002 a cigarette-tax increase that would give the city the highest such tax in the nation, he justified it not on the ground that it would recoup costs that smokers imposed on society, but rather on the ground that it would help force smokers to quit. "This may be the most important measure my administration takes to save people's lives," he said.[142]

Paralleling this trend has been the increasing medicalization of smoking and the conceptualization of smokers as victims of a chronic disease, nicotine addiction, who are in need of treatment and, as a corollary, are fit subjects of paternalistic interventions. The 1994 edition of the American Psychiatric Association's *Diagnostic and Statistical Manual* included the illness of nicotine dependence, and in subsequent years a variety of medical groups and advisory bodies offered clinical-care guidelines for treating smoking as a chronic condition.[143] A wide range of nicotine-replacement therapies, such as the patch and gum, and psychopharmacologies such as Wellbutrin constitute the treatment armamentarium of this new medical model.[144]

As smoking grows more socially marginalized and moves into the realm of medical pathology, the field of public health may be poised to move beyond the avoidance of explicit paternalism that has characterized its efforts over the past four decades. Should this transition occur, it will represent a striking achievement in view of the dominant political ideology and social ethos that privilege the claims of individualism.

The Limits of Tolerance: Cigarettes, Politics, and Society in Japan

Eric A. Feldman

Tobacco-control policy in Japan remains poorly articulated and seldom discussed. Despite a tradition of tobacco cultivation that spans four centuries and smoking rates that exceed those in other industrialized nations, the Japanese government has done little to limit the health consequences of smoking. Japan has neither an educational campaign like the U.S. surgeon generals' reports, nor a legislative framework like Canada's Tobacco Act. Its most important public health organization, the Ministry of Health, Labor, and Welfare (MHLW), depends upon the Ministry of Finance (MOF) for its operating budget, and MHLW has been unwilling to strain interministerial relations by insisting on meaningful tobacco-control policies. Anti-tobacco activists have asserted "nonsmokers' rights" (*ken-en-ken*, literally, the right to hate smoke) for decades, but their rights rhetoric has been defeated by an effective industry campaign that portrays smoking as a matter of "manners" rather than rights. Courts have rejected legal claims brought by individuals allegedly suffering from tobacco-related illnesses or exposure to environmental tobacco smoke (ETS). For now, under the loose banner of "anti-tobacco," scores of groups engage in advocacy but remain marginalized, poorly funded, and easily managed.

Why has Japan done so little about the health consequences of tobacco consumption? Money is generally considered to be the most important reason; tobacco-control policy in Japan arguably reflects the triumph of state financial interests over individual and public health.[1] The key player in this scenario is MOF, which has controlled the growth, manufacture, and sale of cigarettes for most of the past century. By focusing on the business of tobacco, MOF is viewed as guilty of benign neglect or as having intentionally worked to limit the power of public health interests such as MHLW so that it could reap the financial rewards of big tobacco relatively unimpeded.[2]

Despite its appeal, this perspective does not stand up well under closer scrutiny. If the primary concern of MOF were tobacco-related profits, one might expect it to set the price and tax on cigarettes (under the Tobacco Enterprise Law, MOF has such authority) at a level that minimizes drops in consumption and maximizes profits. One might also expect MOF officials to balance profits from the tobacco business and the savings resulting from tobacco-related morbidity—such as lessening the expense of social welfare costs for the elderly—with the medical costs of treating people with tobacco-related diseases. There are debates about both of these issues in the United States and many other nations, but not in Japan.[3] Interviews with MOF officials suggest that they view tobacco revenues as a desirable source of income, but that they have not weighed that income against the various costs of smoking.[4] Money is a significant factor for MOF, and it clearly influences its oversight of Japanese tobacco policy, but there is little evidence that it is the master key to understanding tobacco-control policy in Japan.

A second perspective looks beyond explicit fiscal interests to politics. The most plausible political explanation for the current status of tobacco policy is the Liberal Democratic Party (conservative despite its name). It has retained almost uninterrupted electoral dominance since the 1950s, and has avoided regulating tobacco because it does not want to risk offending one of its core constituencies, agricultural interests.[5] But dramatic declines in the number of tobacco farmers in Japan—from over 200,000 households in 1970 to approximately 20,000 today—suggest the waning influence of what in the past had been an important part of the Liberal Democratic Party's support.[6]

Yet another approach to understanding Japanese tobacco policy has to do with the role of corporations, as distinct from politicians and government regulators. When a private company (Japan Tobacco Inc. [Nihon Tabako Sangyo Kabushiki Gaisha], hereinafter JT, the privatized entity formed when the tobacco monopoly was abolished) was created from the government tobacco monopoly in 1985, the regulatory structure of the tobacco industry was transformed. Employees of JT no longer had explicitly divided loyalties to MOF and JT; they were now able to concentrate on promoting corporate interests and did so by using their strong government connections and by working in concert with other major tobacco companies, such as Philip Morris. In a paper that relies on previously unavailable documents made public as a result of U.S. tobacco litigation, Kaori Iida and Robert

Proctor trace the collaborative efforts of JT and Philip Morris to manipulate the debate on passive smoking, cigarette advertising, and other aspects of tobacco policy.[7] This view of Japanese tobacco policy is consistent with the corporate deceit and malfeasance that have taken place in many other nations. But the recent vintage of Japan's tobacco industry makes corporate influence only a partial explanation for Japan's threadbare tobacco-control policy, and the difficulty of obtaining internal corporate documents in Japanese litigation leaves this exploration largely undocumented.

A fourth theory that could account for Japan's undeveloped tobacco-control policy is sociocultural—Japan's longstanding acceptance of individual behaviors that are negatively sanctioned in the West. In contrast to Western moralism, the Japanese state avoids involvement in numerous areas that it considers to be personal preferences. A wide variety of individual sexual choices, for example, are tolerated without being labeled deviant, and public drunkenness is widely accepted without condemnation.[8] This may help to explain why there is relatively little denormalization of smoking in Japan; unlike the negative image of sick, addicted smokers in the United States and elsewhere, the image of smokers in Japan as engaging in a private, self-chosen act has yet to be negatively recast.[9]

Consonant with this sociocultural view is the explicitly libertarian rhetoric that has come to dominate the Japanese government's pronouncements about smoking. The decision to smoke is consistently described as the expression of an individual preference, and a policy that discourages smoking is viewed as an undesirable infringement on personal choice.[10] What makes this approach to understanding Japanese tobacco policy suspect is that there are, in Japan, many examples of the opposite—of the state's willingness to embrace explicitly paternalistic policies. Japan's criminal justice system, for example, has been described as based on "benevolent paternalism" because it justifies intrusions on the autonomy of prisoners by referencing what is in the best interests of individual offenders.[11] In a similar vein, anthropologist Dorinne Kondo describes how corporations use retreats to shape specific beliefs and behaviors, and legal scholar Frank Upham asserts that the state intentionally shapes the legal consciousness and behavior of its citizens in the service of cultivating what it considers desirable social values.[12] So respect for individual choice as an explanation for tobacco policy in Japan is not compelling. One can equally well imagine just the opposite—the Japanese government acting paternalistically and invoking strong antismoking measures.

Each of the above explanations has some validity, but none of them satisfactorily answers the question of why Japan appears to be so unconcerned about tobacco-related morbidity and mortality. In fact, the complex array of crosscutting interests and pressures makes an understanding of tobacco policy resistant to any single theoretical framework. In the sections that follow, therefore, the topics that are generally considered important by scholars, advocates, and critics of tobacco control support one, or often several, of the approaches discussed above; each is also likely to contradict at least one of the others. In the end, like the characters in the great Japanese film director Kurosawa Akira's *Rashomon,* observers of smoking in Japan will find the theoretical framework that suits their preconceptions and prejudices, and will find sufficient evidence to persuade themselves of their particular truth.

This chapter proceeds in five parts. First, because the cultivation and regulation of tobacco in Japan unfolds in a distinctive historical and institutional setting, I briefly describe its history. Second, I provide an overview of smoking prevalence and tobacco-related morbidity and mortality, highlighting trends in smoking rates among men, women, and minors, along with changes in patterns of tobacco-related diseases. Third, I discuss two events that have shaped Japan's current system of tobacco control—the so-called privatization of the government's tobacco monopoly through the creation of Japan Tobacco Inc., and the opening of the Japanese market to foreign tobacco products. Fourth, I highlight a number of important areas of tobacco-control policy in Japan—taxation, advertising, vending machines, and limitations on where people can smoke. Finally, I describe the challenges brought by the antismoking movement, particularly its attempt to shape tobacco-control policy through litigation.

A Brief History of Tobacco in Japan

The Portuguese brought tobacco to Japan sometime in the late sixteenth century. By the early seventeenth century, open-air stalls sold tobacco. The first legal restrictions on smoking were enacted in 1609. It appears that they were imposed because of concern about fires in wooden houses and a worry that the land required for tobacco cultivation might reduce the rice crop. Tobacco flourished despite persistent attempts to control its cultivation and use, including the imposition of Japan's first tobacco tax in 1624.[13] As Prince Toshihito, builder of Kyoto's famous Katsura Palace, wrote in the early part of the seventeenth century: "Of late a new herb from distant lands across the sea has come to our country—a medicine not listed in the herbals of ancient China . . . Persons who know nothing of one another, who come from different worlds and walks of life, can nonetheless find mutual ground and links of friendship in their common liking for the herb, and those with a taste for poetry can find in it matters to inspire them. Wherever one may walk, there is no quarter of the city unscented by its fragrant smoke."[14]

There was little change in tobacco policy for the next two and a half centuries, until the Meiji Restoration of 1868. This period of widespread social and institutional change had important consequences for tobacco farmers, retailers, and users. Beginning with the Restoration, and continuing for four decades, the practices and structures that shaped Japanese tobacco policy were born. Reconciled to the existence of tobacco as a consumer good, the government levied a tobacco tax. Entrepreneurs started to produce cigarettes, as opposed to shredded tobacco for Japanese *kiseru* pipes. Finance officials implemented the 1898 Leaf Tobacco Monopoly Law, bringing the cultivation of leaf tobacco fully under government control, and the 1904 Tobacco Monopoly Law, governing the manufacture of tobacco products. In 1900, Japan's parliament (the Diet) outlawed tobacco use by minors. By early in the twentieth century, the Japanese state had taken control of the cultivation, manufacture, and sale of tobacco products.

The state tobacco monopoly controlled all aspects of tobacco cultivation, manufacture, sale, and consumption. Japanese tobacco farmers were told exactly how much land they could cultivate and how many plants they could grow. The government guaranteed the purchase of 100 percent of domestically grown leaf tobacco, and set the price by negotiating with the growers' association. Manufacturing facilities owned and operated by the government were located throughout the nation (by the twentieth century, tobacco was grown in almost every region of the country). Licensed by MOF, retailers were required to sell their products at a fixed price. From the formation of the tobacco monopoly in 1904, until its superficial privatization in 1985, MOF maintained an uninterrupted grip on tobacco in Japan. Most important, patterns of patronage, interministry relations, and institutional structures established during those 80 years still endure. I will return to these long-ingrained practices, and how they have shaped contemporary tobacco-control policy, after providing an overview of the public health dimensions of smoking in Japan.

Tobacco Consumption and Public Health in Japan

According to data collected by the Japan Monopoly Corporation (the government tobacco monopoly within MOF) and later by Japan Tobacco Inc. , smoking rates peaked in 1966 at 83.7 percent of men and 18 percent of women.[15] In 1970, 77.5 percent of men and 15.6 percent of women were smokers; by 1980 those numbers dropped to 70.2 percent and 14.4 percent; and by 1990, to 60.5 percent and 14.3 percent.[16] Data for 2003 indicate that 48.3 percent of men and 13.6 percent of women were smokers.[17] The highest rate of smoking among men—over 60 percent—is for those in their thirties; the highest rate among women—over 20 percent—is for those in their twenties. Smoking rates among men have steadily decreased over the past thirty-three years, while those for women have hovered in a narrow range, never exceeding 18 percent or falling below 12.6 percent.[18]

The overall drop in smoking rates among adults may to some extent be offset by an apparent increase of smoking among youths. In 1987, at Tokyo's Sixth World Conference on Smoking, a Japanese researcher announced that 43.2 percent of female junior high school students smoked, as did 60 percent of male students.[19] A series of interviews conducted by the Prime Minister's Office in 1989 reported that two-thirds of 2,339 smokers in their twenties started smoking before they turned twenty, the legal smoking age.[20] MHLW's recent survey indicates that more than half of all Japanese smokers start smoking before they reach the age of twenty.[21] Other data, however, suggest more modest tobacco consumption among youth; a 1990 study indicated that 20.3 percent of eighteen-year-old male high school students and 2.6 percent of female students were daily or almost daily smokers.[22]

In addition to concern about smoking by minors, some observers have claimed that smoking rates among women are increasing, but that does not seem to be the case. In fact, overall smoking prevalence among Japanese women has remained almost unchanged since the late 1950s.[23] What has changed is the age of women who smoke. Between 1965 and 1995, smoking prevalence decreased from over 20 percent to less than 10 percent among women over sixty. During that same period, however, smoking prevalence among women in their twenties increased from approximately 5 percent to more than 20 percent, and by 1999, the prevalence had increased to 23.2 percent.[24]

Although overall smoking prevalence in Japan has been decreasing for decades, both the size of the smoking population and the number of cigarettes consumed have fluctuated. According to JT's recent survey, the 24,140,000 male smokers and 7,380,000 female smokers in 2002 represented a decrease of 1,620,000 smokers from the preceding year. The great majority of smokers—almost 70 percent—smoke twenty or fewer cigarettes per day. On average, men smoke more than women; for example, 13.7 percent of men, but only 2.8 percent of women, smoke over thirty cigarettes per day.[25] Total tobacco consumption has risen from 306.4 billion cigarettes in 1988 to a peak of 348.4 billion in 1996.[26] After a drop to 328 billion in 1997, sales increased again to 336.6 billion in 1998.[27] Per-capita cigarette consumption peaked in 1980 at 3,450, fell to 2,905 in 1995, and increased to 3,023 in 2000.[28]

Because it takes several decades for the health consequences of smoking to become manifest, the public health impact of tobacco consumption in Japan appeared, until recently, to be quite modest.[29] In 1950, stomach cancer (Japan's most deadly) caused the deaths of 19,023 men and

12,188 women, compared to 789 men and 330 women who died from cancer of the trachea, bronchus, and lung.[30] In 1970, 29,653 men and 19,170 women died from stomach cancer, an increase of roughly half, but trachea, bronchus, and lung cancer deaths increased nearly tenfold. Cancer of the trachea, bronchus, and lung became the most deadly form of cancer among men in 1995.[31] Among women, in that same year, deaths from trachea, bronchus, and lung cancer were second only to those from stomach cancer.[32]

Reconfiguring the Japanese Tobacco Business: Privatization and Market Liberalization

In the 1980s, almost a hundred years after the Japanese government monopolized the cultivation and manufacture of tobacco products, finance officials reluctantly moved to abolish the Japan Monopoly Corporation (JMC, so named by U.S. occupation officials in 1949). Reform of the JMC was connected, in part, to the general trend of moving certain enterprises away from state ownership under the banner of efficiency, competition, and privatization. Like railways and telecommunications, tobacco was perceived to be overly dependent upon government subsidies and to lack an incentive to be cost-effective. In addition, as Japan's trade surplus with the United States ballooned, American regulators and corporations became vocal critics of the state-controlled tobacco monopoly. They regularly pointed to the main consequence of government ownership: tariff and nontariff trade barriers made it impossible for foreign competitors to gain market share in Japan. After tobacco was monopolized at the turn of the twentieth century, the market share of foreign brands never exceeded 2 percent.

Although some MOF officials may have been attracted to the flexibility and financial freedom promised by privatization, there were significant interests vested in the long-standing relationships and practices surrounding big tobacco in Japan. Taxes from tobacco sales, for example, had for decades made up a significant share of government revenues, and MOF was clearly interested in maintaining the revenue flow from tobacco taxes and sales.[33] Tobacco farmers benefited from monopolization because the government, for a price several times higher than the international market would bear, was required to purchase 100 percent of their crop. Conservative politicians, meaning those in the dominant Liberal Democratic Party, enjoyed the overwhelming support of farmers generally, and tobacco farmers specifically, because the politicians were credited with pressuring finance officials to maintain a high price for leaf tobacco. Retailers were able to avoid competition because the price of tobacco products was fixed, and all sellers had to be licensed by MOF. The ministry and its bureaucrats maintained jurisdiction, and thereby control, over an important political resource. Each of these practices limited the impact of privatization on the Japanese tobacco industry, and each influenced how far the Japanese government would bend in accommodating U.S. pressure to open the tobacco market.

Pressure started to mount in March 1979, when the Cigar Association of America (CAA) filed a complaint with the U.S. government under Section 301 of the Trade Act of 1964, alleging that Japan was engaged in unfair trade practices.[34] Section 301 allows private parties to petition the U.S. government and request "unilateral action" against foreign governments that unreasonably restrict trade and burden U.S. commerce. Government action generally involves a strong retaliatory threat; the president may impose duties or other import restrictions on the products or services of the offending country.[35] The CAA's primary complaint was that retail prices of cigars in Japan were fixed at too high a level, making it impossible for U.S. producers to sell their products.[36] In addition, the association criticized advertising restrictions that limited the ability of foreign companies to promote their wares.

In October 1979 the Associated Tobacco Manufacturers (ATM) filed a similar complaint.[37] In presenting their case against Japan's restrictions on pipe tobacco, attorneys for ATM invoked Thomas Jefferson (known as the father of the Declaration of Independence, but also, one might add, a tobacco grower). On August 15, 1785, in the midst of negotiating a trade agreement for the U.S. government, Jefferson sent a letter to Louis XVI's secretary of foreign affairs. "The monopoly of the purchase of tobacco," Jefferson wrote, "is contrary to the spirit of trade and to the disposition of merchants . . . where but one person is allowed to buy it, and where, of course, that person fixes its price."[38] The symbolic weight of quoting Jefferson was clear. The pipe tobacco industry had framed the conflict over Japan's monopolized tobacco market as implicating basic American values, specifically the "spirit of [free] trade"—which was no mere question of market share or political strategy. The thrust of the ATM position was that by keeping ATM's tobacco products out of Japan, the Japanese government's tobacco monopoly violated a fundamental belief of the United States' own Founding Fathers, a belief that is sanctified in American accounts of the Boston Tea Party and the War of Independence.

Matching the rhetoric of the U.S. position, Japanese officials referenced deeply rooted sociocultural beliefs. The image of a hostile foreign force preying on a vulnerable Japanese market, like the fear of "outsiders" that resulted in 250 years of isolation during the Tokugawa period

(1615–1868), has cast a long shadow on Japan's tobacco enterprise. A guide-book to Tokyo's Tobacco & Salt Museum, discussing the monopolization of leaf tobacco in 1898, decries the "influx of cheap imported tobacco." It continues:

> Soon after the promulgation of the law, a further crisis transpired when American tobacco cartels made an attempt to take over the entire Japanese tobacco industry. Prompted by this incident, as well as by the need for increased taxation brought on by the Russo-Japanese War, the Japanese government turned its attention to the possibilities of tobacco-manufacture control, and in July 1904 it instituted the Tobacco Monopoly Law.[39]

American bluster about free trade was therefore countered, symbolically if not directly, with accusations that the United States was on a self-serving mission to seize control of a 400-year-old Japanese institution. As the con-flict escalated, Japanese officials could easily predict the outcome; either they would make significant concessions to the United States, or they would end up in a damaging trade war. Only the former was a realistic alternative, so MOF officials began to prepare for the opening of the market—which required a plan for lessening the impact of foreign competition when it arrived.

The Regulatory Regime of Tobacco "Privatization"

Disassembling the tobacco monopoly was not exclusively the result of for-eign pressure.[40] According to Sato Hajime of Tokyo University's Depart-ment of Public Health and Occupational Medicine and colleagues, the privatization of tobacco had been on the government's agenda since the 1970s, as a response to the rapidly increasing administrative costs of running the JMC and as part of the "international trend towards mar-ket liberalization."[41] A 1982 report by the Provisional Commission on Administrative Reform suggested the privatization of three public corpo-rations, one of which was tobacco.[42] Similar to other enterprises once con-trolled by the government, such as trains and telephones, management of the tobacco industry would be physically distanced from MOF and given a corporate identity, but full independence was out of the question. Despite the vocabulary of "privatization," the growth, manufacture, and sale of tobacco would not be left to the principles of laissez-faire economics.

The Japan Tobacco Inc. Law of 1984, effective from April 1, 1985, formal-ized the institutional structure of Japan's new (and only) tobacco com-pany.[43] If there were any doubts about the continuing relationship between

MOF and big tobacco, they were immediately dispelled by the requirement of Article 2 and the "Supplemental Provisions" of Article 13. Together, those articles concluded that "the Government shall hold, for the time being, shares amounting to two-thirds or more of the total number of outstanding shares issued by [JT]." In fact, not a single share of the new company was publicly owned until 1994, and MOF continues to hold a full two-thirds of JT stock.[44] The law contains a variety of other provisions that assure close oversight by MOF. All former employees of the JMC's tobacco unit became employees of JT, and the first three presidents of the company were former MOF officials. The ministry was given the authority to approve all changes to the board of directors. MOF's sign-off was required for the annual business plan. And just in case the relationship was still ambiguous, Article 12 stated: "The Minister of Finance may give orders to [JT] as necessary for the supervision of [JT]'s business if it deems necessary to do so for the enforcement of this Law."

Former beneficiaries of the tobacco patronage system, such as farmers and retailers, had little to fear from privatization. Although the government wanted to make JT competitive with foreign companies, it was also committed to retaining the powerful ties between farmers, politicians, and bureaucrats that constituted the foundation of the tobacco enterprise (and has been described as a crucial element of Japanese agricultural politics generally) for at least a century.[45] The Tobacco Enterprise Law, promulgated concurrently with the JT Law, establishes the outlines for how those ties could be maintained once foreign cigarettes were marketed in Japan.[46]

The Tobacco Enterprise Law sets out the requirements and procedures that govern almost every aspect of contemporary tobacco policy. Chapter 1 of the law states that its goal is "to promote the development of the national tobacco industry . . . thereby procuring treasury revenue and developing the national economy." Chapter 2 makes JT the sole purchaser of all domestically grown tobacco leaf and establishes the Leaf Tobacco Deliberative Council. The council, consisting of eleven members "of learning and experience" appointed by JT, is given the authority to determine both the amount of tobacco to be cultivated and the price it will fetch. Chapter 3 gives JT the exclusive right to manufacture tobacco products in Japan, and places the retail price of tobacco, as well as the tobacco tax, under the control of MOF. Chapter 4 requires all importers of tobacco (except JT) and all tobacco retailers to be licensed by MOF.

Regulations that govern the price of tobacco products are presented in Chapter 5 of the law. MOF will determine the price of all tobacco products sold in Japan. Retailers are required to sell tobacco products at a fixed price. Manufacturers (that is, JT) and importers are required to include MOF's prescribed packet warning about "the relationship between the consumption of tobacco products and the damage to health." In addition, "excessive" advertising is discouraged, particularly when it is aimed at minors, and if a company fails to comply with MOF's advertising guidelines, MOF is empowered to "publicize" the "disobedience."

The detailed conditions of the JT Law and the Tobacco Enterprise Law ensured the continuation of almost every important aspect of the domestic tobacco monopoly. Japanese farmers were assured that JT would purchase all leaf tobacco at a rate several times higher than its value on the international market. Liberal Democratic Party politicians, who could take credit for pressuring MOF to make sure that JT was a generous patron, would retain the votes of tobacco farmers. JT was made the sole tobacco manufacturer, commanded significant benefits from its close ties to regulators, and faced almost none of the risks associated with market competition. MOF retained its authority over the tobacco enterprise. Tobacco-tax revenues were unchanged. Senior bureaucrats could settle into generously compensated jobs in the not-so-private sector when their age led them into mandatory retirement. The number of retailers was still limited, thus insulating them from some of the risks associated with competition. Perhaps most importantly, MOF retained a wide degree of discretion over almost every corner of tobacco operations in Japan. It was this tightly knit structure of tobacco growth, manufacture, and sale that American negotiators confronted when they made their final assault on the Japanese tobacco market and attempted to gain entrance.

Opening Japan's Tobacco Market

In 1985, when the new regulatory structure of big tobacco in Japan was put into place, the foreign share of the tobacco market was less than 2 percent. Although no law prohibited the importation or sale of non-Japanese tobacco, a combination of tariff and nontariff trade barriers provided a strong disincentive to potential importers. Beyond the necessary approvals and paperwork required by MOF (itself a formidable obstacle), until 1982 there was a 90 percent import duty on all foreign tobacco products.[47] Distribution channels were limited, advertising guidelines obscured the visibility of new products, and prices were fixed. The government, in 1903, had expressed concern that the domestic tobacco market might "ultimately fall into the hands of some foreign trust."[48] By 1985, Japan's tobacco system appeared to be exceptionally well fortified.

An article in *Forbes*, revealing the disdain felt by many in the American business community for the Japanese tobacco enterprise, dismissed it as "a bloated and inefficient government-owned monopoly" that operated forty-five factories in the early 1980s when four might have been sufficient.[49] Just five months after the formal creation of JT, and with the U.S.-Japan trade deficit increasing from $21.2 billion in 1983 to $43 billion in 1985, the Reagan administration initiated a Section 301 investigation into the manufacture, importation, and sale of tobacco products in Japan.[50] The United States attacked Japan's high tobacco tariffs, its discriminatory rules on marketing, advertising, and distribution, and its maintenance of a government tobacco monopoly. According to the September 16, 1985, *Federal Register,* those practices led to higher prices for imported tobacco products than for domestic goods.[51] While giving credit to Japan for slightly liberalizing the tobacco market by reducing the 90 percent import tariff to 20 percent, the United States still took issue with the tariff, the manufacturing prohibition, the restrictions on pricing, and the distribution network.[52] In a memorandum from U.S. Trade Representative Clayton Yeutter to Japanese Minister of Finance Utsumi Makoto, Yeutter prods his adversary: "If [the United States' understanding of cigarette pricing in Japan] is at all accurate, it demonstrates to me the persuasiveness of our Section 301 case and the need for further changes in the Japanese system. In a capitalistic society like Japan or the US, why not just let the market operate?"[53]

U.S. manufacturers, represented by the U.S. Cigarette Export Association, were intimately involved with the effort to force open Japan's market. Tobacco consumption in the United States had declined steadily since the end of World War II, and the world's biggest tobacco market, China, was clearly out of reach, so Japan's market, number three in the world, was enticing.[54] American manufacturers argued that foreign tobacco products were being unfairly singled out and excluded from Japan, and they strongly supported a challenge to this trade practice under Section 301.[55] The U.S. government assembled a team of negotiators from the Office of the U.S. Trade Representative, and negotiations with MOF began in the summer of 1986.[56]

In the midst of this tense U.S.-Japan trade negotiation, Senator Jesse Helms, the most powerful political advocate for tobacco in the United States and a member of the Senate Foreign Relations Committee, wrote a letter to Japanese Prime Minister Nakasone Yasuhiro. Helms stated that he had seen "little tangible evidence of efforts on Japan's part to open your doors to more U.S. tobacco products . . . [This inaction] is causing a growing sentiment among my colleagues in the U.S. Congress to take strong action against Japan in matters of trade."[57] In order to more powerfully assert its position, the United States prepared a list of Japanese goods that would be singled out for retaliation if MOF did not accede to U.S. demands.

In October 1986 the White House announced that American and Japanese negotiators had reached an agreement. The Japanese team capitulated to the most important U.S. condition and agreed to eliminate the

20 percent import duty on foreign-made tobacco products by April 1987. The result would be a reduction in the price of U.S. cigarettes in Japan from the equivalent of $1.82 to $1.65 per pack.[58] In addition, Japanese officials agreed to modify the distribution network, which would limit delays and eliminate other impediments; to make JT and foreign corporations subject to the same excise tax requirements; and to simplify the process of obtaining approval for cigarette price changes.[59] Japanese negotiators did refuse, however, to yield on one key issue: they insisted on maintaining a monopoly on the domestic cultivation and manufacture of tobacco products.[60] After almost a century of exclusion from the Japanese market, U.S. firms had mobilized their government to help them gain access to the industrialized world's most voracious consumers of tobacco.

Liberalization had unambiguous consequences. The market share of foreign products rose from less than 2 percent in the early 1980s, to almost 15 percent in 1990, to 20 percent in 1995, and to 23.5 percent in 1999.[61] The value of U.S. tobacco exports to Japan increased fivefold between 1986 and 1989; in 1998 the value of Japan's tobacco imports reached ¥318.44 billion, up from ¥216.12 in 1990.[62] To promote their products, the American companies poured money into advertising. By the end of the 1980s, they were spending 50 percent of their tobacco-advertising dollars in Japan, and introducing 75 percent of Japan's new tobacco products. Whereas Japanese television carried only twenty hours per week of cigarette advertisements in 1985, it was broadcasting seventy-three hours per week by 1987.[63]

Some scholars have suggested that providing U.S. firms with access to the Japanese tobacco market caused an overall increase in smoking prevalence among women and minors. Winder and colleagues trace this change to U.S. firms' more aggressive marketing and advertising.[64] Similarly, Chen and Winder write:

> To achieve their objective in Asia . . . U.S. tobacco companies directed their advertising primarily at youth . . . Thus, American rock stars have been featured as role models, and cigarette advertising is prominently presented in public places where young people congregate; popularly read magazines are full of advertisements by American tobacco companies.[65]

The long-term trend in Japanese tobacco sales, however, is that the number of cigarettes sold has increased steadily since the 1950s—a trend that may well have continued even without market liberalization. Moreover, there is no compelling data that indicates a casual link between opening the market and a change in smoking prevalence among minors or women. High rates of tobacco consumption existed well before the market was open and those rates have been gradually declining for more than thirty years.[66]

It is interesting to note the vilification of foreign tobacco-related interests in Japan—which deflects attention away from potential strategies for domestic tobacco control. In an analysis of the impact of market liberalization on smoking in Japan, for example, two Japanese public health scholars have recently written, "Japanese people began to see the threat to their future that market liberalization might pose."[67] Likewise, a prominent anti-tobacco attorney describes Japan as "victimized" by the United States, "surrendering" to its demands, and "vulnerable" to its pressure, all of which, he believes, handicapped MHLW efforts at tobacco control.[68]

Similarly, Sato Hajime criticizes the U.S. Trade Representative's position that Japan's restrictions on marketing and advertising, as well as its high tariffs, were inappropriate trade barriers. According to Sato and colleagues, "[W]hen the Japanese government tried to enforce a new marketing code on cigarette advertisement in the mid-1980s, US cigarette companies opposed its efforts, with the assistance of US government officials."[69] Consequently, in his view, U.S.-Japan trade negotiations delayed the implementation of domestic regulations that may have reduced smoking prevalence. There is little doubt, however, that the Japanese government's attempt to introduce new advertising restrictions in the 1980s was aimed at limiting the ability of foreign enterprises to compete. Had finance and health officials previously demonstrated a commitment to tobacco control, one might be less skeptical about their sudden enthusiasm for advertising controls. But the timing points strongly toward an interest in market dominance rather than a desire to limit tobacco consumption.

Tobacco Control in Contemporary Japan

Beginning in 1985, tobacco policy in Japan broke from the past in two crucial ways. First, tobacco moved away from total control by the state bureaucracy; the creation of JT brought about a new set of corporate interests that were, at least in some ways, distinct from the government. Second, the health consequences of tobacco could no longer be ignored or dismissed. These changes required Japanese public policymakers to confront new policy concerns not unlike those of other industrialized democracies—taxation, advertising, vending machines, and zoning. But there has been no attempt to craft a unified regulatory scheme. Rather, Japan has emerged with a fractured framework of tobacco control, shaped by such crosscutting forces as the state's legacy as tobacco monopolist; the continuing dominance of MOF; the emergence of JT as an internationally powerful tobacco company (In 1999, JT paid $8 billion for the international tobacco operations of RJR Nabisco, and in the process acquired the worldwide [except US] ownership of branches such as Camel, Winston, and Salem.); party politics; and the underlying tension between traditions of individualism and paternalism. What has emerged, with little debate or interest from the medical community or the general public, is a jumble of unsystematic and informal tobacco-related policies, mostly unenforceable.

Taxation

In the past several decades, public health advocates around the globe have pressed for increases in the tobacco tax as a way to drive up the cost of smoking and reduce the number of smokers.[70] They rely on a formula that is now widely cited by the tobacco-control community—raising the price of cigarettes by 10 percent will cause smoking prevalence to drop by 4 percent—resulting in increased government revenue and improved public health.[71] This approach has had no discernible effect on Japanese tobacco tax policy. From the earliest days of tobacco cultivation in Japan, the government taxed (and later sold) tobacco to fill the public coffers. It continues to do so today, but with no emphasis on the accompanying public health effects. The tax has at times been controversial; foreign tobacco companies and governments, for example, have attacked its structure as disadvantaging non-Japanese tobacco products. So far, however, the Japanese debate over taxing tobacco has been impervious to the view that such taxes should be seen, at least in part, as a public health intervention.

Most politicians, along with MOF and JT officials, have little desire to raise cigarette taxes further because they believe price increases are likely to cause a decline in tobacco sales and a fall in both JT profits and government revenue.[72] In late 1999, when senior Liberal Democratic Party politician Kamei Shizuka proposed a tobacco tax increase, the proposal was immediately and vigorously attacked. Within two weeks it was withdrawn. Mizuno Masaru, JT's president and CEO, reacted angrily to Kamei's proposal:

> We are very surprised at this completely unexpected news. We have made painful decisions in the past to raise tobacco retail prices in two consecutive years in response to the consumption tax hike in April 1997 and the introduction of a tobacco special excise tax in December 1998. The latter, whose main purpose was to reduce the debts of the former Japan National Railway, was especially hard to bear.[73]

Mizuno went on to say that increasing the tax on tobacco would "inconvenience" 33 million customers and damage the tobacco industry in Japan. "We strongly oppose this Liberal Democratic Party initiative," he argued, because "it places too high a burden on a specific industry and its consumers."[74] Such views have helped to maintain the tobacco tax at a relatively constant level since 1986. It currently accounts for ¥141 of the average ¥250 cost of a cigarette pack in Japan, the least expensive cigarettes in the industrialized world.[75] A pack of Marlboros in New York City cost $7.50 in early 2003, for example, but less than $3.00 in Tokyo.

The regressive effect of tobacco taxation has been largely ignored in Japan. In the United States, some economists have argued that since the less well-off enjoy health benefits from a higher tax (because they will smoke less), tobacco taxes are not regressive.[76] In Japan, however, there has been no public or expert discussion about the impact of cigarette taxes on lower-income smokers. This is difficult to explain in light of the debates over the value-added tax (shohizei) in 1989, when the unequal impact of that tax was clearly articulated. In fact, increases in tobacco taxes would have a disproportionate effect on lower-income people.[77] In 1998, those with incomes below ¥4 million per year (representing the bottom five of eighteen income brackets) spent an average of ¥1,362 per month on tobacco, whereas those with incomes over ¥8 million per year (the top five of the eighteen brackets) spent ¥1,068 per month.[78] So concerns about equity have had little, if any, influence on tobacco tax policy; as the price of cigarettes climbs, those with less money will pay even more for a product on which they already spend a disproportionate share of their income.

Advertising

Prior to the U.S.-Japan trade conflict over Japan's domestic tobacco market, and the creation of JT, the advertising of tobacco products was largely unregulated. More formal guidelines on advertising were part of the 1984 Tobacco Enterprise Law, which discouraged "excessive" advertising but contained no sanctions.[79] At that time, more than 98 percent of Japanese smokers smoked domestic cigarettes, and an overwhelming number of them smoked the same brand (Mild Seven). What little tobacco advertising existed was aimed at attracting and retaining customers, but it appears that expensive, aggressive advertising campaigns were unusual, at least when compared to the United States.[80] With smoking rates among men the highest in the industrialized world and no outside competition, "excessive" advertising during that period would have little appeal to government tobacco monopolists, and the voluntary limitation on advertising therefore imposed no undesired curbs.

With the opening of the Japanese tobacco market to foreign products, and the U.S. Trade Representative's attack on Japan's 1984 tobacco advertising restrictions, costly and sophisticated advertising campaigns seemed inevitable. Foreign corporations seeking to increase market share needed to bring their products into public view. To retain its massive base of domestic consumers, JT would have to respond. Indeed, as already discussed, in the mid- and late 1980s spending on tobacco advertising in Japan rapidly increased.

In 1989, MOF issued administrative guidelines to limit tobacco advertising. The guidelines restricted television advertisements from airing between 5:00 A.M. and 10:54 P.M., and also reduced radio advertising. The Tobacco Institute of Japan (TIOJ), an industry association of Japanese and foreign firms, issued a more complete set of regulations in 1998, almost three decades after the U.S. Congress banned cigarette advertising on television and radio. Titled "Rules on Advertising and Sales Promotion Activities for Tobacco Products," it prohibited tobacco advertising in movie theaters and on television, radio, outdoor TV monitors, and the Internet. Mindful of the long-established practice of distributing free cigarettes at busy intersections, the regulations prohibited such handouts in tobacco shops, pubs, restaurants, event sites, and other "closed" locations.[81] The rules discouraged advertising directed at minors and women in several ways: by prohibiting advertising in publications that appeal to those groups, by banning billboards within one hundred meters of schools, and by not allowing advertisements to portray women smoking. Not affected by the rules are the ubiquitous cigarette posters on trains, subways, and buses—which feature alluring women and celebrities, and are clearly intended to attract young, particularly female, smokers.

Although the TIOJ rules go further than previous advertising restrictions in Japan, they are mere guidelines that have no legal force and depend entirely upon the voluntary compliance of industry. Significantly, the industry raised no objection to the guidelines, and MHLW has gone so far as to say that imposing further, more legal restrictions on advertising is unnecessary.[82] The absence of industry protest suggests a familiarity with studies of tobacco advertising restrictions concluding that partial advertising bans and limitations will have no (or very little) impact on tobacco consumption.[83] Such studies make clear that companies can successfully move the advertising dollars they save by not being allowed to engage in certain forms of advertising, and spend them on different media. Moreover, if all companies are prohibited from engaging in certain forms of expensive advertising, each is spared the costs without suffering a competitive disadvantage. It is risky to speculate on the motivations of MOF and the TIOJ, but it is not unreasonable to conclude that their advertising restrictions were more strongly shaped by corporate interests than public health concerns.

Vending Machines

Vending machines are a major source of cigarette retail sales in Japan and have become a lightning rod for anti-tobacco activists, who believe that the easy access the machines provide to cigarettes encourages consumption and facilitates youth smoking. Since 1987, when there were 273,000 tobacco retail outlets, the number of licenses granted by MOF to sell tobacco at retail has grown by only two or three thousand a year. In contrast, the number of vending machines has increased rapidly. The first cigarette vending machine was installed in 1957; the number grew to 268,000 by 1980;[84] to 407,000 by 1987; and to 629,100 by 1999, accounting for more than 40 percent of total retail sales.[85] Clearly, little attention has been paid to the 1975 call by the World Health Organization (WHO) for a ban on vending machines.

Japanese extensively use vending machines *(jidōhanbaiki)* for such products as milk, rice, batteries, beer, pornography, soft drinks, whisky, and cameras. In a move that suggests both diversification and consolidation, JT in 1999 purchased 64.2 percent of Unimat, the nation's leading vending machine corporation.[86] This makes it highly unlikely that JT will support any move to limit the use of such machines to sell cigarettes. The company has agreed to comply with informal restrictions on hours of operation; in 1996, cigarette vending machines stopped working between 11:00 P.M. and 5:00 A.M. in order to limit tobacco consumption by minors.[87] But as one commentator has noted, "One guesses that the late-night shutdown was designed primarily to help retailers reduce vandalism."[88]

In March 2001, the assembly of the small northern town of Fukaura (population 9,000) voted to eliminate outdoor vending machines. There are only 34 such machines in the town, but it took activists months to overcome JT's lobbying efforts to retain them. The assembly's resolution is, in any case, quite weak; if retailers refuse to close down their machines, there is little that the town can do. Lacking penalties for noncompliance, the town assembly can only disclose the names of the shops that refuse to obey the order. It is clear from the experience in Fukaura that local resistance has a long way to go before it has any effect on the prominence of vending machines in Japan's cigarette sales.

Environmental Tobacco Smoke

Interest in environmental tobacco smoke (ETS) was sparked in 1981 by the publication of Hirayama Takeshi's "Non-Smoking Wives of Heavy Smokers Have a Higher Risk of Lung Cancer: A Study from Japan" in the *British Medical Journal.*[89] Hirayama, chief of epidemiology at the National Cancer

Center, studied 91,540 nonsmoking wives, all aged forty and above, in twenty-nine health center districts in Japan over a fourteen-year period. He found that wives of heavy smokers were at a higher risk of developing lung cancer than wives of nonsmokers or light smokers, and concluded: "These results indicate the possible importance of passive or indirect smoking as one of the causal factors of lung cancer." The implications of Hirayama's work were immediately clear to antismoking activists around the world. Before 1981, demands for smoke-free zones had rested on shaky scientific footing, and came dangerously close to pitting the desires of smokers against the preferences of nonsmokers. After Hirayama's study, no longer would the justification for tobacco control be targeted at smokers alone. Third-party harms, now scientifically proven, could be the basis for imposing limits on where people smoked.

How broadly to interpret Hirayama's findings was a critical question. Did they apply only to the home, or to all contained indoor spaces? Did they indicate a health risk for nonsmokers who were exposed to tobacco smoke at work? In public transportation? On crowded city streets? Japanese tobacco-control advocates, like their colleagues internationally, read Hirayama's work broadly, and sought to use it as a justification to limit smoking in a wide range of settings. Government and business interests, however, strongly resisted the science and policy implications of ETS. As a result, Hirayama's work has had a mixed impact on tobacco-control policy in Japan. Litigation focused on ETS has failed, and judges question the data that links passive smoking and cancer. But corporate and government initiatives that limit where people can smoke have grown substantially. The public health justifications for such limitations are of lesser importance than the annoyance that smoke may cause to nonsmokers, but the consequence is that smoke-free environments in Japan have gradually been increasing.[90]

Workplace smoking restrictions, for example, have been spreading, but slowly and without debate about the health benefits of nonsmoking areas. Many companies now limit smoking to particular hours or rooms, and some ban it entirely, but they tend to use reducing the costs of cleaning the carpet, curtains, and ventilation system as the justification. A few government offices have become smoke free. The Ministry of International Trade and Industry and the Ministry of Posts and Telecommunications prohibit smoking, as does the Science and Technology Agency. The Lower House of the Diet went smoke free in 1996. Predictably, MOF is not one of the government agencies to ban smoking; ironically, neither is MHLW.

In a 1996 report, MHLW addressed the issue of no-smoking areas in a way that exemplifies the common understanding of such regulations in Japan. Rather than squarely taking on the question of banning tobacco consumption in certain areas, the ministry used a term of art: *bun-en,* or "divided smoking." MHLW was willing to urge Japanese organizations to create smoking and nonsmoking areas, but it did not want to be perceived as imposing a burden on smokers. Similarly, in 1996, the Ministry of Labor announced guidelines for workplace smoking. The basic message was that smokers and nonsmokers should have mutual respect and understanding, and cooperate in creating both smoking and smoke-free areas.[91]

In 1978, Japanese airlines introduced no-smoking sections. Over the next twenty years those sections gradually expanded. When in 1988 Japan Airlines announced that all of its short-distance flights would become non-smoking, a pro-smoking group, the Committee to Consider the Antismoking Movement, quickly organized a symposium. Questioning the links between smoking and lung cancer, someone complained that "[a]t this pace, the 33-million large smoking population will be ridiculed as society's dregs."[92] Nonetheless, in 1998 all of Japan's airlines banned smoking on domestic flights (a decade later than the prohibition by the U.S. Federal Aviation Agency), and in 1999 that ban was extended to international flights.[93] But those prohibitions were simply in-house directives, so compliance was a significant problem. An article in a major Japanese newspaper cited a survey of flight attendants, 63 percent of whom said the ban was not observed.[94] A spokesperson for All Nippon Airways reported that the company receives 300 reports each month of cigarette butts left in airplane toilets.[95] Tired of simply giving out written warnings to passengers when they violate the rules, in April 2000 Japanese airlines included their smoking-related policies on passenger agreements (the papers attached to plane tickets) in order to strengthen their enforcement powers. The airlines have also requested that the Ministry of Transportation's Civil Aviation Bureau implement no-smoking regulations with clearly defined penalties, but so far the bureau has refused.[96]

Trains have also experienced an expansion of their nonsmoking sections. Smoking is prohibited on subways and local trains, and has been banned or limited on platforms since the late 1980s. Tokyo's Yamanote Line (which circles the city and is the world's busiest commuter train) designated smoking sections on the platforms of two stations (Mejiro and Harajuku) in 1987, and by August 1993 other stations had followed. Regional railways like the Kyushu Railway Company and East Japan Railway have also established smoking areas. More controversial are the long-distance "bullet" trains *(shinkansen),* widely used for both business and leisure travel. Since they were introduced in 1964, these trains have symbolized Japan's technological sophistication, its success at building a national transportation system, and the perfect efficiency that enables the trains to be scheduled seconds apart and operate flawlessly. But to a small, vocal group of antismoking activists, the bullet train is a symbol of the state's failure to accommodate the desires of nonsmokers. Activists insist that no-smoking cars be added to every train, and in order to emphasize the urgency of their appeal, they have brought their grievance to the courts.

Manners, Rights, and Anti-Tobacco Litigation

Since 1974, when it started the "Smokin' Clean" campaign, JT has worked hard to frame the debate about tobacco as an issue of manners. Using a Japanized form of the English word "manner" (manaa)—meaning "etiquette" or "decorum"—JT has highlighted three themes that it considers central to good smoking manners: properly disposing of cigarette butts, showing consideration to nonsmokers, and preventing fires.[97] The meaning of smoking manners can be illustrated with reference to the use of portable telephones. In contrast to the ubiquitous use of cell phones on Tokyo's local trains in the mid-1990s, since 1999 the phones have gone silent. There is an automatic announcement on most trains that asks people to please mind their manners and refrain from using their phones, because it annoys other passengers. (The conductors also mention that cell phones may cause harm to people with pacemakers, but that is presented as the weaker of the two pleas.) Everyone complies.

JT has promoted the importance of smoking manners through television, radio, and newspaper advertisements; public posters; and other media channels. It has placed ashtrays in public areas, distributed individual portable ashtrays, and even sponsored street-cleaning projects. Since 1990, all cigarette packets in Japan have carried two warnings. The health warning tells people that "because it is harmful to your health, take care not to smoke too much" [anata no kenkō sokonau osore ga aremasu no de, suisugi ni chūi shimashō]. The other warning simply states, "Let's mind our smoking manners" [kitsuen manaa o mamorimasho].[98] As Mizuno Shigeru, former president of JT, puts it, "It is a personal judgment whether or not to stop smoking, but it [i.e., smoking] involves a matter of manners. We want to further strive to make smokers and nonsmokers coexist."[99]

To a considerable degree, the campaign seems to have worked to deflate claims of nonsmokers' rights and to cast the smoking debate as simply requiring cooperation and decent behavior from all involved parties. Lawyers suing the train companies in the 1980s, for example, called for the tobacco monopoly to make advertisements telling smokers to watch their manners. The 1989 Prime Minister's Survey found that a majority of smokers thought that they should not smoke when asked to forgo, and that they should ask permission before lighting up.[100] In a recent survey, 74 percent shared the opinion that the campaign to publicize smoking manners is effective.[101] A recent newspaper story decries the poor manners of smokers who light up outside designated smoking areas on train platforms.[102] And a member of the anti-tobacco group Tabakoresu (tobacco-less), Nogami Hiroshi, complains that smokers in Osaka, where the group is located, lack manners and light up in no-smoking areas, train stations, and elsewhere.[103]

The effort to place manners at the heart of the smoking debate, however, has not discouraged all anti-tobacco activity.[104] There are estimated to be a hundred antismoking groups in Japan—including lawyers, physicians, housewives, opposition politicians, and former smokers—most of which were formed after 1978.[105] In February of that year, a group calling itself the Group to Establish Nonsmokers' Rights [ken en ken kakuritsu o mezasu kai] met in Tokyo and decided to start a movement under the banner of ken-en-ken, literally "the right to hate smoke." The meeting resulted in a manifesto that outlined the main features of an anti-tobacco campaign. It called for the elimination or restriction of smoking in hospitals and clinics, trains, workplaces, public facilities, and schools; education about smoking in elementary schools and junior and senior high schools; and a ban on tobacco advertising. The leaders of the group—Asao Shin, Nakata Midori, and Watanabe Bungaku—explicitly sought to avoid attacking smokers, and made clear that they wanted to focus not on the harm of smoking itself, but on the danger of secondhand smoke.

Soon after this meeting, two attorneys—Akiyama Mikio and Isayama Yoshio—decided to "back up the civil movement from the legal side" by bringing a tobacco-related lawsuit to the courts.[106] They first drafted a complaint aimed at tobacco advertising, but then shifted tactics and filed suit against Japan National Railways (JNR, then a state monopoly, now privatized as Japanese Railways), the tobacco monopoly, and the state, which includes both MOF and MHLW. On World Health Day, April 7, 1980, the attorneys submitted their claims to the Tokyo District Court, demanding that one-half of all cars on JNR bullet trains be smoke free, and requesting compensation for four plaintiffs allegedly harmed by tobacco smoke.[107] Their petition read, in part:

> Smokers are not the only people who use public transportation. Babies, minors, pregnant women, people with respiratory or circulatory problems, people with allergies, and nonsmokers who cannot stand the odor of tobacco or its uncleanness also use it. Why do these people have to suffer for the private pleasure of smokers? ... Now is the time for nonsmokers to declare the following rights: the right to breathe clean air unpolluted by tobacco smoke; the right to say that tobacco smoke is unpleasant; and the right to appeal to society in order to restrict smoking in public place. Also, by appealing to

the right to breathe clean air and invoking the pain of nonsmokers, we will clarify that this country has no policy to prevent the spread of tobacco pollution, and that JNR has acted negligently toward non-smokers. In addition, we will prosecute [the tobacco monopoly] for hiding tobacco's harmful influence and endangering people's health and lives.[108]

These legal claims were grounded in a variety of theories, which differed with the defendants. Against JNR the attorneys alleged the violation of "personal rights" *(jinkaku-ken),* which have developed and been litigated since the late 1960s.[109] Personal rights include the pursuit of happiness and the protection of health, freedom, and honor. They are rooted in Articles 13 and 25 of the Japanese Constitution.[110] In the context of tobacco, plaintiffs' lawyers alleged the infringement of personal rights on the basis of exposure to secondhand smoke, and the lack of governmental commitment to tobacco-control policy. Against the state, they claimed that—since MHLW was responsible for public health, the Ministry of Transportation controlled JNR, and MOF managed the tobacco monopoly—all had a duty to non-smokers riding the trains. The tobacco monopoly, according to the lawyers, was required under the consumer-protection laws to prevent harm being caused by their products. Defendants countered with a threefold position: smoking is an individual choice; the impact of secondhand smoke is minimal; and Japanese consumer-protection laws regulate artificial, not natural, substances—which means that tobacco is beyond their scope.

During the first set of oral arguments in the case, lawyers for JNR argued:

Even though there is scientific examination and criticism about smoking and passive smoking, in this country's social life smoking is recognized as a luxury good. We understand that some nonsmokers have something to say about the condition in the trains, but considering the common ideas of this society, we do not think we are causing intolerable harm to the plaintiffs.

In response, plaintiffs' attorneys asserted:

In this case, we are not trying to stop the trains or sabotage JNR's work. We are merely asking that at least half of the train cars be nonsmoking. This is not a tough task for JNR. And, we are not robbing smokers' freedom to smoke. They can smoke in the smoking cars. Therefore, there is no reason why nonsmokers have to bear the harm to their health caused by passive smoking, and we cannot accept that the damage is within the limit of tolerance.

The Tokyo District Court announced its judgment on March 27, 1987, almost seven years after the case was filed. During the intervening period—and beginning, indeed, in 1980, the same year that the suit was filed—nonsmoking cars had gradually been added to the trains, and by the time of the court's decision, almost 30 percent of the cars on the bullet train were smoke free. Against this background the court stated that traveling by train was not the only option for those moving around Japan, and since all trains had no-smoking cars, it was easy for people to avoid smoky cars on trains.[111] Furthermore, and most importantly, the court declared that Japanese society generally accepts smoking, and that passive smoking has only a minor impact that is within the "limit of tolerance" *(jyunin gendo nai).*[112]

The leading lawyer for the plaintiffs, Isayama Yoshio, assailed the court's reasoning, particularly the balancing of public benefit and individual health that the court borrowed from cases such as those addressing airport noise. In Isayama's view, imposing a theory about the "limit of tolerance" mistakenly accepts the existence of a public benefit to smoking, and minimizes the actual harm caused by passive smoking.[113] But the lawyers did not appeal the decision, and it has cast a long shadow on other tobacco-related litigation.

The progeny of this pioneering suit have mostly focused on the harms of ETS.[114] Uniformly, the legal claims are denied on the basis of the theory of tolerable limits. For example, in a 1999 decision involving ten people allegedly suffering from ETS, Nagoya District Court Judge Aoyama Kunio wrote that "the impact of the damage from passive smoke, the suffering it causes, is comparatively slight, and the feeling of dislike and unpleasantness toward tobacco and smokers is within the range of tolerable limits."[115] Similarly, in a 1998 case before the same court that demanded the end of tobacco manufacturing and sales in Japan, Judge Nakamura Naofumi concluded:

> If there is an ongoing infringement of a person's lifestyle and/or body, or a danger that they will be infringed, and if the infringement is not within tolerable limits, then the personal right is infringed, and the court can order that the infringement be stopped. But in this case, it is hard to see the relation between the deed of the defendants and the harms to plaintiffs.[116]

Courts examining the link between ETS and health have, at least so far, ignored the compelling body of knowledge about the link between second-hand smoke and lung cancer. In a 1998 decision, for example, a Nagoya District Court judge (Nakamura) wrote that "the relation between lung cancer and passive smoking is extremely weak."[117] Another judge (Aoyama) points out that drinking water and grilled fish can cause cancer, and cites a 1998 WHO report as evidence that the link between ETS and lung cancer is not statistically significant.[118] His argument directly contradicts a March 1998 press release of the WHO—"Passive Smoking Does Cause Lung Cancer, Do Not Let Them Fool You"—a title that makes further explanation unnecessary.[119]

Underlying most of the tobacco-related legal decisions, and complementing the reliance on a tolerable-limits standard, is a conception of smoking as a matter of personal choice. Starting with the 1987 decision of the Tokyo District Court, judges have consistently described smoking as something that individuals decide to do because it suits their taste. Judges have not only dismissed the idea that smokers are victims (of a pharmacological addiction, for example, or of corporate seduction), but also paid homage to the importance of individualism and free will.[120] Judge Aoyama of the Nagoya District Court, for example, writes: "In Japan, for many years, smoking has been a matter of individual taste, and has become popular at many levels of society . . . Smoking is still, as a matter of principle, something done as an individual freedom, and tolerance of smoking has come to be expected."[121] Similarly, Judge Inada of the same court declares that "until now, the general point of view toward smoking was that it is a matter of one's own taste [shikō]," and Judge Teramoto of the Nagoya High Court opines that "smoking is still considered an issue of one's taste, and many smokers continue with the knowledge that tobacco is harmful to them."[122]

These legal opinions appear to echo the public's conception of smoking. For the antismoking movement and antismoking litigation to blossom in Japan, smokers—particularly sick and dying smokers—would benefit by wrapping themselves in the shroud of victimhood. Unfortunately for them, that is not an easy sell in Japan. Public opinion polls indicate that the average Japanese person does not think of smokers as victims; 90 percent of people in a recent survey agreed with the statement that "smokers are responsible for their decision to smoke."[123] And even tobacco lawyers believe that it is hard to find plaintiffs for their cases because smokers do not think of themselves as victims.[124]

In the most important tobacco case now before the Japanese courts, filed in May 1998 in the Tokyo District Court, plaintiffs are being represented by Isayama Yoshio, the attorney who brought the 1980 claim seeking smoke-free train cars.[125] He is joined by several veterans of the public interest bar: Yamaguchi Toshihiro, who worked on the famous Minamata mercury-poisoning case, for example, and Tani Naoki, who represented HIV-infected hemophiliacs against MHLW, the state, and private pharmaceutical companies. In the present suit against JT and the state (specifically MOF and

MHLW), the lawyers (sixteen in all) represent seven plaintiffs with lung cancer or other allegedly tobacco-related health problems.[126]

The cause of action casts a wide net. Predictably for a case that the attorneys characterize as a tort claim, it seeks damages, specifically ¥10 million for each plaintiff, or a total of ¥70 million. In addition, it goes well beyond individual remedies, and demands a series of policy changes. They include: (1) a ban on vending machines; (2) a ban on tobacco-company sponsorship of sporting events and concerts; (3) a ban on magazine, newspaper, television, and radio advertising; and (4) new warnings (larger type, with more severe cautions) on cigarette packs.[127] During oral arguments, JT questioned whether smoking caused the plaintiffs' illnesses, and asked that the suit be dismissed. In its *1999 Annual Report,* JT minimized this and other litigation, saying that "the Company believes that the ultimate outcome [of the litigation] will not have a material adverse effect on the Company's financial condition or results of operations."[128]

So far, this assessment appears to be accurate. In October 2003, the Tokyo District Court found for the defendants on every allegation put forward in the case.[129] The Court described smoking as a matter of personal preference, nicotine addiction as relatively weak, packet warnings as adequate, and the risk of harm to plaintiffs from ETS as speculative. Plaintiffs have appealed the decision to the Tokyo High Court. The case will probably be in the courts for years, but it is unlikely to become a major legal breakthrough for the anti-tobacco movement. Resting on a shaky doctrinal foundation, unable to rely on precedent, and involving some of Japan's most powerful institutions, an affirmative court decision would be extraordinarily surprising. Only time will tell if the litigation successfully achieves other objectives, such as invigorating the antismoking movement or exerting an influence on the shaping of social norms regarding smoking.

Finally, in November 1996 and March 1997, ten plaintiffs from Aichi, Fukui, Osaka, Tochigi, and Yamaguchi Prefectures sued JT in Nagoya District Court, demanding that domestic tobacco manufacturing be banned. The plaintiffs asserted that their personal rights were violated when JT imported, manufactured, and distributed tobacco knowing that it was toxic. They demanded that JT state clearly that tobacco is addictive and can cause cancer and heart disease, and asked for ¥1.1 million each as compensation for harm, and potential harm, to their health. On March 15, 1999, Judge Aoyama Kunio dismissed the suit. He wrote:

Therefore, first, smokers must be considerate to nonsmokers, and should exercise adequate self-control in terms of where and how they smoke. If smokers do this, then the chance of nonsmokers being exposed to smoke will disappear. Of course, we can't rely on smokers' manners alone to perfectly protect nonsmokers from indirect smoke. Recently, the harm of tobacco has been stressed, and in public institutions, in transportation, and in general workplaces, steps have been taken toward general regulations to *separate smokers from nonsmokers [bun'en]*. So, from now, there is good reason to expect that nonsmokers will be protected from indirect smoke by social regulation.[130]

Although the judge said that it would be "preferable" for JT to strengthen its warning on cigarette packs and to mention the risk of cancer, emphysema, and heart disease, he did not insist that JT do so.

In sum, in trying to use litigation to promote their cause, antismoking activists in Japan have found the tolerable limits standard to be a formidable legal barrier, and the framework of manners to be a conceptual obstacle. Public opinion, moreover, has not been swayed as in the United States, where anti-tobacco activists managed (after decades of legal failure) to reduce their message to a sound bite: big, dishonest companies deceived the public; people got sick and died; and the companies should be made to pay.[131] In Japan, the accused is the state itself—MOF, MHLW, and JT. It may be that in some sense the state is guilty and deserves to be punished for inflicting nicotine dependence and illness on innocent citizens. But for ordinary taxpayers—not only nonsmokers, but smokers who are not interested in seeking compensation for tobacco-related illnesses—the logic of litigation is fuzzy. Why should nonsmoking members of the Japanese public support litigation that would result in their tax monies being given to sick, litigious smokers? There is no clear sense in which equity is served by "punishing" the state and requiring that it compensate so-called victims of smoking when the money being paid is that of nonsmokers and of smokers who have not filed suit. In Japan, it is difficult for anti-tobacco activists to mobilize public support for their cause, and their assault on big tobacco has thus far been unsuccessful.

Conclusion

In October 1998, MHLW suddenly appeared ready to address the increasingly serious public health consequences of smoking in Japan. Lung cancer rates had climbed steadily for decades and other smoking-related illnesses were on the rise.[132] A decade earlier the ministry had issued its first white paper on smoking and health, but it contained few policy recommendations and had little impact on extant policy.[133] When in 1998 MHLW convened a blue-ribbon panel to draft a report like the U.S. government's "Healthy

People" series, it appeared that Japan's public health officials were finally getting tough on tobacco.

In August 1999, a year in which MHLW's total tobacco-related budget was a paltry ¥39 million ($361,000 with a conversion rate of ¥108 = $1),[134] the Committee to Establish a Plan for "*Healthy Japan 21*" issued its interim report.[135] The report roamed widely over the landscape of public health, providing advice on the best way to stretch in a desk chair and how to care for one's teeth. This plan, after all, was intended to be a ten-year blueprint for a healthier nation. When it came to tobacco, it was stunningly direct. The report proposed better school and community education about smoking, and suggested limiting smoking in public places and in offices. It noted that in 1993 Japan spent ¥1.2 trillion, or 5 percent of its total medical expenses, on treating illnesses related to cigarette smoking, and another ¥4 trillion on other smoking-related costs, such as fires. In place of the usual ambiguous data endemic to Japanese government reports, the committee proposed three clear numerical targets: (1) to halve the number of adult smokers; (2) to halve per-capita cigarette consumption; and (3) to eliminate smoking among minors, all by the year 2010.

These were not, of course, the only numerical targets included in the interim report of *Healthy Japan 21*. It also recommended a 20 percent reduction in the number of heavy drinkers and urged people to walk an additional 1,000 steps per day. But proposing clear goals for reducing tobacco consumption was different because it cut directly against the grain of long-cherished state policy. Tobacco was, at least to MOF officials, a political and financial resource rather than a public health threat. With cigarette-related taxes estimated to be ¥896 billion, or 1.8 percent of total tax revenue in the fiscal year ending March 31, 2000, and with the Liberal Democratic Party struggling for control, telling people to stop smoking was not on MOF's agenda.[136]

Immediately following the issuance of the interim report, the criticism began. More than 2,000 comments, mostly complaints, were directed at MHLW. One, coming from a committee of the Liberal Democratic Party's Policy Research Council, declared ominously, "It is inappropriate under the Constitution if a government office sets a numerical target and attempts to alter adults' freedom of choice. Such a move will have a grave impact on the tobacco industry."[137] Japan's 23,000 tobacco farmers, members of tobacco-related industries, and JT together submitted a petition with 53,700 signatures, arguing that numerical targets would lead to administrative control over people's tastes. Sumiya Noriaki, a spokesperson for the Japan Tobacconist Federation, asked: "What about sugar? It's linked to diabetes. The next thing you know we're going to be told how many spoons of sugar we should put in our coffee."[138] And Oshima Tadamori, a Liberal Democratic Party politician, opined: "Tobacco is deeply rooted in local economies, and it is one of this country's most important industries."[139] With such clear opposition from the Liberal Democratic Party, JT, the affiliated tobacco-related industries, and MOF, the numerical targets were in serious trouble.[140]

MHLW issued its final version of *Healthy Japan 21* in February 2000.[141] In incorporating the findings of the draft report, the final plan proposed spreading knowledge of the "influence" *(oyobosu)* of smoking on health to 100 percent of the population, noting that 84.5 percent of Japanese citizens know about the link between smoking and lung cancer, and 40.5 percent about smoking and heart disease.[142] It maintained its targets of "getting rid of" *(nakusu)* smoking among minors, advocated creating no-smoking areas in the workplace and public settings, and endorsed increasing access to cessation.[143] But the targets for reducing adult tobacco consumption were gone, transformed into a mere "slogan" *(surogan)* that led the ministry to announce "let's quickly reduce smoking" without providing any concrete goals.[144] MHLW, under pressure from MOF and dependent upon it for the allocation of its general health budget, abandoned its commitment to numbers and resorted to a set of vague aspirations. Like tobacco-control policy throughout the twentieth century, Japan's new blueprint for a healthy society took a barely noticeable bow to the health consequences of smoking and embraced an almost meaningless set of objectives.

The debate over *Healthy Japan 21* seemed to suggest that tobacco policy in the first decade of the twenty-first century would be much like it was in preceding years. As Yamazaki Masakazu, a writer and member of the MHLW Committee to Establish a Plan for *"Healthy Japan 21,"* stated, "Smoking is a culture that has been cultivated over the centuries. Government should not intervene in this issue simply on the grounds of health."[145] Yet increasingly, the government is intruding on the freedoms long enjoyed by smokers in Japan. One example is a recent ordinance passed by the Chiyoda Ward Assembly. In October 2002, it became a legal offense to smoke on certain streets of Chiyoda Ward, a district of central Tokyo where there are one million workers. First-time offenders are fined $20; second offences warrant fines of up to $200, handed out by uniformed cigarette patrollers. Particularly interesting is how this new legal regime has been justified. No reference has been made to third-party harms implied by Hirayama's findings on ETS, nor to the health benefits for smokers, who may smoke fewer cigarettes and thus be less likely to develop a tobacco-related disease. Instead, the stated goal of the rule is to cut down on cigarette-related litter and to protect small children who could be hurt by burning embers.

More likely to be significant is the Diet's Health Promotion Law, targeted at reducing so-called lifestyle-related disease by urging people to be attentive to good nutrition and other healthy behaviors. The law went into effect on May 1, 2003, and as a result ten private railway companies in the Tokyo metropolitan area promptly banned smoking at all of their 730 stations.[146] No such action was required by the law; it simply asks that operators of public facilities "make efforts to take necessary measures" to reduce ETS.[147] Nor does the law contain penalties for those public facilities (defined by MHLW to include schools, hospitals, department stores, company offices, restaurants, hotels, banks, and museums, among others) that do not comply. But the new law does send a powerful signal that the government now considers ETS a public health issue of sufficient importance to justify a national response.

Even without the bite of sanctions, the Health Promotion Law may be an important step in a new direction. By invoking the harms of ETS as a justification for limiting tobacco consumption, the government has retained its hands-off posture toward individual behavioral choice while at the same time exercising its paternalistic public health powers. In contrast to the judiciary, the bureaucracy appears willing to use the research finding on ETS to justify new smoking restrictions, even in settings where the ETS data are controversial. Whether the health of nonsmoking train riders will be harmed by smokers who congregate in particular sections of outdoor rail platforms appears to be less a question of science than it is the assertion of a new social norm.

Perhaps these new policies indicate a change in the political power of the tobacco interests, and a reconsideration by MOF of the likely effect of particular tobacco-related policies on its bottom line. It may also be that JT's strong move into the international tobacco market has made it more willing to accept changes at home. Maybe these recent tobacco-control initiatives signal the emergence of a new politics of public health, and the decline of smokers' manners as the basis of the social contract underlying smoking. A new agenda has not yet been crafted, but the era of smoker hegemony in Japan may be heading for its final breath.

Rights and Public Health in the Balance: Tobacco Control in Canada

Christopher P. Manfredi and Antonia Maioni

In 1908 the Canadian federal parliament passed the Tobacco Restraint Act, which made it illegal to sell tobacco products to anyone under sixteen years of age. It would take almost sixty years before tobacco regulation would again appear on the federal policy agenda, and yet another twenty years before the federal parliament would take legislative action against smoking and the tobacco industry. Between 1988 and 1997, the federal parliament enacted four major pieces of anti-tobacco legislation: the Non-Smokers' Health Act (entered in force, 1989), the Tobacco Products Control Act (1989), the Tobacco Sales to Young Persons Act (1993), and the Tobacco Act (1997). As Robert Kagan and David Vogel note, because of the powerful combination of material interests and ideas about the appropriate scope of government activity in a liberal state, the establishment of *any* tobacco regulation in such a state is a remarkable achievement.[1] Despite these obstacles, however—which included nine years of a conservative political administration dedicated to deregulation and free trade with the United States—Canada possessed by the end of 2000 a comprehensive, internationally recognized anti-tobacco strategy that combined taxation, legislation, and educational programs.[2]

The story behind the establishment of Canada's anti-tobacco strategy is one of political will, bureaucratic support and expertise, and effective advocacy outside government.[3] It took place against a background that included growing scientific evidence about the negative health effects of smoking; recognition of high rates of cigarette consumption by Canadians; and counterattacks by the tobacco industry. On the domestic front, in 1954 the

Canadian Medical Association issued the first public warning on the hazards of smoking, and in 1961 it concluded that cigarette smoking causes lung cancer. In 1958 and again in 1962, the National Cancer Institute of Canada recognized the causal link between cigarette smoking and cancer. Internationally, in 1962 the Royal College of Physicians of London (United Kingdom) issued its historic report on the harmful consequences of smoking. In view of these national and international developments, the Canadian minister of health and welfare, Judy LaMarsh, took official notice in 1963 of the harm of smoking and told the House of Commons that "there is scientific evidence that cigarette smoking is a contributory cause of lung cancer, and that it may be associated with chronic bronchitis and coronary heart disease."[4] In the following year, the U.S. surgeon general followed suit by issuing a report that smoking causes lung cancer in men. Despite these scientific findings, throughout the 1960s and 1970s the tobacco industry succeeded in avoiding coercive measures by adopting voluntary advertising codes. In the 1980s, however, mounting evidence about smoking-related disease (including the 1986 report of the U.S. surgeon general that defined passive smoke as a major health hazard), coupled with high smoking prevalence and per-capita cigarette consumption in Canada,[5] paved the way for increased federal legislative activity. But then, in the 1990s, public opposition to high taxation, combined with greater judicial protection for civil liberties, enabled the industry to erode the antismoking strategy that had developed in the 1980s.

In this chapter we tell the story of how Canada—a relatively late entrant into the tobacco-regulation field—became in less than a decade the world leader "in restricting cigarette marketing, in deterring use through taxation, and in directly regulating cigarette use."[6] We focus, in particular, on legislation and taxation, since they have been the principal policy instruments utilized by Canadian governments against tobacco use. Litigation also makes an appearance in the story as a tactic utilized by both anti-tobacco forces and the tobacco industry. We begin by looking at smoking as a social phenomenon and health problem in Canada. We then turn our attention to the development of legislation and of tax policies, particularly as they affect advertising, tobacco use, and pricing. We conclude by attempting to identify the factors, including the influence of external developments, that have shaped current policy.

Setting the Stage: Smoking and Contemporary Tobacco Control in Canada

Drawing an accurate picture of smoking in Canada is not a straightforward task. Smoking statistics are compiled by multiple agencies using different measures. In addition, the time lag between measurement and the publication of data affects the timeliness of those data. Nevertheless, by relying on a variety of sources, we are able to identify the key trends in smoking prevalence, consumption amounts, and health effects.

The data for 2000 from the Canadian Tobacco Use Monitoring Survey (CTUMS)—conducted by Statistics Canada on behalf of Health Canada—indicate that smoking prevalence had reached its lowest level since 1965, at 24 percent of the population over the age of fifteen. Smoking prevalence among fifteen-to-nineteen-year-olds decreased from 28 to 25 percent from 1999 to 2000, but was still higher than in 1990 (21 percent). On a provincial basis, the prevalence ranged from a low of 20 percent in British Columbia to a high of 30 percent in Quebec. Smoking is more prevalent among males than females in every age category except fifteen-to-seventeen-year-olds, where prevalence is higher among females (26 versus 20 percent).[7]

These findings are consistent with earlier data. In 1996, Statistics Canada's National Population Health Survey (NPHS) reported that the combined prevalence of daily and occasional smokers among fifteen-to-nineteen-year-olds was 3.4 percent higher among girls than boys (30.9 versus 27.5 percent).[8] Indeed, with the exception of 1979, smoking prevalence has been higher among girls in this age group since 1978. Both sexes in this age group, however, evidence a similar phenomenon: while smoking prevalence decreased consistently from 1965 to 1990 (from 55 to 21 percent for boys, and from 37 to 21 percent for girls), it increased throughout the 1990s.

The 1996 NPHS found overall smoking prevalence among daily and occasional smokers over the age of fifteen to be 28.5 percent. This percentage is significantly lower than the 49.5 percent prevalence found in 1965. The decrease was particularly apparent among men, with prevalence falling from 61 percent in 1965 to 31.2 percent in 1996. Smoking prevalence also decreased among women, from 38 percent to 25.9 percent. Again, these data demonstrate a convergence in smoking behavior between men and women. These data also mean, however, that by the end of the 1990s, more than 6.5 million Canadians still smoked on at least an occasional basis.

The NPHS revealed that smoking behavior differs among the provinces, with Quebec having the highest combined prevalence of daily and occasional smoking (34 percent), and British Columbia the lowest (26 percent). Among males, overall smoking prevalence ranged from a high of 41 percent in Prince Edward Island to a low of 26 percent in British Columbia. The highest overall prevalence of smoking among females was found in Quebec (30 percent), with the lowest found in Ontario (23 percent). Among daily smokers, the highest per-capita cigarette consumption (roughly twenty) was found in Prince Edward Island, with Newfoundland daily smokers consuming the least (roughly sixteen). Quebec had the second highest daily consumption (nineteen cigarettes) to accompany its leading position in the overall prevalence ranking. Consequently, among all the provinces, Quebec arguably faces the greatest behavioral, regulatory, and health challenges.

The health challenges posed by smoking to Canada's comprehensive system of publicly funded health care are significant. The Canadian Centre on Substance Abuse estimated that in 1992 the direct health care costs associated with tobacco use amounted to Can$2.6 billion. In 1996 Health Canada reported that there were 45,214 deaths attributable to smoking—a figure that includes deaths from neoplasms, cardiovascular illness, respiratory illness, fire, and environmental tobacco smoke (ETS), as well as pediatric deaths. The number of deaths represented a 9.2 percent increase over 1991, and a 17.9 percent increase over 1989. Smoking-attributed deaths among women increased an alarming 47.7 percent, from 10,820 in 1989 to 15,986 in 1996. Indeed, the federal government reports that lung cancer rates among women have quadrupled since 1969. Overall, smoking accounts for a large proportion of preventable deaths in Canada—for example, 79.3 percent of such deaths in 1989.

The current regime of tobacco regulation in Canada aims at reducing the health effects of smoking by reducing smoking prevalence and consumption. In particular, recent efforts on the part of the federal government have been directed at encouraging smoking cessation and at deterring young people from starting to smoke—the latter of which is especially important in view of the smoking-prevalence trends in the 1990s. At the provincial and municipal levels, policies have also aimed at reducing ETS by regulating the places where tobacco may be consumed.

The federal and provincial governments currently regulate tobacco and smoking through both legislation and taxation. One of the central elements of Canada's current antismoking legislative scheme is the 1997 Tobacco Act and its associated regulations, which impose general restrictions on manufacturers and distributors; restrict promotion, packaging, and products; and impose point-of-sale restrictions. The overarching purpose of the Tobacco Act

> is to provide a legislative response to a national public health problem of substantial and pressing concern and, in particular,
>
> > (a) to protect the health of Canadians in light of conclusive evidence implicating tobacco use in the incidence of numerous debilitating and fatal diseases;
> >
> > (b) to protect young persons and others from inducements to use tobacco products and the consequent dependence on them;

(c) to protect the health of young persons by restricting access to tobacco products; and

(d) to enhance public awareness of the health hazards of using tobacco products.[9]

Although the Tobacco Act replicates the basic regulatory framework of its predecessor, the 1989 Tobacco Products Control Act (TPCA), it makes parts of that framework more precise in order to address constitutional deficiencies in the TPCA that were identified by the Canadian Supreme Court in 1995.[10] For example, unlike the TPCA, the Tobacco Act distinguishes between "brand preference" and "lifestyle" advertising, and imposes an absolute prohibition on the latter while simply regulating the former.[11] In addition, the act permits tobacco companies to attribute any health warnings included on tobacco packaging to a "prescribed person or body if the attribution is made in the prescribed manner."[12]

Not surprisingly, health warnings play a central role in the regulatory framework established by the Tobacco Act. Indeed, the act provides the statutory authorization for Health Canada to promulgate regulations "respecting the information that must appear on packages and in leaflets about tobacco products and their emissions and the health hazards and health effects arising from the use of the products and from their emissions."[13] Pursuant to this authorization, Health Canada promulgated a new set of Tobacco Products Information and Reporting Regulations on June 28, 2000. These regulations, which went into effect in January 2001, impose labeling requirements that in several important respects surpass those found in other countries. The requirements include the following:

- Exterior health warning messages must occupy 50 percent of the principal display surface of packages (cigars excepted).
- Packages must contain one of sixteen health-warning messages, equally displayed among brands. Examples of these warnings are:
  - Cigarettes Cause Mouth Diseases: Cigarette smoke causes oral cancer, gum disease, and tooth loss.
  - Tobacco Smoke Hurts Babies: Tobacco use during pregnancy increases the risk of preterm birth. Babies born preterm are at an increased risk of infant death, illness, and disability.
  - Don't Poison Us: Second-hand smoke contains carbon monoxide, ammonia, formaldehyde, benz(a)pyrene and nitrosamines. These chemicals can harm your children.
  - Cigarettes Are a Heartbreaker: Tobacco use can result in the clogging

of arteries in your heart. Clogged arteries cause heart attacks and can cause death.

- Tobacco Use Can Make You Impotent: Cigarettes may cause sexual impotence due to decreased blood flow to the penis. This can prevent you from having an erection.

- Health warnings must contain color, graphics, and text.
- Packages must include information about toxic emission yields, including yields of formaldehyde, benzene, and hydrogen cyanide.

Not surprisingly, less than two weeks after these regulations were enacted, Canada's largest tobacco company—Imperial Tobacco—initiated legal proceedings to have the labeling and reporting requirements nullified as unconstitutional violations of freedom of expression. The company also asked the Quebec Superior Court to stay the implementation of the regulations until the constitutional challenge could be heard, but on September 20, 2000, the court rejected the stay application and held that tobacco companies must comply with the regulations until their constitutional validity is determined. On December 13, 2002, after a lengthy trial, the court issued its judgment, upholding the constitutionality of the Tobacco Act in its entirety.[14]

A second statute—the Non-Smokers' Health Act (NSHA)—and its associated regulations also form an important part of the federal tobacco control framework.[15] This statute applies to the federal government as an employer, as well as to all private employers regulated by the federal government under the Canada Labour Code. The NSHA requires every such employer to "ensure that persons refrain from smoking in any work space under the control of the employer" except for designated smoking rooms.[16] In addition to this requirement for employers, the act imposes a parallel requirement upon individuals that they refrain from smoking in any work space except designated smoking rooms or areas. The NSHA applies to financial institutions, broadcasting facilities, public transit, transit stations, commercial aircraft, trains, ships, and other federal government workplaces. Employers who violate the regulations are subject to fines ranging from Can$500 for a first offense, to Can$10,000 for each offense after the third (except for ships, where fines range from Can$250 to Can$1,000). Individuals are subject to fines ranging from Can$50 to Can$100.

The national scope of these two statutes means that the regulatory framework so established applies uniformly across Canada. These federal laws and regulations have also been supplemented, however, by the provinces. One reason for such provincial action is that workplaces under provincial regulatory jurisdiction are exempt from the federal antismoking regulations. A second reason is that the federal laws and regulations act as a kind of minimum national standard, with provinces having the ability to "ratchet up" the regulatory framework. Quebec and British Columbia have been the most aggressive provinces. Quebec's 1998 Tobacco Act establishes a comprehensive regulatory regime that complements and covers the same range of subjects as the federal statutes. British Columbia's 1994 Tobacco Sales Act imposes provincial restrictions on manufacturers and distributors; restricts promotion, packaging, and products; and strengthens the federal point-of-sale restrictions. The British Columbia framework also regulates brand-preference advertising, sponsorship, misleading advertising, and several features of packaging and labeling. Nova Scotia has enacted legislation dealing with promotion/advertising/sponsorship and with packaging/labeling, the latter of which is also covered by provincial laws in Ontario and Manitoba. All provinces have passed restrictions on smoking in public and private places under their jurisdiction (for example, schools, shopping malls, and hospitals), and seven provinces have enacted legislation authorizing municipal authorities to pass smoking bylaws. As a result, there are now over forty Canadian municipalities that ban smoking entirely in restaurants, and twenty-five that ban smoking in bars. The City of Toronto was one of the first large municipalities to attempt to control ETS in the hospitality industry; beginning in 1993, 50 percent of seats have been set aside for nonsmokers. In 1999 the city of Victoria, British Columbia, became the first Canadian municipality to effect a total ban on smoking in public places (including restaurants and bars). In early 2000, the British Columbia government instituted a provincewide ban on smoking in all restaurants and bars, despite the opposition of the hospitality industry, including its union, because of the reluctance to alienate smoking customers, especially tourists.

The federal and provincial governments have also used their taxation powers as a health tool in an effort to influence tobacco consumption. Although there is conflicting evidence as to whether price increases or advertising bans have a greater impact on tobacco consumption, Canadian governments have applied both measures to promote their public health objectives. Available figures suggest that price elasticity for Canadian tobacco consumption is in the range of −0.40,[17] and Canadian and comparative data tend to reinforce the "mirror image" between consumption and real prices for cigarettes. In particular, one claim is that higher tobacco prices are especially effective in deterring smoking among youth, since they have relatively fewer financial resources at their disposal.[18] Canadian public health officials, particularly within the federal government, believe that smoking habits are price sensitive, and that increasing the price of tobacco products through taxation can have a direct effect on tobacco consumption. In 1999, taxes accounted for an average of 65 percent of the price of a pack of cigarettes (Can$2.80 of, on average, Can$4.25), ranging from a high of 75 percent in Newfoundland to a low of 55 percent in Ontario. The federal government does not require provinces to match federal tax increases, and there is an informal convention that the federal government will not increase tobacco taxes without provincial consent. Since 1994, the federal government has increased the federal tax on tobacco products three times (1995, 1996, and 1998), for a total increase of about Can$2.00 per carton, or twenty cents a pack. These increases were matched only in certain provinces, most notably Quebec, which raised tobacco taxes by about 9 percent (adjusting for inflation). In effect, from 1994 until the end of the decade, only in Quebec was there a significant increase—about Can$5.00 per carton, or fifty cents a pack—in the price of cigarettes due to taxes (in Ontario, the increase was about Can$3.00 per carton, or thirty cents a pack). On April 6, 2001, however, combined federal and provincial taxes on a carton of cigarettes rose by an additional Can$4.00, or forty cents a pack, in New Brunswick, Nova Scotia, Ontario, Prince Edward Island, and Quebec. On March 19, 2002, the Alberta government announced that its 2002–2003 budget would include a tobacco tax increase of Can$2.25 per pack.

Taxes on tobacco provide an important source of revenue for governments. Federal and provincial revenue from tobacco taxes totaled Can$36.2 billion between 1991 and 1998, with federal tax revenues accounting for Can$18.8 billion (52 percent) and provincial tax revenues accounting for Can$17.4 billion (48 percent). During the 1990s, annual federal revenues from tobacco taxes reached a high of Can$4.1 billion in 1991, dropped to Can$1.9 billion in 1994, and rose to Can$2.1 billion in 1998. Provincial revenues declined steadily from Can$2.8 billion in 1991 to Can$1.8 billion in 1994, but then began to rise steadily until reaching Can$2.2 billion in 1998. The principal explanation for this fluctuation in tobacco tax revenue in the mid-1990s was a massive increase in smuggling, a phenomenon that we treat in greater detail in the next section.

A third potential instrument for regulating tobacco—litigation—has not been used frequently in Canada.[19] At the end of 2003, three class action lawsuits by individual smokers against tobacco companies were pending in Quebec (two cases) and Ontario. None of the classes had been certified; hearings on certification were scheduled for 2004. Also in 1999, Canada launched a U.S.$1 billion civil fraud lawsuit against R. J. R. MacDonald and the Canadian Tobacco Manufacturers Council (the industry's principal association and lobbying group) in the U.S. District Court for the Eastern District of New York. The suit alleged that tobacco companies had engaged in a deliberate conspiracy to smuggle cigarettes into Canada, thereby violating U.S. racketeering laws. The district court dismissed the suit in July 2000 on the ground that Canada was attempting to use U.S. courts to enforce Canadian tax laws. The court declared such an action to be outside its jurisdiction under an eighteenth-century common law rule (the "Revenue Rule"), even though it also expressed doubts about the contemporary viability of the rule. On July 28, 2000, Canada filed a notice of appeal in U.S. federal circuit court. However, on November 4, 2002, the U.S. Supreme Court ended Canada's hope to recover lost tax revenues in U.S. courts when it refused to review the circuit court of appeal's denial of Canada's appeal. The Canadian government responded by resurrecting this action in domestic courts, where it is pending.

In 1997 British Columbia became the first province to pass legislation to facilitate suits for recovering health care costs (the Tobacco Damages Recovery Act, 1997, followed by the Tobacco Damages Recovery Amendment Act, 1998). The tobacco industry challenged the constitutionality of the 1997 act almost immediately, and in March 2000 the provincial Supreme Court (the highest trial court in the province) nullified the statute for overbreadth because it applied to corporations headquartered outside the province.[20] The court nevertheless rejected the tobacco industry's arguments that the legislation interfered with judicial independence and violated the rule of law. British Columbia responded with a new version of the act in 2000. Newfoundland followed suit, passing its own "act to provide for the recovery of tobacco related health care costs."[21]

In March 2000 Ontario also launched a U.S.$40 billion lawsuit against major North American tobacco manufacturers under the Racketeer Influenced and Corrupt Organizations statute in a New York district court. The suit aimed at recovering costs incurred by the Ontario Health Insurance Plan (the government agency that administers the province's publicly funded health care system) in the treatment of smoking-related diseases. The court dismissed the case in August 2000 on the ground that foreign governments should file such claims, insofar as possible, in their own courts.

Not only is it difficult, as we have seen, to sue Canadian companies in U.S. courts, but several features of the Canadian legal system also discourage litigation against tobacco companies. First, class action suits are even more difficult to pursue than in the United States, where they have not, in any event, been especially successful either. Second, the use of contingency fees is a relatively recent phenomenon in Canada, and was only recently permitted in Ontario (Canada's largest and most economically significant province). Third, punitive damages are more difficult to obtain and are usually, when awarded, very modest. These factors suggest that government-initiated suits will dominate future developments in tobacco litigation in Canada.

Notwithstanding the difficulties encountered in litigation against tobacco companies, the preceding overview indicates that tobacco control in Canada by all levels of government is extensive. The road to regulation has been neither fast nor easy, however. Nor has it been without detours. Indeed, in 1994 and 1995 Canadian tobacco control suffered two important setbacks—out of which the current regulatory regime emerged.

The Road to Regulation

As in most liberal democracies, the regulation of smoking and tobacco in Canada has had to meet the burden of justification imposed by the "harm principle," which was originally set forth in John Stuart Mill's *On Liberty*. In its pure form this principle prohibits government regulation of individual conduct except where that conduct poses "a definite damage, or a definite risk of damage, either to an individual or to the public."[22] Although this formulation does not precisely define the permissible scope of government regulation, it does indicate that simple moral disapprobation is insufficient. Without citing Mill directly, the Supreme Court of Canada endorsed this principle in 1992, holding that independent of some harm to society, governments could not justify limits on fundamental rights in order to enforce "a particular conception of morality."[23]

At the risk of oversimplification, the legacy of this principle is that tobacco control has been most often justified in liberal democracies as a child welfare measure. In Canada the prevention of smoking by children formed the basis for legislation early in this century, and two of the four purposes of the 1997 Tobacco Act refer explicitly to the protection of young persons. Restrictions on tobacco use by adults have been somewhat more difficult to justify, although harm to public health—especially in the context of publicly funded health care in Canada—plausibly falls within the harm principle, at least in a financial sense. At a minimum, the principle justifies warning labels and restrictions on advertising and promotion. More problematic are direct restrictions on where people may smoke, which must be justified with reference to the secondary health effects of ETS.

As in the United States, tobacco regulation in Canada has faced the opposition of powerful interest groups and their allies in the federal government.[24] Historically, the tobacco industry—and in particular Imperial

Tobacco, whose products account for about 70 percent of the cigarette market in Canada—has enjoyed a relatively friendly relationship with senior federal government officials.[25]

In 1914, six years after the passage of the Tobacco Restraint Act, a House of Commons Select Committee on Cigarette Evils debated such measures as banning promotions, disclosing nicotine levels, and restricting tobacco advertisements and sales. Despite these prescient initiatives, it was not until the 1960s that tobacco reemerged as a politically relevant health concern.[26] In 1966 Canada's health minister, Allan McEachen, recommended to the cabinet that the government introduce legislation to

> prohibit false, misleading or deceptive labeling, packaging, selling or advertising of cigarettes and cigarette tobacco or advertisements likely to create an erroneous impression regarding character, merit or safety of cigarettes or cigarette tobacco either generally or in relation to the nicotine and tar content in the tobacco smoke produced.[27]

Four years later the House of Commons' Committee on Health, Welfare and Social Affairs recommended a ban on tobacco advertising and promotion, and in 1971 the government introduced legislation (Bill C-248) to that effect.

Before the bill could be debated in Parliament, however, the federal government and the tobacco industry reached a much more permissive agreement than the statutory proposal's outright ban on tobacco advertising and promotion. The industry agreed to follow voluntary advertising guidelines—including an end to advertising on radio and television (only), the elimination of billboards near schools, and the inclusion of inoffensive warning labels on cigarette packs. This early attempt at tobacco regulation failed for a variety of reasons. Smoking had not yet come to be stigmatized, and smokers were, for the most part, unconvinced of the medical evidence about the dangers of tobacco to themselves and their children. The issue was consequently framed in the context of rights—in particular, the rights of smokers to engage in their habit. In the policy community, there was no strong, organized antismoking lobby, and the prevention of smoking was not of primary and vocal concern for any of the established interest groups. In view of tobacco's economic importance as a cash crop and agricultural export, there were strong incentives to heed the tobacco industry's preference for self-regulation. The concentration of tobacco interests in the vote-rich regions of southwestern Ontario (where 90 percent of the flue-cured, Virginia tobacco produced in Canada is cultivated) and Quebec (where Imperial Tobacco is located) further strengthened the industry's strategic position.[28]

Although this early legislative initiative failed, it did transform the Canadian political landscape with respect to smoking—by encouraging the mobilization of new public interest groups committed to antismoking policies, such as the Canadian Council on Smoking and Health (in 1973) and the Non-smokers Rights Association (in 1974). It also galvanized existing groups—for example, the Canadian Cancer Society and the Heart and Stroke Foundation—to focus on smoking as an environmental health issue. Paradoxically, even though the federal government had balked at restraining the tobacco industry directly, it began to promote antismoking as part of a wider public health agenda. Of particular importance was the publication of *A New Perspective on the Health of Canadians* in 1974 under the auspices of the federal minister of health and welfare, Marc Lalonde.[29] The so-called Lalonde doctrine was considered a breakthrough because it focused on public health in terms of lifestyle and environment, and went beyond traditional concerns with biomedical issues and health care organization.[30] One of the report's most significant conclusions was that smoking is an environmental issue with serious health implications for both smokers and nonsmokers (or, in this context, passive smokers). The report inspired a new focus on health promotion within the federal government, including lifestyle changes such as smoking cessation, that would enhance health outcomes. This focus culminated in the 1986 publication of a policy document entitled *Achieving Health for All: A Framework for Health Promotion*,[31] and in the adoption later that same year—in a conference jointly sponsored by the World Health Organization (WHO) and the Canadian government—of the *WHO Ottawa Charter for Health Promotion*.[32]

The late 1980s marked the beginning in Canada of "no-smoking" regulations aimed at ETS in public spaces and the workplace. In 1988, the federal parliament passed the Non-Smokers' Health Act, which banned smoking in all federal government offices and facilities (later extended to all publicly regulated employers) and on all domestic flights of two hours or less (later extended to international flights on Canadian carriers). Pressure for this federal legislation was spearheaded by the aggressive campaigns of public health groups (including the Canadian Cancer Society, the Heart and Stroke Foundation of Canada, the Canadian Lung Association, and the Canadian Council on Smoking and Health), the Non-Smokers' Rights Association, and Physicians for a Smoke-Free Canada. Labor unions working within the Canadian Labour Congress were also involved, but most industrial unions considered other, more serious environmental issues (such as lead exposure and other work-site pollutants) to be more urgent.

Also in the late 1980s, there was an abrupt turnabout on government subsidies to tobacco farmers. As late as 1985, the federal Department of Agriculture attempted to establish a marketing agency to promote flue-cured Canadian tobacco and encourage its production through farm subsidies. The proposal met with sustained opposition from health groups and the antismoking lobbies, however, and by 1987 the federal government had begun to subsidize farmers to cease growing tobacco and to move toward alternative crops.[33] The expenditures for these new programs were significant: between 1987 and 1993, Can$50 million to cease growing tobacco, and Can$13 million for alternative crops.

On the more difficult issue of tobacco regulation, the federal government continued through most of the 1980s to allow tobacco manufacturers the flexibility to follow a "voluntary code" of self-restraint both in tobacco sponsorship and advertising, and in warning labels about the health effects of smoking. In the absence of government initiatives, grassroots activism emphasized the link between public health and smoking concerns—and was especially critical, in particular, of the widespread sponsorship of amateur and professional sports events by tobacco companies.[34] One important victory during this period occurred in 1985, when Canada's minister of fitness and amateur sports, Otto Jelinek, prohibited amateur sports organizations that received federal funding from accepting new tobacco sponsorships.

The social-democratic opposition party in the House of Commons played a crucial role in building the momentum for the adoption of antitobacco legislation. In 1986, Lynn McDonald of the New Democratic Party introduced a private members' bill (C-204) that proposed to restrict smoking in federally regulated workplaces, as well as on planes, trains, and boats.[35] In addition, the bill proposed that tobacco be placed under the federal Hazardous Products Act, thereby prohibiting all advertising and sales except where specifically authorized by regulation. The bill's initial importance was to some degree the product of chance: it was drawn as one of twenty items for further discussion in a lottery of about 150 private members' bills. From that point on, however, the bill played a critical role in pushing official government action forward. Once it reached the floor of the House of Commons for debate, the "Non-Smokers' Health Act" had become a lightning rod for antismoking activists.

The unexpected emergence of Bill C-204 as viable legislation provided the minister of health and welfare, Jake Epp, with needed leverage to push the government toward enacting its own legislation. Thus, in April 1987, Epp announced the introduction of Bill C-51, An Act to Prohibit the Advertising and Promotion, and Respecting the Labeling and Monitoring, of Tobacco Products. The bill became both the focus of intense public debate and the target of extensive lobbying by the Canadian Tobacco Manufacturers' Council, the Non-Smokers' Rights Association, and the

Canadian Cancer Society. Although many in government were reluctant to support the bill, the health minister actively promoted it within the party caucus, and public support for regulation increased.[36] Despite Epp's efforts to enact strong and broad antismoking legislation, the government's apparent strategy was to defeat C-204 while passing C-51, and every cabinet minister present (except Epp, who abstained) voted against C-204.[37] In the end, however, both bills passed, with C-204 becoming the Non-Smokers' Health Act and C-51 becoming the Tobacco Products Control Act.

The TPCA came into force on January 1, 1989. Section 3 identified three statutory purposes:

1. to protect the health of Canadians in light of conclusive evidence implicating tobacco use in the incidence of numerous debilitating and fatal diseases;
2. to protect young persons and others, to the extent that is reasonable in a free and democratic society, from inducements to use tobacco products and consequent dependence on them; and
3. to enhance public awareness of the hazards of tobacco use by ensuring the effective communication of pertinent information to consumers of tobacco products.

To pursue these objectives, the TPCA contained provisions on advertising, promotion, sponsorship, and health warnings. In sum, these provisions prohibited *all* forms of tobacco advertising in Canada; prohibited the free or discounted distribution of tobacco products; prohibited the use of tobacco trademarks on anything other than a tobacco product; permitted tobacco-company sponsorship of cultural or sporting events only if promotional material did not use specific brand names; and required that one of eight separate health warnings appear in an area covering at least 25 percent of a cigarette pack's surface.[38]

In 1996, following the constitutional invalidation of key sections of the TPCA (discussed below), the federal government introduced the Tobacco Act as Bill C-71. The House of Commons' Standing Committee on Health heard evidence on the bill from twenty-six separate organizations over three days in December 1996. Four of these organizations—the Canadian Tobacco Manufacturers' Council, the National Association of Tobacco and Confectionery Distributors, the Regroupement des exploitants de distributrices automatiques de cigarettes, and the Conseil canadien de la distribution alimentaire—raised general objections to the bill. Thirteen additional organizations, largely representing the beneficiaries of event sponsorship by tobacco companies, raised concerns about the bill's sponsorship provisions. Finally, nine largely health-related organizations (for example, the Canadian Council on Smoking and Health, the Non-Smokers' Rights Association, and Physicians for a Smoke-Free Canada) testified in favor of the legislation. These health organizations carried great weight in the legislative deliberations, and when the standing committee considered the regulations emanating from the Tobacco Act on April 23, 1997, it heard only one witness—an official from the Canadian health ministry's Health Policy Division.

Throughout the 1980s and 1990s, bureaucratic activism combined with pressure from external social movements to push the tobacco-control agenda forward. Without exaggerating their influence, certain individuals within the policy community can be identified as playing especially important roles. For example, Neil Collishaw—who worked on long-range health planning in the federal health ministry during the 1970s—took a position in the health protection branch in 1981 to advocate tobacco control. After moving in 1991 to WHO's "tobacco or health" program, Collishaw became in 1999 the research director for Physicians for a Smoke-Free Canada. Similarly, Louis Gauvin, the cofounder and codirector of the Quebec Coalition for Tobacco Control, worked as a public health professional in the areas of tobacco prevention and smoking cessation. The coalition's other cofounder and codirector, Heidi Rathjen, began her career as an activist in the firearms control movement (after witnessing the shooting massacre of fourteen women—mostly fellow students—at Montreal's École Polytechnique). Gauvin and Rathjen established the coalition in response to the decrease in tobacco taxation that occurred in the mid-1990s. Political pressure from both inside and outside government thus played an important role in moving Canada toward its current tobacco-control regime.

Detouring through the 1990s

Canada's tobacco-control regime experienced two detours in the mid-1990s. First, the rapid increase of taxes on tobacco in the late 1980s, coupled with the introduction of new value-added and sales taxes in the early 1990s (the federal Goods and Services Tax, or GST, and the Provincial Sales Tax, or PST), opened a window of opportunity for tobacco smuggling. Smuggling became a noticeable phenomenon in 1988 and increased substantially in 1991 after large tobacco-tax increases and the introduction of the GST. By the beginning of 1994, tobacco smuggling had become a Can$5 billion-per-year industry. Approximately one-third of all cigarettes consumed in Canada were obtained illegally, and more than two million Canadians purchased cigarettes smuggled into Canada from the United States.[39] Ironically, these cigarettes were manufactured in Canada, exported legitimately to the United States (largely to upstate New York), and then returned as contraband.[40] As the figures cited above suggest, and since the goal of the smuggling was to evade taxes, an obvious result of this illegal activity was a decrease in government tax revenue—by 46 percent from 1991 to 1994.

Concerned by both the decrease in revenue and the generally corruptive impact of widespread illegal behavior, the federal government implemented its National Action Plan to Combat Smuggling in February 1994. The principal component of this plan was a massive rollback on cigarette taxes.[41] Federal excise taxes per carton of two hundred cigarettes fell by 48 percent, from Can$10.36 to Can$5.36. Five provinces where smuggling was especially prevalent—New Brunswick, Nova Scotia, Ontario, Prince Edward Island, and Quebec—also reduced provincial taxes per carton by an average of 54.8 percent. In Ontario and Quebec, the two most affected provinces and also Canada's largest by population, the provincial tax rate per carton fell from Can$28.85 to Can$9.65 and from Can$29.61 to Can$8.61, respectively.

Critics of the tax rollbacks on tobacco (including the Canadian Cancer Society, the Non-Smokers' Rights Association, and Physicians for a Smoke-Free Canada) grounded their opposition on the public health effects of lower cigarette prices (by encouraging Canadians to smoke) and on the fiscal effects of depriving government treasuries of important sources of revenue needed for program funding. And as the critics suggested, the rollbacks did have a discernible impact on smoking prevalence, smoking incidence, quit rates, and the amount smoked, at least during the first year of the rollbacks.[42] Although smoking prevalence continued to decline in all provinces, it declined more quickly in provinces that did not experience a tax cut. Thus, by March 1995 smoking prevalence in tax-cut provinces was 28.3 percent, compared to 24.9 percent in provinces without a tax cut. Similarly, the rate at which people started to smoke was 0.5 percent higher in tax-cut provinces by March 1995. Smokers in provinces without a tax cut also quit at a higher rate (10.7 versus 10.3 percent). Finally, while the mean number of cigarettes smoked in tax-cut provinces was stable between April 1994 and March 1995 (16.5 versus 16.4 percent), it declined from 17.0 to 16.5 percent in provinces without a tax cut.

The second detour for antismoking policy occurred in the 1995 case *RJR-MacDonald v. Canada (Attorney-General)*, in which the Supreme Court of Canada nullified the advertising, labeling, and promotion provisions of the 1989 Tobacco Products Control Act on the ground that the provisions unconstitutionally limited freedom of expression.[43] The court reached this decision even though one provincial government (Ontario) and five nongovernmental organizations (the Heart and Stroke Foundation, the Canadian Cancer Society, the Canadian Council on Smoking and Health, the Canadian Medical Association, and the Canadian Lung

Association) intervened in the case to support the TPCA's constitutionality.[44] Consistent with the broad definition given to freedom of expression in earlier cases,[45] the court unanimously held that the 1989 act limited freedom of expression contrary to the constitutional guarantee set out in Section 2 of the Canadian Charter of Rights and Freedoms. Under Canadian constitutional law, however, such a finding does not end the court's inquiry. Section 1 of the Charter stipulates that constitutional rights and freedoms are subject to "reasonable limits." The test for making this determination under Section 1 contains two elements.[46] First, the government seeking to defend the limit must show that its legislative objective relates "to concerns that are *pressing and substantial* in a free and democratic society" (emphasis added). Second, the limit must be proportionate to the legislative objective, which courts determine according to a three-pronged proportionality test. To pass the first prong of this test, the limit must be rationally connected to the legislative objective. Next, the government must show that, by impairing the relevant right or freedom as little as possible, the limit in question represents the least restrictive means of achieving this objective. Finally, it must be clear that the benefits gained from limiting the right or freedom outweigh the costs of the impairment.

The application of this test in *RJR-MacDonald* resulted in a fractured court and, ultimately, a judgment that the statute was unconstitutional. A majority of five justices found the restrictions unreasonable but were divided over the precise extent of the constitutional violation. All five justices (Frank Iacobucci, Antonio Lamer, John Major, Beverley McLachlin, and John Sopinka) held that restrictions on advertising and labeling failed the minimal impairment test, and two justices (Iacobucci and Lamer) also found this to be case with respect to restrictions on promotional activities.[47] In terms of the two areas of common ground, the majority criticized the TPCA for mandating a complete ban on advertising in the absence of evidence that less intrusive regulations would fail to achieve the government's public health objectives. In particular, they criticized the act's failure to distinguish between lifestyle and brand-preference advertising. In their view, while a complete ban might be justified in the former case, it could not be justified in the latter. The majority also criticized the government for failing to provide evidence that the *unattributed* warnings required under the act would be more effective than *attributed* warnings.

In contrast to the majority, the four dissenting justices accepted the legislation as a reasonable limit on an expressive activity that they found to be far "from the 'core' of freedom of expression values."[48] The minority argued that the sole purpose of tobacco advertising "is to promote the use of a product that is harmful and often fatal to the consumer by sophisticated advertising campaigns often specifically aimed at the young and most vulnerable."[49] In its view, the TPCA was precisely the type of social legislation that merited a high degree of judicial deference. The dissenting justices noted that the complete ban on advertising followed two decades of experimenting with less intrusive measures, and that the unattributed health warning requirement represented only a minuscule burden on the tobacco companies' expressive freedom. The majority obviously rejected this approach, arguing instead that

> to carry judicial deference to the point of accepting Parliament's view simply on the basis that the problem is serious and the solution difficult, would be to diminish the role of the courts in the constitutional process and to weaken the structure of rights upon which our constitution and our nation is founded.[50]

The court's judgment in *RJR-MacDonald* clearly established that there are constitutional limits to the policy instruments that governments can employ to control the public visibility of tobacco. According to the court, government regulation of tobacco advertising, labeling, and promotion intrudes on freedom of expression, despite the purely commercial purpose of such expression. Although the court accepted the public health objectives underlying regulation, it forced the government to redesign the specific form it takes.

At first glance, the 1997 Tobacco Act and its associated regulations seem an odd response to the federal government's constitutional loss in *RJR-MacDonald*. Indeed, particularly in the area of labeling, the post–*RJR-MacDonald* regulatory regime appears more intrusive than the one it replaced. Given the high probability of a constitutional challenge to the new regime (which the tobacco industry transformed into a certainty in July 2000), what factors might explain the government's obvious confidence that its new law and regulations were capable of withstanding constitutional scrutiny?

There are at least two answers to this question. The first is that the government will be defending a new law before a new court. The 1995 decision identified two crucial flaws in the impugned legislation: a failure to distinguish between "brand preference" and "lifestyle" advertising, and a failure to allow tobacco companies to attribute health warnings to government authorities (as a consequence of which, the court said, the companies were forced to express opinions that they did not necessarily hold). The 1997 Tobacco Act addresses both of these flaws by imposing a complete ban only on lifestyle advertising, and by allowing attribution of health warnings to

Health Canada.[51] It is also worth noting that, in defending these new pro-visions, the government will face a court with at least four new justices of its own appointment. Given how narrow its 1995 defeat was—a fragmented, 5–4 majority—the government may anticipate that the combination of an amended statute and changes in judicial personnel could shift the outcome of the court's reasonable-limits analysis. Finally, the government has a bet-ter idea of the evidentiary burden it faces and will be defending a statute of its own creation rather than one enacted by its predecessor.

A second, broader answer to the question involves the court's recent adoption of a "dialogue" metaphor to describe and justify its relationship to other branches of government. This metaphor emerged in the court's opin-ion in *Vriend v. Alberta* (1998), where it held that a province's failure to include sexual orientation among the prohibited grounds of discrimination in its human rights statute is an unconstitutional violation of equality.[52] Given the controversial nature of this judgment, the court devoted several paragraphs to the democratic character of rights-based judicial review. It argued that the Charter of Rights and Freedoms "redefined" Canadian democracy to establish a "more dynamic interaction among the branches of governance."[53] According to the court, the growth of this interactive dynamic demands more active participation by the judiciary in a dialogue with legislatures and executives about the proper balance between indi-vidual rights and common purposes. From this perspective, Charter-based judicial review is simply an integral component of a more comprehensive and sophisticated democratic discourse.[54] An important element of this dialogue, the court would say in 1999, is to recognize that courts "do not hold a monopoly of the protection and promotion of rights and freedoms."[55]

The relevance of this metaphor is that it would seem to apply directly to the sequence of events surrounding judicial review of tobacco-visibility regulations: a government restricts freedom of expression in order to pur-sue important public health objectives; the Supreme Court identifies cer-tain flaws in those restrictions and nullifies the statute; the legislature amends its restrictions in light of the court's judgment; the new statute's constitutionality is challenged by those to whom it applies. The government may be anticipating that this series of events constitutes enough of a legislative-judicial dialogue about the proper balance between expressive freedom and public health regulation to withstand constitutional scrutiny.

The detours of the 1990s illustrate that even the most comprehensive, government-supported tobacco-control regime faces constraints. Whether encouraged by the tobacco industry or not, the Canadian tobacco tax revolt of the early 1990s is, in many ways, evidence of the continued salience of liberal ideas about the scope of government. The willingness of large numbers of Canadians to engage in illegal behavior demonstrates that intrusive government action—especially in the form of taxation—can provoke a counterproductive reaction. Similarly, liberal ideas about freedom of expression constrain the type and scope of direct regulation available to the state. Not surprisingly, the material interests affected by tobacco control are more than willing to exploit the strength of these ideas in order to advance their own agenda.

Conclusion: Lessons Learned from the Canadian Experience

Despite tax rollbacks, constitutional setbacks, and the problems associated with coordinating government action in a federal system, Canadian governments have been willing and able to enact policies that go against the preferred interests of the large and powerful tobacco industry in order to advance a broader public health agenda.[56] More importantly, despite disputes at the margins—over such things as the precise scope and content of advertising and labeling regulations, the level of taxation, and the power of municipal governments to regulate smoking activity—there is a general consensus that extensive government regulation of tobacco is justified on public health grounds. Moreover, tobacco control has been successful, at least as measured by smoking prevalence. In less than forty years, a combination of public policy measures has cut in half the percentage of Canadians who smoke. The precise impact of this reduction on overall health levels is perhaps less clear, but it is certainly an important precondition for creating a healthier society.

What lessons can be learned from the Canadian experience? One is that a comprehensive strategy of regulation, taxation, and prevention programs is necessary to change a pattern of individual behavior that is notoriously resistant to change. A second is that this strategy requires internal and external pressure on governments. Third, in federal systems, formal coordination between national and subnational governments is crucial. Fourth, institutions matter, in the sense that once the basic policy decision was taken to control tobacco, the smaller number of veto points in the Canadian political system (at least compared to the U.S. system) eased implementation of the details of that policy. Finally, even with optimal conditions, liberal democratic ideas about the role of government impose real constraints on what can be done. In Canada, these constraints emerged in the form of a tax revolt and constitutional litigation. While the tax revolt and smuggling problem may now be under control, constitutional challenges to tobacco regulation remain an important arrow in the tobacco industry's quiver.

There is an irony, however, in the recent history of tobacco control in Canada. At the precise moment that tobacco regulation and control have become publicly acceptable, Canada has taken important steps toward liberalizing its policies with respect to another smoking-related substance, marijuana. The federal government has legalized the medical use of cannabis, going so far as to license growers of medicinal-grade marijuana and to create a procedure for individuals to secure medical exemptions from federal laws governing its possession, distribution, and cultivation. Public opinion now supports decriminalization of simple marijuana possession, as do leading law-enforcement interests such as the Royal Canadian Mounted Police and the Canadian Association of Police Chiefs. Ministers of both health and justice have signaled their openness to law reform in this area, and the federal parliament has established an all-party committee to investigate the issue. Thus, while Canada becomes more restrictive than its southern neighbor with respect to tobacco regulation, it threatens to become much more liberal with respect to at least one "soft drug." Substance control in liberal states is undeniably a complex phenomenon.

The Politics of Tobacco Control in Australia: International Template?

John Ballard

> In Australia, smoking is a health issue. There is almost universal acceptance that smoking causes disease, and a very effective anti-smoking movement has a willing audience to which it appears credible and reasonable. In contrast, the industry suffers from negative perceptions and cynical audiences. The industry and our smokers are isolated. The isolation is exacerbated by significant legal exposure. Australia is a template for anti-smoking groups in other countries. Recently, a prominent anti-smoking activist, Nigel Gray, said that the battles all had been won; that the tobacco industry had been defeated and was a spent force. Our goal is to prove that he is wrong and to destroy the template.
>
> — *David Rees Davies (CEO, Philip Morris) to Ann Daw (director of planning), November 30, 1993*[1]

For much of their early history, the Australian tobacco industry and forces opposed to it drew largely on British and American precedents. Only from the late 1960s could Australia be said to provide a source of innovation—arguably, a template—for tobacco control. In this chapter I examine how the situation described in the memorandum quoted above came about, focusing particularly on the sources of policy initiative and innovation.

Australia's record in reducing tobacco consumption is good by most measures. From 1945 to 1998 the prevalence of smoking among males over the age of fourteen in Australia fell from 72 percent to 22 percent. Although relatively little of this change took place after 1991, the percentage of those who had never smoked increased from 23 to 34 percent over that period.[2] The prevalence of smoking among women has fallen from a peak of 31 percent in 1983 to a level equal to that among men. Annual adult per-capita consumption fell by 61 percent to 1.37 kilograms in 1999.[3] Yet tobacco use was still the major cause of drug-related deaths in 1998, with 19,019 deaths attributable to smoking,[4] and it remains the leading cause of preventable death and disability in Australia.

Tobacco politics is a unique species of policymaking. The tobacco industry is not alone in denying its own evidence concerning the negative health impact of its products, but its deception has long been recognized by health authorities and activists, and has recently been confirmed by the release of industry documents. The industry's duplicitous image has shaped policy debate and contributed to a willingness to impose stringent governmental controls rather than rely on self-regulation by the industry and by smokers.

Establishing a Modern Discourse on Tobacco

The supply and marketing of tobacco in Australia was closely linked to British and American industry from the mid-nineteenth century, though Australians developed their own production.[5] At the turn of the century a series of industry mergers produced an Australian manufacturing and import monopoly for the British Tobacco Company (Australia), and trade union agitation for nationalization based on the European model was subdued by the imposition of minimum quotas for the use of Australian leaf. Federation of the Australian states in 1901 put an end to separate tariff regimes, and the new federal government quickly discovered a welcome source of revenue in tobacco excise fees.

Australians developed their own culture of smoking. There was a preference for pipes rather than cigars or chewing tobacco, and a preference for roll-your-own cigarettes persisted through the 1950s. As in other Western countries, the provision of cigarettes to military forces during both world wars consolidated tobacco use as the norm among men and ensured its close identification with masculinity. Anti-tobacco movements of the nineteenth and early twentieth centuries—usually initiated by temperance and evangelical religious groups, often with close links to U.S. counterparts—gave a puritanical taint to arguments based on health and fitness. Apart from taxation, however, regulation of tobacco was slight. During the reform period of the early 1900s, child-protection legislation was enacted in each state, imposing age limits for tobacco purchase,[6] and from 1935 smoking was banned in theaters to protect against fire.

The 1950s brought revolutionary change in the tobacco industry, in

Australian smoking culture, and in evidence concerning the health effects of tobacco use. As Australia emerged in the mid-1950s from an extended period of economic restriction, the monopoly held by the British Tobacco Company (locally, WD & HO Wills) was broken by the establishment of new factories by Philip Morris (its first expansion outside the United States) and Rothmans. The new firms introduced aggressive marketing for a proliferation of new brands, including filter-tipped cigarettes with higher tar and nicotine content.[7] Consumption, which had been rising since World War II, attained new heights (2.49 kilograms per capita in 1960–61).[8] During this same period, distribution through thousands of small tobacco shops was displaced by larger, nonspecialist vendors for whom tobacco was a mere fraction of total sales.

From 1949 to 1972, conservative federal governments, formed by a coalition of the Liberal and Country parties, were strongly committed to the promotion of national industrial and agricultural development; state governments, including those controlled by the Australian Labor Party, were also committed to such development during a period of sustained economic growth. The establishment of a newly competitive industry and the increase in tobacco production to meet new demand received especially strong support from the Country (later National) Party. In 1953 a Central Tobacco Advisory Committee (later the Tobacco Research and Development Council) was established, with representation from government, growers, and manufacturers, to promote the interests of the industry. Quotas for imported leaf were steadily reduced, and in 1955 the first Tobacco Plan established a variety of direct and indirect subsidies for growers through irrigation schemes and research, and also for manufacturers. Under the plan, a tobacco industry trust account was established for research and training, financed jointly by growers, manufacturers, and the federal government.

Government involvement in the industry intensified during the 1960s. The Tobacco Marketing Act 1965 established an Australian Tobacco Board (later the Tobacco Marketing Advisory Committee) and marketing boards in each of the producing states (Queensland, Victoria, and New South Wales), while introducing a series of five-year stabilization plans to control marketing and pricing in an effort to protect the Australian crop against cheaper overseas products. The three manufacturers agreed to purchase 50 percent (from 1977 on, 57 percent) of their leaf domestically in exchange for a concessional tariff on imported leaf, generating extra profit for local growers of 36 percent, or Aus$20 million, by 1993.[9] The shift toward economic rationalism in the 1970s brought the stabilization plans under attack in successive reports of the Industry Assistance Commission (later Industry

Commission), which recommended the phasing out of support for what had become the most highly assisted industry in Australia. The stabilization plans were initially scheduled to end in 1995, but a final plan extended into 2000. Even beyond that date, the tobacco industry continued to receive substantial subsidies.

While the tobacco industry was becoming a focus for government support in the 1950s, the discourse of tobacco as an engine of economic development began to be challenged by an anti-tobacco discourse of health. The first results of British and American research linking tobacco and lung cancer were published in 1950 and were reported not only in the *Medical Journal of Australia,* but also in the popular press. Although Australian medical research on smoking was limited, overseas results were followed closely. In 1957, in the wake of the United Kingdom's Medical Research Council warning of an association between tobacco and lung cancer, Australia's National Health and Medical Research Council (NHMRC)—the advisory body representing the medical profession and Commonwealth and state health departments—issued a set of formal recommendations. The NHMRC called for a national campaign on antismoking education and for the establishment of an advisory council on the means of reducing risk in smoking. Three years later, in view of a 33 percent increase in lung cancer from 1954 to 1958, the council repeated its call for a national campaign and asked for a prohibition on tobacco advertising to the young. Through the end of the decade, however, the Australian medical profession had yet to be fully persuaded concerning the link between smoking and lung cancer; for example, both sides of the case continued to be represented in articles appearing in the *Medical Journal of Australia.*[10]

The documents most often cited as initiating the contemporary debate on tobacco and health are the 1962 and 1964 reports on smoking and health prepared, respectively, by the Royal College of Physicians in the United Kingdom and by the U.S. surgeon general's advisory committee. The authoritative nature of these reports drew media and public attention to tobacco-related disease throughout the English-speaking world, but some policy initiatives were already under way. In Australia, apart from the well-publicized NHMRC reports, Western Australia had launched an antismoking education campaign in 1957, and school programs had begun in several states.[11]

In the mid-1960s, following the U.K. and U.S. reports, pressure for regulation intensified. In February 1964 the states, at a conference of health ministers, asked the Commonwealth to assist in a public education campaign on the health risks of tobacco, but the federal government declared the issue to be one for the states.[12] At the insistence of medical groups, successive Commonwealth ministers for health advised the Cabinet of the need for health warnings and advertising restrictions, but the advice was rejected because of the Country Party's continuing protection of the flourishing tobacco industry. Meanwhile, a shift in the Australian Labor Party was taking place. In 1964 its long-term opposition to raising indirect taxes on goods of mass consumption gave way to a willingness to increase the excise on cigarettes to discourage smoking, and in 1967 the party's national conference adopted a policy of banning all tobacco advertising.[13] This shift was not determinative, however, as became apparent after the party attained office in 1972; its anti-tobacco policies, along with its refusal of campaign contributions from tobacco companies, proved short-lived. Consequently, although the 1960s had seen a mobilization of medical opinion favoring tobacco controls, none were enacted until the mid-1970s, several years after advertising restrictions were imposed in Canada, the United Kingdom, and the United States.

Regulation of Advertising: Stage One

By the 1960s a causal relationship between tobacco and lung cancer had become medical orthodoxy, and a retrospective study shows that evidence of the link had accumulated beyond a reasonable doubt by 1959.[14] Public and political consciousness was rising despite the mobilization of counter-arguments by the tobacco industry and its own subsidized band of scientists; a public opinion poll in February 1969 found 80 percent in favor of health warnings on cigarette packs. In the same year, a survey of smoking in schools led the NHMRC to advocate warnings on packs and advertisements, restrictions on advertising, and a national program to warn of the dangers of smoking. These initiatives were endorsed by a meeting of Commonwealth and state health ministers, despite a substantial lobbying campaign by the industry. When the federal government under the Liberal-National Coalition again failed to act, the states began to move.

Although the Liberal premier of New South Wales blocked uniform action among the states, Victoria and Western Australia adopted pack warnings in 1970 (effective from 1973), and other states required a notice on all tobacco advertisements: "Warning—smoking is a health hazard." In 1972, the final year of the Coalition's long hold on the federal government in Canberra, a group of Liberal backbenchers, advised by the Anti-Cancer Council of Victoria (ACCV), persuaded the government to support the attachment of a warning to radio and television commercials. The tobacco industry succeeded in having this warning watered down from "smoking is dangerous to health;" to "smoking is a health hazard;" 30 percent of children later surveyed in Sydney were found to believe that "hazard" meant "habit."[15] The adoption of health warnings was nonetheless the first substantive evidence that governments had abandoned a prosmoking stance, and it provided anti-tobacco groups with political respectability.[16]

Although public opinion favored health warnings and education campaigns, there was greater reluctance to support a ban on advertising. Polls in 1962 showed 21 percent support for a complete ban, which rose to 39 percent in 1972, when 28 percent also favored *some* restrictions on advertising and only 25 percent fully opposed them.[17] Whereas the United Kingdom and United States had banned cigarette advertising on television in 1965 and 1971, respectively, a voluntary code of advertising adopted by the industry enabled Australian Coalition governments to deny the need for regulation. A new Labor government in 1973 introduced a ban on tobacco advertising on television but, at the request of the television channel owners, granted a three-year grace period to develop alternative sources of revenue. By 1976 the Coalition was back in office. Despite a rare vote in the Cabinet, which produced a majority opposed to implementing the ban, Prime Minister Malcolm Fraser declared it carried.[18] During debate in Parliament, however, the leader of the Country Party succeeded in adding a seemingly innocuous, industry-sponsored amendment permitting "incidental and accidental" display of advertising. This exception was claimed necessary in order to allow the broadcast of anti-tobacco advertisements, but its effect was to open the gate for continuous display of stadium-perimeter advertising in televised sports.

The Australian tobacco industry had begun supporting sports and cultural events in the 1950s. Wills served as a major sponsor of the 1960 Olympic team,[19] and Rothmans set up its National Sport Foundation in 1964 in anticipation of a ban on radio and television advertising.[20] Once the ban was in force in 1976, the industry's large television-advertising budget was diverted to much less expensive print media and to sponsorship of sports and cultural events. Major Australian sports events were effectively taken over by tobacco brands: test cricket by Benson & Hedges; the Australian Open tennis tournament by Marlboro; and a rugby league in New South Wales by Rothmans' Winfield, the most popular brand of the 1970s and 1980s. The industry claimed that it was interested only in competition for brand loyalty, and denied allegations by anti-tobacco groups that sports sponsorship was a blatant appeal to the young—allegations later validated by industry documents.[21] Expecting a threat to sponsorship, Philip Morris in 1976 organized the Confederation of Australian Sport, which became the main body representing sport and was successful in obtaining substantial government funding for sports. From the confederation's inception, Philip Morris covertly paid the salary and office expenses of its president.[22] The confederation proved to be an influential proponent of tobacco sponsorship.

During the 1970s much of the focus of anti-tobacco groups, particularly the ACCV, was on the tar content of cigarettes, which was initially higher in Australia than elsewhere. The ACCV regularly publicized the tar levels of different brands, affecting consumer choice, until the federal government took over the task in 1974. Not until 1982, however, was the industry required, through an agreement with the government, to specify tar and nicotine content on cigarette packs.

A report from the Senate Standing Committee on Social Welfare, *Drug Problems in Australia: An Intoxicated Society* (1977), provided the first overview of tobacco policy in Australia. Its many recommendations for reducing consumption included the progressive reduction of tar and nicotine content, curbs on advertising and sports promotion, and an end to the tobacco industry's trust account. The Australian Medical Association, which had declared smoking a health hazard in 1972, responded to the Senate report with even more radical proposals: a ban on vending machines, taxation by tar content, and a levy on tobacco sales to fund a public education program. The industry, aided by revenue-dependent media and advertising bodies, lobbied vigorously against all these proposals. Three years after the Senate report was issued, the Fraser government's formal response accepted only a general commitment to the reduction of consumption, to the reduction and labeling of tar and nicotine content, and to restrictions on smoking in Commonwealth offices.[23] Apart from these policies, the Coalition government in office from 1976 to 1983 was inactive on tobacco control and provided no funding for education programs.

In line with Coalition ideology, the prevailing federal government view depicted smoking as a problem of individual behavior rather than a public policy issue—a position warmly supported by the tobacco industry. The industry's strategy for avoiding further regulation of advertising was the adoption of a voluntary advertising code, which had been in place since 1965 and meshed with the Coalition government's preference for nonintervention. Following the 1976 broadcasting ban, Commonwealth and state health officials were asked to renegotiate the code; they presented proposals for health warnings attached to all advertising, based on the 1976 Canadian code. The industry resisted this approach, but in December 1977 the Media Council of Australia, usually supportive of the tobacco industry, promulgated a voluntary code that required health warnings in all tobacco advertisements. As of 1978, a year after the television ban took effect, the media were still receiving a substantial proportion of advertising revenue from the tobacco industry.[24]

During the 1980s, a gradual shift in public opinion, as well as in policy, toward control of tobacco advertising resulted in large measure from the mobilization of several anti-tobacco groups to contend with industry lobbying, which had enjoyed a relatively clear field.

Lobbying for and against Tobacco

The Australian tobacco industry's political strategy is revealed in a Philip Morris situation review of February 1978. The Australian chief executives of Philip Morris, Wills, and Rothmans had for ten years been advised by

> the industry ad hoc committee, a small group which actively attempts to stave off any anti-smoking laws and regulations . . . Assisted by 15 specialists, including publicists, media experts and lobbyists, the Committee is in daily contact and meets frequently to monitor current events and plan future campaigns. This Committee has close links with tobacco growers, tobacco unions, the Media Council of Australia, the Association of National Advertisers, the Federation of Australian Commercial Telecasters and Broadcasters, and sporting groups throughout the country. It carries out intense, ongoing lobbying with major federal and local political parties and groups, and a continuous contact program with the media.[25]

Lobbying by sports groups had helped to defeat proposals in Tasmania and South Australia to make health warnings compulsory on all advertising. "We had little trouble in persuading sports writers to defend our sponsorship, as many of them are closely involved in corporate promotions."[26] Contracts with sports associations contained escape clauses allowing for the withdrawal of sponsorship if legislation interfered with advertising.[27] The next stages of industry political action were to be undertaken by the Tobacco Institute of Australia, established in December 1978 to coordinate public relations in Australia with the efforts of parallel organizations in other countries set up under an international tobacco industry strategy.

Medical prestige was a significant force in mobilizing political support for anti-tobacco measures. In Melbourne, Dr. Bill Keogh, the medical director of the long-established ACCV, was a force behind the NHMRC statements of the 1950s. He helped persuade the Liberal Party of Victoria in 1957 to call for health warnings on cigarette packs and, four years later, to deplore the failure of governments to act.[28] In Sydney, Dr. Cotter Harvey, president of the New South Wales Medical Board and of the National Tuberculosis and

Chest Association, organized in 1966 the Australian Council on Smoking and Health (ACOSH), modeled in part on the U.S. Interagency Council on Smoking and Health, which had been set up two years earlier. Although its membership was broad, ACOSH was led by physicians and established its roots primarily in New South Wales, Western Australia, and South Australia. The involvement of prominent doctors such as Keogh and Cotter was maintained by those who succeeded them in the battle for further restrictions on advertising.

Unlike most Australian nongovernmental organizations (NGOs)—which have, since the 1970s, depended on government grants for much of their funding—the ACCV was well endowed financially. Its door-to-door campaign, the first in Australia, raised £1.3 million in 1958, and donations and bequests raised its annual income to Aus$1.1 million in 1977, ensuring independence from governments.[29] The council's resources were devoted primarily to research, but Keogh pushed it into public education on the risks of tobacco. His handpicked successor, Dr. Nigel Gray, became the most prominent anti-tobacco activist in Australia, with strong support from an eminent board closely connected with the Melbourne establishment. Gray, who was active in the International Union against Cancer and later served as its president, helped win Liberal Party support in Victoria for the 1970 health warnings. The council also developed the first imaginative anti-tobacco campaign for television—a series of short clips satirizing the glamour of industry advertisements and using well-recognized faces. These clips were considered to have had an impact both on Labor Party policy in the early 1970s and on Fraser's determination to carry through on the advertising ban in 1976. Meanwhile, the council's David Hill became Australia's leading authority on social research on tobacco. In South Australia and Western Australia, doctors in local branches of ACOSH mobilized medical professionals behind a series of campaigns. At a meeting of the Public Health Association in 1979, ACOSH leaders and Gray agreed to concentrate their political efforts on opposition to the tobacco industry's sports sponsorship.

Other anti-tobacco groups formed during this period. The Non Smokers' Movement of Australia (NSMA), modeled on a California group, was organized in Sydney in October 1977 to protest the failure to enforce rules on smoking in public transportation; the industry responded with covert sponsorship of the Smokers' Rights League and funded its advertisements.[30] The NSMA developed a tradition of embarrassing public officials and supporting occupational health litigants, winning media coverage for its cause. It attracted a young doctor, Arthur Chesterfield-Evans, who became its president and produced for several years a radio health program with emphasis on tobacco. Although the NSMA had some support in other capitals, it remained primarily a Sydney group.

In 1978 a small group of Sydney public health activists organized a group called the Movement Opposed to the Promotion of Unhealthy Products (MOP UP). It targeted Rothmans' advertising campaign for Winfields—a campaign featuring Paul Hogan, who had achieved national icon status as a television entertainer. Under a provision of the voluntary code specifying that "[n]o advertising for cigarettes may include persons who have major appeal for children or adolescents,"[31] MOP UP registered a complaint with the Advertising Standards Council against the Winfield advertisements. After eighteen months, and in light of audience research supporting MOP UP's case, the council's chairman ruled that the Hogan campaign violated the code. Rothmans, faced with the alternative of undermining the code's credibility, withdrew its campaign.[32] Annual MOP UP protests in Melbourne were also credited with the termination of Marlboro's sponsorship of the Australian Open tennis tournament.

Initially an offshoot of MOP UP, the more anarchic BUGA UP (Billboard Utilising Graffitists against Unhealthy Promotions) achieved greater notoriety, becoming an international model for effective civil disobedience. Over a period of eight years, BUGA UP was best known for its spray-paint "refacing" of billboards advertising tobacco products, most often to alter their lettering. "Mild" and "Marlboro" became "Vile" and "a Bore"; "Dunhill" became "Dunghill"; and the ubiquitous slogan "Anyway, Have a Winfield" became "Anyway, Have a Wank, It's Healthier." The spontaneous humor of BUGA UP caught the public imagination, and its work was credited with a swing in opinion toward the regulation of advertising.[33] In their campaigns, all of the anti-tobacco groups developed expertise in achieving media coverage, and their lessons were documented by Simon Chapman, himself a leading activist, for emulation by the growing international anti-tobacco movement.[34]

The difference in approach between Melbourne and Sydney—represented by the contrast between the ACCV and BUGA UP as leaders in the anti-tobacco movement—is notable in other areas of public health. Melbourne has long had a progressive social and political establishment in which physicians are prominent. Its teaching hospitals, which give substantial power to professors, have a tradition of research and innovation in public health, leading to major initiatives in government regulation. On child care services in the 1920s, car seat belts in 1970, and in vitro fertilization in the 1980s, Melbourne set world precedents; its model legislation on road safety and sanitary reform, and even the wearing of uniforms in public schools, maintained the State of Victoria's preference for regulation—which dates back to its advocacy of tariff protection and labor arbitration from the late nineteenth century. All of the health initiatives were pushed through with the support of Melbourne's elite. In other states, particularly New South Wales, social and political power is more diffuse. Sydney's libertarian traditions fitted with the loose structures of ACOSH and the spontaneous action of MOP UP and BUGA UP, while public health programs remained almost exclusively a government concern.[35]

In the 1970s the health department of New South Wales delegated substantial initiative to regional offices. The North Coast region, taking seriously the new concept of health promotion, set up a community-intervention project focusing on healthy lifestyles, including tobacco education. Its novel feature was the introduction of a social-marketing approach through media-based campaigns in three communities, each receiving a different level of public health intervention between 1978 and 1982. The "Quit for Life" antismoking campaign, though suspended after formal complaints from the Tobacco Institute, had already proved itself highly effective[36] and served as the basis for a statewide "Quit" campaign in 1983, which was widely copied elsewhere.[37] The North Coast Quit for Life campaign was also seen in Australia as a turning point in the reorientation of public health policy toward health promotion—which subsequently had a significant impact not only on Australia's approach to tobacco education, but also on its response to AIDS.[38]

Shortly after the Labor Party took federal office in 1983, government funding was sought for a national antismoking organization that would serve as a national voice corresponding to the Tobacco Institute of Australia. When nothing was forthcoming from government, state cancer councils and the National Heart Foundation organized and subsidized from 1984 a small advocacy office, Action on Smoking and Health (ASH) Australia. Based initially at the ACCV, ASH moved in 1988 to the New South Wales Cancer Council. Its executive officer, Steve Woodward, who had run Western Australian campaigns for ACOSH, coordinated national campaigns until 1993. After successfully working to enact federal legislation in 1992, ASH discontinued operations and gave way to state-level organizations that had developed, but the organization was revived in 1997 for both national and New South Wales lobbying.

Regulation of Advertising: Stage Two

While broadcast advertising is subject to Commonwealth regulation, the states have the power to control local advertising through cinemas, billboards, shop fronts, and point-of-sale displays. Various attempts were made through private members' and government bills to ban these forms of cigarette advertising and also local sports sponsorship (in South Australia in 1980, 1983, and 1985; in Western Australia in 1982 and 1983;[39] and in Tasmania in 1983). In each case, the Tobacco Institute of Australia succeeded in blocking action—by lobbying Coalition parties and through its intensive media campaigns. The industry was also able to shift its print advertising between states, which enabled the industry to focus its efforts wherever regulation was being seriously considered.[40] Nonetheless, a determined health minister with an experienced advisory team pushed through legislation in South Australia in 1986.[41]

In 1987 Victoria adopted one of the most significant innovations in Australia's anti-tobacco history. In February of that year, the ACCV's medical director, Nigel Gray, received an invitation from David White, minister for health in the state's Labor government, to push through tobacco reform. The minister's father had recently died of emphysema. Gray's account describes the nature of the campaign.

> Thus, opportunistically, began the coalition which was to drive the Victorian Tobacco Act through Parliament on November 17 that year—one of the most serious political defeats suffered by the tobacco industry . . . The [act] banned those forms of advertising susceptible to State control, such as billboards, competitions, giveaways, and applied [an earmarked] tobacco tax to Victorian cigarettes. This tax was pioneering legislation, which was quickly copied by South Australia, Western Australia, California, Massachusetts and others. The idea of earmarking tobacco tax for buying back sport had surfaced in my correspondence as early as 1981 . . .
>
> This Victorian campaign started in February 1987 with a detailed plan which involved me meeting weekly or fortnightly with David White. Mark Birrell, a long-time supporter and Liberal Leader of the Upper House (as well as Shadow Minister for Health), was apprised early and planned much of the second half of the campaign. It was understood at the beginning that the hardest hurdle was likely to be the Liberal Shadow Cabinet, in which 11 out of 20 votes were needed in order to carry the party room [which controlled the upper house of Parliament]. The plan required us to persuade Cabinet and the Labor Party by August of the need for a Bill, and for the Bill to be drafted within the Health Department by then. It would then be announced and followed by a 6–10-week public debate, during which time we had to persuade the Liberal Shadow Cabinet and back bench, then generate a vocal lobby as Parliament debated the Bill.

The plan was military in style, with set times, targets and mar-shalled resources. We conducted an opinion poll which showed clearly that tobacco tax increases were popular, that tobacco advertising was not, and that tobacco sponsorship of sport, while less unpopular, could be replaced by a tobacco-tax-funded body (which eventually was the Victorian Health Promotion Fund) without upsetting the voters. This impressed Cabinet and Parliament. *The Age*, after a visit to the editor, published a five-day intensive coverage of tobacco on the requested date (to coincide with a key Cabinet meeting). This gave both sides much publicity and allowed our public health case to be seriously contrasted with the rather ugly and certainly specious case of the tobacco industry . . .

. . . [I]ndustry blunders helped. One tobacco company reacted to the announcement of the Bill by asking their large staff to telephone, write or visit their parliamentarians. They blocked the parliamentary switchboard, often leaving the company switchboard as the call-back number, thereby enraging many politicians. Our 140,000 donors were requested to do the same and a large but unknown number did so, somewhat more temperately it seemed, but clearly representing grass-roots opinion. We solicited support from innumerable community organisations and were rarely refused.

The then Opposition Leader, Jeff Kennett, may or may not have been surprised to receive about 20 calls from senior Liberals, includ-ing his [party] Treasurer. They were organised by one phone call to a well connected businessman. Two calls to the Anglican and Catholic Archbishops (men I had never met) triggered contacts from them to five important members of the Shadow Cabinet [who had expressed concern about limiting the right to advertise] just before the crucial vote.

So the Bill came to Shadow Cabinet, was passed, passed the Liberal Party room, and went to Parliament, where it was the object of a filibuster attempt by the National Party. Mark Birrell merely told them Parliament would sit until the Tobacco Bill had been dealt with. I watched the tobacco industry people leave Parliament about 5:30 pm, visibly angry, and stayed to see the Bill passed by a unanimous Parlia-ment late on the night of November 17, 1987. Afterwards, the tobacco industry took their money away, at least temporarily, from the Liberal Party, and I was mortified to discover it was the equivalent of only about 10 per cent of our research budget. Should we have been spend-ing our money on political party contributions instead of research?[42]

The element of surprise was significant. The minister's office maintained a war room to manage the joint campaign, and succeeded in concealing activity from the industry until the bill was introduced in Parliament. The Tobacco Institute of Australia, successful in stifling earlier efforts in other states, was caught off guard with insufficient time to mount a countercampaign.[43]

Established with funding from the act's tobacco-tax increase, the Health Promotion Foundation of Victoria (VicHealth) financed Victoria's Quit program for antismoking education (run by the ACCV) and undertook to wean Victorian sports and arts bodies from industry funding. Ron Casey, Melbourne's leading sports commentator, helped organize this stage of the campaign. Most sports associations were happy to substitute Quit advertising for tobacco sponsorship, while others remained loyal to the sponsors that had seen them through an important stage in the commercialization of Australian sport.

Victoria was quickly followed by South Australia,[44] Western Australia, and the Australian Capital Territory in restricting local forms of advertising and in setting up health promotion foundations to fund Quit campaigns. New South Wales was a different matter. ASH had moved its offices to Sydney, where the Liberal state government was closely aligned with the industry (its premier, Nick Greiner, later became chairman of Wills and of its successor, British American Tobacco Australia), but where minor parties and independents held the balance of power in both legislative houses. When an independent state legislator, Rev. Fred Nile, proposed a ban on local advertising and an end to sports sponsorship, the Labor Party agreed, and ASH orchestrated strategic support and lobbying against a massive industry campaign.[45] At the last moment Greiner, in an effort to disable the legislation, persuaded Nile to accept an amendment requiring all other states to enact equivalent measures within twelve months in order for the law to take effect.

There was consequently increasing pressure on the Commonwealth government to close the loophole for stadium-perimeter advertising in the Broadcasting Act of 1976 and to ban print advertising, which lay within federal jurisdiction. Although the Hawke Labor government had been in office in Canberra since early 1983, it was inactive on tobacco issues apart from a ban on importing smokeless tobacco. It was also loath to offend Australia's media barons, Rupert Murdoch and Kerry Packer: tobacco provided 10 percent of Packer's advertising income; Murdoch joined the board of Philip Morris in 1984; and both were heavily involved in commercializing major Australian sports. The minister for health, Neal Blewett, was preoccupied with the reintroduction of national health insurance, battles with the medical profession, and the AIDS epidemic. In 1986, following the U.S. precedent, the Commonwealth government launched its National

Campaign against Drug Abuse. Despite its nominal responsibility for reducing tobacco consumption, the campaign focused—with full support from the tobacco industry—on the rising use of illegal drugs.

At meetings of Commonwealth and state health ministers, it was agreed in principle that further action on advertising was needed, but when the Commonwealth minister announced in October 1988 that he would proceed with legislation only if he had the support of all the states, he did so knowing that such a consensus was unlikely to develop. What forced the government's hand was a declaration by the minority Australian Democrats in August 1989 that they would table legislation banning all remaining forms of tobacco advertising. Public opinion polls showed strong support for a ban, and the government, about to face an election in which it sought Democrat voting preferences, decided to support their bill.

Steve Woodward, director of ASH, coordinated the first national lobbying campaign against smoking, much of it focused on extending the ban on sponsorship. The Tobacco Institute of Australia presented its usual case: that advertising neither entices children nor increases consumption; that it merely affects each brand's market share; and that bans are a form of censorship restricting commercial and individual freedom—a precedent for further incursions.[46]

Government amendments effectively rewrote the Democrats' proposed legislation, deleting all reference to sports sponsorship and perimeter advertising on television, and focusing only on the issue of print advertising (while the government quietly assured print media of continued self-regulation with respect to alcohol advertising). Cabinet held up action until after a Queensland election in November, which returned a Labor government. The Coalition parties were badly divided on the issue, but were forced under intense media scrutiny to abandon a filibuster and accept the bill, the last piece of legislation enacted before the 1990 federal election.

The issue of sports sponsorship remained on the agenda. By the time the Commonwealth government came to act, there were legislative precedents from several states, as well as from Hong Kong, to draw on. The primary concern was that of removing the exemptions implanted in the 1976 broadcasting ban. Early in 1992 the federal minister met with ASH representatives to work out a political strategy, and ASH proceeded to prepare a massive portfolio of relevant research. Support was readily available from the Ministerial Council on Drug Strategy, which brought together the federal minister and state ministers of health and of police affairs. As this group turned its attention to tobacco, Philip Morris urged that it be subjected to "political attack" for its "misplaced priorities" and "usurpation of political authority."[47]

Two pieces of research were of considerable importance in persuading the new Keating Labor Cabinet to support the legislation. First was the publication of a major study of the direct and indirect costs of both licit and illicit drug use. Commissioned by the National Campaign against Drug Abuse and given wide publicity, the research found that the use of tobacco and alcohol resulted in greater social costs than the use of illicit drugs.[48] What was even more important for closing off advertising through sports was ACCV research that undercut industry claims by showing that brand preference among school-age smokers varied markedly according to brand football sponsorship in each state. This evidence was crucial in swinging the support of some ministers. Written into the legislation, however, was authorization for the minister of health to grant exceptions for international sports events that might move away from Australia if tobacco sponsorship were discontinued. Under this provision, international motor racing continues to be broadcast with peripheral tobacco advertising; only in 2000, in conjunction with international action on this issue, was legislation enacted to terminate the exemption in 2006.

Further control of advertising was imposed through expanded warnings on cigarette packs and restrictions on point-of-sale displays. Following a rigorously researched ACCV report on the need for clear warnings on all sides of cigarette packs, the Ministerial Council on Drug Strategy adopted such warnings in 1993. A newly elected Liberal premier in Victoria then reneged on this agreement, insisting, instead, on the industry's preferred European Union warnings and rejecting compromise proposals. The issue was settled when compromise arrangements were mandated by the federal government in 1994 under the Trade Practices Act. In 1999, New South Wales introduced stringent restrictions on the size, placement, and format of point-of-sale advertising, and in 2001 Tasmania's government passed comprehensive tobacco legislation that made it the first state, and perhaps the first jurisdiction globally, to ban all point-of-sale advertising.

Restricting Smoking in Public Places

Prior to World War I, indoor smoking was customarily confined to specified spaces such as smoking rooms and public bars, but after the war, it became the norm for smoking to occur in workplaces, restaurants, and public transportation. Complaints by nonsmokers led gradually to the segregation of nonsmoking space in public transportation, which was largely under governmental control, but only in the 1970s were trains and buses declared smoke free, in part because of cleaning costs. The question of enforcing these bans in each state was the focus of campaigns in the late 1970s by the NSMA and its industry-sponsored opponent, the Smokers' Rights League.

Litigation for compensation for the effects of passive smoking was unheard of until the mid-1980s. As of that time, even cases brought by smokers were unsuccessful—except for claims pursued under veteran-rehabilitation legislation and specifically for having taken up smoking during military service. In 1986, however, various reports on the harmful effects of passive smoking were published, including reviews by the U.S. surgeon general, the World Health Organization's International Agency for Research on Cancer, and the Australian NHMRC. The NHMRC report, referring to U.S. precedents, called for the restriction or prohibition of smoking in workplaces and in enclosed public spaces, hospitals, restaurants, and transportation.

In July 1986, a month after publication of the NHMRC report and the implementation of a ban on smoking in federal government offices, the Tobacco Institute of Australia published an advertisement in major newspapers: "A message from those who do . . . to those who don't." The advertisement claimed that "there is little evidence and nothing which proves scientifically that cigarette smoke causes disease in non-smokers." The Australian Federation of Consumer Organisations (AFCO) had recently been stirred, through its participation in a congress of the International Organisation of Consumers Unions, to take an active role on tobacco. AFCO complained to the Trade Practices Commission, responsible for enforcement of the Trade Practices Act of 1974, which offers protection against false advertising. When the Tobacco Institute refused to give an undertaking not to repeat its claims, AFCO sought an injunction. Its suit became a marathon public-interest test case, with 6,000 pages of evidence, twenty Australian, U.S., and British expert witnesses, and a 211-page judgment issued in February 1991. The Federal Court of Australia, reviewing the evidence on passive smoking, ruled that it is a cause of lung cancer, asthma attacks, and respiratory diseases. In so doing, the court set a global legal precedent that received wide publicity.[49]

From the mid-1980s, there were several workers' compensation cases on passive smoking. In the most publicized of these, a transportation company paid a settlement of Aus$65,000 to a bus driver who claimed that his lung cancer arose from exposure to passengers' tobacco smoke.[50] After the 1991 AFCO judgment on passive smoking, states enacted occupational health legislation in relation to passive smoking, and in 1992 a New South Wales court awarded Aus$85,000 in damages for asthma resulting from nonenforcement of an office-smoking ban; this award was the first of its kind based on a jury verdict. In view of the litigation risk, most large companies had by this time adopted policies to make workplaces either entirely or partially smoke free.[51]

In 1992 the NHMRC began a process of reviewing its 1986 report on passive smoking and was challenged at each stage by the Tobacco Institute of Australia, which submitted a large volume of material largely comprising papers written by scientists with established links to the industry.[52] The new NHMRC report, based on a conservative view of the scientific evidence, recommended that all workplaces and confined public places become smoke free. Through legal action, the Tobacco Institute succeeded in 1996 in delaying publication of the report on the ground that the council's working group had refused to take account of non-peer-reviewed evidence, which was interpreted as a procedural violation of the NHMRC Act.[53]

In the area of public transportation, pilot and flight attendant unions had, beginning in 1982, recommended a ban on smoking on airplanes, but the airlines themselves were reluctant to take up an invitation from the federal government to impose a ban on short flights. Then, in December 1987, a new federal minister for aviation—factionally aligned with the flight attendant union within the Labor Party—announced an immediate ban on smoking on all domestic flights. As regulations increasingly banned smoking in all forms of public transportation, including taxis, and as restaurants became smoke free, the Tobacco Institute of Australia and its partner, the Australian Hotels Association, promoted the international tobacco industry's preferred alternative, air conditioning. Governments seeking to avoid antagonizing hotels, restaurants, bars, and their smoking patrons were encouraged to divert the issue of environmental tobacco smoke into one of air-quality standards. The success of this approach was most apparent in New South Wales, where a bill introduced by Fred Nile, proposing a ban on smoking in public places, was accepted by the government. The government, however, added an amendment, making the legislation dependent on the adoption of a new air-quality standard, on which no further work was undertaken.

The first jurisdiction to introduce comprehensive legislation banning smoking in enclosed public spaces, including restaurants and hotels, was the small and progressive Australian Capital Territory, which did so in 1994, with a grace period of a year for restaurants and three years for licensed premises such as pubs. Following pressure from the Australian Hotels Association, exemptions were allowed for those portions of restaurants and bars meeting air-quality standards that had been introduced for comfort rather than health and safety. Since polling showed a shift in public opinion, other governments followed, usually with lead times and conditional clauses. In 2000 a new Labor government in Victoria brought in legislation covering restaurants, with pubs to follow. The New South Wales government seized the occasion of the 2000 Sydney Olympics to introduce a ban on smoking in enclosed public spaces. Even tobacco-growing Queensland, which had previously avoided regulation and which lacked a strong anti-tobacco NGO, used the National Tobacco Strategy of 1999 as a basis for proposals to catch up with the other states by 2001. Each of these initiatives was welcomed by the unions, which had fully accepted passive smoking as a health risk. In opposition, the Hotels Association (whose chief executive officer transferred from the Tobacco Institute of Australia when the latter ceased operation) made unsubstantiated claims that business, especially tourism, would suffer.

The Beginnings of Comprehensive Tobacco Planning

The last year of Labor's long reign in federal government, 1995, saw the publication of two major reports summing up the state of play in tobacco policy. *Tobacco in Australia: Facts and Issues,* initially prepared by ASH as a briefing document, became a comprehensive review of all issues, sponsored by the Commonwealth Department of Human Services and Health, ASH, and three state health departments. The Senate Community Affairs References Committee, following a 1994 Industry Commission review of the tobacco industry, was asked to review the level of regulation and explore potential cost-recovery mechanisms. In December 1995 the committee issued its report, *The Tobacco Industry and the Costs of Tobacco-Related Illness* (also known as the Herron Report).

The Herron Report made recommendations on a wide range of issues. It proposed that smoking not be permitted in enclosed places, including restaurants, hotels, and sporting venues. It sought an end to exemptions from the ban on sports sponsorship and recommended establishment of a national health promotion foundation to provide alternative sponsorship for sports. It also called for an annual listing of additives in tobacco products, for removal of tobacco from the consumer price index, and for regular increases in excise duties and license fees on tobacco products (along with a commitment of the funds raised thereby to a wide range of new education programs). Although Senator Herron, a doctor, was a future minister in the incoming Howard Coalition government, a minority report from Senator Minchin, shortly to become Liberal minister for industry, provided a better indication of the incoming government's preference for deregulation of business. On publication of the report, the future prime minister, John Howard, echoed tobacco industry rhetoric by referring to the dangers of the "nanny state," though he promised not to roll back existing tobacco regulation. His new government's official response to the Herron Report, tabled in September 1997, referred most of its proposals to the states. The remainder were either set aside for further study or rejected outright.

In view of the stalled decline in smoking prevalence during the 1990s, the

Coalition minister for health provided substantial funding for the first National Tobacco Campaign. Launched in 1997, this collaborative educational effort among federal and state governments and NGOs appears to have had a measurable impact on smoking incidence.[54] The federal government also worked with state governments and NGOs under the aegis of the Ministerial Council on Drug Strategy to formulate the National Tobacco Strategy 1999–2002/3.[55] This, the first comprehensive approach to national tobacco control in Australia, set targets for each state across a range of issues.[56] It shaped planning by states (especially those lagging behind) and by NGOs, and provided benchmarks for best practice in the control of environmental tobacco smoke.[57]

Taxation

Excise duties on tobacco, imposed by the federal government from federation in 1901, have been particularly favored both for their low administrative cost relative to income generated and for the perceived inelasticity of demand for tobacco. Following British precedent, the tax was assessed on a "per weight" rather than ad valorem basis until 1999, when the federal government changed its tobacco-excise assessment to a "per stick" basis. This change reflected anti-tobacco arguments—based on meticulous research by the ACCV's Michelle Scollo—that the industry was producing high-volume, low-weight cigarettes to escape taxation. In the end the tobacco industry itself supported the shift. As of 2000, the Commonwealth collected Aus$5.1 billion in tobacco excise taxes alone[58] and over Aus$8 billion in total revenue from the importation and sale of tobacco products.[59]

The states began to raise substantial revenue from tobacco license fees required of retail outlets from the mid-1970s, and there were substantial rate increases through the 1990s. In August 1997, however, a High Court decision concerning the constitutionality of state tobacco-license fees invalidated all state business-franchise fees, which amounted to over 16 percent of state and territorial revenue. Although the Commonwealth stepped in to compensate the states, the judgment provided the occasion for a review of state/federal fiscal relations.

Given Australia's geographic position, its highly taxed governmental regime has not provoked smuggling on a European or American scale, but has led to the illegal marketing of leaf tobacco known as "chop-chop," thus escaping both taxation and measurement of consumption. Estimates for 2001 put the equivalent value of chop-chop at Aus$600 million (a figure that includes excise losses of Aus$450 million).[60]

The Impact of U.S. Tobacco Litigation

The success of litigation in the United States in the late 1990s led to several initiatives in Australia. A class action by smokers was rejected by the Federal Court in March 2000, ruling that their claims for damages for tobacco-related disease could not be grouped together. The size of the financial settlement obtained by the U.S. state attorneys general in their litigation against the tobacco industry led to calls by the Australian Medical Association and others for comparable action. There was debate as to whether the relatively high level of tobacco taxation in Australia covered publicly funded health costs incurred from tobacco.[61] Because of the significant costs borne by the Australian economy, state attorneys general gave lengthy consideration to the question of whether to pursue litigation—a strategy that they ultimately rejected at the end of 2000.

Also spurred by the success of the U.S. litigation, a coalition of NGOs led by the New South Wales Cancer Council launched proceedings in the Federal Court to recover their past health education costs and to obtain various injunctions. In July 2000, after the court required the coalition to provide security of Aus$100,000 for the costs of each of the three companies, the coalition discontinued the suit.

The wider impact of the U.S. settlement derives from one of its by-products: the availability of industry documentation showing a systematic campaign both to deny and undermine evidence that smoke and smoking endanger health, and to cater to youth smoking and addiction. The most convincing evidence of an international conspiracy—specifically, 1977's Operation Berkshire—was unearthed by Australian activists.[62] That operation, coupled with widely publicized documents concerning the industry's covert activities in Australia, convinced anti-tobacco groups that there are grounds for prosecution. The leading members of a new coalition (Cancer Council Australia, Heart Foundation, ASH, and ACOSH) promoted a September 2001 Senate motion from the Labor Party and Australian Democrats calling on the Australian Competition and Consumer Commission to hold the industry fully accountable under the Trade Practices Act. New impetus was given by a Melbourne court decision in April 2002 striking out all defenses against a claim for damages for lung cancer, on the grounds that British American Tobacco Australia had systematically destroyed documents in anticipation of litigation.[63] The revelations from industry documents—coupled with their intentional destruction—have effectively radicalized strategies for containing an industry that is increasingly seen as a public nuisance and a threat to both good governance and a healthy society.

A Note on Rhetoric and Ethics

The rhetoric of Australian tobacco politics varies somewhat from that of Canada and the United States. Unlike Canada, Australia rejected a bill of rights in a 1988 referendum. The discourse of rights is also much less entrenched in Australia,[64] though since at least the 1970s, it has regularly been adopted by groups combating disadvantage.

> [I]n Australia public political discussion of these matters, like political life generally, is dominated by lawyers, not philosophers. This both expresses and encourages the Australian emphasis on practicality and the suspicion of abstract ideas, unless they can be fully expressed as symbols or simple slogans. Australian perspectives on human rights thus derive their specific character from Australia's legal and political traditions and institutions.[65]

Although Australian courts have found in favor of freedom of expression in relation to public affairs and political discussion, they have not established an absolute right that would override legislative restriction on commercial expression.

The tobacco industry—particularly Philip Morris and the Tobacco Institute of Australia—imported the U.S. language of freedom and rights in arguing against restrictions on advertising and on smoking in public places. The Tobacco Institute's 1983 anti-control campaign in Western Australia against an advertising ban was entitled "The Right to Choose." Its 1991 campaign in New South Wales insisted "Enough is enough!" and warned against government control of private lives. Since the industry has supplied much of the material for opponents of tobacco-control legislation, some of the rhetoric of parliamentary opposition has been framed in these terms. The industry picked up complementary British rhetoric in the form of Margaret Thatcher's denunciation of the "nanny state,"[66] a phrase also deployed by Prime Minister John Howard. In rejecting the antismoking recommendations of a Senate committee, he noted that there "does come a time when you can't protect people against themselves, and perhaps the State shouldn't."[67]

The distinction between U.S. and Australian linguistic usage is nicely caught by an instance of nomenclature. In 1977, leaders of the NSMA met resistance from their membership to perceived radicalism in their proposal to adopt the name of California's nonsmokers' rights movement, though Philip Morris readily set up and funded a Smokers' Rights League to oppose the NSMA. Later, in response to its legal defeat on passive smoking in the AFCO case, the Tobacco Institute of Australia launched a campaign attempting to convert the public issue from one of tobacco versus health, to one of basic freedoms versus bureaucratic control. For this purpose, the Tobacco Institute recruited Australia's best-known manager of advertising campaigns, who invoked the Universal Declaration of Human Rights.[68] When new health warnings were required on cigarette packs in 1993, Philip Morris released a new brand, Freedom, with a quotation from John Stuart Mill on each pack. The tobacco industry deliberately sought to introduce an American rhetoric of rights into the Australian debate on tobacco control, foreshadowing the import of American terminology used in opposing fire-arms control.

Industry attempts to mobilize support among civil rights groups have been unsuccessful. Harm-minimization strategies have had considerable purchase in Australia: needle-exchange programs were readily accepted as a means of dealing with HIV/AIDS, and state governments have considered both decriminalization and controlled administration of heroin. Libertarian groups have generally supported these strategies and have even expressed an interest in implementing strategies designed to reduce smoking—which, as these groups note, causes even more social damage than HIV/AIDS and hard drugs. During the New South Wales campaign of 1991, the Gay Rights Lobby declared that anti-tobacco legislation sponsored by Fred Nile, one of its most vocal opponents, was "the only anti-fag legislation [we] would ever support."[69] The New South Wales Council on Civil Liberties in October 1993 adopted an explicit policy on the issue:

> This Council believes that any individual's liberty should only be cur-
> tailed when it impinges on the liberties of others. We do not oppose
> the sale of tobacco products to adults. It is a person's right to use any
> legal substance, but the context of use should be dependent on the
> comfort of others. Smoking should only be allowed where there is no
> possibility of passive smoking causing harm or discomfort to others.
> The onus should be on the smoker to prove no discomfort or irrita-
> tion to non-smokers. We support the decision of institutions to
> declare enclosed public areas smoke free. Similarly we support the
> right of private ownership to declare "smoking permissible" areas pro-
> viding such areas are well signposted.[70]

Nevertheless, several think tanks and journals that are aligned with the Liberal Party and that take libertarian stances on social issues have occasionally branded heavy taxation and regulation of tobacco as an infringement of rights.[71]

More recently, differences have emerged among anti-tobacco activists over the value of espousing a ban on smoking outdoors. Simon Chapman, former president of ASH and editor of the international journal *Tobacco Control*, has taken a strong line against such a ban on both ethical and tactical grounds, most notably in a debate in the pages of *Tobacco Control* itself.[72] He aligns himself with the ethics of John Stuart Mill and would limit restrictions on tobacco consumption to those based on hard evidence of deleterious health effects. In maintaining this position, he is supported by public health professionals but opposed by Brian McBride, the long-term leader of NSMA, and by activists who argue that outdoor smoking preserves public acceptability for tobacco in the eyes of children and adolescents. Still others regard tobacco as more than a health issue, and seek to remove what is perceived as the malign influence of the discredited tobacco industry from Australian society.

Conclusion

Up to the 1970s Australian tobacco control drew on British, American, and Canadian precedents and provided little in the way of innovation. Exchanges of NGO staff with Britain and visits to Australia from U.S. anti-tobacco luminaries Stan Glantz and James Repace helped shift opinion in Australia.

During the 1970s Australian tobacco policy began to set the pace. Among several Australian innovations, the most celebrated are the Quit campaigns and the health foundations established to displace the tobacco industry's sports sponsorship. Since 1988, the two programs have been a source of inspiration for California's successful antismoking programs.[73] The precedents set by BUGA UP, by the AFCO case on passive smoking, and by the national strategy of the late 1990s have also proved to be of wider significance.

In 1986 the British Medical Association (BMA) published an analysis of its early anti-tobacco work, stressing the importance of "the Australian connection."[74] Simon Chapman had briefed the BMA on campaigns against advertising, while a visit by Arthur Chesterfield-Evans of the NSMA was credited with spurring the formation of the first British direct-action groups, modeled on BUGA UP. Fifteen years later, the executive officer of ASH U.K. urged the British minister for public health:

I believe there is much we could borrow from the Australian experience, and I know your officials have been exploring links and exchanging experience with senior figures in the Australian campaign. In particular, I think we can take the following from Australia.

- The use of harder messages is effective, and behaviour change is driven by discomfort. When Massachusetts used the Australian advertisements, they achieved a 6-fold increase in calls to their help line . . .
- The Australians draw heavily on experts and stakeholders outside the government to shape the campaign, and have formed a Ministerial Advisory Committee, to provide top quality input to the Minister . . .
- Australia's [near-total] ban on tobacco advertising means each dollar spent in Australia is more effective than in the United States, where public health expenditure is dwarfed by tobacco industry promotional expenditure.[75]

Currently, much of the regular exchange of information on new forms of legislation is with Canada and New Zealand, while the advent of Globalink, a tobacco-control network on the Internet, has created a fully international community, albeit primarily among English-speaking countries.

Nonetheless, most of the significant comparative experience that has informed Australian policy has been drawn from different regions within Australia itself. The small number of discrete political cultures in the Australian federation—six states and two territories—has enabled different, innovative approaches to develop within close proximity of one another, thus creating frequent opportunities for cross-pollination. Perhaps even more important is the concentration of Australian society in only a few cities where, as Nigel Gray indicates in his account of Victoria's 1987 legislation, a few well-placed telephone calls, a nice sense of timing, and a carefully planned strategy can, on occasion, enable a group (or a small miscellany thereof) to outflank the resources of a powerful industry. Certainly, the capacity of the anti-tobacco movement to mobilize media, public, and political opinion with limited resources is facilitated by the scope and culture of Australia, in general, and of its urban centers, in particular. The next steps, which could involve criminal prosecution of the industry and its removal from a commercial relationship with consumers, will determine whether Australia remains a creative, leading force in tobacco control.

Militants, Manufacturers, and Governments: Postwar Smoking Policy in the United Kingdom

Virginia Berridge

Most of the extensive literature on smoking in the United Kingdom has focused on the epidemiological "web of causation," not on social science investigation and analysis. With some notable exceptions, there has been little research on smoking culture.[1] The history of smoking as a cultural habit is better served,[2] but there is still surprisingly little on the post-World War II years.[3] This period has been, instead, the province of journalism and political science.[4]

In this chapter, I focus on the development of British smoking policy in the postwar years and analyze four broad stages of policy development. In particular, I show how traditions of voluntary regulation in policymaking, supported by some public health interests, came increasingly into conflict with a militant healthism that began to emerge in the 1970s. The role of science and new "scientific facts" was of central significance in this struggle, and I analyze how and why that scientific battleground has changed over time. I outline some themes that have marked this recent history, together with an agenda for further historical research on health and science policy.

The analysis presented in this chapter is based on traditional historical sources—published sources, interviews with key protagonists, and access to manuscripts, including government archives and those of the main activist organization, Action on Smoking and Health (ASH). The goal, unlike that of much policy writing on smoking (and other current health issues), is not to convey direct policy advice or a policy message, but rather to identify the nature and determinants of issues and to raise historical questions about policy.

At the outset, the basic demographic story of recent smoking in the United Kingdom needs to be quickly outlined. Time series for all adults aged sixteen and over have existed since 1974.[5] There has been a substantial reduction in the proportion of cigarette smokers, from 51 percent of men and 41 percent of women in 1974, to 28 percent and 26 percent, respectively, in 1998. Prevalence declined steadily throughout the 1970s and 1980s, but leveled off during the 1990s. Figures for the second half of the 1990s, however, showed smoking falling again among both men and women. Among men, the reduction in prevalence has been due more to their not having started smoking than to a rise in the proportion of ex-smokers, whereas among women, just the reverse has been true.[6] This difference is itself the result, in part, of smoking having been, until relatively recently, more common among men than women. Prevalence varies among different age groups. In 1998, cigarette smoking was highest among those aged twenty to twenty-four (42 percent for men and 39 percent for women), and lowest among men and women over sixty. A clear class gradient in smoking has developed since the 1970s, when smoking was a cross-class activity. In 1998, men who lived in "unskilled manual labor" households were nearly three times as likely to smoke as those who lived in professional households.

Women's smoking increased in the immediate postwar years but, like that of men, began to decline in the 1970s. In the early 1970s a higher proportion of men than women (at all ages) were smokers. Since then, prevalence at all ages has fallen faster for men than for women, so there is currently (in 2000) a similar prevalence at all ages for men and women. Prevalence fell most for those over fifty years of age and least for those under twenty-five. Whereas in the 1970s smoking was equally prevalent at all ages between twenty and sixty, with lower rates for those under sixteen and over sixty, prevalence now peaks (for both men and women) from twenty to twenty-four and falls progressively with age.

The social profile of smoking has also changed for both men and women; smoking has increasingly become a lower-class, rather than a cross-class, activity. This trend has been especially marked for women. About 40 percent of women in all social classes were smokers in the 1960s. By the early 1990s, only 13 percent of women in the highest social groups smoked, versus 35 percent in the lowest. This figure is 60 percent for lone mothers—a level that has been stable since the 1970s.[7] Martin Jarvis, a leading smoking researcher, has commented that "deprivation and family circumstances are major predictors of smoking, with similar associations to current cigarette smoking in men and in women."[8] The point overall was the increased marginalization of smoking and its closer association with poor people, both men and women.

Chronology of Smoking Policy in the United Kingdom

The chronology assigned to postwar smoking policy has been unclear in most published accounts. Most analysts to date have not been writing with historical change in mind. They have been concerned either with "heroes and villains" history,[9] or with the operation of networks and theories of policy influence, using static models of analysis.[10] The latter type of work has stressed the operation of rival "issue networks" and "producer networks" in policymaking. Historical work has dealt with the industry[11] and the immediate postwar years, concentrating on the 1950s and the early epidemiological "discoveries."[12]

I emphasize a different aspect of the smoking story and specify four distinct policy phases. In the first phase, the 1950s, smoking policy was marked by the cultural normality of smoking and by scientific and governmental uncertainty about the legitimacy of the new epidemiological "facts." In the second phase, the 1960s and 1970s, policy began to emerge at the governmental level, premised on the need to reduce harm from, and the risks associated with, smoking. Policy efforts included health education campaigns, voluntary agreements between government and industry, and scientific research on the development of "safer smoking," which was a strategy that also won support in public health circles. But overlapping with this phase came a new activist policy agenda that put the tobacco industry center stage as "the enemy" and that stressed the role of the media, both as an agent of indoctrination and as a vehicle of public enlightenment about the risks of smoking. In the 1980s, the third phase, science caught up with these new policy agendas: ideas about risk expanded through the concept of passive smoking. In the last of the four stages, the 1990s, the rediscovered concept of "addiction" underpinned both new scientific alliances and a medicalized approach to smoking policy.

The 1950s: Uncertainty in Science and Policy

The story of the "discovery" of the relationship between smoking and lung cancer through the epidemiological research of Austin Bradford Hill and Richard Doll at the London School of Hygiene and Tropical Medicine has often been told.[13] The key paper was published in the *British Medical Journal* on September 30, 1950. This was a case-control study based on twenty London hospitals. Its conclusions were cautious. There was a "real association" between the rise in lung cancer and smoking: the authors concluded that "smoking is a factor, and an important factor, in the production of carcinoma of the lung."[14] Further papers expanded the evidence; the results of a prospective study of British doctors that Doll and Hill started in

1951 continued to inform smoking policy into the 1990s. These conclusions about causation did not go unchallenged. One prominent opponent was the eminent statistician Sir Ronald Fisher, from whose work at Rothampstead agricultural station in the 1920s Hill had derived the original methodology for the randomized controlled trial. Fisher was a eugenist whose scientific framework was the dominant hereditarian and genetic paradigm of British statistics of that time. Other scientists also took up this issue, concentrating on the interpretation of the effects of inhalation and of giving up smoking.[15]

The Hill/Doll work established or refined new technical developments—large population-based surveys, and case-control and prospective studies. The concept of "relative risk" was first introduced in the smoking and lung cancer work, replacing an earlier emphasis on the importance of childhood in adult disease with an emphasis on the risk factors for a specific disease. The importance of this shift of scientific gaze has been underlined by historians of the American smoking story. Both Allan Brandt and John Burnham have argued that the developments marked major changes in the relationships between epidemiology and laboratory science.[16] Changing patterns of disease after the war—in particular, the move from infectious to chronic disease—led to a search for different models of causality and different techniques and styles of work.

Explanations of disease focusing on epidemiological risk came to be accepted, but this process was a gradual one of building scientific claims and did not automatically translate into a change in health policy. Other authors—most notably, Charles Webster—have traced the interactions between the Ministry of Health and its advisory committees in the 1950s, and also those within the Medical Research Council itself, culminating in the council's 1957 special report accepting the causal link between smoking and lung cancer. Shortly thereafter, a Ministry of Health statement in the House of Commons expressed support for the conclusions. Webster has characterized this period as one of delay, with a late, and weak, policy response.[17] A Ministry of Health circular encouraged local authorities to develop health education on the risks of smoking. This response has been ascribed to the smoking habits of key politicians and scientific advisers. The tobacco companies funded research, at arm's length, through the Medical Research Council, and a tobacco tax was an important part of government revenue (16 percent of central revenue in 1950).[18] In 1956 Minister of Health Ian Macleod remarked, "We all know that the Welfare State and much else is based on tobacco smoking."[19]

But there were other factors that inhibited effective action. Politicians and civil servants were, like scientists, uncertain about how to assess the epidemiological evidence. Sir John Charles, chief medical officer of the Ministry of Health, commented that "what I was looking for was evidence apart from the analogous or purely statistical. As far as I am aware, there is no *purely* pathological evidence of this long incubation period in lung cancer."[20] Since the evidence lacked the apparent certainty of laboratory evidence, what kind of proof was it? The most politically sensitive public health issue in the 1950s was clean air and coal pollution, not smoking, as the governmental and Medical Research Council debates make clear.[21] Smoking and lung cancer did not, moreover, fit easily into the contemporary conception of public health. Policymaking was oriented toward the containment of epidemics of infectious disease. Health advice was traditionally aimed at women and children rather than at men, yet more men than women were smokers. And in the wake of World War II, the connotations of "propaganda" made policymakers wary of intervening in matters of individual habit and preference in order to prescribe preferred patterns of behavior. Health advice was consequently notable for "stating the facts" about smoking and leaving individuals to make up their own minds. Finally, health education, which had been handled by the central government during the war, was again a responsibility of local government. Since such education was now funded by local taxes, the Treasury was not anxious to resume control and mount a central campaign on smoking.

The 1960s and 1970s: Risk Reduction and Voluntary Agreements as Contested Public Health Strategies

The medical profession played a crucial role in presenting the new, epidemiological way of seeing public health and its goals to policymakers. Indeed, the 1962 report by the Royal College of Physicians (RCP), *Smoking and Health*, effectively and vividly presented the epidemiological case to the general public and in the policy arena. The RCP committee, whose original mandate was both smoking *and* air pollution, began meeting in 1959. Its work was significant in a number of ways. Although the original goal was to educate doctors, the publicity given to the committee's published report also brought the smoking-cancer link to the attention of policymakers and more broadly into public awareness. Air pollution was a much more politically sensitive issue, and the committee explicitly rejected any environmental association with the rise in lung cancer deaths. Its view was that although individuals could not avoid the dangers associated with pollution, they could avoid those associated with smoking. The committee thus was moving toward a less politically contentious concept of public health—one that emphasized individual responsibility.[22]

The RCP report had mentioned the possibility of restricting advertising, and it was this issue that the government initially focused on. In response, the Tobacco Advisory Committee (subsequently renamed the Tobacco Advisory Council and now known as the Tobacco Manufacturers' Association) agreed to implement a code of advertising practice that was intended to take some of the glamour out of cigarette advertisements. The code was based on the former Independent Television Authority code governing cigarette advertisements on television. Shortly thereafter, in 1965, the government used the powers vested in it under the terms of the 1964 Television Act to ban cigarette advertisements on television. In 1967 the minister of health, the Labor Party's Kenneth Robinson, announced the government's intention to introduce legislation to ban cigarette-coupon schemes, to control or ban other promotional schemes, and to limit other forms of advertising.

Robinson's desire to extend controls even further was frustrated, however, by the opposition of Richard Crossman, who was minister of the Department of Health and Social Security (DHSS).[23] When Robinson presented a draft bill to the Cabinet Home Affairs Committee in July 1968 to outlaw cigarette coupons, Crossman's reaction was brusque. He

> simply blurted out that this was another of those Bills which we simply couldn't afford to pass when we were running up to an election because bans of this sort made us intensely unpopular, particularly with children and families. If you're going to deal with the cigarette-smoking problem you should not try this kind of frivolous but intensely unpopular method. There was a tremendously violent reaction with everyone saying that here we must stand on moral principle. I heard it from Eirene White, Dick Taverne, and Edmund Dell, representing the Board of Trade which has switched its Junior Ministers round, and, indeed, I only had two or three people on my side. However, I'm still just powerful enough to hold the thing up and finally I suggested that instead of forbidding coupons we should ration the amount of money to be spent on advertising and leave it to the cigarette manufacturers to decide how they should spend their money. I found this infinitely preferable. Harmony achieved.[24]

The episode underlined the dominance of electoral considerations, rather than industry influence, in policy strategies. Crossman's opposition was founded on a long-standing belief in the importance of smoking as a working-class habit that had to be approached carefully for electoral reasons. His opponents included Dell, a minister at the Board of Trade who might have been expected to have industry interests more at heart; but he did not take a pro-industry line.

The only formal legal restrictions concerning smoking remained those on sales to children, which dated from very early in the century and were enacted out of the fears of national degeneracy in the wake of Britain's defeat in the Boer War.[25] The Children's Act of 1908 imposed penalties on selling tobacco to children and young persons under the age of sixteen, with a fine of up to £2 for the first offense, £5 for the second, and up to £10 for third and subsequent offenses. It was the duty of any park keeper to seize cigarettes or cigarette papers from any person under sixteen found smoking in a public place. The park keeper could search any boy found smoking (but not any girl). Vending machines used extensively by children could be removed. If a retailer did not know that the cigarettes were for use by someone under the age of sixteen, the retailer was not guilty of an offense. This act was replaced by the Children and Young Persons Act 1933, whose provisions were similar to those of the 1908 act.[26]

The 1971 publication of the second RCP report, *Smoking and Health Now,* led to government action. That action was based on the concept of voluntary regulation, with informal, nonstatutory agreements between government and industry. Those agreements, which have been the norm in British smoking policy, concentrated on three areas: advertising and sports sponsorship; health warnings on cigarette packs; and product modification (the last of which was also connected with the possible regulation of tobacco and tobacco products or substitutes as pharmaceuticals). These policy initiatives are further discussed below. The policy goal was to reduce risk or limit harm.

The regulation of these three areas through voluntary agreement dated from 1971, when Sir Keith Joseph, a Conservative, was secretary of state for health. Joseph initiated a cross-government study of smoking policy and its economic consequences—which was never officially published—and had initially planned an antismoking bill. He scaled down his demands, however, after receiving only moderate backing from his Conservative colleagues.[27] What ensued was the first of the voluntary agreements between the tobacco industry and government: all cigarette packs for sale in the United Kingdom were to state, "Warning by HM Government: Smoking can damage your health;" all press and posters advertisement were to state, "Every pack carries a government health warning;" and the industry agreed to establish a scientific liaison committee consisting of scientists designated by the industry and by the DHSS to explore less dangerous forms of smoking and to devise a way of measuring tar and nicotine levels.[28] That committee was replaced in 1973 by the Independent Scientific Committee on Smoking and Health (ISCSH), which comprised public health and other scientists, and advised both the government and the tobacco industry on the development of tobacco substitutes and "lower risk" cigarettes. The ISCSH produced two reports in the 1970s on these topics. Tar and nicotine tables were produced during the 1970s; subsequent voluntary agreements led to their inclusion on cigarette packs.[29]

Discussion of this period has focused on the roles of Dr. Robert Hunter (chair of the ISCSH throughout the 1970s) and the committee secretary, Andrew Nelmes, who subsequently accepted jobs with the tobacco industry. The context within which the committee operated was also highly significant, however. The parallels were with (medical) drug safety and regulation, where cooperation with the industry was the norm. In particular, the ISCSH's activities paralleled those of the Committee on the Safety of Medicines (CSM), which also established a voluntary relationship with industry. Hunter and Frank Fairweather, chief scientific adviser to ISCSH, both had connections with the CSM, and in terms of policy responsibility, smoking came under the same area (food and drug safety) of the DHSS.[30]

In addition to the voluntary agreement reached between government and industry in the 1970s, the other main policy initiative during this period was the attempt by Dr. David Owen, the Labor Party's minister of health in the mid-1970s, to bring tobacco products under the licensing provisions of the 1968 Medicines Act. Control and monitoring would have been vested in the ISCSH, which would have taken on a more extensive statutory role. After Owen's departure from the DHSS, however, these initiatives petered out. There was also legal opposition from one tobacco company.[31] A few years later, the issue of tobacco substitutes became an academic one; tobacco substitutes such as Cytrel and New Smoking Material were resounding commercial failures.

In the 1960s and 1970s, antismoking forces supported risk reduction, including the concept of safer smoking, as a policy goal. Changing to pipes and cigars—as safer than cigarettes—was included in both the 1962 and 1971 RCP reports, and when Action on Smoking and Health (ASH) was established in 1971, smokers who were invited to join the new committee but were reluctant to do so were told that the organization's main target was cigarettes, not pipes or cigars. This "hierarchy of objectives" (a policy phrase later used in relation to both AIDS and drugs) paralleled the early nineteenth-century temperance movement, which aimed to eradicate spirit consumption rather than stopping all drinking. During the 1970s this harm-reduction objective became much less important in relation to smoking, however, and abstention emerged as the major aim. The tobacco industry became the enemy—rather than a collaborator in a shared agenda.

The roots of this significant change in the stance of public health were complex. New players entering the arena of smoking policy had a significant impact on policy aims. The foundation of ASH, which was modeled on the United States' National Interagency Council on Smoking and Health, provided one impetus for change. ASH was a new style of health pressure group. It was primarily government funded; civil servants had argued that the impetus to introduce antismoking measures would be stronger if there were a voluntary movement pressing government from outside to take action. ASH itself was a London-centered organization with few members. Its major focus—especially under its director from 1973 onward, the professional activist Mike Daube—was on media publicity to generate hostility toward the tobacco industry. Although ASH cooperated in Owen's strategy for tobacco-product licensing, the organization became increasingly disenchanted and, by the end of the decade, came to believe that the Labor government strategy had achieved little.[32]

Also by the end of the 1970s, a new conception of public health was emerging, both within the United Kingdom and internationally. This conception, which stressed the role of individual prevention and responsibility for health, had its roots in the earlier, epidemiological "paradigm shift" of the 1950s epitomized by linking lung cancer to smoking. The "risk-avoiding individual" replaced the mass-vaccination campaign characteristic of public health in the 1950s. Smoking was a central, paradigmatic issue. And in the latter part of the 1970s, a series of government documents on prevention gave authority to these concepts. The agenda presented to the House of Commons Expenditure Committee's investigation into preventive medicine in 1977 gave the essence of the components of this "new public health," recommending an advertising ban, annual price increases, the abolition of cigarette coupons, restrictions on cigarette machines, a stronger health warning on cigarette packs, more nonsmoking areas, targeted health education, and more research into the problem of physiological addiction.[33]

Based on this new (or revived, turn-of-the-century) ideology, ASH and the Health Education Council (HEC) were at the center of a new, distinctive public health alliance that developed around smoking. This alliance was deeply opposed to safer smoking. In one of its advertisements, the HEC portrayed safer smoking as equivalent to jumping off the thirty-sixth rather than thirty-ninth floor of a building. In his dissenting memorandum to the ISCSH's second, 1979 report, Dr. Donald Ball—a public health member of the committee—argued that the "only adequate response to the tobacco disease problem is preventative; this requires measures which stop people smoking or prevent them starting."[34] Public health researchers quoted science back at the committee and its conclusions. Leading smoking researchers Martin Jarvis and Michael Russell pointed out that people smoked to maintain their nicotine levels, so that low-tar/low-nicotine cigarettes might actually cause more harm rather than less, through "compensatory smoking."

By the end of the 1970s, distinct policy positions had thus developed. The "new public health" lobby pressed for more stringent action through an agenda focused on fiscal measures, the control of advertising, and the use of the mass media for health campaigns. By contrast, industry and government shared the objectives of product safety and voluntary regulation. These two approaches have been characterized from the political science perspective as rival "issue" (public health activists) and "producer" (industry/government) networks.[35] The situation was actually more complex, however, because public health and medical specialists were also involved in the product-modification side through their membership in the ISCSH.

The 1980s: Passive Smoking and the Rupture with the Industry

The election of a Conservative government in 1979 led to a hardening of the stances on all sides. Initially, the signs of antismoking interest in the new government were promising. Secretary of State Patrick Jenkin and Under Secretary Sir George Young, who was a keen antismoker and a member of the Commons All-Party Group on Smoking (along with the Conservative Member of Parliament [MP] Lynda Chalker), used the threat of legislative action against advertising as part of the negotiations around a new voluntary agreement. There was no reason why Conservative MPs should not take up the issue. Numerous private members' bills had been introduced over the years by MPs from both parties. In the 1960s, both the Conservative Sir Gerald Nabarro and the Labor MPs Laurie Pavitt and Dr. John Dunwoody had introduced bills (all of which were unsuccessful). Nevertheless, commitment to beliefs in the freedom of the individual and the primacy of market forces tended to be held more widely in the Conservative than in the Labor Party, and antismoking sentiment in the Department of Health was soon defused. Both Jenkin and Young were moved to appointments elsewhere in Prime Minister Margaret Thatcher's reshuffle of September 1981. The possibility of legislation was lost, and the one remaining health minister sympathetic to their concerns, Gerard Vaughan, was subsequently replaced by Kenneth Clarke, a Nottingham MP with constituency interests in tobacco.[36] Daube was later prevented from moving from ASH to a post at the HEC; a subsequently leaked civil-servant memorandum said his appointment would have been a disaster.

This political change arguably placed the public health alliance in a policy cul-de-sac. Members played no part in the main agenda of government, which was focused on the negotiation of voluntary agreements.

Government, in its involvement in the establishment of the Health Promotion Research Trust in the early 1980s—which was funded by the tobacco industry and provided support for health research largely unrelated to smoking—seemed almost deliberately to be ignoring the alliance's concerns. And the risk of smoking was, after all, voluntary.

The prevailing view on the risks associated with smoking was overturned in 1981, when papers by Takeshi Hirayama and others in the *British Medical Journal* showed that the nonsmoking wives of smoking men had a higher risk of lung cancer. A steady stream of evidence subsequently appeared to support this claim. In the United States, the surgeon general's 1986 report accepted the health consequences of what was termed "involuntary smoking," and a National Academy of Sciences report of the same year assessed and measured its health effects. In Britain the government accepted in 1987 an Interim Statement on the subject from the ISCSH (under the chairmanship of Sir Peter Froggatt). In March 1988, ISCSH produced its fourth and last report, in which the committee recognized a small increase in the risk of lung cancer for nonsmokers from exposure to environmental tobacco smoke (ETS). Despite the uncertainties about quantifying this risk, the strategic significance of the concept of ETS risk was considerable. As Froggatt later commented, "The argument that smokers poison only themselves (or their unborn children) can no longer be convincingly sustained. The conceptual framework within which government, industry and the profession have worked, is fundamentally changed."[37]

As has been noted in analyses of smoking policy in both the United Kingdom and United States, smoking control moved from being a matter of individual free will and the regulation of self-control, to a potential harm to the whole community and a threat to "innocent victims."[38] Smokers were individuals who harmed not only themselves, but also the environment and the community at large. This shift in perception was congruent with changes in the "new public health" that incorporated an environmental dimension in addition to the 1970s focus on individual lifestyle. I have called this "environmental individualism." In analyzing passive smoking and its emergence, I have argued, in particular, that the health risk of passive smoking was a "scientific fact waiting to emerge," given that ASH and other anti-tobacco organizations had already begun to argue in the latter half of the 1970s that nonsmokers should be protected against passive smoking; it was an example of the interpenetration of "scientific fact creation" and policy. These "new public health" arguments tended to be on the basis of "rights"—a development of the "nuisance" argument of the earlier, interwar antismoking organization, the National Society of Non-Smokers—rather than on the basis of science.[39] The changes of the early 1980s gave this position the authority of science, however, changing a moral issue into a scientific one, albeit with continuing moral overtones.

The "fact" of passive smoking has continued as a subject of debate, generated in part by organizations related to the tobacco industry. For example, the pressure group FOREST (Freedom Organisation for the Right to Enjoy Smoking Tobacco) argued in a 1991 pamphlet that not all the associations (for example, between ETS and lung cancer) were causal. It argued, too, that the tobacco smoke in the air was not as dangerous as tests in the artificial atmosphere of a laboratory might suggest. And when the figures on passive smoking were analyzed in terms of actual risk rather than increased risk, the number of people affected was negligible. FOREST also argued that the right of people to smoke was as important as the right of nonsmokers to a smoke-free environment. There were many other habits that, like smoking, caused irritation, but, for the most part, people were able to organize their lives accordingly and to reach compromises.[40] The statistician Peter Lee, in a study funded by the tobacco industry, criticized the conclusions drawn from the data on passive smoking. But leading anti-tobacco researchers also looked with disfavor on the conclusions that had been drawn. Richard Peto, for example, pointed out that it was still the individual smoker who was, by far, at the greatest risk. Finally, in 1998, the Scientific Committee on Tobacco and Health—the expert committee that had replaced the ISCSH— published a further report on passive smoking. The committee's meta-analytical study reaffirmed its status as a "scientific fact." It linked ETS to lung cancer, heart disease, SIDS, asthma, and, in children, disease of the middle ear. It recommended, among other things, that smoking in public places be restricted.[41] In 2003 *The Lancet* went further, calling for a total prohibition.[42]

What was the overall impact of passive smoking as a scientific fact? It certainly symbolized a final rupture with the tobacco industry. One epidemiologist noted in an interview that the industry "wouldn't cooperate with me now. Passive smoking was the big watershed."[43] Passive smoking brought heightened pressure on issues concerning public visibility, both in public spaces and in the workplace. Nevertheless, the tradition of voluntary agreements remained strong. Britain deliberately avoided the route of legal regulation, and there was also much less emphasis on lawsuits against tobacco companies.

Public Visibility

Control of public visibility had been central to the voluntary agreements between government and the tobacco industry that had begun under Sir Keith Joseph in the 1970s. And in the 1980s, there were also separate agreements defining and limiting the parameters for the industry's sponsorship of sporting events.[44] During this same period, the antismoking public health alliance focused ever more strongly on the banning of advertising—which became a symbolic objective, despite some dispute about what the impact of advertising actually was. The industry position was presented in 1985 in a Tobacco Advisory Council document,[45] which argued that advertising of tobacco products encouraged brand switching as part of the competition among manufacturers, and that it created incentives for manufacturers to improve existing brands and develop new ones. Consumers of tobacco needed information, and advertising provided it. Advertising was, moreover, a legitimate marketing tool that promoted a legitimate product. The council argued that there was no clear evidence to show that advertising caused anyone to start smoking. Advertising could not, by itself, increase or decrease total consumption of tobacco products in a mature market such as that of the United Kingdom. Banning advertising would result in competition on price, not quality; low-cost foreign brands would gain a further competitive advantage over domestic brands and adversely affect the country's jobs in the industry. The council also argued, as would the House of Commons Health Committee in 1992, that restrictions on advertising would serve to encourage smuggling. In particular, the removal of border controls in the European Community in 1993 would leave the U.K. market especially vulnerable to smuggling because of the price differentials across the EC (resulting from tobacco taxation).

In contrast to this stance, ASH, in the evidence it presented to the Commons Health Committee in 1992, argued that advertising predisposed children to smoking and reinforced the habit in those who already smoked. ASH also argued that a ban would not be an infringement of liberty; it would, instead, be a standard public health intervention. It would, that is, marginally limit the freedom of a minority so as to achieve a much greater good for the majority. It would also protect children from taking up the habit. ASH argued that voluntary controls were ineffective and inappropriate, working against health interests in the long term because they granted legitimacy to tobacco advertising and thus, in turn, legitimated the whole tobacco industry.[46] The 1992 Smee Report on advertising, produced by the government's chief economic adviser, broadly accepted this symbolic view of advertising. In 1999, however, a report by the Institute of Economic Affairs—a radical right think tank—came to a different and more equivocal assessment of the evidence.[47] It concluded, "Even if there remained some shadow of doubt, a prohibition on advertising would be wholly disproportionate. It should furthermore be wholly unacceptable to all who cherish liberal values and decry the process by which individual freedoms have been progressively eroded by political expediency during the present century."[48]

Public Space and Workplace Space

Although passive smoking was the "scientific fact" that had the most recent and direct impact on the control of public space, ETS had been an issue much earlier. The National Society of Non-Smokers, the interwar predecessor of ASH, mounted campaigns against the environmental aspects of smoking, but the arguments were based on nuisance and the selfishness of smokers in inflicting their habit on others—an essentially moral position. There is evidence from post-World War II surveys—in particular, the results of an early health education campaign in Edinburgh—that there was public support for this nuisance-based position rather than for the science of the lung cancer link.[49] Nevertheless, this moralistic agenda was one from which the antismoking campaigners of the 1950s and 1960s were anxious to distance themselves. Until the 1980s, most actions to restrict public smoking had been carried out on a voluntary basis by individual companies. For example, in 1971, after a campaign by ASH, London Transport increased the proportion of cars in Underground trains reserved for nonsmokers from 50 to 75 percent and banned smoking on single-deck buses. In the same year, Rank, a leisure business, began to provide smoke-free seating in most of its cinemas. In 1973 the airline British Overseas Airway Corporation (BOAC) began to reserve a number of its seats for nonsmokers. Much of this activity took place at the local level. For example, Glasgow 2000, a campaign to make Glasgow smoke free by that year, was launched in 1983, and the Tyne and Wear County Transport Committee agreed in 1987 to make all public transportation in the area smoke free.

But it was safety rather than risk that brought about major change in the 1980s. The key safety issue concerned the 1987 Kings Cross fire. After earlier fires, London Transport had been increasing restrictions on smoking on the Underground network. The Kings Cross fire, said to have been started by a cigarette igniting dirt accumulated under an escalator, saw the deaths of thirty-one people. London Transport banned smoking and tobacco advertising throughout the network. British Rail banned smoking on a section of commuter line running through a deep tunnel in central London. Further restrictions followed.

Safety issues brought smoking bans, but the issue of risk through passive smoking continued to be addressed through voluntaristic policies. In 1991, for example, the Department of the Environment published guidelines for the introduction of restrictions on smoking in public places. Nonsmoking, along with the segregation of smokers, was to be the norm inside buildings. Targets for the reduction of smoking in public places were included in the *Health of the Nation* white paper of 1992. Commercial space in shops and restaurants began to be divided. The trend was, in general, permissive. Attempts to include control of smoking in public places in the 1990 Environmental Protection Bill were defeated. The focus was on governmental advice and guidance, and this style was maintained by the succeeding Labor government, elected in 1997, in *Smoking Kills,* its white paper of 1998.[50] Control of smoking in public continued to be an aim of the antismoking alliance, however, as is apparent from the discussions of the 1992 RCP committee on smoking and young people.

> Dr. Stewart-Brown suggested that there could be a recommendation that smoking should be restricted to private places, which would in effect mean a ban on smoking in public places. The aim would be to encourage the same attitude to smoking in public places as to drinking alcohol in public. It was agreed that a recommendation that there should be a trend towards this would be included, but that such a policy was unlikely to be enacted for some time.[51]

Local action was important. For example, in 1995 Oxfordshire ASH and Yorkshire ASH urged magistrates—when implementing the Deregulation and Contracting Out Act, which allows children's certificates to be issued to pubs and bars[52]—to include the condition that areas of pubs and bars licensed for children be smoke free. As another example, institutions made efforts to control the space around their buildings and its use for smoking.[53]

Passive smoking also brought the workplace more centrally into smoking policy. There was local action, and individuals filed legal claims against employers for the long-term effects of passive smoking at work. One case that was lost in 1998 paradoxically established that employers did have a duty to protect employees from the excessive consequences of ETS. But, as with public space, the government's emphasis was on permissive guidance. In 1988, for example, the Health and Safety Executive—the government agency responsible for safety at work—published *Passive Smoking at Work,* which relied on the voluntary action of employers rather than legal action under the Health and Safety at Work Act. The succeeding Labor government also declared that it would not ban smoking at work. The Health and Safety Commission consulted, instead, on a new Approved Code of Practice in the workplace.[54] In general, there seemed to be public support for such restrictions; a 1998 *Guardian* survey found that 73 percent of respondents approved of a ban on smoking at work. The issue concerning passive smoking, public space, and the workplace was clearly important in re-energizing anti-tobacco forces. A 1996 survey of smoking policies in the workplace found that 77 percent of organizations had written policies, compared to less than 50 percent in 1992.

Voluntary Regulation versus Anti-Industry Activism

As we have just seen, passive smoking was to some degree incorporated into the dominant voluntary traditions of governmental policymaking. Those patterns of voluntary regulation continued in other areas—for example, with agreements on advertising and on sports sponsorship. Cooperation between government and industry, with the involvement of leading researchers, also continued; most notably, the ISCSH worked, at arm's length, with industry through the Tobacco Products Research Trust, which had been established with industry money under the 1980 and 1984 voluntary agreements.[55] The work of that trust, which was disbanded in 1995, focused on the association of tar with smoking-related conditions, on compensatory smoking (compensating for the use of low-tar/low-nicotine cigarettes by smoking more), and on how best to reduce the ratio of tar to nicotine in designing a safer cigarette. The program produced significant work on the role of nicotine, concluding that the toxicity of cigarettes might be reduced more if nicotine levels were reduced less than those for tar.[56] The advent of EC regulation in these areas superseded the product-modification program.

At the same time that voluntary regulation was maintained within the government/industry/science nexus, concern about passive smoking underpinned both a harsher stance by anti-tobacco activists and the formation of new anti-tobacco alliances. The developing role of the British Medical Association (BMA) was one example. In the 1980s the organization reconstructed its rather fusty and doctor-focused image through its involvement with public health issues such as smoking (1984) and AIDS. In the case of smoking, the BMA—like the HEC and ASH, with which it worked closely—assumed a high-profile, media-conscious stance, opposing any notion of risk reduction. This absolutist position was demonstrated in 1985 in the furor over Skoal Bandits (a form of chewing tobacco). Public health activists took pride in having them made illegal in 1989; after a campaign led by ASH Scotland, regulations were introduced under Section 11 of the Consumer Protection Act.[57] This rare example of legal restriction was, significantly, of a product aimed at children. The issue of passive smoking was also addressed by Bobbie Jacobson and Amanda Amos in a 1985 BMA/HEC report on cigarette advertising in women's magazines—symbolically entitled *Smoke Gets in Your Eyes*. It was followed in the spring of 1986 by the first mass public health campaign on the hazards of passive smoking. The BMA also launched, with great public relations flair, a report on smoking called *The Big Kill*, a statistical analysis of smoking-related deaths and disease in fifteen regional volumes. The organization credited itself with having produced a much more hostile attitude to smoking as a result of the campaign.[58]

In the 1990s, the anti-tobacco forces, looking to the United States, also turned their attention to litigation, although with little success. One of the first mentions of legal action had come in 1975 when, in a submission to the Royal Commission on Civil Liability and Compensation, ASH had called for tobacco manufacturers and retailers to be made legally liable for compensation in respect to death or illness caused by smoking. That call was part of an effort by anti-tobacco activists in the 1970s to reconstruct the movement along more militant lines.

It was not until 1992, however—in the wake of a U.S. Supreme Court decision in the *Cipollone v. Liggett Group*[59] product-liability case—that there was, for the first time, marked interest in filing such suits in the United Kingdom. Two firms of U.K. solicitors reported that they were inundated with inquiries after they advertised for test cases to bring a similar lawsuit against the U.K. tobacco industry. Suit was eventually filed on behalf of fifty-five lung cancer victims on the ground that the tobacco companies had known since the 1950s that it was the tar in the cigarettes that was causing the cancers, and that they could have taken steps to reduce tar intake. Legal aid was granted for a short while but then withdrawn because the case did not meet the merits criterion—namely, that the case had a good chance of success. Eventually, the solicitors and claimants decided to go ahead on a conditional-fee basis, and legal proceedings on behalf of about fifty claimants were initiated at the end of 1996 against Imperial Tobacco and Gallaher. The fee arrangement was for 100 percent of costs and 25 percent of damages. The case eventually came to court in February 1999. After Lord Justice Wright ruled that the majority of claimants had exceeded the three-year time limit for personal injury claims, the lawyers for the plaintiffs decided that it would be too risky to pursue the case for the remaining claimants. No direct-smoking (versus passive smoking) cases have been won in the United Kingdom.

Taxation—A Class Strategy?

The government and anti-tobacco forces still had one antismoking strategy in common: the important role for taxation as a tool of smoking control. Here, again, the 1970s had been the crucial decade for a change in policy.

The taxation of tobacco had a long history, with significant changes in the 1970s after Britain's entry into the European Economic Community.[60] Although the tax revenue from the sale of cigarettes was a declining proportion of central government revenue, the issue of taxation was to become a central plank of anti-tobacco strategy. In 1950 tobacco tax formed

16 percent of central revenue. This figure was 8 percent in the late 1960s, and fell to 4 percent in 1987, and to 3.6 percent in 1996.[61] The role of taxation figured in the first two RCP reports on smoking (1962 and 1971), but the emphasis was on differential taxation, imposed to discourage more hazardous forms of smoking. This approach was in line with the general emphasis at that time on "harm reduction" in smoking policy. The 1971 report suggested that government should undertake an inquiry into the economic consequences of current smoking habits and into the potential results of a general reduction in cigarette smoking. An interdepartmental inquiry was subsequently conducted, although the results were never officially published. As the 1970s progressed, an argument on taxation became an important plank of the anti-tobacco position. Taxation came to be seen as a tool for achieving the potential abstention from smoking, rather than as one for reducing harm. The Commons Expenditure Committee argued in 1977 for increased taxation, a position that was taken up in the subsequent white paper. As Daube—then director of ASH, and otherwise critical of the government's antismoking record—commented, "Cigarette taxation is the one area in which the Labour administration can be fairly proud of its record."[62] Chancellor of the Exchequer Dennis Healey introduced regular annual increases in cigarette taxes from 1974 to 1977, and in 1978 introduced a supplementary tar tax.

This reliance on tax as a tool in smoking policy was a significant reversal of earlier postwar political attitudes, which had stressed the potential detriment to poor and also elderly smokers from high tobacco taxes. Health economists were beginning to have influence in health policy discussions in the 1970s. For example, Joy Townsend, then chief research officer at the University of Essex's Department of Economics, argued strongly for increased taxation. Her argument was that taxation would advantage rather than disadvantage working-class smokers. If the price of cigarettes were raised, consumers would buy fewer of them and have more money available for other purposes. The end result would be a proportionate reduction in the cost of living for poor families.[63] Smoking was, in Townsend's words, a "waste of working-class life"—a waste that policies involving taxation could help to prevent. High prices would stop working-class consumers from smoking.

This emphasis on taxation continued. In the 1992 policy document *The Health of the Nation,* the government committed itself to raising the tax on cigarettes by at least 3 percent a year in future budgets, thus raising the actual price of cigarettes by about 2.5 percent. This change was justified on various economic grounds. In addition to helping to reduce smoking, the tax increase was needed because of the cost of smoking-related diseases (estimated to cost the National Health Service £610 million in 1993); the

ares caused by smoking (£20 million a year); the loss of productivity
borne by the smoker (30 million working days a year); and transfer
payments such as retirement pensions, pensions to dependents, and sickness and invalidity welfare payments (£190 million a year).

By the 1990s, the growing class differential in smoking brought about the realization that tobacco price and taxation had different effects on different socioeconomic groups, as was highlighted by the 1994 report *Poor Smokers,* by Alan Marsh and Stephen McKay of the Policy Studies Institute.[64] The policy dilemma was that tobacco taxes were, indeed, reducing smoking, but that they had had little or no effect on those who smoked most and could least afford it—the poorest families, whose smoking rates had remained high. Tobacco taxation had therefore been a means of amplifying, rather than reducing, disadvantage. Townsend, who had argued in favor of increased cigarette taxes, suggested that special measures might be necessary to reduce the impact on the poor. This focus on the class implications of taxation carried over into the activities of the Labor government and was a major factor in the discussions concerning the newly revived concept of "addiction" to smoking (see below). The issue of taxation has also been bound up with the role of the European Union and cigarette smuggling (see below).

The 1990s: Addiction and a Medicalized Public Health

The advent of a Labor government in 1997 gave the issues of inequality and "social exclusion" a higher policy profile, the implications of which were soon apparent in the area of smoking policy. The late 1990s saw reorientation of the anti-tobacco forces and of public health interests in government. The 1970s lifestyle agenda for public health, already modified by the environmental individualism of the passive-smoking case, took a new turn. A more medicalized public health was the result, one based on the "rediscovery of addiction."

The concept of dependence or addiction (the two were distinct historically) had not been absent in the smoking field in the postwar period, or even before then, but it had not had any particular policy significance.[65] In earlier times, the idea of the cigarette as "enslaving" had been part of general discourse. The concept of enslavement had not been in tune, however, with the key public health emphasis since the 1970s—which was on self-determination and individual responsibility. But addiction did become a central public health concept in the 1990s. Epidemiology was forming new scientific alliances as its own ability to provide explanations came under increasing attack; these new relationships between different scientific arenas had already been demonstrated in the development of the scientific case for passive smoking, where the discovery of "markers" for smoke intake had helped strengthen the case.[66] For addiction, the evidence came from the field of psychopharmacology, which had been largely separate from public health epidemiology in previous decades. Smoking researchers accepted the inequality arguments in relation to the impact of tobacco taxation, but argued that the root cause was dependence or addiction, and that "treatment" was therefore needed. The medical "magic bullet" was to be nicotine replacement therapy (NRT), free to those having low incomes. This policy paralleled the provision of methadone to drug addicts, another medical public health strategy that had attained increased priority in the wake of the AIDS epidemic.

The prescribing history of NRT had been a tortuous one.[67] Initially viewed as a "quack" remedy, it came to be "owned" by psychologists in the 1970s and 1980s. And as is apparent in the Labor government's policy documents—the smoking white paper, the National Health Service National Plan of 2001—it emerged in the 1990s and 2000s as a central response to the issue of teenage mothers and their smoking habits. NRT was to be provided both within primary care and over the counter. This policy linked teenage mothers and primary care, which were two focal points of government health policy, and provided greater commercial freedom to pharmaceutical companies, which was another emphasis within public health policy at both the national and international levels. The RCP gave its authority to this rediscovered scientific fact through its report *Nicotine Addiction*, published in 2000. Its cover shows a woman avidly drawing on a cigarette. Antismoking interests, which had been hostile to the idea of risk reduction since the 1970s, embraced it anew. The idea of a nicotine regulatory authority was floated in policy documents, including the Commons Health Committee report *The Tobacco Industry and the Health Risks of Smoking*, published in 2000. There were similarities between policy issues concerning NRT and the product-control issues that arose in relation to tobacco substitutes in the 1970s, in that NRT was regulated by medicine-control legislation and the Medicines Control Agency.

The policy developments concerning addiction and NRT have been lower profile, but perhaps more significant, than the more symbolic issues concerning advertising and the advertising ban. The EC's involvement in tobacco issues in the 1990s (see below) resulted in a directive to harmonize national provisions on tobacco advertising. Despite initial U.K. opposition, the Labor government that came into power in 1997 soon rejected that position. Antismoking activists were heartened when, at an antismoking summit held in 1998, cabinet ministers declared their intention to implement the advertising ban. But even by 2001, no ban had been implemented.

The government's desire to exempt Formula One racing from the immediate ban proved controversial because a major donor to Labor Party funds, Bernie Ecclestone, was involved. Moreover, the tobacco industry overturned the ban in the European Court of Justice. Labor subsequently promised to introduce new legislation to ban advertising; the ban was introduced in 2003 and will be fully implemented in 2005.

Themes and Agendas

In this final section I highlight some issues that emerge from the changing nature of relationships within smoking policy during the last half century.

Reconfiguring Public Health and Public Health Science

The changing ideology and focus of public health and public health science have been central animating forces in smoking policy. Smoking was the prime issue that marked the redefinition of public health around lifestyle issues, and the history of smoking policy since the 1950s mirrors the evolution of the broader public health alliance, whose emphasis moved away from risk reduction and toward abstinence in the 1970s. The "new public health" policy program focused on fiscal (taxation) and media strategies (advertising bans and mass-media campaigns), with a new and distinctive role for health activist groups, such as ASH, that took a strong anti-industry stance. This type of public health activism was replicated in other areas—for example, diet and heart disease. Epidemiology became the central public health science, but redefinitions in public health in the 1980s and 1990s—toward greater environmental and biomedical emphases—were reflected in new scientific alliances and new (or reborn) concepts such as passive smoking and addiction. It has been the argument of this chapter that these scientific facts and policy positions were constitutive of each other. At the same time that the pharmaceutical industry was becoming an ally of control, the 1970s hostility toward the tobacco industry was deepening.

The Nature of Policymaking

The particular case study of smoking throws light on the nature of British health policymaking. It has been my argument here that neither the "insider/outsider" models of political science nor the "heroes and villains" analysis presented in journalistic accounts does justice to the complexity of interactions within policy. The tradition of voluntary agreements to make and implement health policy was used by the government not only for smoking policy, but for other, related areas of policy—most notably, the regulation of medicine, where government-industry cooperation was also the norm. The role of the expert committee, a key site of interchange between science and policy, has been an important dimension in the British smoking story—both in the RCP committees outside government and in the role of the ISCSH and its successor, the Scientific Committee on Tobacco and Health. Public health interests and scientists have been involved in these government committees, some of which have also established links with industry. The agenda of risk reduction has come in and out of focus, but has always maintained a presence despite the hostility of antismoking interests since the 1970s.

Local Dimensions of Policy

The central/local dynamic is an important element in British health policy-making. For smoking, policy has often been a matter of local responses—over workplace regulation, or the control of public space, for example. There have been initiatives from Scotland, a country that has a significant role as a dynamic force in British health policymaking; the role of ASH Scotland was important in bringing concern about women and smoking to the fore and in initiating the movement to ban Skoal Bandits.

European and International Dimensions of Policymaking

Increasingly, the European and international dimensions of policymaking have come to the fore. European Union law and directives have, for example, affected domestic policies on taxation and on advertising.[68] The disparity in price between highly taxed, British cigarettes and those in other European countries has created incentives for smuggling, and the price differential for tobacco used in hand-rolled cigarettes is even more marked. The smuggling of tobacco is also becoming a major international problem. There is evidence that tobacco smuggling is a large-scale, organized, global activity, and there are even allegations that British American Tobacco is party to these activities. At the international level, the most significant recent development is the proposed Framework Convention on Tobacco Control, in which the initial protocols cover advertising, smuggling, and treatment. The issues involved—smuggling, industry involvement, and international control mechanisms—are reminiscent of the early stages in the historical development of international drug control and of the trade in illicit drugs. The interwar years were marked both by the expansion of that trade into new markets and by the complicity of pharmaceutical manufacturers in the illicit trade. The very existence of efforts to impose international controls, so historians have argued, fostered excess production, illegal manufacture, and illicit trading.[69] Unfortunately, this history of the international drug trade and of efforts to control it appears to have had little impact on current discussions of tobacco smuggling and control.

Cultural Change, Substance Definition, and the Impact of Policy

A more intangible theme within smoking policy, both in Britain and in other countries, has been the impact of cultural change, the relative marginalization of tobacco, and its "denormalization"—a shift that relates to the concept of the "tipping point" discussed by Allan Brandt.[70] Along with that cultural redefinition of tobacco, there have been various attempts to recategorize and redefine it as a substance. Are tobacco and its active principle—nicotine—a medicine, substance, or illicit drug? Tobacco has been a "borderline substance" (a term used within government), and this definition has both reflected and contributed to the nature of the policy response.

And what impact has that policy had? Can both the decline in smoking and its growing association with social inequality be attributed to formal government policy—that is, to voluntary regulation—or to health activism and its public and media focus? Have voluntary regulation and taxation achieved more than legal bans? The assessment of the combined impact over time of the multiplicity of factors involved presents many difficulties; at present, the question is rarely asked, let alone assessed in terms of future policy formulation.

Conclusion: Historical Analyses of Policy

Even though historical work on postwar smoking policy remains relatively scant, what is known about that period has recently begun to have a significant impact on British politics and public policy.[71] In particular, anti-tobacco activists have been using archival material as a tool in their ongoing political struggle. What can be termed an "official" anti-industry history of tobacco has been developed in a way that pays little attention to normal standards of historical assessment. A heavy "presentism" informs the conclusions that have been drawn. Also apparent in the "findings" of activists is an ahistorical assumption that there have always been "ideal models" of public health response and that past behavior, whether of individuals or organizations, should be judged by reference to such ideal models. The notion of contingent, time-specific, path-dependent responses is absent.

The point of historical analysis is to attempt to interpret events within the context of their own time, not ours. This standard mind-set of the historian appears not to have informed the use of the material on British smoking policy to date. As I have attempted to show, the "problem" of tobacco and its science, together with the problem-solving strategies that were therefore considered appropriate, has changed over time. Such changes are matters for analysis rather than for moral posturing—which incorrectly presupposes a progressive, linear development from past to present. There is also, however, a larger issue concerning the writing of contemporary history. Can the even-handed approach that is standard in analyzing earlier periods of history hold its own in the study of recent, contentious events?[72] As I have attempted to demonstrate, there is more to postwar British smoking policy than a framework of government/industry collusion. To that extent, at least, the failure to observe standards concerning historical research and interpretation has distorted our understanding of our own history, and potentially distorted contemporary public policy.

Liberté, Egalité, Fumée: Smoking and Tobacco Control in France

Constance A. Nathanson

The left-bank intellectual with a Gauloise drooping from the corner of his mouth has virtual iconic status as a symbol—if not to the French themselves, at least to the tourist soaking up culture and smoke in equal parts at every café and on every street corner. This image is, nevertheless, of relatively recent date and, in some sense, misleading.[1] Not until after the Second World War did cigarettes become the dominant form of tobacco consumption in France, and it is only very recently that the prevalence of smoking has come close to that in the United States. Even more counterintuitive, perhaps, is that France was among the first countries to pass, in 1976, stringent tobacco-control legislation, including controls both on advertising and on smoking in places "open to the public." Reflected here are multiple contradictions: not only do symbol and reality collide, but what is symbol and what is reality are often unclear. Underlying these contradictions is a story about the politics of public health, with implications—certainly for France and possibly for other countries as well—that go far beyond the limited arena of smoking and tobacco.

The story is complicated, and the chronologies overlapping. For purposes of exposition, I have divided the basic facts into three sections: (1) the history of tobacco use in France, including current data on consumption and tobacco-related mortality; (2) the relationship between tobacco and the French state, including a brief history of the French tobacco monopoly; and (3) the story of French tobacco-control legislation, a narrative that necessarily overlaps with that of the French tobacco industry. The final two sections consider the background and nature of anti-tobacco militancy in

France, as well as the ideological conflicts that underlie French ambivalence when it comes to reconciling smokers and nonsmokers.

Tobacco Use in France

History tells us that tobacco was first introduced into France in 1556 by a holy father, André Thevet, who had observed and recorded its properties and manner of use in the course of his voyages to the New World.[2] A far more prominent exponent was the French ambassador to Portugal, Jean Nicot, who in 1560 sent seeds and plants (originating, most likely, in Brazil) to the French court. Promoted as a "wonder plant"—an herbal remedy for countless ills, from the migraines of the French queen mother to ulcers and epilepsy—and legitimized by its royal and noble associations, tobacco use was rapidly incorporated into European culture, permeating "all European social classes at about the same time."[3]

Tobacco made the transition from herbal remedy to an essential element in the colonial political economy of Europe during the course of the seventeenth century. For the French (and English) it became the sine qua non of settlement—grown in the colonies as a cash crop, exported to the mother country, and re-exported to the rest of the world.[4] Duties imposed on tobacco imports were an increasingly important source of revenue to the state, and finance ministers, from Richelieu in the early seventeenth century to Necker just before the French Revolution in the late eighteenth century, took steps to ensure the size and continuity of these receipts. In 1674 Colbert declared the manufacture and sale of tobacco products a monopoly of the state. On the eve of the revolution, Necker wrote that "tobacco taxes are of all such contributions the easiest and most imperceptible, and they are included with some reason among the most useful of fiscal inventions."[5] Although the monopoly lapsed for thirteen years following the revolution, it was reinstated by Napoleon in 1810.

The bulk of tobacco consumed in France in the nineteenth century was imported, directly or indirectly, from North America. It was in the fiscal interest of colonial powers to discourage domestic cultivation, although some were more successful in doing so than others, and France seems always to have had some domestic growers. A sense of the relative importance of different sources may be obtained from the composition requirements for *caporal* (coarse tobacco): 40 percent from the United States (Kentucky and Maryland); 24 percent from Hungary; 4 percent from Turkey; and 32 percent from France.[6]

Consumption of tobacco products grew slowly, but continuously, during the centuries following its introduction. Sales of about 7,500 tons per year were reported just prior to the revolution, increasing to 9,000 tons in 1815 and 48,000 tons in 1914.[7] Until early in the nineteenth century, the principal form of tobacco consumed in France was snuff, either in manufactured form or in *carottes* (dense blocks of tobacco) from which individuals grated their own snuff. "Cold" tobacco (to sniff or chew) was displaced by "warm" tobacco (to smoke) in the course of the nineteenth century: at first in pipes, later in cigars, and finally in cigarettes.[8] As measured by their relative position in the sales of the tobacco monopoly, however, cigarettes did not become France's most popular form of tobacco consumption until after the Second World War.[9] From then on, their popularity continued to increase, a trend that has only recently abated.

With the increase of tobacco consumption in the late nineteenth century, there was also an increased denunciation of its dangers.[10] Confronted by the twin threats of German expansion and French population decline, eminent politicians and scientists joined in blaming tobacco, along with alcohol, for the weakness of the military and the poor reproductive performance of women. The first organization against tobacco was founded in 1868. In 1872 the group added alcohol to its purview and became the *Association française contre l'abus de tabac et des boissons spiritueuses*. At its height in the early 1880s, the organization had close to one thousand members, counting among them Pasteur, Dumas fils, and other leading figures of the time. Despite its high profile, the nineteenth-century anti-tobacco movement was unsuccessful in stemming the tobacco tide. By the First World War, it had—unlike the movement against alcohol—essentially disappeared.

Two measures are currently employed to estimate how much a country's population smokes: annual grams of tobacco sold per person fifteen years and older ("consumption"), and smoking prevalence based on population-sample surveys.[11] To give these data some context, I compare French consumption and prevalence patterns with those of the United States. In 1964, the year of the U.S. surgeon general's report on smoking and cancer, annual sales of tobacco in France were less than half of those in the United States. French consumption rose steadily until the early 1990s, dropped between 1991 and 1997, and has since shown signs of leveling off, converging with that of the United States (which had dropped steadily since the mid-1970s). The current prevalence of cigarette smoking based on survey data is substantially higher, however, among French than among U.S. adults: 35 percent of French men and women aged eighteen and over report smoking, as compared with 25 percent of Americans.[12]

In 1990, there were 60,000 deaths in France attributable to tobacco.[13] Among men aged sixty-five and over, lung cancer mortality rates increased fivefold between 1950 and 1992 (from 65 per 100,000 to 336 per 100,000) but have since showed signs of leveling off.[14] Rates among women in the same age group have also increased substantially (and continue to increase), but from a much lower level and at a much slower pace. By comparison with other industrialized countries, however, French lung cancer rates are actually quite low.[15]

Tobacco and the State

By the end of the eighteenth century, the French tobacco monopoly yielded 7 percent of total state revenues. This figure was a weighty one "in that it created both a state interest and private interests that could not readily be ignored when relevant policy questions came to be decided."[16] This state of affairs remained relatively stable until about 1970. In the past thirty years, the interrelated pressures of market, consumer, and regulatory change have led to the monopoly's gradual privatization and, in 1999, to a merger between the tobacco industries of France and Spain. Tobacco nevertheless continues to be an important source of revenue for the French state, and to engage substantial public and private interests.

The *Societé nationale d'exploitation industrielle des tabacs et allumettes*, or SEITA—best known as the manufacturer of Gauloises and Gitanes—was created in 1926. SEITA had the monopoly not only on the manufacture and wholesale distribution of tobacco products and matches, but also on tobacco farming; further, the state was under an obligation to purchase the tobacco harvest. This obligation was ended in 1971, along with SEITA's farming monopoly. In 1976, under pressure from the European Community, SEITA gave up its monopoly of wholesale sales and distribution, opening the French industry to multinational competition. The immediate results were substantial declines in the industry's market share and its revenue. In 1971 SEITA had 97 percent of the French tobacco market. By 1986 its share had dropped to 58 percent; on the date of its merger with Tabacelera (the Spanish tobacco monopoly) in 1999, SEITA's market share was down to just over a third.

SEITA's weaning from the state was a gradual process, lasting nearly twenty years. In 1980 it became a nationalized industry, no longer under direct government control. It was privatized in 1995, although the government retained 5 percent of the stock, along with considerable influence, if not control. By 1999 the government had divested itself of its stock, but it retained a seat on the board of the company created by the merger (Altadis) for a period of one year. Further, the French government continues to have exclusive control of retail sales of tobacco products through 35,000 tobacco shops.

SEITA's economic and political power derived from its contribution to the French treasury, its importance as the sole employer in some of the more impoverished regions of the country, and the elite status of its directors. The latter, graduates of the *grandes écoles,* were fully enmeshed in "the network of links [among these graduates] established across the boundaries between the state and private sectors."[17] SEITA's economic reverses were due, among other things, to the increasing unpopularity among French consumers of the dark *(brun)* tobacco for which its cigarettes were known. Once the French market was opened to competition, sales of American *blonde* cigarettes (principally Marlboros) took off. The industry was slow to respond, but respond it did. *Gauloises Blondes* were introduced in 1984; tobacco cultivation in France has shifted toward light tobacco; and all but a single manufacturing plant have been closed.[18] By the mid-1990s, when SEITA was privatized, the industry's economic health had improved, and the merger announcement in 1999 was upbeat.[19]

Under the French tobacco regime, both tobacco taxes and the total price of cigarettes to the consumer were controlled by the state. Taxes have consistently hovered around 75 percent of the total price (a percentage not atypical for Europe). Until 1991, however, the overall price of cigarettes was about half their cost in other countries of the European Union. The Finance Ministry's interest in holding down the price of cigarettes was dictated by tobacco's inclusion in the cost-of-living index. The index played a major role in employer-employee negotiations over wages and salaries. As long as the index included tobacco, any price increase would immediately have been reflected in demands for higher salaries contributing—from the ministry's perspective—to the threat of inflation. In 1992, as part of a broader legislative initiative to regulate both tobacco and alcohol (see below), tobacco was removed from the cost-of-living index. In the ensuing nine years, cigarette prices have been increased eleven times, by a total of 122 percent. The parallel, if not wholly commensurate, decline in smoking has been attributed to these increases.[20] Higher prices have, of course, redounded to the benefit of the French treasury (tax revenue from tobacco sales doubled between 1991 and 2000) and contributed to the health of the French tobacco industry.[21]

French Tobacco Control in Theory . . . and in Practice:
The *loi Veil* and the *loi Evin*

In 1972 the French National Academy of Medicine passed a unanimous resolution calling attention to the nefarious consequences of smoking.[22]

Nevertheless, detailed knowledge of the reports of the British Royal College in 1962 and of the U.S. surgeon general in 1964 was confined to the few specialists who read English, and there was essentially no public or media attention to this issue until the mid-1970s. Based on the account of, among others, Maurice Tubiana—a distinguished oncologist, member of the French Academy, and chair of a government commission on cancer appointed by the then minister of health, Simone Veil—the catalyzing event took place in 1975 when Tubiana saw the minister being interviewed on television with a cigarette in her hand. Tubiana wrote to Veil and was invited to her office for further discussion, with the end result that Veil became an enthusiastic convert to the cause of smoking and health (although she did not, herself, stop smoking). France's first tobacco legislation, the *loi Veil* —as it became known, after its principal sponsor—was passed with relatively little fanfare in June 1976.[23] The gist of its provisions, described below in greater detail, was to restrict tobacco advertising and to place limitations on smoking in places *affectés à un usage collectif* (open to the public).

As in other parliamentary democracies, legislative proposals come to the French Parliament in the form of government or private bills. The *loi Veil* was a government bill and, as such, had the support of members of the (center-right) party in power. Nevertheless, the government appears to have done its best to minimize what opposition there might have been. The bill was sprung on the General Assembly on a Friday evening with many members absent (a tactic that elicited relatively mild complaint). Government spokespersons took what appears in retrospect to be extraordinary pains to reassure members present that the law would have no adverse economic consequences for tobacco growers and retail outlets, and that there was no intention of "discriminating" against smokers. Parliamentarians congratulated themselves that *tabagisme* was an issue that crossed party lines, since so many members smoked. The most contentious issue was the government's proposal to end tobacco sponsorship of sporting events, resolved by the inclusion of an exception for auto racing.[24] Indeed, the only organized opposition to the government's bill was from the *groupe communiste* on the ground that this "preventive" legislation was largely cosmetic in the face of the real problems facing the country.

Specifically, the *loi Veil* prohibited advertising for tobacco or tobacco products on radio and television, in theaters and movie houses, and, with some exceptions, on posters and billboards. Tobacco sponsorship of sporting events was prohibited, with the exception noted above. Advertising was allowed in retail tobacco sales outlets (small, mom-and-pop stores) and in the print media under specified conditions. Package warnings *(abus dangereux)* and requirements for content labeling (specifics to be determined) were imposed, and pertinent health information was to be provided for schools and the army. Both in the government's presentations to Parliament and in the wording of the foregoing legislative provisions, primary emphasis was on the protection of youth from industry blandishments.

Among the many curious aspects of this legislation (for example, a warning limited to tobacco "abuse"), none are more so than the provisions that refer to smoking in places "open to the public." These provisions consist of two sentences under the heading *"dispositions diverses"* (more or less equivalent to "miscellaneous"). The first sentence reads, "Without prejudice to measures that may be taken by the police to preserve public order and tranquility, decrees of the *Conseil d'état* will determine the conditions under which smoking prohibitions will be established in places open to the public where this practice can have consequences dangerous to health."[25] The second sentence states that in locations and in vehicles where smokers and nonsmokers might be differently affected, the space designated for the nonsmokers cannot be less than half of the total space.

The *loi Veil* was implemented by a series of *décrets* (by the *Conseil d'état*, with the force of law) and *arrêtés* (administrative regulations issued by the Ministry of Health) in 1977 and 1978. The first *décret*, published in September 1977, dealt with smoking in places "open to the public," for the first time making clear (or clearer) what was meant by places *affectés à un usage collectif*. Under the *loi Veil* this phrase referred to educational establishments, hospitals, kitchens where food was *prepared* for sale, and laboratories that dealt with germs or "toxic substances." Also included were modes of public transportation: buses, trains, airplanes, and ships. There was no mention of restaurants and bars, or places of employment. They were excluded by omission. Even within the "places" that were included, however, the rules were far from simple. For example, smoking in schools and colleges was prohibited only where and when students were present. Smoking in hospitals was prohibited only where there were patients. Unless used primarily by students, modes of public transportation were subject to the rule of "no more than one-half:" no more than one-half of the places in buses, trains, airplanes, and so on could be given over to smokers.

Details of the regulations governing advertising and labeling (cursory to the vanishing point by American standards, covering no more than a page of two-column text) were spelled out in subsequent publications. Enforcement of these and the "public places" regulations was delegated to various government ministries, "each one in the area of its concern;" there was provision for a commission composed of officials and representatives of television and the press to oversee the regulation of advertising and to "reconcile opposing interests." In case of violation, the law itself spelled out fines and even authorized, in the extreme, prohibition of product sales.

As a piece of legislation, the *loi Veil* law was ahead of its time, banning most outdoor advertising and restricting smoking in places of public accommodation years before anything comparable was passed elsewhere.[26] In practice, however, the Veil law amounted to little more than an intellectual exercise, honored far more in the breach than the observance. The law was the work of one person, Simone Veil. While it had the support of President Valéry Giscard d'Estaing, the powerful Finance Ministry—ever mindful of tobacco's contribution to the treasury and fearful of what any increase in tobacco prices might do to the cost-of-living index—was opposed.[27] French authorities took few or no steps to enforce the law; industry evasion of its provisions with respect to advertising was widespread; and the law's limitations on smoking in places open to the public were essentially ignored.

The pattern I describe—a law is passed but neither implemented nor enforced with any rigor—is not unusual in France. Indeed, I was told more than once that the French "don't have much respect for law." This statement is something of an oversimplification, however. The law in France has a tutelary function: it is a statement of the norms to which French citizens are expected to adhere, much as a parent sets normative boundaries—"behave respectfully to your elders," "come home before midnight"—for a child. It is not only understood, but expected, that reality may not conform to the norm, but the norm itself is no less valid.[28]

The *loi Evin*

The *loi Veil* was replaced in 1991 by the *loi Evin*, named for the health minister who shepherded its adoption, Claude Evin.[29] Credit for this law belongs in large part to a group of five physicians—the *cinq sages* as they came to be known—who came together out of common frustration with what they saw as government complicity to weaken or evade existing laws for the protection of public health.[30] Following a path very similar to the British physicians who prodded the Royal College into action, the group formed on the basis of prior social and professional connections among these doctors and drew its influence from preexisting sets of distinct, but overlapping, relationships with members of the French medical elite, government officials, and politicians. Chronologically, their story begins not with tobacco, but with alcohol.

In the 1950s the government had established a commission on alcoholism, reporting directly to the prime minister. In the mid-1980s the members of this commission included Claude Got, a professor of anatomy at one of the Paris hospitals and a frequent consultant to the French government on a wide range of public health issues, and Gérard Dubois, a professor of public health in Amiens and adviser to the French system of national health insurance.[31] In 1987, following a decision by the prime minister to authorize alcohol advertising on television, Got made a highly public resignation from the commission, and he and Dubois recruited the cream of the French medical establishment (Nobel Prize winners, current and former presidents of the Academy of Medicine, medical school deans) in support of an intensive media campaign to get this decision overturned. Within three months the authorization for television advertising was withdrawn, and Got and Dubois had discovered the power of medical lobbying.[32]

At much the same time, there was a revival of action on the tobacco front, which had been largely moribund since the passage of the *loi Veil* in 1976. On the advice of Maurice Tubiana and an Italian colleague—advice transmitted directly to their respective prime ministers—the European Community launched Europe Against Cancer, a program that included a war on tobacco. In this context, Albert Hirsch, a professor of medicine and a specialist in lung diseases at a Paris hospital, was asked by a friend, who was then the minister of health, to do the first official evaluation of the *loi Veil*. Hirsch commented (years later) that "I was completely new in this field. I was already very sensitive to public health, but I did not know the field."[33] The 1987 report, *Lutter contre le tabagisme*, was a year in preparation and reflected the work of four teams of specialists. Hirsch sees it as the French equivalent of the Royal College and U.S. surgeon general's reports. "Nothing new, of course, but new in this country. [It was] the first one in France and in French."[34]

The report by Hirsch was scathing in its denunciation of the French government's response to open and widespread violation of the Veil law's provisions with respect to tobacco advertising.[35]

> Ten years after the law's adoption, the inadequacies in its implementation are notorious . . . The authorities have continuously held back, and the fight against tobacco *[tabagisme]* has not, up to now, been a serious object of public policy *[l'objet d'une volonté politique fermement déclarée]*.[36]

The report and its series of recommendations received substantial media attention—due, in part, to a carefully timed article in *Le Monde*, "*Le tabagisme, un véritable désastre sanitaire*" ["Smoking, a health disaster"], signed by medical heavyweights Maurice Tubiana and Jean Bernard.[37] The report was, however, essentially ignored by a government then caught up in the approaching elections. It was at that point that, as described by Hirsch, the advocates of alcohol and tobacco control determined to join forces:

> So, because nothing happened, I decided to join my efforts with a friend, Claude Got.
>
> I knew Claude Got very well, who was at that time involved with alcohol control. And because nothing happened in alcohol and nothing happened in tobacco, Claude Got and I decided to join our efforts in order to lobby. This was completely new in France. We decided to increase the number of the group to five. Claude Got introduced me to Gérard Dubois, because they were both involved in the alcohol program. And we decided to ask Maurice Tubiana because he is very representative of the medical establishment, [which is] very strong in France. And he was at that time the Chairman of the group of European experts from the program, Europe Against Cancer.[38]

Hirsch subsequently asked François Grémy, another friend who, like Dubois, was a professor of public health, to join the group.

In addition to medical eminence and political connections, a third consideration in the formation of the *cinq sages* was their diverse political affiliations (two right, one center, two Socialist):

> This was very important. Each time we met someone, a member of Parliament or a politician, we were always at least two from different affiliations. It was important to present the issue not as a political problem [or rather] as a political problem, but not in the sense of belonging to the right or the left.[39]

From early 1988, just before the French presidential election of that year (which brought in the Socialist government of François Mitterand), until after the passage of the Evin law in 1991, the *cinq sages* followed a strategy that alternated intense public pressure on the government through the media with "insider" lobbying of parliamentarians, civil servants, and politicians. Thus, in a classic ploy of public-interest lobbyists, their first step was to address a series of questions to the presidential candidates—doing so, however, not simply in a letter, but in a press conference that received wide coverage on television and in print. With the exception of Jacques Chirac, who was then prime minister, all the candidates committed themselves to a complete ban on tobacco advertising.[40]

Following Mitterand's election, the new minister of health, Claude Evin, asked the *cinq sages* for recommendations for the control of smoking (along with other "unhealthy" behaviors). Much as had been the fate of Hirsch's earlier report, this report (completed in 1989, and officially considered confidential) was in danger of being buried; the "insider" strategy was proving to be unsuccessful. As Dubois noted, Evin

> asked us to lobby the government, that is, his own administration. That's quite unusual, and we were quite uneasy with that. And, after some months, we realized that it doesn't work because you have to be silent, we were underground, official but underground, and that's not the right way.[41]

So, again, the *cinq sages* went public with their report, publishing it in *Le Monde,* the French equivalent of the *New York Times.* This last démarche was, finally, successful. The five doctors were courted by influential members of Parliament and of Mitterand's administration; within a year and a half, the Evin law—written in its essentials by the *cinq sages* —became law. The economic interests that had worked within the government to keep the issue under wraps were at least partially defeated. The prime minister, Michel Rocard, is reported as having said to his colleagues responsible for budget and finance, "*Écoutez, de toute manière, vous avez perdu; les médecins ont gagné. Nous n'avons plus le choix.*" ["Listen. In any case, you have lost. The doctors have won. We no longer have a choice."][42]

The physician-architects of the *loi Evin* were concerned as much with alcohol as tobacco, and they deliberately combined the regulation of both in the same bill. Their rationale—repeated ten years later in the report of the commission to evaluate the law's implementation—was that the introduction of tobacco in France was relatively "recent," and that tobacco was therefore less burdened with the weight of history, altogether less important than alcohol as a "collective representation" of what it meant to be French.[43] Parliament, the drafters calculated, would take so easily to the regulation of tobacco that it would not notice the threat to wine and cognac. Nevertheless, and in striking contrast to the *loi Veil* experience, the *loi Evin* was extremely contentious. Although tobacco was not ignored, the most prolonged and heated debate was on the proposals for regulation of alcohol advertising, and those regulations have never been implemented. Debate continued over a period of nine months in multiple sessions of the General Assembly and the Senate. Like the *loi Veil,* however, the *loi Evin* was a government bill, and it ultimately passed with the unanimous support of the *Groupe socialiste* (the party in power). Opposition (almost equally united) was from the unlikely combination of conservatives opposed to limits on the free market and of communists opposed (again) to legislation that ignored underlying social and economic problems.

Insofar as it concerned tobacco, the *loi Evin* was intended to shore up existing provisions of the *loi Veil*, as well as to add additional measures. The tobacco industry's evasion of the Veil law had taken a variety of forms: placing the familiar brand name of its cigarettes (for example, Camel or Marlboro) on products (cigarette lighters, watches, boots) that were not, literally, tobacco products as defined by the law; sponsoring entertainment through organizations whose names incorporated the product name (for example, "*Fondation Philip Morris pour le cinema*"); and imaginative visual images using cigarette packages (the law limited print advertising to representations of the package itself). The Evin law, in consequence, both strengthened the Veil law's prohibition against indirect advertising by specifically defining "indirect" as "all advertising or publicity for a group, a service, an activity, a product or article other than tobacco, or a tobacco product, which, by its graphic design, its presentation, or its use of a trademark, emblem, or other distinctive symbol, recalls tobacco or a tobacco product."[44]

There is, however, a loophole. To avoid the application of the statute to certain products that had been on the market for many years and that had names identical to those of cigarette brands—for example, Gitane bicycles—the article prohibiting indirect advertising did not apply to

> advertising or publicity for a product other than tobacco or a tobacco product put on the market before January 1, 1990, by a business entity legally and financially independent of any entity that manufactures, imports, or sells tobacco or tobacco products. Any legal or financial connection between these entities removes this exception *[rend caduque cette dérogation]*.[45]

The meaning of this arguably obscure paragraph was left to the interpretation of the courts. Other pertinent changes included: an increase in fines; a provision that the business entity itself (as well as its individual directors) may be sued; a provision that the attorney general *(ministère public)* or a judge may issue a preliminary injunction against illegal advertising; further limitations (but no ban) on advertising in the print media; and the removal (since reinstated!) of the exception for automobile racing.

Parliamentary debate focused almost entirely on the potential threat of these advertising restrictions to French economic interests—the tobacco industry, mass media, and automobile racing. From the public's perspective, however, the law's principal innovation was not in its strengthened advertising bans, but in a single sentence (pithier even than comparable provisions of the *loi Veil*) that, for the first time, privileged the rights of nonsmokers over those of smokers: "Smoking is prohibited in places open to the public, including educational institutions, and in public transport, *except* in locations expressly designated for smokers."[46] In comments in the course of parliamentary debate, Evin made his intentions explicit: "Our aim is the reversal of current logic. Smoking [now] is allowed everywhere except in places reserved for nonsmokers. Henceforth it will be forbidden to smoke except in places reserved for smokers."[47] The devil, of course, was in the details. The meaning of this provision was spelled out in a *décret* issued at the end of May 1992. Specifically mentioned as locations where smoking was prohibited were: "closed and covered" spaces open to the public; workplaces (except private offices); unenclosed spaces in schools and colleges; and public transportation. Provisions for smokers were left to be determined by each location, given specified ventilation requirements and "the necessity to assure the protection of nonsmokers." "Eating and drinking" places have their own paragraph, calling for "flexible" arrangements to accommodate smokers.

Given the vagueness of this regulatory framework and the government's reliance for its implementation on a multitude of unspecified authorities with, by and large, little to gain from compliance, it is unsurprising that on June 1, 2000, marking the occasion of France's annual "day without tobacco," the headline in *Le Monde* proclaimed that the "Evin law is badly applied." The article goes on to explain that "while advertising is markedly reduced, the division of space between smokers and non-smokers is poorly respected."[48] The commission constituted to evaluate the law's operation reached much the same conclusions.[49] Where smoking prohibitions exist, and where their implementation is required, compliance is variable, at best.[50] Restrictions on smoking in trains and airplanes are largely observed (not, however, in stations and waiting rooms). Bars and restaurants are another matter altogether. Perhaps most striking to the American observer is the absence of enforcement in hospitals, not to speak of educational institutions, where smoking goes on in corridors, classrooms, and private offices. Workplace restrictions are not uniform and (at least as reflected in newspaper accounts and in complaints by nonsmokers to anti-tobacco groups such as the Comité national contre le tabagisme (CNCT)) have, indeed, encountered the greatest resistance. Nonsmokers have generally been reluctant to assert their right to protection (repeated several times in the 1992 *décret*), and it was not until 1997 that CNCT began a systematic effort to bring these complaints to the attention of the courts, with some success.[51]

Insofar as the *loi Evin* was intended to reduce smoking, its most influential provisions were not those concerning either advertising or bans on smoking, concluded the *Conseil national de l'évaluation*, but the decision to take tobacco out of the cost-of-living index, making it possible to raise the price of cigarettes. The evaluation attributed declines in smoking primarily to these increases (more than doubling the price of a package of cigarettes between 1992 and 2000), arguing that advertising had been limited under the Veil law but that no significant decline in smoking had resulted. Advertising bans were nevertheless important, in the evaluators' view, as a statement of the government's position: any change in the law would be taken by the public as a "strong signal" that the authorities no longer considered smoking dangerous.

The most powerful opposition to the Evin law has not been from smokers or even directly from the tobacco industry itself, but from advertising agencies, media outlets, and the press—all of which had historically depended on the industry for much of their revenue. The law grants standing as private attorneys general to qualified associations, allowing them to bring suit against the law's violators,[52] and the bulk of the litigation under the *loi Evin* (over 130 lawsuits) has concerned illicit advertising. A recent legal commentary on the Evin law credits CNCT, the association that brought these suits, not only with ensuring respect for the law, but also with forcing the courts to define exactly what the law allowed in the way of advertising and what it did not.[53] As noted above, there has been little or no parallel effort to give legal precision to the law's smoking bans.

The complex and—at least to the outsider—unpredictable character of tobacco-control politics in France is indicated by the fact that the *loi Veil* was promulgated by a government of the right and the *loi Evin* by a government of the left. While I cannot fully unravel these governments' underlying agendas, two points may be relevant. First, as I noted earlier, SEITA's monopoly of tobacco imports and sales ended in 1976, the year of the *loi Veil*. Given the enormous advantage in advertising budgets enjoyed by the multinational tobacco companies, the government may well have seen an advertising ban (but not, at the time, a price increase) as in SEITA's—and therefore the government's—financial interest. Second, more than one observer has suggested that an important factor in obtaining the Socialist (Mitterand) government's support for taking tobacco out of the cost-of-living index in 1990 was the state's need for revenue to offset large deficits in the social security system.[54]

Other Actors, Other Means

While the European Union has become a major player in Europe's tobacco wars, evidence of its influence on French tobacco policies is conspicuous by its absence, both from public commentary and from my interviews with the architects of French tobacco policy. The French see their legislation as a model for their European neighbors (one of the *cinq sages* noted to me that "the French law is the most drastic and the European Union has two or three times voted the equivalent of the French law"), but also as one that some of those neighbors (Britain and Germany, in particular) have been reluctant to follow.[55]

Recent French activity on the tobacco front has taken two quite disparate directions. The first involves an effort to medicalize smoking issues. Tobacco, along with alcohol, has been designated a drug (joining cocaine, heroin, and marijuana) within the purview of the national drug-control agency (the Mission interministerielle de lutte contre la drogue et la toxicomanie). In addition, over-the-counter sales of nicotine patches and gum are now permitted. These changes are in striking contrast to the more politicized approaches that led to passage of the Evin law: *tabagisme* has been redefined from a problem of industry skullduggery to one of individual addiction, and the battlefield has shifted from the legislature to the consulting room. According to one tobacco-control professional with whom I spoke, this shift in emphasis, heavily backed (with money, not just words) by the pharmaceutical industry, "suited a lot of people." Practicing physicians—a powerful interest group in France—are more comfortable with tobacco as a medical, rather than political, issue, and the government is able to avoid unwanted confrontation with the industry and its media allies.

The second major recent change is that litigation has been initiated by a local branch of the French national health insurance system *(Caisse primaire d'assurance maladie de Saint-Nazaire)* against four tobacco companies—SEITA (now Altadis), Philip Morris, Reynolds, and Rothman—to recover 51 million francs (approximately US$10 million) in compensation for costs associated with the treatment of smoking-related illness.[56] As one journalist described, France is "timidly, very timidly, adopting American methods in the struggle against *tabagisme.*"[57]

Perhaps the most interesting road not taken in France is prohibition of cigarette sales to minors. The need to protect "our children" from the dangers of tobacco was a major theme in the parliamentary debates surrounding both the *loi Veil* and the *loi Evin,* and the percentage of smokers among adolescents is high (among eighteen-year-olds, 60 percent report that they smoke). Nevertheless, restriction of sales to persons seventeen and over was considered and rejected on both occasions. Many of the arguments are familiar: for adolescents, prohibition will be an additional incentive to smoke; restrictions "don't work" and will be evaded. At least two other arguments are less familiar, at least to those not living in France: a prohibition limited to children might imply that smoking is not dangerous for adults, and the government should not impose regulations that it fears will not be enforced. These two arguments have deep ideological roots, akin to the roots of French ambivalence toward the privileging of nonsmokers (see below).[58]

Anti-Tobacco Militancy

Doctors and Politics

The difference between the *loi Veil* and the *loi Evin* was less in the content of the two laws than in the campaign on behalf of the *loi Evin* that was mounted by a small, but determined, band of medical specialists, the *cinq sages*. Their campaign was unique in France—as reflected in the level of media and parliamentary attention it received—and thus of questionable sustainability over the long term. To comprehend this uniqueness, it is necessary to understand the broader medical and public health context in which it occurred.

In *Le Prix de la Fumée [The Price of Smoking]*, Albert Hirsch (one of the *cinq sages*) and Serge Karsenty set out a telling, even poignant, characterization—clearly written from experience—of the physician advocate of tobacco control in France and of the response he can expect.

> He will be highly atypical. He will understand the limits of medicine in the field of health. Tired of intervening too late in illness that frustrates his efforts, he will want to act in advance, to influence the transition from health to sickness. He will know the obstacles he will confront. He cannot count on the recognition or on the support of his peers; on the contrary they will sometimes be hostile. He will struggle against powerful economic interests and can scarcely hope for the sincere support of politicians. He can expect no more than modest results, in the long term, obtained as a result of determined effort on many fronts. This exceptional physician, this health activist, this militant must have clear objectives; otherwise his militancy will accomplish nothing except to please himself.[59]

Nonetheless, when all is said and done (these authors argue), the consequences of smoking are the province of medicine, and the thankless task of advocacy—"to defend the interests of the citizen and the community" against tobacco—belongs to doctors.[60]

The almost plaintive tone of this description reflects what is, by universal consensus, the unfriendly climate for preventive medicine and public health in France.[61] This difficult climate is attributable to public health's institutional weaknesses, to its generally low status relative to curative medicine, and, more specifically in the case of tobacco, to what is perceived as the "unscientific" nature of advocacy on behalf of tobacco control. Within the government, "Health" is a relatively small entity located administratively within the much larger Ministry of Solidarity, Health, and Social Protection (responsible, among other things, for the state system of health insurance). While individual health ministers have acted effectively—Simone Veil is a notable example—the office itself has few resources and little power. A second institutional weakness emphasized by my informants is the absence in France of a graduate-level school of public health comparable to the London School of Hygiene and Tropical Medicine or to the schools of public health in the United States.[62]

There is considerable irony in the low status occupied by public health in the land of Louis Pasteur, an irony by no means lost on the various actors in this drama. The explanation offered for this low esteem is twofold: first, the powerful position held by what is called in French the *clinique* —the highly individualized assessment of each patient by his or her own doctor—as the supreme medical act;[63] and second, a well-developed suspicion of public health as, on the one hand, an infringement on the liberty of the individual and, on the other, a government penny-pinching scheme. The image of an authoritarian government trampling on the liberties of the people draws, of course, on deep roots in French history and culture. Its continuing resonance is reflected not only in the elite intellectual status of this frame's proponents—"the philosophers are not with us," lamented one of my informants from the world of tobacco control[64]—but in the frequency with which this image is raised and its applicability contested by advocates of action on behalf of public health.[65] Suspicion of government penny-pinching—that the state advocates disease prevention not out of any altruistic motives, but solely to avoid paying for its cure—may possibly have deep roots, too, but its immediate context has been the French government's vocal concern with the rising cost of its state-supported system of medical care.

A final factor influencing French attitudes toward preventive medicine and public health—particularly with respect to smoking—is that the issue of smoking and health has not been a "respectable" topic for academic research (much less advocacy) in France.[66] There was no unit of INSERM (the French equivalent of the National Institutes of Health) devoted to smoking. Despite France's role as host of the 1994 International Conference on Smoking and Health, relatively few French scientists attended (only 10 percent of the delegates were French, and as one of the organizers said to me, "we had to beat the bushes to find them"). While INSERM provided some funding for the conference, strict limits were placed on how the funding could be used (in particular, not for anything that smacked of advocacy). A leader of the French medical profession with whom I spoke (himself one of the *cinq sages* and highly supportive of the "smoking and health" cause) used the analogy of microbes and sewers in the late nine-teenth century to describe the relative status of smoking as a target of medical attention: smoking is—as were sewers then—beneath the dignity of physicians to address.[67]

Given this background, what accounts for the (relative) success achieved by the *cinq sages?* Their strategy had four elements critical to what they were able to accomplish. First was their discovery of "outsider," media-based lobbying. British physicians played an equally key role in that country's tobacco story, but their strategy relied much more heavily on Britain's long tradition of "insider" negotiations between civil servants and the medical elite. The second crucial element in the French doctors' strategy was their use of medical luminaries (Nobel Prize winners and the like) as props to reinforce the scientific authority and legitimacy of their case.[68] Third was the link created between tobacco and alcohol, a strategy difficult to under-stand outside of France: tobacco was employed as a stalking horse to get legislation limiting alcohol advertising. As explained by Hirsch, referring to the notorious failure of Mendés-France's campaign in favor of milk, "In this country it was absolutely impossible to do anything in alcohol . . . So, we decided to mask the wine problem behind the tobacco problem."[69] The final element and, indeed, the coup de grâce for a Socialist government, accord-ing to Hirsch, was the social inequality of sickness and death (that is, higher morbidity and mortality among the poor than the rich)—an inequality, stated the *cinq sages,* created by diseases associated with tobacco and alco-hol.[70] For a "government of the left," this inequality was an argument impossible to ignore.[71]

A Story of David and Goliath

There are, in France, organizations that correspond to the American Cancer Society *(la Ligue nationale contre le cancer)* and the American Heart Asso-ciation *(la Fédération française de cardiologie).* For most of their history, these groups have been even more conservative than their American counterparts—oriented almost exclusively toward raising funds for medical research. Within the last few years, the Ligue, under new leadership, has become much more active and visible in tobacco control and is now a dominant player. The vanguard of the French tobacco wars, however, was the *cinq sages* and the small group of militants organized as the CNCT.[72]

It is telling that in their otherwise detailed account of the struggle for tobacco regulation in France, Hirsch and Karsenty never mention CNCT even though Hirsch was its president from 1991 to 1993, when Gérard Dubois took over. The most likely explanation is that "activists" in France are more likely to be regarded with suspicion than admiration, and lay advocacy on behalf of what is seen as properly a "medical" or "scientific" question is particularly suspect.[73] For this reason, anti-tobacco militancy in France has proceeded over much of the past fifteen or twenty years along two tracks, intersecting at various points and mutually aware, but also mutually wary: a "respectable" track represented by the *cinq sages* and a less respectable track, that of CNCT.[74] CNCT has been almost solely responsible for what legal action has been taken to enforce the provisions of the *loi Evin*.[75]

CNCT traces its origins to the nineteenth-century *Association contre l'abus de tabac*. When the organization celebrated its centenary in 1977, the Veil law had recently been passed (1976), Simone Veil (the minister of health) was the celebration's keynote speaker, and CNCT itself, after a hundred years, had finally received the all-important recognition of its "public utility" by the *Conseil d'état*. The revival of CNCT in the early 1970s is, of course, largely attributable to an increasing, worldwide recognition of cigarette smoking as dangerous to health. This revival also owed much, however, to the French National Academy of Medicine's prior recognition of smoking as a public problem *in France*, and to the receipt of public funds for CNCT's antismoking campaigns from the French national health insurance system.[76]

During most of the 1970s, CNCT was dominated by physicians, and it pursued a fairly conventional agenda of health education and smoking-cessation programs. In the late 1970s, however, observing that the *loi Veil* was violated more often than it was observed and that the state prosecutorial system remained quiescent, CNCT launched its own campaign of legal action against violations of the Veil law. That campaign was largely responsible for CNCT's visibility in France and for its status as the industry's number-one enemy. The organization underwent another major transformation in the 1990s, essentially throwing out the (relatively) moderate leadership in place since the mid-1970s and replacing it with a highly politicized set of activists (through what the French industry group, *Centre de documentation et d'information sur le tabac* (CDIT), described as a "putsch"). These activists included the more overtly "militant" of the *cinq sages* (Hirsch and, later, Dubois) as unpaid *présidents* and, following the same path as the British ASH (Action on Smoking and Health), a salaried lay director with advocacy experience.[77]

In its incarnation of the 1990s, CNCT presented a familiar picture to American eyes—a small group of young, highly dedicated activists working out of a renovated old house, surrounded by computers, telephones, fax machines, file cabinets, and overflowing cardboard boxes. From the French perspective, however, the organization was an anomaly: a "health" association staffed by nonphysicians; an activist public gadfly supported at least in part by recoveries in court; an American-style lobbying group. CNCT's dues-paying membership was, in fact, very small (no more than a few hundred). The organization appeared, indeed—apart from its partial public funding (about half of its revenue)—to be a modern public-interest lobby, grafted uncomfortably onto French soil.

The other half of CNCT's income was generated by its success in court against the tobacco industry and its advertisers.[78] From 1991 through the middle of 1994, CNCT reported initiating 120 lawsuits against violators of the French statutes against tobacco advertising, and from 1991 through 1993, recovered close to US$1.5 million.[79] Perhaps the most credible testimony to CNCT's impact was the hostility that it generated from the tobacco industry. In a 1994 internal memo to its members describing the "antitobacco lobby" in France, CDIT gave CNCT equal billing with the *cinq sages;* the March 1995 issue of the industry publication *Revue des tabacs* devoted its cover article and an accompanying editorial to an excoriating attack on CNCT.[80]

One of the principal themes of this attack was that in initiating its lawsuits—"substituting itself for public officials in matters of public health"—CNCT's motives were wholly pecuniary, to "get money, more money, and still more money."[81] CNCT was, as a matter of fact, acting in place of a judiciary that had proved extremely reluctant to act in its own name, either against violations of the earlier *loi Veil* or against the *loi Evin.* Clear evidence of CNCT's key role as a government surrogate was the latter's response when, in late 1997 and 1998, CNCT confronted a legal and financial crisis. In late 1997 CNCT's director was forced to resign on suspicion of serious financial improprieties—which was no doubt taken by the tobacco industry and many others as confirming that CNCT was a sleazy organization. In the wake of that resignation and also a devastating report by government inspectors on CNCT's management, financial and otherwise, the group confronted bankruptcy. It was rescued by the timely intervention of the minister of health and reorganized under government auspices.[82] The government's 1999 report on the operation of the Evin law recognized "the important role of associations (i.e., CNCT) in implementation of the law," but also suggested that the state should take a more active prosecutorial role in the future.[83] There is no evidence that the state has followed this advice, and CNCT continues to be an active, successful litigator. Its focus has shifted, however, from advertising violations to smoking in the workplace.

Passive Smoking: La Liberté versus La Santé Publique

The meaning of cigarettes and smoking in France is thrown into sharp relief by a comparison with the meaning of narcotic drugs. French horror of *illegal* addictive drugs is no less than that of Americans. The bases for the French aversion are, however, culturally specific:

> Youth that escapes from guardianship, a private life without social or political connection are the sources of French anxiety about drugs: this anxiety has much more to do with the supposed isolation of the drug addict from others and from the world . . . than it does with dangers of drug use to the addict's health.[84]

The danger of narcotic drugs lies in their association with the *rejection* of social ties. In sharp contrast, cigarettes and smoking are associated with the *creation* of social ties. "Tobacco makes a connection . . . To offer a cigarette is to create a connection, a sociable (friendly, companionable) space."[85] The *loi Evin* attempted to redefine this space from friendly and companionable to dangerous. Further, and even more ideologically problematic, it aimed to transform smoking from a basis of inclusion to one of exclusion. In the French ideological lexicon, there are few worse sins than the sin of *exclusion,* by which is meant the construction of barriers between one French citizen and another. *Exclusion* is socially and politically illegitimate.[86] It is the opposite of *solidarité*—understood as the minimization of inequalities among different segments of the population. Promotion of *solidarité* is a central principle by which policies are judged. Insofar as the protection of public health is perceived to undermine this principle, it swims against powerful ideological currents and is extremely difficult to implement or enforce.[87]

In the immediate aftermath of the *loi Evin,* this ideologically based resistance was expanded by some French left-wing intellectuals and members of the press into a broad attack on public health as the entering wedge of the totalitarian state and on tobacco control as a new form of racism. The target of this attack was not the law's advertising bans, which are largely accepted, but the new privileging of nonsmokers. The gist of these attacks, along with the comments and responses of the major public health actors in the case—Simone Veil, Claude Evin, and Albert Hirsch—have been collected in a volume entitled, significantly, *Public Health and Individual Liberties (Santé publique et libertés individuelles)*.

The American left is friendly to public health, identifying it as among the few government-financed and -run programs that directly serve the poorest and most vulnerable members of the population (poor mothers and children, drug users, persons with sexually transmitted infections, and so on). "No smoking" rules, furthermore, are largely self-enforcing. The French left, by contrast, sees public health—and, in particular, the "new" public health focused on what are perceived to be "lifestyle" choices—as requiring unacceptable intervention by the "hygienic" state into individuals' most personal decisions. "Medicine wants to direct our life, dictate our conduct, rule over us by 'the medical light.'"[88] Invasion of privacy, health "fascism," discrimination, setting smokers and nonsmokers at one another's throats, and victim blaming are among the major themes of this discourse. In these polemics, the United States serves as an all-purpose *bête noire*. It is used by the left as a horrible example of what is in store for France—not only "a new prohibition," but also new forms of segregation reminiscent of Jim Crow. And it is used by public health advocates as an instructive example of what not to do: the unreconstructed smoker will not, in France, be pushed outside the social pale.[89]

Not far beneath the surface of this debate are conceptions of the non-smoker and of the relation between smokers and nonsmokers that are very different from those in the United States. Advocates of smoking restrictions portray nonsmokers as victims especially in need of the state's protection. "Legislation must above all protect nonsmokers . . . [T]he right of the most vulnerable [e.g., children, pregnant women] to breathe clean air must be respected."[90] By the same token, to protest against another's smoke is to cast *oneself* in the role of victim—a victim, furthermore, who is prepared to interfere with another's "small pleasures" for what are perceived by smokers and many others to be specious reasons: "The smoker—I know, I've been there—does not for a moment believe that the non-smoker is truly bothered. No, he simply wants to annoy, to deprive the smoker of a little pleasure." "*[Le fumeur—je sais, j'en suis parfois—ne pense pas une seconde que le non-fumeur est vraiment gêné. Non, il veut simplement l'embêter, le priver d'un petit plaisir].*"[91] This construction of smoking as *un petit plaisir* with which it is simply churlish to interfere largely explains why smoking restrictions are more readily respected aboard buses, trains, and airplanes than in cafés and restaurants. The latter are defined as zones of pleasure, whereas the former are not.

Just as the principle of *solidarité* dictates that children should not be discriminated against, so—and even more powerfully—it dictates that smokers should, insofar as possible, not be segregated. Images of the smoker out in the cold, of "civil war between smokers and nonsmokers," are invoked to argue against any overzealous enforcement of restrictions on when and where smoking will be allowed. Ideally, smokers and nonsmokers will resolve their disagreements through dialogue and negotiation, and will arrive at a solution equally satisfying to all parties. This process is likely to take a while, however, and there is no guarantee that it will be continuous. "In the end, France will change like everyone else: the whole world has come to know that the Marlboro cowboy died of smoker's cancer. But we have a long way still to go." "*[Enfin en France, on finira par évoluer comme partout: tout le monde commence à savoir que le cowboy Marlboro est mort du cancer du fumeur. Mais on est encore loin]*."[92]

In March 2003, six years after this young woman's words were written, the President of the Republic, Jacques Chirac, declared "*la guerre au tabac*" in the larger context of a renewed "*mobilisation nationale*" against cancer.[93] Included in the President's plan were a steady increase in cigarette prices, more rigorous implementation of the *loi Evin,* and—in greatest contrast with earlier policies—the prohibition of cigarette sales to minors fifteen and under. Among the more interesting aspects of Chirac's statement is the framing of antismoking policies as on a par with increases in breast-cancer surveillance and the availability of medical imaging equipment, as contributing to the larger struggle against cancer, not as an end in itself and certainly not as a war against smokers. At least as reported by the French media, Chirac made no reference to passive smoking: the enemy was tobacco and the smokers were the potential victims.

Between Paternalism and Voluntarism: Tobacco Consumption and Tobacco Control in Germany

Günter Frankenberg

The Overlapping Discourses on Smoking

Even before the world—first New, then Old, with Germany being part of the latter—had capitulated to the "wonder plant tobacco," four overlapping discourses determined the development of tobacco production and consumption within the German territories,[1] and shaped the social construction of smoking there. *Civilizatory* discourse focused on tobacco consumption as a status symbol and matter of taste and lifestyle. It was intricately linked with the *fiscal* discourse on tobacco manufacture, commerce, and consumption as a source of state income—from taxing what was considered conspicuous consumption and luxury. The regulatory aspects were captured by the *politicolegal* discourse, which focused on the dangers of smoking as a public pastime. The *medical* discourse was concerned with the pharmacological properties of tobacco and with smoking as a threat to private and public health.

After the Huguenots introduced tobacco from France to their German places of refuge in the seventeenth century, the tobacco herb soon came to be perceived as a cure-all in the medical discourse. Throughout the century, numerous treatises recommended it as a panacea against such diverse illnesses as infections (of all kinds), wounds, fever, headaches, asthma and other pulmonary diseases, and constipation and other gastrointestinal ailments.[2] The universal medicinal effects ascribed to the tobacco herb were also reflected in the variety of forms in which it could be used or applied—for example, compresses, enemas, ointments, powders, and juice.

Toward the end of the seventeenth century, the tobacco mystique began to be deconstructed by analyses of the toxic side effects of tobacco therapies and by references to the repercussions of tobacco abuse. Criticisms of smoking from the medical profession remained isolated and were primarily concerned with the hazardous effects of additional substances used to refine the taste of tobacco. It took almost another hundred years and the triumph of the natural sciences to completely end tobacco therapy in Germany. Only in the early twentieth century did tobacco consumption begin to be recognized as a health problem—first, for tobacco workers; then, for smokers; and finally, for nonsmokers.

Whereas the concept of tobacco as a medicinal plant was introduced into Germany by the Huguenots, the habit of pipe smoking and snuffing was almost simultaneously imported during the Thirty Years' War by English (some authors claim Spanish) soldiers; "eating fire and smoke,"[3] they laid the foundation for civilizatory—today one would prefer to say "lifestyle"—discourse. Although the habits of snuffing and pipe smoking were soon to be cultivated by the aristocracy, hedonist tobacco consumption was by no means an exclusively aristocratic pastime. The triumph of the cigarette in the second half the nineteenth century led to the ultimate "democratization" of tobacco hedonism.

From the very beginning of tobacco consumption, the rulers of the German territories recognized its fiscal potential, thus initiating the intimate dualism of fiscal and regulatory discourse.[4] Ever since the beginning of the seventeenth century, state revenues stemming from tobacco taxes or tobacco monopolies have been on the increase. Subsequent tobacco regimes oscillated between license and prohibition, depending on the enthusiasm or aversion of the monarchs and their bureaucracies to smoking in public and on their need to tap new sources of income for the state. Initially, the formula "license and taxation" was supported by the mercantilist spirit of the epoch.

From the early days of tobacco consumption to this very day, the fiscal discourse has been uneasily related to the regulatory discourse. Fiscal interests call for the promotion of tobacco production and consumption, but the rapid spread of the smoking habit was accompanied by critical voices and prohibition measures in some regions and towns. The primarily moral criticisms—the "dry drunkenness" and the "gradual suicide" of smokers—were impotent against the spread of this new enthusiasm for tobacco. Tobaccophiles prevailed throughout the seventeenth and eighteenth centuries in most of the German territories, usually with the blessing of tax-conscious governments.

On the other hand, from the early decades of the eighteenth century, there was also evidence of the spirit of prohibition supported by a motley and changing coalition, comprising the greater part of the clergy,[5] dissident aristocrats, and high-ranking bureaucrats, chiefly under the banners of fire prevention and morality. Until the last part of the nineteenth century, smoking was prohibited in towns, forests, barns, bedrooms, and other locations, each according to its presumed fire hazard.[6] Soldiers were not allowed to smoke "in action" or while standing guard. Thus, under the state's police power, regulatory schemes followed the logic of averting dangers. A second strand relating to prohibition was based on the immorality of tobacco abuse. Notably, smoking by women was considered to violate the *boni mores* of society. This moral discourse on tobacco consumption was supported by what had come to be the dominant view of tobacco as a luxury item rather than a medicinal herb—which brought smoking within the range of social-disciplinary policies executed by the *Polizey*, the specifically German mix of comprehensive regulation and provision of public services organized and supervised by state authorities.

The relationship between this regulatory discourse and civilizatory discourse has always been tense. From the beginning, the implementation of prohibitive strategies met with major cultural obstacles. For one, the habit of smoking persisted—most notably, in aristocratic and bourgeois circles—even under smoking bans. Moreover, public health officials and doctors recommended that smoking be permitted during the cholera epidemic because of its presumed anti-miasmatic and sedative qualities. When the Prussian administration reinstituted the ban on smoking in public places after the epidemic had subsided in 1840, the greater part of the population—being used to the widespread tolerance and even official recommendation of smoking—continued to resist prohibition. Popular resistance was strengthened by the liberation movements of the *Vormärz* to the Revolution of 1848—which elevated tobacco smoking to the ranks of emancipatory action, much like the rebellious students of the 1960s in the United States and Germany who integrated pot smoking into their liberation agenda and finally succeeded in ending the ban on smoking in public places. Therefore, it comes as no surprise that bans on smoking were moderated and that it took another fifty years for the first private associations against tobacco abuse to come into being in Germany. With the proliferation of the cigarette in the second half of the nineteenth century, tobacco consumption increased dramatically. By 1927, Germans consumed 32.5 billion cigarettes, 6.5 billion cigars, 3.8 million kilograms of pipe tobacco, and 2.3 million kilograms of snuff per year.[7] In the meantime, the German state, in pursuit of its mainly mercantile economic policy and in an effort to fill the treasury's coffers, had successfully established a tobacco monopoly—and had unsuccessfully attempted to nationalize tobacco production.

Under the National Socialist regime, the process of gradual liberalization came to a sudden stop.[8] Tobacco consumption, though not banned in general, was "racialized" by its characterization as the vice of degenerate Africans, "genderized" by excluding women (as well as minors) from consumption, and "domesticated" by directing consumption to the home or pub. The Nazi regime launched an ambitious antismoking campaign in the name of popular health *(Volksgesundheit)* and social discipline. After studies by two German doctors claimed to have established a statistical correlation between smoking and lung cancer, the Nazi government issued sanctions against smokers, prohibited smoking in hospitals and public offices, demarcated special compartments for nonsmokers in trains, and restricted certain forms of cigarette advertising—all drawing from an earlier generation's eugenic policies and combining them with the ethics of bodily purity and effective performance at work.[9] It is crucial to note the complicity between medical science and politics in the campaign against this "un-German habit." Even so, the resulting, massive campaigns did not curb cigarette smoking, which rose to a staggering 75 billion cigarettes in the war years of 1940 and 1941—more than doubling since 1927.[10]

It is fair to assume that the main reason tobacco was not banned altogether was that smoking was not only quite widespread, but especially popular among men. In the 1930s, 80 percent were smokers.[11] A strictly implemented, rigid regulatory regime might therefore have provoked more resistance than did the racist and anti-Semitic agenda. Furthermore, the Nazis were well aware of the importance of tobacco consumption for the state budget—12 percent of which was financed through tobacco taxes—and were willing to compromise their health policy for fiscal reasons. So, once again the imperatives of fiscal discourse triumphed over public health discourse.

After the Second World War, the use of tobacco continued to grow, pushed by an odd combination of lifestyle, public health, economic, and regulatory factors. Against the background of a country in ruins and a destroyed economy, imported cigarettes, notably Camels, were used on the black market in lieu of the inflationary official currency. And though tobacco had once been a luxury good that distinguished the ruling classes from their subjects, it now turned into a means of survival for everyone; in addition to being widely considered as one of the basic human needs, smoking was idealized by smokers as "the last tiny bit of a dignified life."[12] This demand for tobacco products could not be met by domestic production, which had dramatically declined during the war. Imports were ruled out for financial reasons. Rationing, which had already been introduced in 1939, could not solve the problem inasmuch as there was very little to ration. Tobacco had become a scarce commodity (and not the only one in postwar Germany). The whole cycle of tobacco production—growth, manufacture, and sales—was therefore submitted to strict state controls, which invited deviancy and generated an extensive black market.[13]

Even after the monetary reform of 1948, the importation, domestic production, and consumption of cigarettes—more so than cigars and pipe tobacco—continued to increase, supported by the traditional state interest in tax revenues and by the image of smoking as an expression of a modern, liberal lifestyle. Only in the early 1980s did things begin to change. Inspired, in part, by mounting criticism of tobacco consumption and increasing public health concerns in the United States, the federal and state governments in Germany engaged in new initiatives to protect nonsmokers.[14] There were resurgent antismoking campaigns—the weekly *Der Spiegel* referred to the new movement as the "rebellion of the nonsmokers"[15]—and more general campaigns against drug addiction. The image of the cigarette-smoking Marlboro man or the good-looking, successful, and dynamic manager or executive was displaced by a new representation of smokers as asocial, irresponsible, and self-destructive.

From Agriculture to Technology: The Development of the German Tobacco Industry

Although the habit of smoking tobacco spread in Germany after the Thirty Years' War in the first half of the seventeenth century, and was soon followed by the cultivation of tobacco primarily for medicinal purposes, the first German tobacco company producing cigars was established only in 1788, and the first manufacturing facility for hand-rolled cigarettes, in 1862.[16] While the overall economic impact of domestically produced tobacco remained modest, small firms processing mostly tobacco from the Osmanic Empire (a region that included what is now considered Turkey) and Virginia spread rapidly throughout Germany during the eighteenth century under the influence of the Huguenots in Prussia. Due to the labor- and time-intensive production of cigars and cigarettes,[17] the tobacco industry developed at a slow speed until the middle of the nineteenth century, when several independent German states joined the German Customs Union (1834), thus providing free access to a much broader market for tobacco products.

Subsequent developments, which have yet to generate any systematic interest of historians, may be divided into four phases. During the second half of the nineteenth century—encouraged, in part, by the introduction of machine-operated production in 1878—an increasing number of tobacco growers and manufacturers entered the market.[18] Dresden was soon to become the center of the German tobacco industry. Almost half of the cigarette production was concentrated there because of the availability of cheap labor, the favorable transportation routes linking Germany with eastern Europe and Italy, and the entrepreneurial spirit of Russian immigrants.[19] The Dresden cigarette producers were able to sustain their leading position for almost thirty years on the basis of their technologically advanced production methods.

The second phase began around the turn of the century. This period of growth and market extension, which was accompanied by the first antismoking (and anti-alcohol) organizations,[20] lasted until the global economic crisis of the 1930s. Further mechanization and the revenue stamp, both of which overburdened the financial resources of small firms, enhanced a concentration process; some of the large companies came to employ more than one thousand workers. The decline of the cigar in favor of the cigarette, coupled with economic development in the unified Germany, led to a diffusion of tobacco production away from Dresden and toward several other cities. Before long, Berlin—the capital and by far largest city and regional market—soon dominated the domestic tobacco industry.

After the interim period—a compulsory cartel to curb overproduction and high prices in the 1930s, followed by the establishment of new companies after the end of the Second World War—the third, maturation phase from 1950 to 1980 witnessed an even more dramatic concentration process than the one in the first third of the century. Though not in the same monopoly position that Dresden once had had, Berlin was able to sustain its position of dominance, not least because of the constant flow of federal subsidies for its economy.

The year 1980 witnessed what has been characterized as the saturation of the domestic market. German companies were forced to export tobacco products (primarily cigarettes) and start joint ventures with foreign companies. Due to the superior quality of tobacco of foreign origin, the contribution of the German tobacco industry consisted more and more in providing the know-how for machine-operated production lines. Thus, the life cycle of cigarettes "processed" in Germany ended just how it had started in the middle of the nineteenth century: with the export of technological knowledge concerning tobacco production. In 1999 the German market for tobacco products had a volume of more than DM 40 billion, compared to a market of DM 22 billion for sausages. In the tobacco market, which is dominated by factory-produced cigarettes subject to sales tax, the multinational corporation Philip Morris holds a comfortable lead (with a share of 38.9 percent), followed by the German company Reemtsma

(23.5 percent) and British American Tobacco (23.3 percent). Lesser players are Reynolds (4.2 percent) and smaller companies such as Austria Tabak of Vienna and Landewyck of Luxembourg (altogether, 9.2 percent).[21]

Patterns, Trends, and Costs of Tobacco Consumption

The "usual suspect" for intensive tobacco consumption in Germany is male, a graduate from the elementary school system, unemployed, and under forty years of age. He is likely to smoke more than twenty cigarettes per day—preferably Marlboros or Marlboro Lights—and has seriously attempted to give up the addiction at least once. This image may be constructed from the statistical data gathered by the Federal Office for Statistics, the Federal Center for Health Information, private associations, and the tobacco industry.[22]

Demographic and Social Patterns

The demographic and gender profile of smokers in Germany reveals that roughly 40 percent of men and 25 to 30 percent of women are regular smokers.[23] Projected onto the population between eighteen and fifty-nine years of age, 17.8 million Germans can be considered smokers, and 6.7 million of them as "heavy smokers" consuming twenty cigarettes or more per day—compared to 2.5 million alcohol abusers and 100,000 drug abusers. According to the diagnostic criteria of the International Classification of Diseases, 70 to 80 percent of the German smokers would be considered "nicotine dependent"—eight to nine million men and five to six million women. The percentage of German men who smoke is average for Europe—between Greece's 51.5 percent and Sweden's 28.1 percent—whereas the percentage of German women who smoke is significantly below the European average.

Tobacco use and abuse follow a somewhat different pattern among juveniles (twelve to seventeen years old) and young adults (eighteen to twenty-five years old). In a recent study on drug affinity and drug abuse, 41 percent of the juvenile tobacco consumers referred to themselves as regular or occasional smokers. From 1993 to 1997 the number of juvenile smokers increased by 5 percent overall (but faster among young women living in the East German states), whereas juvenile alcohol consumption has declined.[24] The picture is a little brighter if one takes into account the percentage of teenagers and adolescents who never smoked, which increased from 20 percent in 1970 to 42 percent in 1997. The conditioning age—that is, the age at which minors start to smoke—is gradually decreasing, however, which reflects a European trend, as does the increase in juvenile cigarette consumption by 8 percent from 1990 to 1995.[25]

There is a distinct social pattern for tobacco consumption in Germany: 36.1 percent of the lower middle class and below, versus 23.8 percent of the middle class and above, consume tobacco products. Almost half of all unemployed persons[26] have identified themselves as regular smokers. Again, there is a gender difference: the percentage of unemployed males who smoke is nearly 20 percent higher than that for unemployed females. Tobacco consumption is also inversely related to education, at least in the age group ranging from fifteen to forty years. Higher, and especially university, education contributes significantly to the reduction of smoking. Among Germans who graduated from a university, 27 percent identify themselves as regular smokers, compared to 48.7 percent of those with only an elementary education.

Recent Trends of Tobacco Consumption in Germany

Of late, tobacco consumption has followed a surprising pattern.[27] On the one hand, tobacco products have dramatically increased in popularity since the mid-1990s. After decades of steady decline, the consumption of tobacco products increased by 7.5 percent from 1996 to 2000. The use of cigarettes and cigars accounts for this questionable success story; the use of pipe tobacco has stagnated. Much to the benefit of the industry, international trade, and the treasury, Germans spent DM 38.8 billion on tobacco products in 1998—DM 5.4 billion more than in 1993. Despite antismoking campaigns and stricter regulatory measures taken by the European Union (EU),[28] the market for tobacco products—especially cigarettes—has boomed in the 1990s. With a consumption of over 170 billion factory-produced and 19 billion hand-rolled cigarettes in 1999, the German market ranks fifth worldwide, after China (1,632 billion), the United States (420 billion), Japan (329 billion), and Russia (249 billion).[29]

On the other hand, influenced by the antismoking campaigns in the United States, which were extensively covered by the media, Germans have apparently grown more health conscious. The increasing demand for medium, light, and ultralight cigarettes has reduced the market segment of full-flavor cigarettes to 62.5 percent, and corresponds to growing support among smokers for measures to protect nonsmokers generally (such as "zoning" smoking in public areas), as well as children (no smoking in their presence) and the unborn (no smoking during pregnancy). Eight percent of all smokers even advocate an increase of the tobacco tax. And in what may be interpreted as a gentle turn away from nicotine use, the attraction of smoking has been on the decline—at least over the longer term—among adults. The percentage of male smokers (age eighteen and over) dropped steadily from 61 percent in 1980, to 46 percent in 1997, to 40 percent in 1999. Although women were generally more resistant in the 1990s to "kicking the habit," the percentage of female smokers (age eighteen and over) dropped from 44.5 percent in 1979 to less than 30 percent in 2000.[30]

Social Costs of Tobacco Consumption

While the consumption of tobacco products has been connected with a number of diseases, there have recently been few specifically German studies on the development and prevalence of diseases related to smoking. German reports on the correspondence between tobacco consumption and health hazards mostly refer to Anglo-American studies or to a recent survey concerning tobacco-related mortality in the EU.[31] Causality between smoking and certain diseases—in particular, cancers of the lung and larynx, and pulmonary and coronary diseases—cannot be established with certainty but can be estimated and determined with high probability. Recently, several studies confirmed a correlation between passive smoking and lung cancer, as well as other impairments.[32]

Estimates regarding the health costs of smoking have recently stirred a rather macabre controversy. The standard figures cited are that private and public insurers spend almost DM 40 billion annually to cover the costs of smoking-related diseases,[33] and that economic losses caused by smoking amount to roughly DM 2 billion annually. Countering these calculations, however, is that the health costs of smoking-related diseases have to be balanced against the "savings" for the social security system—notably of health insurance and pension systems—due to smokers' reduced life expectancy.[34] While the estimated "lifetime health costs" of a male smoker amount to roughly DM 150,000, the average male nonsmoker, living eight years longer, requires DM 20,000 more.[35] Critics of regulation and prohibition therefore argue that "smokers do not cause external costs for nonsmokers in the public health system,"[36] and that a total ban on smoking would lead to a breakdown of the social insurance system in Germany. These calculations and figures are almost impossible to compare since the protagonists operate with different points of reference. If one looks at the public health system, smoking and smoking-related diseases constitute a major financial problem. Those who primarily consider the situation of the tobacco industry and the fisc will accentuate the "benefits" of smoking. Hence, it is questionable whether a total ban would actually lead, as some have argued, to a net loss of over DM 50 billion per year for the national economy.[37] It is interesting to note that health insurers, which ultimately have to foot the "smoking bill," do not publish statistical data concerning the health costs of tobacco consumption.[38] Their silence suggests that they reject "cost-benefit analyses" of smoking because of the complexity or inherent cynicism of such analyses. Only one figure seems to be beyond dispute: epidemiologists estimate that each year in Germany, a staggering 100,000 deaths are directly or indirectly related to the consequences of smoking.[39]

Prevention, Therapy, and Lobbying against Tobacco Consumption

Following the example of the United States, antismoking organizations, health insurers, and government agencies have recently intensified their campaigns against the consumption of tobacco products—and primarily against cigarette smoking. In particular, they have launched several campaigns in the past decade to enlighten the general public about the dangers of smoking, to change the image and the assessment of smoking, and to generate a more critical attitude toward tobacco products. Most activities are chiefly addressed to juveniles and young adults since it is at these ages that smoking habits are developed. Prevention has also become part of both the school curriculum and basic medical care. Evaluation of preventive measures has shown their effectiveness to depend mainly upon the number, intensity, and combination of strategies.[40]

Many ex-smokers claim that they quit smoking without professional therapeutic help. Their desire to "kick the habit" was influenced most by the advice of their doctor or pharmacist, by concerns regarding the exposure of family members to tobacco smoke, by pressure from nonsmoking family members and friends, by tobacco-tax increases, and by public warnings regarding the hazards of smoking.[41]

Tobacco Production—Booming despite the Head Wind

The tobacco industry experienced a remarkable boom in the 1990s, based only to a marginal extent on domestically grown tobacco, which holds a market share of 5 percent versus 95 percent for imported tobacco. In 1999 tobacco companies, which are overwhelmingly foreign owned, produced 204.6 billion cigarettes in Germany, significantly more (over 12 percent) than in the previous year. Even though the number of companies and factories is gradually declining, the tobacco industry reported net income of almost DM 31 billion in 1998.[42] The balance of trade concerning cigarettes has always been and still is significantly positive: in 1999 only one out of four cigarettes consumed in Germany was imported, which means that the German cigarette industry is mainly an export industry.[43] Consumer expenses for tobacco products amounted to roughly DM 40 billion in 1999, and increased by 17 percent from 1994 to 1999.[44]

Compared to the world's leading tobacco producers, such as China (1.4 million tons per year) and the United States (800,000 tons), or even to lesser producers such as Italy (150,000 tons), tobacco cultivation and the manufacture of crude tobacco in Germany (11,000 tons) is relatively insignificant.[45] Even within Germany's own national economy, tobacco production and processing are not important factors. They are of some economic importance, however, due to their geographic concentration in disadvantaged areas, mainly in the east and in rural regions throughout the country. In general, domestic tobacco is produced and processed by small, family-owned enterprises. Due to their labor intensity, these enterprises contribute significantly to the preservation of local economic and social infrastructure. Altogether, almost fifteen hundred tobacco-producing and tobacco-processing enterprises are located in Germany, employing four thousand regular workers and ten to fifteen thousand seasonal ones.

Core Issues of Tobacco Control

Tobacco regulation in West Germany underwent a dramatic change in "philosophy" after the Second World War. Whether a reaction to Nazi Germany's rather prohibitive and racist tobacco propaganda or a product of the "Camel lifestyle" that was promoted during the immediate postwar years, a much more liberal approach prevailed during the following three decades. Based on agreements between the government and the influential German trade association of cigarette manufacturers, the Verband der Cigarettenindustrie (VdC), the regime combined a policy of selective prohibition with voluntary self-control by the tobacco industry. The consumption of tobacco products, primarily cigarettes, was regarded as a "private sin," "harmless pleasure," or, at worst, an annoyance for nonsmokers. As such, tobacco consumption was to be taxed, but not forbidden—with the exception of minors and areas expressly demarcated "off limits."

In the late 1960s and early 1970s, the libertarian spirit of the time was reinforced by the student movement's critique of the repressive capitalist system, state, and culture, and also, more generally, by a widespread lack of support for more restrictive public health measures against smoking. Only in the 1980s was the dominant official strategy of "taxation rather than prohibition" beginning to be seriously challenged by increased attention to problems of environmental pollution and growing support for a healthy lifestyle. Cigarette smoking was still very much part of popular culture and highly visible in the print media and in some other forms of advertising. Nevertheless, criticism informed by cancer research and by environmental and public health concerns was gradually but steadily mounting. These forces, coupled with the advances of antismoking groups in the United States, inspired a range of regulatory measures.

Public Health in Germany: Between Paternalism and Voluntarism

In order to understand today's controversies in the field of public health and tobacco regulation in Germany, it is necessary to take a brief look at the development of the country's paternalist health regime. An institutionalized system of public health came into existence only after the demise of the medieval state and the feudal order of society in the fifteenth century. It was at that point that the experiences of recurrent epidemics and less dramatic diseases could be translated into health policies to be executed by the state administration.[46]

Three discourses shaped the early institutions of public health and its field of action. Though distinctly different, they were interconnected through the organization of the state administration, governmental policies, and their effects. The discourses followed different cycles over time, and they overlapped in various ways—depending on public health priorities and policies, the division of labor within the federalist system, the type of cooperation between the state and the medical profession, and funding. Half a millennium later, their influence continues; the three discourses provide, indeed, a thematic outline of today's antismoking regulatory policies.

The discourse of *control* was almost exclusively located in the state administration and was based on traditional police law, which in more current terminology would comprise police law, social law, and public health law. It focused on police measures in the widest sense, which were geared toward prohibiting unhealthy behavior and imposing a duty upon people to preserve their health.

The discourse of *prevention* was again state-based and relied on medical and scientific elites for input. It was and is still characterized by its concern with enlightening the general public about how to avoid diseases and unhealthy life conditions (in today's Germany, such matters as the hazards of active and passive smoking).

Finally, the *curative* discourse was less statist and state-based since it was carried on primarily by the medical profession and to a lesser extent by public health institutions. It focused on regulations concerning the training of medical personnel and the provision of health care by physicians and institutions (hospitals).

Three other factors, not directly related to the discourses outlined above, also influenced the early history of public health and social hygiene as a field for state action—and, in so doing, helped to establish the foundation for tobacco control and health care in Germany. First, for purposes of internal consolidation, the absolutist state sought to use and increase its national resources as a means, in turn, of increasing its economic, financial, and military power. According to the mercantilist principle *"que le nombre des peuples fait la richesse des Etats"* (King Frederick II of Prussia), the policy of consolidation was aimed at preserving and augmenting the population. Developing the human capital would necessitate that the state supervise the training of medical personnel and organize a system of public health care.

Second, the politicization of health as a public task was enhanced by the developing concept of the state as a rational institution for the welfare and security of its citizens. The new statist philosophy defined the improvement of health and hygiene as a duty of the state, and referred to the subjects as "members of the state." Preserving the people's health, moreover, justified the existence and powers of a centralized, responsible state administration (in contrast to an irresponsible aristocracy that was still indulging in excesses and luxuries such as smoking).

Third, the increasing health consciousness on the part of the administration and the citizens was reinforced—even very early on—by the strategy of physicians to monopolize the market for health services and to propagate a new curative philosophy that was designed to extend the field of professional medical control and thereby to lay the foundation for a professional association organized and administered under the authority of the state. The medical profession thus succeeded both in establishing its members as the officially recognized providers of curative medical treatment and in supplanting the traditional (nonmedical) barber-surgeons, midwives, and healers.

Until the first decades of the nineteenth century, state interventions to provide health services and to curb smoking were limited to "soft" forms of public health control and indirect provision of health care. This approach was called into question, however, by the rapid industrialization that displaced the mainly agrarian structure of German society, ended the compulsory membership in, and protection by, guilds, and therefore caused a dramatic pauperization of the working class. The sheer number of the poor, as well as their miserable living conditions, overstrained the main institutions traditionally charged with dealing with poverty and its consequences—poorhouses and hospitals. Discourse on public health changed radically as it became clear that the destitute masses presented a political threat to social peace and political stability rather than constituting the wealth of the state. Poverty and disease became synonyms. Nevertheless, the economic bourgeoisie resisted state paternalism to promote public health, and instead favored voluntary health insurance as well as savings banks founded by workers' and journeymen's associations. Before long, these associations proved to be insufficient either to replace the feudal social system or to ease the burden on the local institutions providing relief to the poor.

During the second half of the nineteenth century, the German states, led by Prussia, developed and supported health insurance despite criticism by the liberal segments of society. Nevertheless, Prussia was unable to keep under control the side effects of the processes of social and economic transformation—or even to limit the growing impoverishment of the working class and the resulting social misery. After a series of failed attempts to curb the politicization of the "social question" through police measures and political persecution of workers' organizations, first the Prussian government and later the imperial government shifted their policies from exclusion to integration of the politically organized workers; a system of semipublic social insurance was consequently instituted in the 1880s—including programs in health insurance (1883), accident insurance (1884), and old-age and invalids' insurance (1889). In the following decades, these programs were extended from the industrial workers to all workers and, during the Weimar Republic (1918–1933), were complemented by a system of public assistance for the poor.

By the beginning of the Weimar Republic, two of the three pillars of today's public health system had thus been created: (1) medical health control administered by the state agencies and (2) the curative system of semistatist health care provided by doctors participating in "legal health insurance."[47] The third pillar—health prevention and health information—began to be built in the 1920s, simultaneously with the rise of "social hygiene" as a new medicoscientific discipline. According to the basic maxims of social hygiene, reflecting a social Darwinism that was soon to triumph in Nazi Germany, the population was regarded as a biological system, and only the strongest and fittest "social bodies" ("Volkskörper") were deemed to be suitable for propagation. Interestingly enough, this survival of the fittest called for a preventive approach to public health—an approach geared toward calling a halt to all social conditions that might be hazardous to the "social body" and to the German germ plasm.[48]

In the 1930s this doctrine was implemented and carried to its extreme for the sake of "racial hygiene" and "racial health."[49] The official Nazi propaganda resuscitated and radicalized the duty of all members of the "social body" to care for their health. The National Socialist regime ended the long era of soft interventions by centralizing the public health system, including the organization of the medical profession, and by placing it under direct control of the health bureaucracy. The regime also supported preventive medicine—in particular, cancer prevention—and initiated national campaigns for a healthy diet and against the hazards of smoking.[50]

After the Second World War, the organization of the public health system was revamped within the context of the newly established welfare state *(Sozialstaat)* of the Federal Republic. The "social state" was no longer geared toward fighting diseases so as to consolidate the state and to secure the fitness of the people to fight. The new system of public health could be considered liberal insofar as it decentralized the system of health care, restricted police measures to the direct supervision of hazardous professions (for example, prostitution) and trades (for example, pharmacies, groceries, and restaurants), granted the medical profession the right to self-organization, and abstained from establishing a legal duty to preserve one's health. A combination of direct control and provision of ambulatory health care was and is to be provided by the medical examiners on the municipal level. Indirect control is exercised over both public (or "legal") and private health insurers. Comparatively weak still is the third pillar of the public health system—the principle and institutions of prevention, which have always been opposed by health insurers as being too costly and inefficient. Only in recent decades could the traditional resistance against preventive medicine be partly overcome for the sake of cancer prevention, and could the "uneasy triumph" of a pragmatic and preventive strategy displace the potential use of repressive measures—such as compulsory testing, the duty of notification, and quarantine—in the battle against AIDS.[51] The crucial institutions for public health information, however, are still underdeveloped; it can hardly be said that the *Bundeszentrale für gesundheitliche Aufklärung*, the central agency for health information of the federal government, is adequately funded and staffed to meet the demands of a modern society.

Tobacco Consumption and Public Health: The Politicolegal Framework

In a country like Germany—with its high level of juridification—any conflict is likely to be settled, or at least acted out, in the legal arena. The controversies over tobacco regulation have been no exception. Once the health of the people *(Volksgesundheit)* was nationally recognized as a particularly important object of legal protection that justified far-reaching restrictions, legislatures, and other public authorities were deemed to be entitled to take a wide range of protective measures under the law of the states. By the same token, restrictive health policies and measures were negotiated by the Conference of State Health Ministers. On the national level, however, public health powers and policies were more or less limited to the fight against communicable diseases, to the supervision of foodstuffs, narcotics, and pharmaceutics, and to "soft interventions" such as health information and education.

In the mid-1980s, a third public health regime—on the supranational level—was established under the law of the European Community (EC). In particular, under Article 95 the new EC Treaty, the authorities of the EC—which, since the Maastricht Treaty of 1992, has been reconstituted as the "European Union"—were granted the general power to maintain a "high level of protection" in the areas of health and consumer protection.

The extent to which Germany's state legislatures, the Federal Diet *(Bundestag)*, or EU organs are empowered to enact appropriate legislation still remains controversial, however. There is a question whether nonsmoking laws might violate what one might refer to as smokers' "right to the free development of their addiction"—their right to self-impairment. There are also questions relating to the economic rights of restaurant owners, entrepreneurs, tobacco manufacturers, and advertising agencies under Germany's Basic Law, and to free competition under the provisions of the EC Treaty. Since the early 1980s, numerous law review articles and court decisions[52] have accompanied the growing awareness of the hazards of smoking, and they testify to a significant antismoking activism within the legal class.

In the last two decades, antismoking initiatives in Germany, though historically weak, gained considerable momentum in the legal and political arenas: first, through the EC's determination to fight tobacco abuse[53] and to achieve a high level of health protection;[54] second, through a series of court decisions in the 1980s that protected the rights of nonsmokers in the workplace; third, through more recent legislative initiatives, primarily by the Green and the Social Democratic parties; and, finally, through the assertion of jurisdiction by the Federal Constitutional Court, which construed the individual right to life and health—in general, and not just in relation to smoking—as a "protective duty" to be implemented by all public authorities.[55]

In 1989 the European Council recommended the prohibition of smoking in public places and in places accessible to the public, and in 1996, in Berlin, the Green Party introduced a bill providing for the sweeping protection of nonsmokers. Nevertheless, the federal government and the Federal Diet—both dominated by the Christian Democratic Party and the Liberal Party, and shying away from unpopular policies that would also provoke opposition by the tobacco industry—remained hesitant to pursue this regulatory path and denied federal competence to enact extensive regulations. Recently, a similarly comprehensive federal bill initiated by the Social

Democrats and Greens failed to obtain the required majority in the Federal Diet. That is why to this very day the regulatory scheme consists of a political program to improve the quality of the air in rooms open to the public[56] and a mosaic of prohibitions on the federal and state levels (which will be discussed below), but no general antismoking law—thus singling out Germany as the only EU country lacking comprehensive statutory protection of nonsmokers. The official approach may still be characterized as a mixture of prohibition (pursuant to the principle of health paternalism) and of appeals to the tobacco industry for self-regulation, to smokers for sensitivity to the interests of nonsmokers, and to nonsmokers for tolerance of smokers, all pursuant to the principle of voluntarism.

Restricting the Visibility of Tobacco Products: Bans on Advertising and Sponsoring

During the past thirty years, restrictions of the public visibility of tobacco products and smoking have been among the most contested political issues. Four years after the 1971 agreement between the minister of health and the tobacco industry to limit television advertising, a strict legal ban was imposed on all advertising of tobacco products on all public radio and television programs.[57] Since the mid-1970s, small antismoking organizations have been pressing in vain for a total ban on cigarette advertising; the tobacco industry has succeeded in dodging such a ban, however, by intensive lobbying and by voluntary (but not overly restrictive) "gentlemen's agreements"[58] to limit the design and presentation of advertisements. For example, the tobacco industry has discontinued advertising in youth magazines and in the vicinity of sports stadiums.

Governmental procrastination testifies not only to the fiscal interest in high tobacco taxes and to the veto power of the tobacco industry, but also to the strong resistance from the print media and movie theatres, which depend heavily on cigarette advertising. Although the amount spent on advertising tobacco products has declined over the last two decades, the total sum is still impressive. In 1997 the tobacco industry invested nearly DM 500 million in tobacco (mostly cigarette) advertising in the print media, movie theatres, and outdoor advertising (billboards). Despite its high visibility—using familiar campaigns for Marlboros and Camels, for example—such advertising constituted only 1.1 percent of the total amount spent for product advertising in Germany. The market of border-crossing (notably media and Internet) advertising for tobacco products in Germany reveals a remarkable asymmetry of the advertising expenditures by the tobacco industry. Due to the ban, television and radio (both public and private) received nothing. Internet and online services received less than 1 percent, and daily newspapers and other print media, roughly 4 percent each. These amounts were far overshadowed, however, by the 83.4 percent that went to illustrated magazines.[59] The costs of stationary advertising of tobacco products in Germany amounted to roughly DM 350 million in 1997: DM 255.8 million for outdoor advertising, DM 52.4 million for advertising in cinemas, and DM 39.4 million for indoor advertising (for example, sales displays).[60]

This situation may change, though, since the EU seems to be advancing toward more stringent restrictions on advertising—energized by a new policy outlined in the European Commission's program "Europe against Cancer." A 1998 directive that would have imposed a virtual ban on tobacco advertising and promotion was resisted by a tobacco company, advertising agencies, and the government, which all filed a suit before the European Court of Justice (ECJ). The economic plaintiffs claimed that the directive violated the rights of tobacco manufacturers and advertising agencies under EU primary law, notably the EC Treaty, by restricting free trade and the free flow of services, and the German government argued that the EU acted ultra vires—outside its area of competence—because the EC Treaty did not transfer regulatory powers to EU authorities in the area of public health.

After the court's advocate general had stated that he shared the view of the German government (and the tobacco industry), the ECJ followed suit by rescinding the directive in its decision of November 2000—thereby confirming the more restrictive interpretation of the EU's role in the area of health policy. Limitations on advertising and sponsoring will therefore have to be imposed by the member states.

We may not have seen the last act of the battle concerning an EU advertising ban. Of late, members of the European Parliament and the European Commission indicated that they were ready to initiate an amendment to the EC Treaty that would establish the EU's regulatory power in the area of public health and allow for the harmonization of tobacco regulations, including restrictions of the public visibility of smoking. For the time being, however, anti-tobacco paternalism cannot be implemented directly by EU authorities. They therefore have to resort to indirect measures such as the recently drafted directive to prohibit the export of "unhealthy" cigarettes with high nicotine or tar content.[61] This directive, which again caused a stir among the tobacco companies, has been challenged—even before its passage—as an unlawful interference with free trade. Unless the EC Treaty's free trade provision is changed, this export ban is likely to share the same fate as the advertising ban.

The paternalist protection of the population against the risks of tobacco consumption is regularly reinforced by considerations regarding the necessity to protect juveniles, who are said to be encouraged by advertising to take up smoking. The tobacco and advertising lobbies, however,[62] base their legal defense strategies on the protection of free choice, of the free market, and of commercial speech. The lobbies disregard or play down the impact of public imagery, the role models for smoking who declare "I like to smoke," and the overrepresentation of young, beautiful, and dynamic cigarette smokers. Indeed, the lobbies claim that the advertising of tobacco products is neither addressed to young people nor scientifically proven to promote their desire to smoke. Opponents of advertising restrictions further claim that bans or similar measures do not lead to a decrease in smoking.[63] In light of the "disastrous economic consequences," especially for the media—which may suffer, it is claimed, a loss estimated at DM 6.6 billion, leading to the collapse of one-quarter of all movie theatres—opponents of the restrictions demand that no total ban be established.

The politicolegal environment in Germany suggests that the tobacco industry, whose strategies are orchestrated mainly by the "big players"— Philip Morris, Reemtsma, and British American Tobacco—and its supporting actors may prevail. It is interesting to note that the Economic Committee of the Federal Diet rejected the recommendation of the Federal Council (Bundesrat) concerning additional restrictions of advertising for tobacco and tobacco products.[64] Hence, because state support appears to be lacking, the national legislature is not likely to follow up on the dictum of the Federal Constitutional Court that a ban on advertising is within the regulatory powers of the states.[65]

Shaping the Image of Smoking and Tobacco Products through Public Warnings and Regulation

During the last three decades, the strategy of restricting the public visibility of tobacco products has been connected with measures to shape their image and to inform consumers about the hazards of smoking. The same national statute that established restrictions on advertising also required the tobacco industry to indicate on all cigarette packs the nicotine and tar content of the cigarettes, and forbade labeling tobacco products as "natural" or "naturally pure." These provisions were complemented by warnings of the health hazards of smoking, which were first issued under national statutes and then, beginning in 1989, pursuant to an EC directive.[66] Prior to the advertising directive, European health paternalism also led to a directive limiting the admissible tar content of cigarettes.[67] It is interesting to note that the strategy of promoting public health within the EC (and later the EU) did not persuade the European Commission to discontinue subsidies for growing tobacco.[68]

Initially, the tobacco industry was successful in its court challenges of legally required warnings—such as "Cigarette smoking is hazardous to your health," "Smoking causes cancer," and "Smoking causes heart and circulatory diseases"[69]—as violations of tobacco companies' constitutionally protected commercial speech, emanating from the freedom of speech under the Basic Law. Therefore, national and EU ministers of public health revised the warnings' text to clarify that the ministers, not the companies, were the authors. Under EU law[70] cigarette packages and tobacco advertisements have to carry the general warning: "The EC Health Ministers: Smoking/ tobacco is hazardous to your health" *["Die EG-Gesundheitsminister: Rauchen/Tabak gefährdet die Gesundheit"]*. Cigarette packages have to carry the additional message: "The EC Health Ministers: Giving up smoking reduces the risk of serious diseases" *["Wer das Rauchen aufgibt, verringert das Risiko schwerer Erkrankungen"]*.

The European Commission rejected the intervention of the German minister of health, who was obviously influenced by the tobacco lobby, to modify the warning by including the word "may." The commission referred to a "Declaration on Labeling" issued by the expert Committee on Cancer in 1989 and emphatically stated that such a conditional modification was scientifically incorrect.

In 1997 the Federal Constitutional Court confirmed the constitutionality of the above-mentioned warnings and dismissed the constitutional complaints of several cigarette manufacturers as unfounded. The court held that according to the present state of scientific research, smoking causes cancer and coronary diseases, and that the government is therefore entitled to issue warnings that adequately dramatize the dangers of smoking.[71]

During the period leading up to the Constitutional Court's decision, politicians, legal scholars, and the tobacco industry had criticized the EC directive for dogmatically restating the opinion of cancer experts who based their judgment on "questionable statistical" data provided primarily by the U.S. surgeon general and who accepted that there is a "monocausal correlation" between smoking and lethal diseases. Instead, the directive should have taken into account, or so critics argued, "more sophisticated and reliable research studies" that are based on statistical and experimental methods relating to genetically oriented hypotheses, and that question the validity of causal explanations.[72] In addition to challenging the sufficiency of the evidence, the legal controversy once again concentrated on the EC's competence to take regulatory action in the field of health policy under the guise of harmonizing the national regulations governing the labeling of tobacco products, and on the negative freedoms of commercial speech, trade, and advertising. Legal scholars who supported the tobacco industry's position argued, too, that the directive "unreasonably" restricted those freedoms by the medically unproven content of the warning. Presently, this controversy over labeling is quiescent, but it may be reignited should the European Commission or Parliament decide to move toward an amendment of the EC Treaty that would allow *regulation* rather than just *promotion* of public health.

The cigarette industry has always tried to avoid more explicit warnings, especially ones addressed to juveniles, by voluntarily advertising "Cool kids can wait"—a slogan much criticized by drug experts, who demanded that the message should be "Cool kids don't smoke."[73] In the future, this appeasement strategy may not be enough to sustain voluntarism over paternalism. Incensed by the lost battle for a total ban on advertising, the commission declared in early 2001 that it was determined to put into effect a policy of stricter warnings.

"Zoning" the Freedom to Smoke

The approach of "zoning" smoking—that is, of designating nonsmoking or smoking areas—redirects the goal and attention of regulatory policies. Instead of trying to influence the behavior of smokers and potential smokers, zoning is intended to protect nonsmokers. Passive smoking thereby becomes the crucial battleground. From the very beginning of the battle over the health risks of smoking, however, the German Association of Cigarette Manufacturers (VdC) has done everything in its power to dismiss, and to suppress scientific evidence concerning, the claim that tobacco poisons released into the air endanger the health of nonsmokers.[74] The VdC orchestrated its own research, whose goal was to demonstrate that causality had not been established; for example, it supported a study by a scientist who had promised to produce favorable results. The VdC also discontinued research projects likely to "open the door for prohibitionists;" recruited expert consultants who would support their general policy; set up subsidized front groups; staged conferences to cast doubt that passive smoking was anything more than a nuisance or, at worst, a risk. It even went so far as to pension off the "uncooperative" head of its research institute in 1975.[75] These actions, together with public relations campaigns and intensive lobbying, paid off. One of the former presidents of the Federal Health Office held back "dangerous scientific data" on passive smoking and delayed the final decision on the cigarette additive coumarin.

Hence, it may be no coincidence that zoning policy for smoking was implemented somewhat differently in the Federal Republic of Germany than in the United States. In Germany the implementation was slow, but steady, in the face of the mainly covert, and not very energetic, resistance of the tobacco industry. Among other things, zoning had already been firmly established in pre-World War II Germany. Furthermore, the industry may have realized, informed by the American experience and by international anti-tobacco campaigns,[76] that a stance of total opposition would be unsuccessful. Finally, there was considerable support for moderate zoning; even most smokers agree that nonsmokers, especially within the family or at the workplace, are entitled to a reasonable amount of protection against the risks of exposure to smoke.[77] Interestingly enough, the judiciary was here, again, more energetic than the Federal Health Office, the Federal Diet, and the federal government generally in protecting the health of passive smokers. In a series of decisions, courts—mainly labor courts—issued injunctions against smoking in the workplace. The typical situation was one in which employees went to court after management had failed to meet their demands either for a smoke-free workplace or some kind of zoning. By 1994 roughly sixty courts had ruled in favor of the plaintiffs based upon either labor law or civil service law.[78]

Legal battles over the significance of data concerning passive smoking were accompanied by political and scientific controversies regarding the associated health hazards. The prozoning group relied on the views of some U.S. scientists that passive smoking ranks among the most frequent causes of death (next to active smoking)[79] and therefore presents a serious danger to nonsmokers.[80] This group invoked the constitutional duty of public authorities to reduce health hazards for nonsmokers, including unknown or uncertain risks.[81] Furthermore, the group argued that it was legally and ethically absurd to claim that smokers have a right to develop their personality at the expense of endangering the health of others—or, as it was claimed, at the expense of annoying others, but causing them no actual harm. On the other side, legal scholars, scientists, and politicians who opposed stricter zoning measures—such as a general ban on smoking in all public areas—claimed that "passive smoking does not cause health hazards under normal room-air conditions"[82] and that the annoyance of passive smokers is legally irrelevant. They charged nonsmokers with being "oversensitive" and held that to follow what it characterized as the "fundamentalist American approach" would amount to a disproportionate state intervention into the private sphere. (There is no evidence that they invoked the precedent of Nazi Germany's interventionist public health policy.) Finally, they claimed that under the principle of subsidiarity, the state should regulate only when agreements between the unions and the employers' associations cannot be reached, and when no other type of conflict-resolution process has been successful. Smokers and nonsmokers should, that is, be entitled to negotiate adequate solutions and to accommodate their conflicting interests and rights—and to do so free of state intervention.

Critics of the existing regulations can hardly claim that the federal regulatory scheme is too rigid or too prohibitive, or that it leaves no space for the principle of subsidiarity. The decentralized and fragmented network of zoning provisions primarily addresses public or publicly accessible rooms, buildings, and areas (hospitals, public offices, subway stations, airports); means of transportation (buses, trains, airplanes,[83] taxis, and so on); and restaurants. The Ordinance Governing Workplaces and the Labor Protection Statute of 1975 provides that workers and employees are entitled to a sufficient amount of healthy, smoke-free air during work and leisure hours, and places responsibility upon the employers to take appropriate measures for the protection of nonsmokers.[84] The ordinance also obligates smokers to take into consideration the health of their nonsmoking colleagues, who may suggest proposals for their protection and may appeal to legal authorities should the measures taken by the employer be insufficient. In addition, employees may request under civil law or civil service law that they be assigned workplaces not hazardous to their health. The Federal Labor Court decided in 1998 that workers and employees are entitled to a "tobacco-free" workplace if so required by reasons of health; for example, because they suffer from pulmonary disease.[85] In addition, many business enterprises are covered by regional or local regulations contracted by the "social partners" (employers and trade unions), which act flexibly to safeguard the health of nonsmokers.

The recent revision of the Statute Governing the Restaurant Business (1998) follows the general lines of the regulations on labor protection. The statute, however, is connected with, and may be restricted by, the "nature of the service." If the "nature" of a pub or restaurant implies the entertaining of smoking guests, neither the guests nor the waiters and waitresses may claim that smoking should be legally prohibited there. The statute provides only that local legal authorities may require appropriate improvements or adjustments such as the installation of a ventilation system or the demarcation of nonsmoking areas. During the last decade many, if not most, restaurant and pub owners have voluntarily established nonsmoking areas.

Antismoking leagues have been critical of this piecemeal approach and have called for stricter, more comprehensive and centralized regulation. Legislative projects of the Green Party and of the Social Democratic Party have made the same demands. In 1996, and as noted earlier, the Greens initiated, but failed to enact, a sweeping bill governing the protection of nonsmokers. It included a ban on smoking in all interior rooms open to the general public or used as public workrooms.[86] While almost everyone agreed that the purpose—protection of passive smokers—was legitimate,[87] critics kept pointing to legal problems: lack of competence of the federal (and even the state) government; the infringement of the civil rights of restaurant and hotel owners; the questionable appropriateness of extending nonsmoking zones beyond rooms open to the public; and the impracticality of a nearly complete ban. Public health officials declared that they were unable to effectively implement and supervise such sweeping provisions. A similar, multiparty initiative by a number of deputies of the Federal Diet was introduced and debated in the German parliament for the first time in 2000, but has not passed yet.[88] Its main goal was to prohibit smoking in public rooms of the federal government, the states, and municipalities, as well as in all modes of public transportation and in all workplaces. Opponents claimed that the bill was overly broad and too indeterminate, especially because of its unclear exception for "rooms without office hours"—a phrase that means "not accessible to the public." With regard to workplaces, the draft reiterates a well-known "privilege:" the ban has to be justified by the "nature" of the service in question.[89] This legal scheme, while allowing local conflict resolution, is not without drawbacks for nonsmokers. First, any ban would have to be supervised by the entrepreneur/ employer and therefore depends on his or her sensitivity to the interests of nonsmokers. Second, the scheme requires that an employee not happy with the supervision and the measures taken must go to court—which means that the protection of nonsmokers against passive smoking depends ultimately on the willingness of nonsmokers to defend their health even under adverse circumstances.

The Regulation of Smoking by the Price of Tobacco

As noted earlier, smoking was, from the very beginning, subject to taxation. Taxing tobacco itself (the leaves) or the trade of tobacco products was meant to create a new source of government revenue or to regulate the behavior of smokers. In 1949 the former imperial tax *(Reichssteuer)* was transformed into a federal excise tax in the form of a stamp duty.[90] Pursuant to the EC Treaty, national excise taxes are indirect taxes that fall within the regulatory competence of the EU insofar as they affect the common market. The EU has therefore attempted to harmonize these taxes since the early 1970s—as part of its effort to establish a market without border controls—but has met with a great deal of resistance from the member states, which feared that they might be deprived of a crucial source of income.[91]

In the tradition of "moral taxes," the purpose of an excise duty on tobacco products is not to cover or compensate public health costs caused by smoking, but to "punish" luxury expenditures and to redirect the ethically reproachable social behavior of smokers. The tobacco tax is therefore officially and counterfactually classified today as a social-purpose tax with a secondary fiscal purpose—a label that is clearly belied by the determination of the federal government, with respect to the EU, to defend the tobacco tax and maintain the resulting revenue, which in 1999 amounted to DM 22.7 billion, or 2.57 percent of the total. Nevertheless, the prevailing opinion in the tax field seems to be that the tobacco tax is justified by reasons of public health as a method of disadvantaging those who behave in a manner that causes health hazards to others and has social costs for the whole of society.

It is interesting to note that the tobacco industry opposes tax increases with the arguments that taxes, in general, fail to change human behavior, and that the tobacco tax, in particular, does not reduce smoking but enhances the black market and smuggling. While the behavioral effects of taxation are hard to prove or disprove, smuggling has, indeed, increased in the EU over the past decade.

During the past decade almost all EU member states have increased the tax burden on tobacco products. Having increased the tobacco tax by only 32 percent, Germany still ranks among the few European countries that have abstained from dramatic increases. The German tobacco tax now constitutes about 57 percent of the retail price for cigarettes (DM 0.26). If one adds the value-added tax of 13.8 percent, the overall tax burden on the price of cigarettes amounts to a little over 70 percent.[92] Tobacco tax constitutes one of the most important sources of income for the federal budget: the total amount rose from DM 6.1 billion in 1968 to DM 21.6 billion in 1998[93] (and as noted above, to DM 22.7 billion the following year). Since 1993, total tobacco-tax revenue has increased 12 percent, with the lion's share— slightly over 90 percent—being provided by cigarettes.[94]

While the revenue from the tobacco tax may explain why the government has generally pursued a lenient regulatory approach to tobacco control, taxing tobacco products has clearly failed to curb the "undesirable habit" of smoking. The fiscal logic of tobacco control may also explain why the availability of tobacco products, mainly cigarettes, has not been reduced, not even for the sake of the widely declared goal of protecting juveniles: over the last decade, the number of cigarette vending machines, many of them openly accessible to the general public, has doubled from 400,000 to 800,000.

Incentives or Punishment? Other Issues

Aside from efforts to influence the consumption of tobacco products through the use of public warnings, designating smoking areas, and increased prices, the German regulatory scheme is complemented by a number of more or less indirect strategies that reflect a similar mix of *Ordnungspolitik* (regulatory policies) and soft interventions, if not a shift from policing tobacco consumption to a policy of providing incentives to reduce usage. Along the lines of its policy of required warnings, the federal government initiated several antismoking campaigns that targeted primarily children and adolescents, and were carried out by the Federal Agency for Health Information. Due to the agency's limited funds, these campaigns had little impact on tobacco consumption in Germany. Other measures, such as limiting the sale of tobacco products to minors and restricting the smoking age, focus on the same target group. More recently, members of the federal government suggested that health insurers should play a more active role in the campaign against tobacco abuse. With reference to the United States, the former minister of health proposed that nonsmokers be granted a discount on insurance. Neither public nor private insurers have so far reduced insurance contributions, however, most likely because of the difficulty in determining and controlling the smoking/nonsmoking behavior of particular individuals.

Members of the Federal Diet, as well as legal scholars, have recently suggested that, following the model contracts between the American tobacco industry and some of the states, the tobacco industry should cover the health insurance costs[95] caused by smoking-related diseases. This suggestion was criticized for not considering the savings of the social insurance system due to the reduced life expectancy of smokers and for disregarding the specific situation in the United States, where only two-thirds of the population are covered by health insurance.[96] So far, strategies to establish product liability—beyond the obligation of the tobacco industry to inform consumers of the health risks of smoking[97]—have not been pursued energetically. This state of affairs may change in the near future as legal scholars urge that the Product Liability Law be applied to tobacco products. They argue that despite warnings on cigarette packages and information about tar levels and nicotine content, tobacco consumers are still not adequately aware of the hazards of smoking. One may therefore infer, they claim, that cigarette producers are liable under the said law because of the "complexity of the harmful substances contained in cigarettes" and because of the "constructional defect" of cigarettes. Quite persuasively, experts claim that many of the health risks might be eliminated or minimized by an improved "product design."[98] If courts follow this lead and establish product liability, they would invigorate the antismoking campaigns within and without the legal arenas.

Unlike what has happened in the United States, there has been in Germany no significant litigation against tobacco producers. This difference may be due less to the formerly more restrictive liability law in Germany[99] than to the fact that smoking-related health costs are covered by health insurance. Hence, there is little incentive for the insured to go to court and sue a tobacco company. Insurance companies are reluctant to litigate because the carriers of public health insurance are also carriers of old-age insurance and therefore would have to show proof that, on balance, the smoking-related health costs are not compensated by a reduction in their payouts for health and social security pension insurance. Due to this combination of factors, the tobacco industry has been reluctant to contribute to a fund to cover potential damage awards. A change in the law of liability, however, might motivate the industry to reconsider its attitude.

Conclusion

Tobacco control in Germany can be said to be different from policies in other European countries and the United States in several crucial respects. First, the German antismoking agenda has never been supported by a strong social movement or by a viable and vocal coalition of groups and organizations. Historically and currently, the move to prohibit or even restrict tobacco consumption has been and still is a concern of "enlightened" expert groups that recruit their activists primarily from the ranks of the medical profession, the state administration, the legal profession, and recently also from ecologically minded and health-conscious organizations and political parties. While there are no simple explanations for the virtual absence of civil-society protest relating to public health and tobacco consumption, one may assume that the state's public health paternalism and the courts' legal activism, taken together, at least partly account for this deficit. Quite obviously, the weak antismoking "movement" did not stand a chance of competing with the powerful pro-tobacco lobby and with the media that have been dependent on tobacco advertising.

Second, the government's use of its power to tax and price tobacco—which means to use indirect interventions rather than strict and direct antismoking measures—is likely to have been prompted by its overriding interest in tobacco-tax revenues, which so far have not been significantly affected by zoning and advertising regulations. For lack of clear evidence, one can only assume that the lenient attitude, comparatively speaking, of the government toward matters of smoking hazards may have resulted from intense lobbying by the tobacco industry, from the division of labor in the area of public health between the state governments, the federal government, and the EC, and from a widespread popular acceptance of smoking. A more prohibitive course of action, though legally possible, is not likely to be followed by the public authorities due to the lack of popular support and the effective defense strategies of the tobacco industry. This situation may change, though, if the EC pursues a stricter prohealth and antismoking course of action, or if product liability becomes a serious legal threat.

Third, globalization may in the long run play into the hands of the anti-smoking "movement" in Germany. Developments in the United States and in other countries are carefully observed both by the defenders of the status quo and by those who would change it. The success of antismoking efforts there and in other countries may very well create prohealth momentum; efficient antismoking campaigns may very well spill over into Germany, help politicize the issue of tobacco control and tobacco consumption, and consequently de-legitimize the present combination of regulatory measures, with its soft interventions and reliance on the cooperation of the tobacco industry.

Fourth, like many previous campaigns and paternalist public health and anti-tobacco measures, even a full-fledged crusade against smoking, wholeheartedly supported by the media and not undermined by pro-tobacco lobbying, is prone to fail unless the smoking majority in Germany demonstrates at least a minimal willingness to question, and then "kick," the "habit." Notwithstanding the piecemeal character of governmental policies and the slick counterinsurgency tactics implemented by the tobacco industry, one has to note that most German smokers have proven resistant to well-intended and well-designed attempts to help them change their positive attitude toward tobacco consumption. Many of them avoided more expensive cigarettes by buying cheaper products; some shook off the tobacco-tax burden by shopping on the black market. A significant number of smokers tried to escape from some of the health hazards by switching from "full flavor" to "light" or "extra light," and from "high tar" to "low tar." And a majority of smokers appeased criticism from nonsmokers by conforming to "zoning" regulations. Despite a greater—even if still limited—awareness of what tobacco consumption can do to one's health, smoking is still rather popular. As a drug that causes what remains a widely accepted dependency, tobacco produces its own "market power of demand."[100] This power cannot be broken by repressive measures and words alone. To make antismoking matters worse, since the fall of the Iron Curtain and the extension of the EU to the east, more and heavier smokers have joined the ranks of tobaccophiles already in Germany. A new "philosophy," lifestyle, and attitude are consequently called for.

8

Holy Smoke, No More? Tobacco Control in Denmark

Erik Albæk

Foreigners visiting Denmark often find the country's tobacco-control policies appallingly lax. When they arrive at Copenhagen International Airport, they find the designated smoking areas to be a joke, separated from non-smoking areas by nothing but (impure) air; they find it virtually impossible to find a smoke-free section even in Denmark's most upscale French restaurant, let alone cafés or bars; and they learn with disbelief that nonsmoking employees in Danish private workplaces are not even protected from smoke during lunch. Many Danish health policymakers share this gloomy view that Danish tobacco-control policies lag behind those of most "civilized" countries.

It is debatable, however, whether Danish tobacco-control policies, in general, lag behind policies in comparable countries. It may appear so when one focuses exclusively on Denmark's weak restrictions on public smoking, but the country's tobacco-control policymakers use all of the available policy instruments in efforts to reduce smoking: carrot (economic incentives), stick (regulations), and sermon (information). If the whole spectrum of policy instruments is considered, Denmark does not fare badly. In fact, the country has for decades been a front-runner in tobacco-control policies, and it still has some of the world's toughest policies. For instance, in the late 1920s, when Denmark dramatically increased its excise duty on tobacco products (a duty first imposed in 1912), the country became a world leader in tobacco taxation. Moreover, it remains a leader today; its taxes on tobacco are the third highest in the European Union (EU). Also noteworthy is that the country has never permitted tobacco advertisements on the broadcast media.

The introduction of such restrictive policies is a puzzle because the configuration of interests favored the well-organized, prosmoking forces. It is well known, however, that once a policy is introduced, it is likely to stay on the same path for an extended period,[1] which is precisely what happened in Denmark. New tobacco-control policies were accepted as long as they were based on two fundamental principles implicitly informing the initial Danish introduction of excise duty on tobacco products: tobacco consumption is considered a private matter, and voluntary agreement is preferred to legal regulation. On the one hand, the acceptance of these principles allowed for the introduction of ever more restrictive policies to reduce active smoking. On the other, these same two principles would effectively preempt any attempts to introduce policies intended to protect nonsmokers from involuntary exposure to smoke—that is, passive smoking.

Nevertheless, Danish policies on passive smoking have become more restrictive, and the proposals for tobacco control put forward by the Danish health authorities during the last decade suggest a shift in policy over a very short period of time. We are thus faced with a second paradox, since conventional wisdom has it that once a policy path has been staked out, it is very difficult to change.

Danish tobacco-control policies are consequently marked by a number of puzzles, on which this chapter attempts to shed light.

Background and Context

From the very beginning, an asymmetrical configuration of interests militated against the introduction of tobacco-control policies in Denmark. Those who favored restrictions on smoking were not, and to this very day still are not, well organized. There are various nongovernmental health organizations, the most important being the Danish Cancer Society, the Danish Heart Foundation, and the Danish Lung Association. All three of them, but the first in particular, have large budgets to run information campaigns and to support research. They are also heard when proposals for new policies or regulations are introduced, but none is an especially powerful interest group.

Tobacco consumers are also not well organized. Hen-ry—an abbreviation of "*hen*synsfulde *ry*gere," the Danish term for considerate smokers—was formed in 1987; the world's first organization of its kind, Hen-ry's explicit aim was to counterbalance the Council on Smoking and Health, established by the Danish Parliament the same year. Hen-ry's membership, however, as well as its political clout, has always been limited. And the organization was compromised in 2000 when the Danish press revealed that Hen-ry receives heavy financial support from Philip Morris.[2] In addition to Hen-ry, there are a few other very small, and likewise insignificant, smokers' associations.

In contrast to health organizations and tobacco consumers, the small group of tobacco manufacturers can be easily mobilized for collective action, making it an influential interest group. The number of manufacturers reached its peak in 1921, with 1,518 registered, 1,200 of which were one-man or small-family businesses. At the same time, there were a number of what were—on a Danish scale, at least—very large companies. In Copenhagen alone, fourteen tobacco manufacturers each employed more than one hundred people in 1914. Over the years, tobacco manufacturing has become even more concentrated. Membership of the Tobacco Manufacturers Association of Denmark decreased, primarily through mergers, from thirty-eight in 1950 to merely seven in 2000, with Scandinavian Tobacco Company as the dominant member; there are only two small firms (which primarily produce marginal tobacco products) in which Scandinavian Tobacco is not involved. The Danish manufacturers satisfy 97 percent of the domestic cigarette market. They are also major exporters of tobacco products and are involved in tobacco manufacture in a number of European countries.[3]

When, at the beginning of the twentieth century, Danish tobacco policy was initiated through the imposition of duties on tobacco products, tobacco workers were also a significant force. An estimated 8,270 persons were employed in the tobacco industry in 1921, representing 0.54 percent of the total workforce and 2.2 percent of industrial workers.[4] In 1918, the chairman of the Cigar Sorters' Union became Denmark's first Social Democratic minister, and in 1924, he became the country's first Social Democratic prime minister. His sixteen years as prime minister has not been exceeded in the history of Denmark's parliamentary government. The number of employees in the tobacco industry decreased dramatically, however, from 7,536 in 1946, to 783 in 1999, at which point they represented only 0.027 percent of the active workforce.[5]

With this particular, asymmetrical configuration of interests in the area of tobacco policy, "client politics" was the likely result;[6] tobacco manufacturers and workers would organize and lobby to prevent costly policies from being imposed on them. Even so, a duty was imposed on tobacco products, and from the late 1920s on, it was one of the world's highest, if not the highest, excise duties on tobacco. In that initial, formative moment of Danish tobacco-control policy, the tobacco industry accepted the imposition of the duty but also ensured the establishment of an institutional arrangement that prevented a violation of its fundamental interests. The two basic principles thus laid down—as noted earlier, that tobacco consumption is considered a private matter, and that voluntary agreement is preferred to legal regulation—would inform Danish tobacco-control policy for decades.

Throughout the twentieth century, smoking and alcohol consumption (from 1917) were viewed as private matters. During the past forty years, while Denmark's welfare state expanded, Danish decision makers abandoned restrictive legislation by "privatizing" decision making about a small but important set of issues like abortion, pornography, and domestic partnership arrangements.[7] The Danes take pride in this liberal feature of Danish politics and look skeptically at countries where they think moralism informs political decisions, as in the United States or neighboring "Prohibition Sweden," so nicknamed because of its restrictive alcohol policies.

A 1992 survey showed that Danes were less inclined to favor restrictions on smoking in public areas than citizens of other EU countries.[8] With two out of three Danes indicating in 2000 that smokers should be allowed to smoke as long as they do so "considerately," Denmark has a far more tolerant attitude toward smoking than other Nordic countries. Danes are also more likely than citizens of other Nordic countries to find the talk about passive smoking exaggerated.[9] When the *Lancet* in 2001 accused Denmark's Queen Margrethe II of causing the high prevalence of smoking among Danish women, Danes almost unanimously defended their queen's right to smoke.[10]

In both the public and private sectors, Denmark prefers voluntary alternatives over legal regulation. If the state wants to change people's behavior, one legitimate policy instrument is information. If that fails, the next option is voluntary agreement. In the public sector, the attempt to impose state regulations concerning the consumption of tobacco on local government premises would be contested as violating the principle of local autonomy. With respect to the private sector, Denmark has a long tradition of governing with, rather than against, organized interests. For instance, ever since the late nineteenth century, labor regulations in Denmark (such as working hours and minimum wages) are almost exclusively based on voluntary agreements between labor unions and employers' associations, with no state involvement; in many other countries, such matters are legally regulated by the state. In other policy areas, the state is involved, but the outcome—the means of control—is not legal regulation, but a voluntary agreement between the state and the relevant parties.

Tobacco Consumption

Per-capita tobacco consumption in Denmark increased through much of the twentieth century; only in recent decades did it begin to decline (see Figure 8.1). Consumption did decrease significantly during World War II due to a shortage of tobacco products, but immediately after the war, tobacco consumption increased sharply and grew constantly over the next forty years before peaking in the late 1970s and early 1980s.

The prevalence of smoking in Denmark has constantly decreased since 1953 (see Figures 8.2 and 8.3). While almost 78 percent of all Danish men over fifteen years of age were smokers in 1953, the number dropped to 50 percent in 1987 and to 42 percent in 2000. For women, smoking rates increased from 40 percent in 1953 to 46 percent in 1976, and then dropped to 42 percent in 1987 and 37 percent in 2000. The decrease in the overall percentage of adult smokers is explained by the decrease in the number of pipe and cigar smokers. In 1970, 26 percent of male smokers smoked tobacco products other than cigarettes, compared to 7 percent in 2000. The corresponding figures for women were 11 percent in 1970 and 1 percent in 2000.

After increasing rapidly following World War II, from 1970 to 2000 the prevalence of cigarette smoking decreased slightly, from 39 percent to 36 percent. A larger decrease can be observed among men, from

Figure 8.1 Annual per capita cigarette consumption in Denmark, 1920–2000

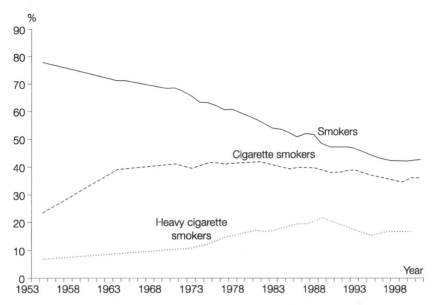

Figure 8.2 Patterns of smoking among Danish men, 1953–2000

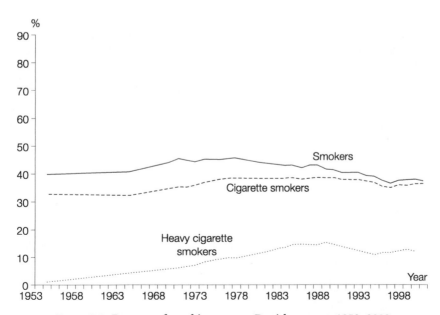

Figure 8.3 Patterns of smoking among Danish women, 1953–2000

41.5 percent to 35 percent. Among Danish women, 36 percent are smokers (a higher percentage than that for men). The prevalence of heavy smoking (fifteen or more cigarettes per day) also increased rapidly in the years following the war, peaking in the late 1980s. In 2000, 15.3 percent of men and 11.9 percent of women were heavy smokers.

Denmark's overall smoking rate of 36 percent is one of the highest in the EU.[11] A notable feature of the Danish population is the close parity in smoking rates of men and women (35 and 36 percent, respectively, in 2000); for many years, the prevalence of smoking among women has been higher in Denmark than almost anywhere else in the world. (And now the rate of tobacco-related deaths among women is also higher in Denmark.)[12] One explanation for the country's high proportion of women smokers is that, in cross-country comparisons of secularization, the country consistently stands out as occupying the secular extreme,[13] and increased secularization tends to reduce moral restrictions on women's behavior. Another factor is that male/female differences in behavior and attitudes have decreased because Danish women joined the labor force at an earlier stage and in greater numbers than women in most other Western countries.[14]

Denmark is one of the few countries where the estimated annual mortality due to tobacco is similar for men and women. An estimated one-fifth of all deaths—13,000, with 40 percent being women—are caused by tobacco.[15] Female mortality from tobacco has increased more than tenfold since the mid-1960s. Lung cancer mortality in Danish women (35 per 100,000 in the early 1990s) is by far the highest in Europe.[16] Estimates of costs vary considerably. When considered in terms of hospitalizations, medical care, sickness allowance, cessation programs, and so on, costs are enormous[17] and often used as an argument for more restrictive tobacco-control policies. When also taking into account both smokers' contributions to the public coffers and the costs saved (for example, on pensions and elder care) given the reduction in smokers' life expectancy, there may be a net economic gain to Danish society from the present level of tobacco consumption.[18]

Tobacco-Control Policies

Although the parameters of Danish politics have generally disfavored restrictive tobacco-control policies, restrictive policies have nevertheless been introduced, some dating to the early years of the twentieth century. In the end, all instruments available to policymakers are now applied to tobacco control. The individual instruments used are presented chronologically below, in the order that they were introduced. Most instruments were intended to reduce active smoking. Only in the late 1980s were measures introduced to protect primarily nonsmokers from passive smoking.

The Price of Tobacco

Whereas the import duty on tobacco has been used in Denmark for centuries, an excise duty on tobacco was introduced only in the early twentieth century. In 1891 the Danish Parliament passed an old-age pension act that was structured according to the principles that were later seen as characteristic of the special Scandinavian model of the welfare state.[19] Using general taxation to fully finance pension payments was one of the special features of the Danish old-age pension scheme. Revenues were procured primarily by imposing an excise duty on beer (there was already a duty on distilled spirits). Although temperance movements were gaining momentum at the time, Parliament focused on the fiscal and distributional consequences of excise duties, not on moral issues.[20] In 1902, the year prior to the introduction of an income tax in Denmark, excise duties on beer and distilled spirits constituted 12 percent of public revenues.[21]

An ever-increasing need for state revenues rendered new objects of taxation necessary, and in 1912 the Danish minister of finance decided to imitate a German excise duty on cigarettes.[22] The finance minister asserted that "new revenues for the Exchequer" were needed.[23] No other arguments were put forward during the parliamentary readings. The industry, which was used to heavy import duties and saw the excise duty not as a dramatic, but as a fair, shift in policy, even assisted the finance minister in the technical drafting of the duty.[24] During that period—the late nineteenth and early twentieth century—the industry's main concerns were, instead, the distributional consequences of specific duties and the protection against international competition.[25] World War I rendered new regulations and taxes necessary,[26] and in the end turned tobacco regulation and taxation into a complicated jigsaw puzzle. In 1917 a tobacco commission was established to conduct an analysis and to draft a proposal for comprehensive tobacco-taxation reform. Four years later the commission sent a comprehensive report to the minister of finance.[27] When, in 1922, Parliament passed a bill on tobacco taxation, repealing all existing tobacco acts, it followed the principles laid down in the tobacco commission's report.[28]

The commission was a truly corporatist body in line with the principles of corporatist policymaking that had been established around the turn of the century and then reinforced during the government's World War I crisis-management efforts. Manufacturers and distributors, as well as workers,

were represented on the commission. They were to consider control mechanisms, the effects of various types and levels of duties on specific tobacco
products, and how this all affected various groups of manufacturers, distributors, workers, and consumers. This task was not an easy one. For
instance, the committee members knew that their suggestions would lead to
a drastic reduction in the number of tobacco manufacturers. In 1922, the
year the reform came into effect, no less than two thousand tobacco manufacturers closed down—primarily tobacco workers who also had a small
home production. This consequence was acceptable to the chairman of the
tobacco workers' union—a commission member—only because compensation was promised to manufacturers who had to close down and because
the overall reform would result in a consolidation of production in fewer,
large production plants that would entail improvements in working conditions and wages for the workers.[29] The Agrarian-Liberal minister of finance
was overjoyed that the settlement was supported by all parties in the
tobacco industry and trade, as well as the major parties in Parliament.
During the parliamentary debate he noted:

> Let me say to the honorable speaker before me that to my knowledge
> no tax bill ever presented in [the Parliament] has come about after so
> much cooperation among the most important actors in the trade that
> is the intended object of taxation. In conjunction with the state
> authorities, fully competent representatives of industry, commerce,
> and workers have, through extended and thorough negotiations, pro-
> duced this bill and agreed among themselves on its provisions. I
> believe this is the only time a tax bill has been introduced here after
> such careful preparation, already consented to, and applauded, by the
> main actors in the trade in question.[30]

In the first two decades of the twentieth century, membership in the
Danish temperance movements increased dramatically,[31] and they did, at
least marginally, concern themselves with the harmful effects of tobacco.[32]
Nevertheless, health concerns were mentioned neither in the tobacco commission's reports nor in the extensive parliamentary debates—which were
exclusively focused on developing a technically effective and politically
acceptable system of tax collection. The bill was passed by a vote of 95 to 2.[33]

World War I and its immediate aftermath became a "formative
moment,"[34] setting out the path for future Danish tobacco policies.
First, the 1922 tax reform definitely established that the use of tobacco,
like the consumption of alcohol, had become a public issue that the state
had a legitimate right to tax and regulate. Although tobacco manufacturers,
distributors, and workers were well organized, they had not been able to

effectively oppose taxation on tobacco. In the end, the state had to procure its revenues from somewhere, and interests related to "luxury" (such as sugar or tobacco) or even "harmful" (such as alcohol) products were in a less fortunate bargaining position than others. Second, the new policy regime was one in which the taxation of tobacco and alcohol products, as well as the regulation of their production and distribution, became a legitimate public concern, whereas consumption of either was defined as an exclusively private matter. Third, the formulation and implementation of tobacco policy became a corporatist matter; rather than legislating unilaterally, the government collaborated with the industry and distributors in order to generate a mutually acceptable outcome.

Throughout most of the century, the price of tobacco was discussed primarily in fiscal terms. In 1928, when excise duties on tobacco were increased dramatically to finance state loans to the Danish bank sector (which had been at the brink of collapse),[35] the spokesman of the Agrarian-Liberal party argued: "I will not go into the harmful effects of tobacco smoke—most likely all tobacco is evil in terms of health—but, after all, we do not introduce tax legislation primarily for ethical reasons."[36] The spokesman's last sentence could have been an epigram on Danish tobacco-taxation policy.

Two separate sets of actors, with little mutual contact, are responsible for taxation and health policies. As phrased by Carsten Koch, a former minister of taxation and later of health: "When the budget of the Ministry of Health is decided, excise duties on tobacco are never discussed. When the budget of the Ministry of Taxation is decided, health policy is never discussed."[37] Only rarely and on a purely ad hoc basis does the Ministry of Taxation contact the Ministry of Health or other health policy actors. In fact, the Ministry of Taxation was flabbergasted when, in the mid-1990s, the minister of health sent a letter to the Ministry of Taxation asking it to consider an increase in tobacco excise duties.[38] It is apparent from the very nature of this request, however, that the minister of health had limited knowledge of taxation policy. Danish tobacco duties are primarily imposed for fiscal reasons, not to reduce tobacco consumption, and since the introduction of the EU's Single European Act in 1986, the main concern of the Ministry of Taxation has been an adaptation of Danish tobacco duties to duties in other EU member states, thus preventing increased cross-border trade and, with it, revenue losses for the Danish government.

Both the state and the Danish tobacco industry profit from the Danish tobacco-taxation system. The state profits significantly in monetary terms: taxation (excise duties and value-added tax) constituted 79.2 percent of the price of a cigarette in 2000.[39] The proportion of central government revenues raised through tobacco excise duties varied widely over the course of the twentieth century. In 1913, the year that excise duties were first introduced, excise duties on cigarettes made up 0.34 percent of central government revenues. In 1920, they grew to 3.4 percent, and in 1950, to 21.14 percent.[40] Not even the Danes, however, could smoke their way through the massive expansion of the welfare state that began in the mid-1960s. For the rest of the century, duties on tobacco were a declining share of total revenues for the central government (local governments do not impose excise duties). In 2000, the Dkr 7.6 billion duties on tobacco (roughly US$988 million, with Dkr 1 = US$.13) constituted 1.7 percent of central government revenues; if value-added tax (VAT) is added, revenues generated from taxation on tobacco amounted to Dkr 10.1 billion. By way of comparison, during the same year, the central government spent Dkr 20.3 billion on the armed forces and Dkr 10.4 billion on the police force.[41] Consequently, from the perspective of Parliament and the central government generally, tobacco is an important source of revenue.

The domestic tobacco industry also benefits from the tax system. The Danish excise duty on cigarettes comprises a fixed specific excise duty (imposed as a fixed amount per one thousand pieces) and a variable ad valorem duty (proportional to the final retail price); in 2000, there was, in addition to a VAT of Dkr 6.20, a specific fixed duty of Dkr 12.14 and an ad valorem duty of Dkr 6.58 on a pack of twenty cigarettes, which sold for Dkr 31 (approximately US$4). Denmark's fixed specific duty, which is comparatively high, has kept foreign tobacco companies from seriously trying to conquer the Danish market: (1) the duty leaves little room for competition; (2) consumer loyalty to specific brands entails large initial costs when marketing a new foreign product; and (3) the Danish market is too small to be of serious interest to foreign companies. Consequently, Denmark's domestic industry currently has a 97 percent share of the domestic market, and the industry's profits from its de facto monopoly are enormous. In 2001 Skandinavisk Tobakskompani was Denmark's eighteenth largest company.[42]

Following Denmark's decision to join the European Community (EC) in 1972, Danish policymakers gradually lost the option of using taxation as an instrument to reduce tobacco consumption (assuming that they had wanted to do so). At the point of entry, cigarette prices in Denmark were the highest in the EC, and they are still among the highest, surpassed only by those in Great Britain and Ireland.[43] Due to rising levels of income and reduced duties, however, the price of cigarettes in Denmark has fallen dramatically—in relative terms—to half of what it was in the early 1970s. Whereas an average manual worker had to work fifty-three minutes to earn enough to buy a pack of cigarettes in 1970, only twenty-four minutes were needed in 2000.[44] Moreover, only if prices in other EU countries are raised dramatically will the Danish government be able to uphold the high Danish tobacco prices. In January 2004, the so-called 24-hour regulation was abolished; it required EU citizens to stay abroad for at least twenty-four hours before they could import more than one hundred cigarettes without paying duties in their home country. The Ministry of Taxation estimates that cigarette prices must be lowered from the present Dkr 31 to Dkr 25 to prevent increased cross-border shopping.[45]

Although the introduction of the Single European Market may have increased the average price of tobacco products in the EU as a whole, it has de facto decreased tobacco taxation (and thereby prices) in member states that have traditionally imposed high duties on tobacco products. In these countries the introduction of the Single European Market appears to contradict the EU's increasingly tough anti-tobacco policies.

This claim is contingent, however, upon a correlation between price and consumption. The history of high taxation in Denmark indicates that if the correlation exists, it is not a simple one. First, even though Denmark has long had the highest excise duties on tobacco in Europe, the Danes have also had some of the highest, and even increasing, rates of smoking. Second, it is not clear what effect an increase in tobacco duties has had on the use of tobacco in Denmark. As indicated in Figure 8.1, each Dane (age fifteen and over) consumed 1,622 cigarettes in 2000, compared to 385 in 1920. As is apparent from the same figure, there have been various increases and decreases in per-capita consumption during that time period. The marked reduction in consumption in 1929 (34.1 percent) and in 1932–33 (12.9 percent) followed significant price hikes stemming from increases in the excise duties on tobacco. At that time the government had the ability, at least for short periods, to influence cigarette consumption by means of its taxation policy; there was still considerable price elasticity because of what were, by present-day standards, modest incomes. The next period of significant decline occurred during World War II, but the decline was the product of shortages and wartime rationing rather than having any relation to taxation. After the war, excise duties periodically increased but without having any significant, long-term impact on consumption, indicating that the general increase in income that the Danes began to experience after the war reduced the price elasticity of relatively inexpensive luxury goods such as cigarettes.[46] Despite high excise duties, consumption continued to grow until the early 1980s. Cigarette consumption then began to decline, but excise duties were also declining in an effort to bring Danish duties more in line with those in other EU countries.

All things considered, Danish taxation policies indicate that excise duties may, in certain circumstances, have an effect on the consumption of relatively cheap luxury goods such as cigarettes and alcohol. In particular, duties would have to be high compared to the population's income level. It is an open question, however, whether the Danish population would accept the extremely high duties on tobacco that would be required to bring net prices to the level they were at in the late 1920s and early 1930s. And even then the duration of the effect is uncertain.[47] Moreover, a substantial increase in excise duties would demand consensus at the EU level. When Sweden increased tobacco duties heavily in August 1997, the country faced increased smuggling and cross-border trade. In 1998, exactly one year after imposing the higher duties, Sweden rescinded the increase.[48]

The Public Visibility of Tobacco

Another policy instrument intended to reduce tobacco consumption is the regulation of tobacco advertisements and warning labels. In Denmark, restrictions on advertisements were first imposed on the broadcast media. Only much later were such restrictions imposed on the print media, along with requirements for warnings on product labels.

Tobacco advertising was never allowed on radio or television in Denmark. In 1926 the Danish Broadcasting Corporation, which was to be financed solely by a radio license paid by the listeners (and later a television license paid by the viewers), was given a monopoly on broadcasting.[49] When the monopoly finally ended in 1988 with the establishment of a second public television channel, that channel was, under specific regulations, allowed to earn some of its income from advertisements. The Ministry of Culture had already issued an order, however, that prohibited the broadcasting of tobacco advertisements.[50]

By contrast, tobacco advertising has always been permitted in the print media. The wisdom of this approach was seriously questioned, however, in the early 1960s. In 1961, prior to the equivalent British (1962) and U.S. (1964) reports on smoking and cancer, an expert committee formed by the Minister of the Interior, then responsible for health, delivered a report that concluded that, based on the available evidence, "there is a causal relation between smoking—primarily cigarette smoking—and lung cancer."[51]

The committee was not alone in reaching this conclusion. In early 1961 a large anti-cigarette campaign was launched to change Danes' smoking habits. It included material for schoolchildren and for forty radio shows.[52] In 1963 the minister of the interior formed another expert committee to consider measures to reduce cigarette consumption in Denmark. The committee's 1964 report cited widespread attention to the link between smoking and cancer in the printed press, as well as on radio and television.[53] An expert opinion printed in the report ascribed a stagnation in tobacco consumption in the mid-1950s to Danes' increased concern about the harmful effects of smoking.[54] For example, the Danish Cancer Society had run extensive anti-cigarette health education programs in the 1950s, and a couple of general descriptions of the problem had been published, such as "Smoke Less—Live Longer" in 1954.[55]

The committee members for the 1964 report were professionals from the medical sector, the educational sector, and the Danish Cancer Society. Although they had been asked to consider possible measures to reduce cigarette consumption, the committee members explicitly interpreted their mandate to mean that they were not to consider the ultimate measure: a total ban on the manufacture and sale of cigarettes. And the members themselves would not have supported such a far-reaching interference with consumers' free choice.[56] The report made a number of proposals, some major, some minor. First, the report suggested a massive upgrading in health education programs on the harmful effects of cigarette smoking, along with the establishment of a permanent expert council to plan and implement anti-cigarette education programs. Second, the report suggested restrictions on advertising. The committee considered but ultimately did not follow the opinion of one expert who had studied cigarette advertising in Denmark and determined that it had little effect on consumption.[57] The committee noted that "measures against cigarette advertisement can be said to be experimental. However, the committee does not think that the fact that the positive effects of such measures cannot be determined beforehand with certainty should stop a responsible society from using all available options to reduce cigarette consumption."[58]

Restrictions on advertising considered by the committee included a total ban, regulating the form and content of advertisements, media-specific restrictions, and an obligation to print warning labels on advertisements and cigarette packs. The committee opted for the most far-reaching solution—a total ban on cigarette advertising—and therefore proposed a draft bill, which was included in the report. The committee's other recommendations included the following: that excise duties be raised to a level at which the individual consumer would have a tangible economic incentive to switch from cigarettes to other tobacco products; that cigarettes not be made available at governmental meetings; that cigarettes be sold only during ordinary business hours; that only tobacco products other than cigarettes be sold at restaurants, bars, and cafeterias; that cigarettes not be allowed as prizes in lotteries; and that smoking be banned on public transportation.[59]

These policy proposals may have been politically naïve; at the time they were presented, they gained no hearing outside a rather narrow group of experts. But they were also far ahead of their time. Among countries with a social fabric comparable to that of Denmark, only Italy and the Soviet

Union had a total ban on cigarette advertising in place then, and West Germany was regulated by a voluntary agreement to reduce tobacco advertising in general and also not to target youngsters.[60] Similarly, the committee's other proposals also were implemented only in rare cases. Nevertheless, no matter how naïve the committee members may have been, and no matter how radical their ideas were for that particular time, the report put into print a number of ideas that, over the next forty years, were transformed into policy in Denmark, just as they were in many other countries.

Although the committee's recommendations were too radical for their time, it would be wrong to infer that there was no support for less radical interventions to combat smoking. Even prior to the publication of the report, the first efforts to restrict cigarette advertising had already been made in Denmark. In April 1962, the Danish tobacco industry promised the Ministry of the Interior to abstain, for the rest of the year, from certain types of advertising. This commitment was later extended,[61] and in 1972 the Tobacco Manufacturers Association signed a formal, voluntary agreement restricting the form and content of cigarette advertisements.[62] In particular, the agreement restricted the media, location, and occasion of cigarette advertising, as well as the categories of persons that might be visually presented in advertisements. Manufacturers were required to stop deliveries to wholesale or retail dealers who did not comply with the agreement's provisions. For years, it had been obvious to the tobacco industry that both nationally and internationally, the wind was blowing in the direction of restrictions on advertising. Rather than being presented with a parliamentary fait accompli in the form of an act on which they had no say, the industry preferred to negotiate their way to an agreement. In addition, a voluntary agreement avoided the unfortunate precedent that might arise from allowing Parliament to regulate advertising.

There were good reasons for the tobacco industry to fear parliamentary interference. In 1971 three parliamentarians of the Nordic Council proposed that the council "recommend to the [Nordic] governments that tobacco advertising be prohibited in the Nordic Countries."[63] In its twentieth session, in February 1972, a majority of the council recommended that the governments of the Nordic countries "introduce uniform regulations and restrictions on the access to tobacco advertising, and introduce effective health education on the harmful effects of tobacco smoking, particularly directed towards young people and by means of exhaustive informative labels on tobacco packaging."[64]

In 1974 the relevant ministries from the Nordic countries decided to form an inter-Nordic committee to survey existing regulations on the advertising and labeling of tobacco products in the Nordic countries and to formulate a proposal for a possible inter-Nordic health education program on the harmful effects of smoking. Prior to this initiative, the Norwegian Parliament had introduced a total ban on tobacco advertising in 1973. Of the three remaining Nordic countries, Denmark had developed the most restrictive regulations. Over the years, the Danish tobacco industry has negotiated and signed voluntary agreements on advertising and labeling, all expanding the scope of the 1972 agreement in accordance with international developments. A 1980 agreement regulated the advertising of all tobacco products, not only cigarettes, and prohibited indirect advertising in the marketing of products or services other than tobacco products. A 1986 agreement determined that cigarette advertisements and packs must carry information on nicotine and tar yield, plus the warning: "The National Board of Health calls attention to the fact that tobacco smoking is injurious to health." Finally, a 1991 agreement regulated tobacco industry sponsorship of sports and cultural events, among other activities.[65]

From the mid-1980s the Danish Parliament, as well as the EC, also began to concern itself with tobacco advertising and labeling. In the 1987–88 parliamentary session, the left-wing Common Course party introduced a resolution to prohibit the advertising of tobacco and alcohol products.[66] In the same session, during the committee debate on two bills on smoke-free environments and labeling,[67] the minister of the interior was asked to draft a bill that would prohibit the advertising of tobacco products. Both the resolution and bills lapsed at the call of a new election.

Advertising and labeling issues now moved to the EC level and to other international forums such as the European Council and the World Health Organization. In the late 1980s and early 1990s, the EC Council issued a number of directives on advertising and labeling. The very first of these directives (89/552/EEC of October 3, 1989), which harmonized a ban on television advertising of tobacco products, did not conflict with existing Danish legislation. Indeed, with its existing ban on the broadcasting of tobacco advertisements, Denmark was one of the countries that stood to gain the most by a directive that would prevent the broadcasting of tobacco advertisements to Danish viewers from abroad. The Danish government nevertheless objected on grounds of principle (similar to Germany's successful objections to Council Directive 98/43/EC of July 6, 1998, on the "advertising and sponsorship of tobacco products"):[68] provisions intended to improve the conditions for the establishment and functioning of the internal market could not be an appropriate legal basis for measures intended to regulate cultural matters.[69] Denmark therefore put a "pending veto" on the directive; that is, if the EC Commission brought a case against Denmark for noncompliance before the European Court of Justice and won the case, Denmark would claim a vital interest and veto the directive.[70]

Neither the government nor the Parliament had problems with the EC directives on the labeling of tobacco products and on the maximum tar yield of cigarettes. These directives were soon implemented in Danish law.[71] Moreover, despite Germany's successful objections to Directive 98/43/EC, the Danish government decided to introduce a bill to the same effect in December 2000, prohibiting most types of tobacco advertisements in Denmark. Both the tobacco industry and retailers objected before the parliamentary health committee, but in vain: the Parliament passed the bill in May 2001.[72]

The gradually tighter Danish regulation of advertising and labeling came with no great controversy. In the beginning, the Danish population was mostly skeptical about a ban on cigarette advertising. A 1988 survey found that 43 percent of all Danes (47 percent of women and 39 percent of men) favored a ban, while 49 percent were opposed.[73] Nevertheless, since the tobacco industry was fully aware of international developments in this field, it voluntarily agreed, step by step, to restrict advertising and to label its products. The voluntary Danish agreements were mostly in accordance with later EC directives, and their implementation in Danish law therefore merely a codification of existing voluntary regulations. The industry has generally complied with the provisions of the voluntary agreements; only rarely has tobacco advertising been interpreted as being in breach. One such example was in 1996, when cigarette manufacturer House of Prince had to withdraw a lifestyle magazine that allegedly catered to young people.[74] The voluntary nature of the agreements, in contrast to the bans in both Norway and Sweden, may help to explain why the Danish tobacco industry generally complies with the regulations; in Norway, for example, the ban on advertising was fiercely disputed in the late 1980s.[75]

Health Education

From the 1950s on, the main efforts to inform the public about the harmful effects of smoking were handled by nongovernmental health organizations, such as the Danish Cancer Society, the Danish Heart Foundation, and the Danish Lung Association. In 1979 the Danish Parliament established *Forebyggelsesrådet*, an independent council to promote public health (in general, not just with regard to smoking).[76] When the relevant act was revised in the mid-1980s, there was widespread agreement that more had to be done to reduce the number of smokers and to prevent the harmful effects of smoking in Denmark. There was some dispute, however, as to whether these goals could be achieved through the existing public health council. Inspired by a Norwegian model, the Parliament decided in 1987, against the government, to establish the independent, expert Council on Smoking and Health, which is precisely what had been suggested in 1964 by the expert committee.[77] The council's overall objectives are to reduce the number of active smokers and to prevent involuntary exposure to passive smoking. It advises the government and has, over the years and often in close cooperation with other health organizations, launched a broad range of programs to prevent recruitment of new smokers, to establish smoke-free environments, and to motivate and help smokers quit smoking. Specific projects undertaken by the council include ones to prevent smoking during pregnancy, to involve dentists in encouraging young people not to smoke, to train facilitators for smoking cessation in the workplace, and to organize direct-mail campaigns to heavy smokers.

The council has been highly conscious of its political legitimacy. It has avoided extremist positions and has promoted, instead, a dialogue based on facts. Likewise, it has avoided stigmatizing smokers or smoking. Had it taken a tougher line, the council would have lost legitimacy among Danes and become politically impotent.[78]

When it was first established in the late 1980s, the council's budget was approximately Dkr 4.5 million (less than US$600,000). After a government led by the Social Democrats took over in 1993, appropriations were more than doubled and have been roughly Dkr 10 million since 1995. It is often noted in public debate that this amount is a small fraction of the Dkr 10 *billion* that the government collects each year in tobacco taxation (excise duties and VAT), but there is no tradition in Denmark for directly linking central government taxation to spending. Moreover, according to a former minister of taxation who later became an outspoken anti-tobacco minister of health, linking taxation to spending would be unwise since spending decisions would thereby become inflexible.[79] Finally, it should be mentioned that Denmark's anti-tobacco programs are not limited to those of the council; Danish county and local authorities also run many such programs on their own.

Regulating Tobacco Products

Unlike other measures, which are intended to reduce the number of smokers and cigarettes smoked, regulations on cigarette content are intended to reduce the harmful effects of cigarettes themselves. In the 1986 voluntary agreement with the Ministry of the Interior, the Tobacco Manufacturers Association committed its members to reduce the tar yield in cigarettes, and as of the end of 1992, the maximum tar yield in Danish cigarettes would come close to the maximum tar yield of 15 mg per cigarette specified in

Council Directive 90/239/EEC of 1990. The additional reduction specified in the directive—to 12 mg by the end of 1997—caused no controversy in Denmark. The market share of full-flavor cigarettes (11–12 mg tar yield) gradually decreased during the 1990s.[80]

In March 2000, the Ministry of Health and the Tobacco Manufacturers Association signed a voluntary agreement on additives.[81] In the agreement, the tobacco industry committed itself to submitting an annual report to the ministry listing the additives used in cigarettes sold in Denmark. For a number of years the tobacco industry had been hesitant to make such a list public, claiming that doing so would infringe manufacturers' rights, but the industry changed its position (not only were similar lists being published in other countries, but the EU was known to be planning a directive making such reporting mandatory). Immediately after the agreement was signed, the left-wing Red-Green Alliance moved a parliamentary resolution requesting the government to draw up an approved list of additives; those increasing smokers' dependence on tobacco, increasing the absorption of nicotine, easing the initiation of smoking, increasing the injurious effects of smoking, or damaging the external environment were to be prohibited.[82] The motion was defeated—and was actually opposed by the Ministry of Health. It seems inevitable that the EU will issue a directive on additives in the near future, and implementing such a directive in Danish law will be easier for the ministry if a voluntary agreement alone, and no prior parliamentary act, is in place. When the Danish tobacco industry issued its first list of additives in July 2000, there were no surprises; the additives were all known from similar lists abroad.[83]

The tobacco industry's publication of the additives list may lead to the first legal action for damages against a tobacco manufacturer before a Danish court. In contrast to the American common law system, there is neither tradition nor incentive for court cases in the Danish civil law system. In general, social conflicts in Denmark are solved in the corporatist-bureaucratic, rather than the judicial, system. As a result, litigation in Denmark is not conducive to political mobilization supported by judicial activism, contrary to what has been seen in many countries with common law systems,[84] and there has been virtually no mobilization either of non-smokers or of present or past smokers suffering from tobacco-related illnesses. It is against this background that a recent Norwegian court case and subsequent developments in Denmark need to be understood.

In 1999 a Norwegian tobacco manufacturer was sued for damages caused by smoking. The case was ultimately dismissed, but it drew much media attention in Denmark—in part because the Norwegian manufacturer had recently been taken over by a Danish tobacco manufacturer (which now potentially faced serious economic losses if the case was lost), and in part because the outcome of the Norwegian case, due to the similarity of Norwegian and Danish law, would indicate whether similar actions for damages might be won in Danish courts. The claims of the Norwegian plaintiff were ultimately dismissed in November 2000, but prior to the dismissal, and after the Danish tobacco industry had made public its list of additives in July 2000, a Danish attorney—as an initial step in a liability action—applied for free legal aid on behalf of a client for the purpose of bringing such an action against two Danish tobacco manufacturers. The application explicitly noted that the plaintiff did *not* hold the two manufacturers liable for known illnesses related to tobacco smoking. In this respect the plaintiff's claim differed fundamentally from the Norwegian case. The plaintiff argued, instead, that the manufacturers were liable for damages because additives, which increase the consumer's addiction to nicotine, were—unknown to consumers—used in the production of cigarettes. As a result the plaintiff could not stop smoking even though, after severe illness and surgery, he had wished and attempted to do so over an extended period.[85]

Protection for Nonsmokers

The tobacco-control strategy that has caused the most controversy in Denmark is the restriction of when and where smoking is permitted. Taxation, regulation of advertising, labeling requirements, tar and nicotine yields, and other measures have been accepted by Danes as fully legitimate means to improve and promote public health, whereas restrictions on smoking have been seen as an infringement on the individual citizen's right to free choice. There have always been restrictions on smoking for hygienic reasons, but only in the late 1970s and early 1980s did the idea begin to emerge that nonsmokers had a right to protection against smoke. The Danes only hesitantly accepted the idea, but today there is widespread agreement that nonsmokers must be protected. Disagreements arise over whether protection for nonsmokers can be accomplished only by bans on smoking in public areas.

In the parliamentary arena, efforts to protect nonsmokers started in the spring of 1986, when four members of the centrist Social Liberal Party moved a parliamentary resolution on (1) a bill affording protection against passive smoking and (2) an initiative to induce management and labor to draw up voluntary regulations on smoking in the private sector.[86] A mid-1980s public health campaign on passive smoking had not, according to the resolution's movers, achieved sufficient protection for nonsmokers. Except for the right-wing Progress Party—whose spokesman inveighed against "Prohibition, prohibition, prohibition, always prohibition!"[87]—members of Parliament widely agreed that passive smoking was a serious problem calling for concrete actions. What divided the members were the appropriate means for promoting smoke-free environments. The minority, including the government parties, moved for rejection of the motion because "information and voluntary agreement give the best results." In addition, the minority "considered it unsatisfactory that the Parliament did not wait for comments from the local authorities' organizations and from the labor market organizations."[88] The motion was adopted in a vote that saw many members of Parliament on both sides of the chamber either departing from their parties' positions or abstaining from voting.[89]

The bill, which was introduced in January 1987, prohibited smoking in the public sector in rooms functioning as a workplace for more than one employee, and also in employee common rooms. Smoking would also be prohibited at meetings in the public sector; in hospitals, day-care centers, residential institutions, and educational establishments; and on public transportation. The bill provided for exceptions under specified circumstances—for instance, if separate premises designated for smoking could be established.

The Parliament was deeply divided, with the left predominantly supporting the bill, and the right predominantly rejecting it. The readings were heated and attracted much media attention. As observed by a member during the first reading: the debate "is apparently a matter of great public interest. It is a long time ago since the press gallery, except in situations of crises, has been so crowded and with so many cameras on both sides of the chamber as we see today."[90] As observed by another, it also engaged the members of Parliament: "It is, in fact, seldom to see that many people present in this chamber."[91] The readings indirectly revealed smoking practice at the time. The Liberal spokesperson mentioned that it was only on the very day of the first reading of the bill that her own party had introduced a rule against smoking during the first half hour of party meetings.[92] Another Liberal member, whose party rejected the bill, remarked to a newspaper how smoking made meetings in, of all places, the parliamentary Environmental Committee totally intolerable.[93] Other signs of the members' mixed feelings about the bill were the extraordinary number of amendments and the political parties' release of their members to vote their conscience.

In the end, the bill was defeated by an 81–67 vote (with three abstentions). Those opposed to the bill repeated their arguments from the parliamentary readings of the previous year that the bill was too restrictive on smokers and that it violated the traditional preference in Danish politics for voluntary means over legislative prohibition. In the wake of the bill's defeat, the government decided to issue a departmental circular on smoke-free environments through the Ministry of Health.[94] Although the wording of the 1988 circular mirrored the bill, the circular regulated only central government premises, and its exemptions were broader than those in the bill. A 1990 departmental circular from the Ministry of Social Affairs requested local authorities to ensure that children in day care and the like were not exposed to passive smoking, and a Ministry of Labor departmental order from 1992 determined that nonsmokers must be sufficiently protected against smoke in cafeterias at work.[95]

There is no legislation in Denmark that regulates smoking in workplaces in the private sector, although there has been much encouragement for the private sector to adopt restrictions similar to those in the public sector; in Denmark, such issues are regulated exclusively through voluntary agreement between labor unions and employers' associations without state involvement. In 1989, at the request of the newly founded Council on Smoking and Health, and with the expectation that the failure to act would potentially lead to unilateral action by Parliament or the government, the Danish Confederation of Trade Unions and the Danish Employers Confederation—through their Cooperation Board—agreed to call on the liaison committees in Danish firms covered by collective agreements to draw up sensible smoking regulations. (All Danish firms with thirty-five or more employees covered by collective agreement must have liaison committees, which are responsible for personnel policies, including smoking regulations.) The Cooperation Board stated:

> Choosing to smoke is a private matter. The same cannot be said for passive smoking, i.e., when nonsmokers are exposed to smoke from smokers. The Cooperation Board therefore encourages the liaison committees to introduce the issue on the agenda and to discuss a reduction of the discomforts smokers might cause nonsmokers.[96]

Since no survey of such voluntarily adopted smoking regulations has been conducted, little is known about their content—only that they vary considerably. Total bans on smoking are rare. Many cafeterias do not have smoke-free sections; instead, smokers must abstain from smoking during the first fifteen minutes of the lunch break.[97] In 1995, an industrial arbitration considerably extended the circumstances under which smoking may be considered exclusively a matter of management policy (rather than personnel policy to be decided upon by joint, labor-management liaison committee). The management of a Danish company, which had been taken over by an American corporation with a smoke-free image, had unilaterally introduced regulations that came close to a total ban on smoking on the company's premises. In this particular case, the arbitrator found that the firm's wish to convey a "green image" could not be dismissed as irrelevant from an operational viewpoint, and the regulation of smoking therefore was properly considered to be a management matter.[98]

With the 1987 bill defeated and the departmental circular on smoke-free environments issued, there was little incentive for Parliament to make a new attempt at passing a bill on passive smoking. In the early 1990s, however, the pendulum started to swing toward further restrictions. The Organisation for Economic Cooperation and Development (OECD) published a report that sent shock waves through the media and the political establishment. Danes had dropped from the fifth highest mean life expectancy in the OECD in the late 1970s to thirty-fifth place in the early 1990s.[99] The OECD report alarmed health professionals and policymakers. Mean life expectancy in Denmark had virtually stagnated for fifteen years, a development found in no other Western country. In 1992, the Ministry of Health therefore decided to form a Mean Life Expectancy Committee, which proceeded to launch a series of research and review projects. In the fourteen reports published by the committee, tobacco consumption stood out as a major explanation of low mean life expectancy in Denmark.[100] Suddenly, health professionals who had been involved in tobacco control for years no longer felt that they were considered fanatical health freaks by their fellow medical professionals (many of whom were themselves smokers) or by policymakers. In the mid-1990s, tobacco smoking had definitely placed itself on the national agenda as a serious health problem.[101]

The Ministry of Health also took action by launching a series of initiatives to control tobacco consumption and to promote smoke-free environments, and in 1995, the ministry's 1988 circular became law through an act of Parliament. In one important respect, the act extended the provision of the circular: local and county authorities were now required to draw up smoking policies, although the act did not specify their form or content. Interestingly, the preamble of the act states: "The purpose of the law is to reduce—considering the interests of smokers as well as nonsmokers—the discomforts of passive smoking in public buildings, public transportation, and the like, and to reduce the associated health risks."[102] The explicit mention of smokers in the preamble illustrates how highly divisive restrictions on smoking in public areas were at the time that the act was passed. The act was not, to be sure, optimal from the perspective of those who advocated tough antismoking measures, but it did indicate a decisive shift in attitudes among members of Parliament.[103]

Parliamentary anti-tobacco advocates found a government ally in a Social Democratic economist who became minister of health in 1999. He knew how to read figures and personally became deeply convinced that tobacco consumption was the major health problem in Denmark. At political rallies he missed no opportunity to mention the tobacco problem and soon annoyed many of his fellow Social Democrats in Parliament. In May 1999, during his tenure as minister, he launched the government's Program on Public Health 1999–2008. For the first time, all available antismoking policy instruments were formulated into a coherent program, and other future initiatives were listed. Since this program was the government's, not the ministry's, it had already been accepted by the cabinet and by the government coalition parties. It is possible, however, that the minister's cabinet colleagues and the members of the coalition parties may not have read the program very carefully. It turned out that the minister had every intention of launching the initiatives mentioned in it, including a bill prohibiting smoking altogether in hospitals and in all institutions for children and teenagers. His initiative met fierce opposition, even in his own party, which was as divided on the issue as it was on the 1987 bill on smoke-free environments. Some members of Parliament argued, for example, that a bill prohibiting smoking altogether in hospitals and in all institutions for children and teenagers might have negative side effects; if smoking were prohibited in youth clubs, low-resource youngsters, who might particularly benefit from the educational and social services offered by youth clubs, might stay away because such youngsters are often smokers.[104] Others argued that the intention of turning health care workers into role models was unacceptable; not only did it violate individuals' rights, but it was uncertain what would happen to health care workers who would not or could not comply. Yet others argued that the initiative violated the principle of local autonomy.

Even before the minister of health had a chance to draft a bill, the prime minister refrained from reappointing him during a reshuffling of the cabinet in February 2000. His replacement, however, continued the same tough stand on tobacco control (as did the next minister of health) and in October 2000 introduced a bill prohibiting smoking in institutions for children and teenagers. The bill forbids children and teenagers to smoke altogether, while adults are forbidden to smoke whenever they are with children and teenagers. The bill has an exemption clause that may come into effect in, for instance, institutions for dysfunctional children and youths, where enforcing the smoking ban might give rise to conflicts.[105] The bill caused a public dispute between the Social Democratic minister of health and the Social Liberal minister of education. The Social Liberals are traditionally the firmest anti-tobacco advocates in Parliament; they also oppose central government interference, however, in local decisions concerning education. In the end, the anti-tobacco arguments prevailed, and Parliament passed the bill in December 2000.

Initiatives to promote smoke-free environments have undoubtedly been the most controversial aspect of Danish tobacco-control policies, and they are still highly disputed. Initiatives to control the price, visibility, and content of tobacco products caused little opposition and are considered fully legitimate means to reduce tobacco consumption. Policies to control smokers are a very different matter. They clash with the principles of free choice and voluntary agreements, which are deeply rooted in Danish politics (although proponents of tough policies to create smoke-free environments argue that nonsmokers are not offered the same free choice *not* to be exposed to smoke). There is, however, no doubt in which direction the pendulum is swinging. Health policymakers have advocated still more restrictive measures and most likely will continue to do so—which may well be in line with popular opinion. Although, as indicated above, surveys show that the Danes are less inclined than citizens of other EU countries to favor restrictions on smoking in public areas, Danish attitudes may be changing. Yearly surveys done by the Council of Smoking and Health demonstrate that a constant number of Danes, over time, report that they are bothered by smoke all day in the workplace.[106] As an objective matter, however, that cannot be true. Although compliance with smoke-free restrictions is sometimes low, it is generally fairly good, and the regulations themselves have actually become more stringent. Consequently, as a matter of fact, fewer Danes should be bothered by smoke *all day* in the workplace. A reasonable interpretation is that Danish nonsmokers have become increasingly intolerant of smoke—and that they therefore *feel* bothered. They may therefore support and push for further restrictions on smoking in the workplace.

Initiatives to create smoke-free environments were greatly helped by concerns in the early and mid-1990s over the causal relation between active smoking and low mean life expectancy in Denmark. It is ironic, however, that these same concerns have led to few new initiatives targeted at reducing active smoking. Instead, the focus of tobacco-control policies in the late 1990s remained on the promotion of smoke-free environments, which is first and foremost a protection against passive smoking alone—a comparatively insignificant risk compared to that of active smoking.

Moral Politics

The vast majority of decisions in the Danish Parliament are taken along party lines. Sometimes the parliamentary parties allow their members to deviate from the party line, however, and to vote in accordance with their "conscience." In everyday political parlance, the issues at stake in such cases are "ethical" or "moral." It is quite unclear what makes some, but not other, issues "ethical." They appear to be issues on which the political parties have taken no official position and on which the parties' fundamental phi-

losophies or perspectives do not lead to an unambiguous position. Whenever members of the Danish Parliament have cast votes of conscience
during the last forty years, the Parliament has generally privatized decisions
by leaving them to individual (as opposed to collective) choice—examples
include abortion, consumption of pornography, and domestic partnership
arrangements. A conspicuous exception concerns the artificial insemina-
tion of lesbians and single women.[107]

The promotion of smoke-free environments is the only aspect of Danish
tobacco-control policies that has been subject to votes of free conscience. In
this context, it is worth noting that quite apart from party affiliations, a
substantial and apparently growing minority of the Danish Parliament
chooses to move in the direction of greater regulation. That is, smoking is
no longer to be considered a private matter, but something that calls for
public regulation—the argument being that insofar as nonsmokers are
involuntarily exposed to tobacco smoking, smokers' choice infringes on
nonsmokers' choice to live and work in smoke-free environments.

Smoking has also moved from the private to the public arena in quite
another sense, and here, too, has become a moral issue. The individual's
decision to smoke is not (yet) considered morally objectionable. Nevertheless, profiting from tobacco production and trade *is*. In 2000 Danish newspapers ran numerous articles critical of tobacco production, trade,
consumption, and policy, and one newspaper[108] launched what appeared to
be a well-orchestrated campaign to discredit both the industry and the
minister of health. As its point of departure, the newspaper campaign
defined tobacco production as morally objectionable. As a matter of logic,
representatives of the tobacco industry were therefore morally corrupt, and
steps by the industry to defend its interests, morally repugnant. Included in
this judgment were efforts to approach politicians or civil servants in the
manner that any other Danish industry would do in order to protect its own
interests. Another target was the Danish Doctors' Pension Fund, which had
to sell its shares in Scandinavian Tobacco Company after critical press coverage. Even the Danish government came under attack; it had to withdraw
its financial support to House of Prince for the company to begin manufacturing tobacco in the Baltic countries. It was deemed irrelevant that the
company had applied and obtained government support on the exact same
conditions as other Danish companies. In these and other cases, the press
coverage came close to a moral crusade of the type to which the Danes
usually think themselves immune.

There is no longer anything sacred about smoking in Denmark. From
having been a private matter—the scope of which the government, by indirect means, might legitimately attempt to reduce—tobacco consumption
has not just become one public health concern among others, but arguably

what is felt by many to be the single most urgent health concern for the Danish people. As a result, there is little moral room for arguments in favor of tobacco consumption. Smoking has almost become a "valence" issue—that is, an issue to which there is essentially only one side in the public debate. One may still argue that, as a matter of principle, the state should not make decisions on behalf of its citizens and therefore should not deprive smokers of a choice. Or one may argue in utilitarian terms that, for instance, restrictions on smoking in youth clubs might be detrimental to the clubs' efforts to reach out to socially disadvantaged youngsters.[109] Apart from these arguments, there are few left.

It is worth noting that alcohol consumption has not become a morally one-sided issue. Although the estimated annual mortality due to alcohol is far below the mortality related to tobacco, Danes do drink more than people in most other Western countries,[110] and there are severe health problems related to alcohol consumption. Not nearly as many people are exposed to passive drinking as to passive smoking, but fetuses, children, and spouses of alcoholics all experience the harmful consequences—whether physical, psychological, economic, or social—of that particular form of substance abuse. Nevertheless, the harmful effects of alcohol consumption get little attention in the Danish media, and media coverage of alcohol is void of the moral objections made to tobacco. The social constructions of tobacco and alcohol at the beginning of the twenty-first century are thus almost the reverse of what they were at the beginning of the twentieth century. One explanatory factor may be that early in the twentieth century, alcohol consumption was clearly more prevalent in the lower classes and tobacco consumption more prevalent in the upper classes; whereas today, tobacco consumption has become a lower-class phenomenon,[111] while education and income level are positively correlated with alcohol consumption (and negatively correlated with attitudes toward more restrictive alcohol policies).[112]

Why did popular opinion and tobacco-control policies in Denmark shift toward ever more restrictive measures even though the configuration of interests and policy history would suggest that just the opposite would occur? First, international scientists, experts, and policymakers have managed with great authority to promote the view that smoking is a serious public health problem, and that tough measures must be taken to control it. These actors have gained an institutional position from which they can speak with a concentrated voice, and they have been instrumental in moving international bodies, such as the WHO, the OECD, the European Council, and the EU, to take an increasingly tough stand on tobacco control. As far as Denmark specifically, there have been public health experts in the relevant government agencies dealing with tobacco consumption for a very long time, supported by the Danish Cancer Society and the Danish Lung Association. Their institutional basis was extended and strengthened by the establishment of the Council on Smoking and Health, and they enjoyed increasing support from international actors. These developments have gradually shifted the interest configuration of tobacco-control policies away from being primarily a matter of "client politics," and toward "entrepreneurial politics"—that is, a situation in which a proposed policy will confer general benefits at a cost to be borne chiefly by a small segment of society, in this case the tobacco industry.[113] In the late 1990s and the early years of the new century, a political climate has emerged in which there is a willingness to change the path that was embarked upon in the early twentieth century: tobacco-control policies are today legislated unilaterally, and smoking is no longer a private matter when it may harm nonsmokers.

Policy Effects?

Except for excise duties, tobacco-control measures have gradually become tougher in Denmark, but their effects are debatable. To the extent that they have been complied with, measures to control passive smoking have had the immediate effect of reducing the discomfort that smoking causes nonsmokers. It is unclear, however, whether such measures have any direct effect on mortality related to smoking.

The same is true for most of the measures introduced to control active smoking. A dramatic increase in excise duties on cigarettes in the late 1920s and early 1930s had a marked influence on consumption. After World War II, increases in duties had a short-term, but no long-term, effect. Ironically, consumption per capita and the total number of smokers fell at a time when Danish excise duties were decreasing due to EU adaptation. And despite the comparatively high duty level, Danes still smoke more than people in most other Western countries. If there is a relation between duties and consumption, it is most definitely circumscribed by other factors. The same is true for advertising. Although broadcast advertising for tobacco products was never allowed in Denmark, and although the Danish tobacco industry voluntarily restricted other forms of advertising before most other countries, the Danes still have had a much higher level of tobacco consumption than people in comparable countries. In addition, it is unclear whether the reduction in tar and nicotine yield has reduced tobacco-related diseases and mortality as intended. The reduction in yield may well have had the opposite effect. The number of cigarettes sold in Denmark remained constant during the 1990s[114] and, as mentioned, with a decreasing share of full-flavor cigarettes and an increasing share of milder cigarettes being sold. Nevertheless, as we saw in Figures 8.2 and 8.3, the number of cigarette smokers in Denmark decreased during the same period. The inference to be drawn is that heavy smokers today smoke more cigarettes than before in order to get their daily doses of nicotine. Thus, an analysis of tobacco-control measures in Denmark yields ambiguous evidence concerning the impact of such measures. The case of Denmark illustrates not only the complex social and political problems, but also the difficult problems of factual assessment, that governments may encounter in attempting to address public health issues within the framework of the liberal state.

Despite the possible failure of each of the above government measures to reduce tobacco consumption and its injurious impact on health, the overall number of smokers and the number of cigarette smokers have, in fact, declined in Denmark during the 1990s. These declines most likely reflect changes in public attitudes, but whether these attitudinal changes are an effect of government policies, or vice versa, is difficult to determine. It may well be, however, that a series of increasingly tough measures to reduce active, as well as passive, smoking has had a combined effect on Danes' attitudes toward smoking, making them less and less inclined to smoke.

9

Tobacco-Control Policy in the European Union

Anna Gilmore and Martin McKee

In 1993 Gerard Wirz of Philip Morris fearfully posed the question: "Are European smokers destined to suffer the same intolerant experience as their American Brethren? Does the [European Community] cigarette market risk as precipitous a drop as the one experienced in the [United States]?"[1] Those traveling from North America to Europe will testify that Philip Morris's fears have yet to be realized: "The bottom line is Europe is awash in a sea of cigarette smoke . . . [Y]ou'd better get used to sharing your breathing space with tobacco-scented gases and particulates."[2]

Although progress in tobacco control throughout most of Europe has been less marked than in North America or Australia, some positive steps have been taken, particularly in the last twenty years. As highlighted in other chapters, the degree of tobacco control varies widely between countries in Europe, but since the advent of European legislation in the late 1980s and early 1990s, there are now common features. That legislation made a positive contribution to tobacco control in Europe, especially by providing an opportunity to address tobacco-control issues in countries whose national governments had not taken action.

The European Union (EU) is a grouping of European countries. The events in this chapter concern the period prior to 2004, when the EU consisted of fifteen countries and had a population just over 377 million; in May 2004 it will expand to include an additional ten countries. The EU, as the EC became after the Maastricht Treaty on European Union in 1992, is quite different from the national governments explored in other chapters. Given that the fifteen member states differ linguistically, culturally, economically, and, more specifically, in their attitudes toward tobacco control, this chapter does not explore each country's cultural attitude toward tobacco, but instead briefly reflects on their tobacco interests and smoking prevalences. It then explores the EU's decision-making mechanisms and public health powers before examining the history of EU action in the field of tobacco control, as well as the factors that have influenced that action. Finally, the chapter examines specific policies on tobacco control, exploring the role that the industry has played in undermining these policies.

Tobacco Interests and the Prevalence of Cigarette Smoking in EU Countries

Western Europe is the world's second largest cigarette-manufacturing region. It accounted for 15.4 percent of world production in 1997, well behind Asia's 48.5 percent and just ahead of North America's 15.2 percent.[3] Europe's main *manufacturing* regions, with large, export-oriented tobacco-processing industries, are in the northern countries—especially Germany, followed by the United Kingdom and the Netherlands. The main regions for tobacco-leaf *production* are in the south. Italy and Greece are the leading producers, followed by Spain and France, with the other countries each producing less than ten metric tons per year.[4]

Accurate data on cigarette-smoking rates among EU residents as a whole are difficult to obtain. Eurobarometer data suggest that from 1987 to 1995 there was a gradual decline in smoking prevalence across the EU.[5] More recent World Health Organization (WHO) data suggest that since then, smoking prevalence has leveled off at approximately 30 percent in those aged fifteen and over,[6] although this figure hides wide variations among individual countries.[7] In general there is a north-south difference, with the epidemic starting earlier in the northern countries, where male smoking became common in the early 1900s and then peaked in the mid-1900s. Among women, smoking became common somewhat later, reaching its peak in the 1970s to 1980s.[8] In many of these countries, smoking rates have now started to fall, the decline being more marked in men; male and female smoking rates are now very similar.

In contrast, the epidemic is at an earlier stage of development in the southern countries. Smoking among men in these countries remains common, with little decline yet seen. Prevalence in women continues to rise,[9] but there is still a large gender gap.

Socioeconomic differences in smoking behavior—which become more marked as the epidemic progresses, largely because the middle classes respond more quickly to health promotion messages—are more pronounced in the northern countries.[10] Similarly, deaths from tobacco are substantially more common among the lower classes, making tobacco a leading cause of health inequalities in Europe.

Tobacco is the EU's single largest cause of avoidable death, accounting for over half a million deaths each year and over a million deaths in Europe as a whole.[11] In 1995 an estimated 25 percent of all cancer deaths and 15 percent of all deaths in the EU were attributed to smoking.[12] Although male deaths from tobacco are now steady, the number of female deaths continues to increase. This gender difference is largely the result of the epidemic's later start in the southern European countries—and the resulting delay, from an epidemiological perspective, in deaths among female smokers.[13]

Surveys show that there is widespread public support for policies to reduce smoking, even among smokers. A 1995 survey found that approximately 80 percent of EU citizens favored legislation to prohibit smoking in public places, and between 44 and 77 percent in each country favored a complete advertising ban.[14] A further survey of ten thousand smokers in representative samples from the fifteen EU member states plus Poland and Russia found that the majority of smokers want to quit.[15] Fifty-four percent of men and 60 percent of women wanted to stop, while an additional 15 percent of each sex were undecided. The proportion that wished to stop varied widely by country, exceeding 60 percent in countries where the anti-tobacco lobby is relatively strong, but under 40 percent where it is weak.

The European Union and Its Decision-Making Processes

The EU comprises a number of bodies (Table 9.1) whose functions are set out in a series of treaties, from Rome in 1957 to Nice in 2000. The European Council brings together the heads of government in regular summit meetings that provide direction and political impetus for EU policies. The European Commission performs the executive functions for the EU but also has a significant role in policy initiation. The Council of Ministers and European Parliament perform the EU's legislative function, while the European Court of Justice (ECJ) serves as guardian of the treaties and has assumed political significance through its exercise of judicial review, particularly since its jurisprudence has established the primacy of European law over domestic law (a unique feature of the EU).

The Commission comprises twenty commissioners[16] and is structured into Directorates General. It is headed by a president, whom member states nominate by common accord. Member states appoint commissioners

Table 9.1 Bodies of the European Union

Body	Members	Function
European Commission	Twenty commissioners appointed by member states and supported by international civil servants	Initiates and develops policies Executes decisions of the council
Council of Ministers	Ministerial representatives of national governments Comprises a general council on which foreign ministers sit and a series of specialist councils (e.g., health) attended by relevant ministers	Sole decision-making powers in some areas, joint powers with Parliament in others
European Parliament	Directly elected representatives of the people of Europe (= members of the European Parliament)	Joint decision-making powers with council in some areas, consultative role in others Scrutiny role with regard to Commission
European Court of Justice	Judiciary drawn from member states (thirteen judges and nine advocates general appointed for five-year terms) Advocate-general role is to submit opinion reviewing arguments and recommending action for court to take	Judges matters concerning the interpretation of community law Can quash any measures adopted by Commission, council, or national governments that contravene the treaties
Economic and Social Committee	Representatives of employers, of employees' organizations, and of special-interest groups of member states	A consultative body that offers opinions on proposed legislation in relevant areas
Committee of the Regions	Regional and local representatives from member states	A consultative body that offers opinions on proposed legislation in relevant areas

who are independent of their national governments. All appointments are subject to approval by the European Parliament. The president attends the European Council and is responsible both for allocating portfolios to individual commissioners and for chairing the Commission's meetings. Moreover, since all member states and the Parliament approve the president's appointment, he or she is in a position to influence major policy developments throughout Europe. The standard term of appointment is five years, although Jacques Delors (France) held the office for an unprecedented ten years, from 1985 to 1995.

Responsibility for tobacco control lies within the Directorate General of Health and Consumer Protection,[17] but the Directorates General of Agriculture and of Taxation and the Customs Union also have a significant impact on tobacco policy. Agriculture has historically played a far more important role within Europe than has health. Almost half of the Community's budget is earmarked for agricultural subsidies—making the Agriculture Directorate General very powerful. In 2000, subsidies totaled nearly €41.5 billion, or 46.4 percent of the total EU budget,[18] compared to approximately €14.4 million allocated to combating cancer, approximately €2 million of which goes toward smoking prevention. Among the factors that exacerbate problems of tobacco control are the poorly coordinated communication and administrative arrangements among directorates, as we see later with the disastrous attempt of the Agriculture and Health Directorates to jointly administer a budget. The policies of different directorates may also be in direct conflict, as is apparent in the Agriculture Directorate's providing subsidies to tobacco farmers while the Health Directorate attempts to control tobacco consumption.

Policies can be implemented through a range of methods: *regulations, directives,* and *decisions* (all of which are binding), and *recommendations, resolutions,* and *opinions* (which are not binding). Regulations have immediate force of law in their original wording. By contrast, directives—which are more commonly used—must be adopted into national law within a specified period, allowing adaptation to specific national circumstances. If not adopted within the time specified, they, too, assume force of law in the original wording. Once enacted, regulations and directives become part of the *acquis communautaire,* or the accumulated body of European legislation. All newly joining states must adopt the *acquis* in its entirety.

In the late 1980s, a loose coalition of governments led by the United Kingdom became increasingly concerned about the extension of the EU's competence and about what they saw as the emergence of a "European superstate." The principle of subsidiarity was therefore introduced and formally incorporated in Article 3(b) of the Treaty of Maastricht, which states that the EU may act "only if and in so far as the objectives of the proposed action cannot be sufficiently achieved by the Member States and can therefore, by reason of the scale or effects of the proposed action, be better achieved by the Community." This condition was seen by some as a considerable scaling back of the potential for European action. Overall, however, other changes—in particular, the introduction of co-decision and qualified majority voting—have increased the EU's power in relation to that of its member states. Power battles between the two continue, with the Parliament continuing to demand more power in a call for greater democratization of the EU, and thus popular support for its institutions. It was only after the ratification of the Single European Act in the late 1980s that health-related issues such as tobacco moved firmly onto the EC's agenda. As we shall see later, the provision that European policies should promote a high level of health protection was used both to develop a Europe-wide policy on tobacco that was based on considerations of health rather than merely market or agricultural concerns, and to enact a series of legislative changes in the field of tobacco control.

The Community's Role in Tobacco Control: Structure, History, and Influences

The first attempted Community involvement in smoking dates back to the 1983 Asbestos Directive.[19] Recognizing the synergistic relationship between smoking and asbestos in the etiology of lung cancer, Commission staff sought to introduce a ban on smoking in workplaces where there was also a risk of exposure to asbestos. Since this prohibition was not supported by member states, the directive's final text simply required the display of "No Smoking" signs. Public health staff next became involved in 1985, when the Commission was exploring harmonization of excise duties and requested advice on the impact on tobacco and alcohol consumption. A Dutch academic offered assistance but was later discovered to be reporting to Philip Morris.

The major stimulus to action on tobacco came with the 1987 establishment of the "Europe against Cancer" program (EACP), one of the first visible outputs of a "social" Europe. In 1986 the Commission had become involved in cancer through its response to the explosion at the Chernobyl power station. At that time, institutional responsibility for cancer was linked with that for exposure to ionizing radiation via a unit that was accountable to two directorates—a situation that was recognized as undesirable. Simultaneously, there was pressure from several well-connected cancer experts for EU action. President François Mitterrand of France[20] (persuaded by his close friend Professor Maurice Tubiana) and Prime Minister Bettino Craxi of Italy (under the influence of Professor Umberto Veronesi) jointly proposed the establishment of an EC program on cancer.

Initially, an expert committee on cancer was established to provide advice and recommendations for action. Tubiana was appointed as its first chair. A proposal concerning the EACP was adopted by a resolution of the Council of Ministers during the Luxembourg presidency in July 1986. Pursuant to that resolution, the EACP was established the following year—under the dynamic leadership of Michel Richonnier, a French commission official. At a time when tobacco control in France was being reactivated, this important French axis was completed with the support of Jacques Delors, the Commission president whose interest in the social aspects of Europe has already been described.[21]

The launch of the EACP was to act as a catalyst for EC action on tobacco. Established at the start of the EC's new public health competence (the Single European Act was not adopted until July 1987, a year after the Council of Ministers' resolution to establish the EACP), it initially functioned as a relatively independent unit in Brussels and reported directly to the Directorate General of Social Affairs. Free from bureaucratic restrictions, it enjoyed a privileged position and strong staffing base. Its first "Action Plan to Combat Cancer" (1987–89)[22] made smoking a priority area and outlined a series of actions based largely on the proposals of Tubiana's committee of experts. This action plan, which the industry referred to as a "kind of Bible . . . in the EEC's fight against tobacco,"[23] underpinned initial EC action on tobacco.

In 1988 the EACP began developing its first legislative proposals; realizing that it would face considerable opposition, it issued a call for tenders for an expert information service on tobacco control in Europe. By the end of the year, the Bureau for Action on Smoking Prevention (BASP) was commissioned to fulfill this function. Headed by Luk Joossens, BASP played a vital role in European tobacco control. BASP's unusual position—in which it both received funding from, and also essentially lobbied, the Commission—left a gap in Europe for nonpartisan advice on cancer. The Association of European Cancer Leagues (ECL) spotted this gap and, in conjunction with the International Union against Cancer/Union Internationale Contre le Cancer (UICC), agreed to fund an EU liaison office in Brussels; in 1990 Andrew Hayes took the post of tobacco program liaison officer for Europe. The objectives were to secure effective tobacco-control legislation at the EU level and to help ECL member organizations secure national legislation, primarily by coordinating lobbying activities and regional anti-tobacco interests.

By the late 1980s, key figures were thus in place to lead efforts in European tobacco control. The introduction of qualified majority voting and also new provisions in the Single European Act on health and safety (designed to balance some of the consequences of the internal market) made it possible to pass legislation. A period of rapid progress followed, facilitated no doubt by the enthusiasm and dedication of the key players, the good links between them, the commitment of an influential president, and the lobbying power of Tubiana, whose expert committee proved to be extremely influential, having frequent access to heads of government. Between 1989 and 1992, seven directives and one nonbinding resolution on tobacco were adopted (Table 9.2).[24] Careful consideration had been given to the options of a single, all-embracing directive versus a series of more focused ones. The latter course was chosen because of concerns about the substantial power of the industry, but one Commission official has said that opposition was actually somewhat less than had been anticipated, suggesting that the industry was not yet devoting significant attention to EC policy.

Table 9.2 Tobacco-control directives and resolutions adopted by the EU between 1989 and 1992

Directive names/year	Directive number	Requirements
Labelling Directives (1989, 1992)	89/622/EEC 92/41/EEC	Require tar and nicotine yield to be printed on side of pack, to cover at least 4 percent of pack
		Require health warning on front of pack, to cover at least 4 percent of pack
		Require warnings for packaging of tobacco products other than cigarettes
		Ban the marketing of certain tobacco products for oral use
Advertising Directive (1989)	89/552/EEC	Bans all forms of TV advertising for tobacco products
Tar Yield Directive (1990)	90/239/EEC	Approximates laws governing the maximum tar yield of cigarettes and sets a maximum tar yield of 15 mg per cigarette by December 31, 1992, and of 12 mg per cigarette from December 31, 1997
Tax Directives (1992)	92/78/EEC 92/79/EEC 92/80/EEC	Set minimum levels of duty on cigarettes and tobacco
Resolution on Smoking in Public Places/ 1989		Invites member states to adopt measures banning smoking in public places and on all forms of public transportation (nonbinding)

At the time, these legislative changes had a considerable impact on tobacco control. The first of the labeling directives led countries with almost no tobacco-control legislation, such as the Netherlands and Greece, to strengthen their health warnings. Similarly, the United Kingdom chose to enact legislation to supersede its voluntary agreements. The tax directives led to a reduction in price differentials among EU member states and an increase in price in countries with cheaper cigarettes, although price increases did not occur in those countries with more expensive cigarettes. The overall impact was greatest in countries with limited legislation; countries such as France, which had already introduced more comprehensive tobacco-control legislation, were less affected. Of course, the impact also depended on the degree of enforcement, which continued then, as it does now, to vary between member states, but over which the EU has little power.[25]

After 1992, progress on tobacco control slowed considerably. Thus, although EACP's subsequent Action Plans (1990–1995,[26] 1996–2000,[27] and 2001)[28] continued to highlight action on tobacco, only three directives were proposed between 1992 and 2001. These directives included the Advertising Directive, whose path to legislative enactment was so long and tortuous that Commission staff may have been unable to dedicate sufficient time to moving forward other tobacco-control measures. However, other changes were also under way—both generally in Europe and more specifically within the EACP—and are likely to have played a more fundamental role in delaying progress.

In late 1992 a new mood of caution about the pace of change in Europe developed in the wake of the Danish decision to reject ratification of the Maastricht Treaty, and the very narrow French majority that voted in favor of ratification. This treaty introduced the principle of subsidiarity, which some have suggested made it more difficult to propose new directives,[29] although it also considerably expanded the previously limited public health competence. Eight new public health programs were launched, with the result that cancer became only one part of a much larger set of activities.

Also in 1992, after a series of internal disagreements about control of the EACP, the program, which had been functioning as a relatively independent unit in Brussels, was moved to the Commission's Public Health Unit in Luxembourg (within the Social Affairs Directorate General). The move brought EACP more firmly under the control of the Commission's civil servants. The EACP had been identified as a great success, and many saw the move as a deliberate attempt to stifle EACP's independence and to weaken the program. Others suggest, however, that there had been concerns that in acting so independently, EACP had sometimes failed to adhere to EU procedures—which then led the new social affairs commissioner, Padraig Flynn, to bring EACP under tighter control by the Commission. During this same period, the program's initial, highly successful team was effectively dismantled. Richonnier, who had proved a dynamic leader, left the unit in 1991; and Régis Malbois and Stelios Christopoulos, his deputies, in 1993 and 1992, respectively. It is unclear whether staff were pushed out or left willingly as a result of the infighting and the threatened move to Luxembourg. Shortly after the move, there was a major change in the role of the expert committee. Rather than meeting twice a year (during meetings of the European Council) and having a strong, independent role, the committee was reduced to a merely advisory function. Tubiana, the committee's influential chair and a leading light in the French tobacco-control movement, resigned.

In 1995, BASP's contract was not renewed; its closing undercut progress still further. As in the case of EACP, explanations differ. One Commission official reports that a call for tenders was issued, but BASP, to his surprise, did not apply. Internal records suggest, however, that the same official, who had pushed for the EACP move to Luxembourg, had previously written to the Directorate General responsible for public health to express concern that BASP had become the key anti-tobacco lobby in Europe, and that its activities had less and less to do with the needs of the Commission and served, instead, to bring pressure against it.[30] It appears that the call for tenders was issued sometime after BASP's initial funding had ceased, making it financially impossible for BASP to continue long enough to apply for the new funding. Externally, it was reported that Germany, the Netherlands, the United Kingdom,[31] and the Agriculture Directorate General[32] had all influenced the funding decision. At the Ninth World Conference on Tobacco and Health in 1994, Joossens (the head of BASP) had gone on record to highlight the EU's hypocritical stance of continuing tobacco subsidies while funding the EACP. He had been careful to stress that it was the EU's stance, not that of the Commission, that he was criticizing. Nevertheless, it seems that Joossens's decision to make this speech was used to justify BASP's closure; Commission officials (seemingly those within the directorates responsible for health and agriculture) argued that it was inappropriate for Joossens to criticize the Commission when funded by it. Internal industry documents show that the tobacco transnationals correctly identified Joossens as "a key figure in the European anti-smoking movement,"[33] included him among a list of "leading activists,"[34] and continued to monitor BASP's activities closely.[35] Nevertheless, while the industry had clearly identified Joossens as a threat[36] and made efforts to undermine BASP's activities,[37] there is little to implicate them directly in the dismantling of the dynamic tobacco-control team that was initially in charge.

What is clear from the documents, however, is that, although the industry had been closely monitoring developments within European institutions since 1975—with Philip Morris commissioning monthly reports from consultants (initially Ernst Hernig[38] and later Douglas Herbison[39])—it was not until the mid-1990s that the industry had its lobbying activities in place and fully functioning. It is therefore our hypothesis that in addition to the facilitating factors illustrated above, the initial progress in tobacco control was made possible through the relative inaction of the industry. Although the Confederation of European Community Cigarette Manufacturers (CECCM) was established in the late 1980s as a way to bring industry groups together, it took some time before animosity turned to cooperation. We do not mean to imply that the industry had been inactive until that time (it had not, as we shall see below in exploring particular areas of legislation). But in the words of their adviser David Bushong of Gold and Liebengood, in 1991 the Philip Morris lobby remained "understaffed, under experienced, disjointed, and uncoordinated."[40] In reviewing Philip Morris's lobbying strategy, Bushong made recommendations to David Greenberg (vice president of corporate affairs, Europe) on how to influence European policymakers—thereby providing some insight into their direct lobbying tactics. Bushong highlighted the importance of the staffs of the permanent national representations,[41] and of the members of the Committee of Permanent Representatives[42]—who have an important influence on national politicians, including members of the Council of Ministers. The commissioners, their cabinets, and Commission bureaucrats were also identified as important points of influence. Bushong made more specific recommendations on how Philip Morris should enhance its European influence to ensure that it was perceived as a "long-term corporate [citizen] involved in the Community and its leadership." These recommendations included funding a think tank, recruiting an "*eminence gris* (from the ranks of former Presidents and Vice Presidents of the Commission) to help you maneuver with subtlety at the highest levels of the Community," linking lobbying at the member-state level with that in Brussels, and cultivating the U.S. ambassador to the EC.

Later industry documents (plus our discussions with European officials and politicians) confirm that these recommendations were generally implemented. The role of each national lobby was to influence the Council of Ministers representative.[43] Its form varied according to established industry contacts in each country (as will be explored below with respect to the advertising ban) and was mindful of national issues and concerns.[44] In the mid-1990s the governments of Denmark, Germany, Holland, and the

United Kingdom were seen as supportive and were encouraged to oppose action on the basis of subsidiarity.[45] The United Kingdom, described as "a key ally of the tobacco industry in the European Community," was seen as an important "vehicle for Philip Morris to communicate its position on issues to the European Community." The United Kingdom was also a place where, by virtue of its "hybrid of American and Continental European systems and cultures," programs that had been successful in the United States could be tried out before export to mainland Europe.[46]

At the European level, just as at national level, the industry used "favourable contacts,"[47] as well as pan-European groups such as the CECCM,[48] to enhance its lobbying position. Lobbying was targeted at all stages of the European legislative process.[49] Plans to introduce company experts to influential European players[50] were achieved in part via the "think tank" that Bushong had recommended: the Philip Morris Institute for Public Policy Research, headed by Giles Merritt,[51] was established in 1993. Describing itself as "a non-profit organisation which aims to stimulate debate by publishing discussion papers that address major policy issues confronting today's European decision-makers," it held semiannual meetings (in the country then holding the EU presidency) on subjects key to European interests.[52] Through its invitations to political leaders and its sharing a platform with them, Philip Morris staff were able to establish contacts at the highest level and to give Philip Morris the aura of respectability that it needed to be seen "as a solid EU citizen."[53] In a similar vein, attempts were made to build coalitions with free-market public-policy organizations throughout Europe.[54]

The trade unions were identified as important allies, particularly the tobacco workers' and growers' unions. The aim was to mobilize unions and employers to lobby both at national and European levels. Particular emphasis was placed on those who were represented on influential EC committees, such as the European Confederation of Employers and of Unions,[55] and the European Trade Unions Confederation—the latter of which, the industry noted, had a great influence on the Economic and Social Committee, which has to be consulted on legislation.[56] Other allies were cultivated according to the issue under discussion and their degree of European influence:[57] the hospitality industry, on public-smoking bans; the Union of Industrial Employers and Confederations of Europe, on secondhand-smoke issues; and, of course, advertising and media organizations, including the International Federation of Advertising Agencies, on advertising issues.

Smokers' rights groups were seen as an essential medium for presenting the industry view because "they have no commercial interest and as such are a more credible voice than the tobacco industry."[58] This "arm's length" relationship with manufacturers was clearly seen as vital for such groups' credibility.[59] Yet it is clear that the industry not only funded these groups across most of Europe,[60] but played a role in organizing their activities.[61] The key role of smokers' rights groups appears to be the promotion of personal liberty, which has particular relevance to the issue of secondhand smoke. For example, FOREST (Freedom for the Right to Enjoy Smoking Tobacco), a U.K.-based group, was keen to stress what it called the "domino effect:" restrictions on tobacco use would lead to restrictions on other areas of personal choice.[62] The industry also sought to promote these libertarian debates via other channels.[63]

Information was another key issue. Bushong observed that Commission civil servants respond to "information and access to non-EC national sources of data, intelligence and leverage." The development of a Brussels-based tobacco-information office or a "BASP-style 'information bureau'" was first suggested in June 1993 by Gerard Wirz in response to the "threat" of restrictions relating to environmental tobacco smoke.[64] His aim was to build an EC network of national information centers in order to defend the position of smokers and to maintain the social acceptability of smoking. The existing IDTs (Information and Document Centres on Tobacco) would form the model; European operations would be coordinated by a central office. The network would play a role in publicizing all favorable findings and would "generate favourable public opinion survey data."[65] Interestingly, Wirz suggested structuring the network in the same way as antismoking organizations—an indication, perhaps, that at this time the health lobby was better organized.

Indeed, by 1993 the European health lobby had a well-developed network. Philip Morris identified it as one of the three strongest regional tobacco-control groups, with the largest number and broadest range of activists.[66] Aiming to influence the same European decision makers as the industry lobby, the health lobby had, insofar as possible, overcome its funding disadvantage through good organization and coordination. A number of international groups—including the UICC (Geneva), the International Union of Health Promotion and Education (Paris), the International Union of Tuberculosis and Lung Disease (Paris), and the International Organisation of Consumers Unions (The Hague)—have their headquarters in Europe. Along with the European groups described below, this range of organizations not only gives antismoking forces a strong physical presence within the region, but also provides more direct access to the WHO, both via its Geneva headquarters and its regional Copenhagen office. The presence of the International Agency for Research on Cancer

2(IARC, a scientific arm of the WHO) in Lyon, France, also helped ensure that health issues remained high on Europe's political agenda.

Through the 1990s the tobacco-control lobby in Europe gradually strengthened. This change can be attributed, in part, to the development of new nongovernmental organizations (NGOs) in the southern European countries (where for both cultural and political reasons, NGOs were not as well established) and to the emergence of activists in Austria and Germany. Better coordination of NGO action to ensure that lobbying on European issues occurred at the national level was also important; improved links enabled NGOs to learn from each other and gradually led the southern European NGOs to take a more activist stance.

The closure of BASP in 1995 left a serious gap in the European tobacco-control movement. EACP attempted to fill this gap by establishing two networks in 1997: the European Network on Smoking Prevention (ENSP) and the European Network on Young People and Tobacco. Given the background to BASP's closure, the role of these networks is more circumscribed than that of BASP. ENSP's remit is to coordinate the approach to tobacco control within Europe (not just the EU)—which has been achieved through facilitating the development and collaboration of national coalitions against tobacco (as alluded to above), and through its work with other European institutions, including WHO Europe. Both organizations are involved in the development and coordination of smoking-prevention and research projects funded by the €2 million allocated annually for this purpose. A further source of funding, the Community Fund for Research and Information on Tobacco, was created in 1992 through a 1 percent (subsequently increased to 2 percent) levy on the financial support given to tobacco producers as part of the 1957 Treaty of Rome's common agricultural policy (CAP, see below), but the funds have rarely been used. Created to help pacify opponents of the tobacco subsidies, half of this money is earmarked for public-information projects on the dangers of smoking, aimed particularly at improving young people's knowledge, while the other half is controversially targeted at research into developing less dangerous varieties of tobacco. Not only is there scant evidence of the benefit of pan-European projects aimed at young people, but due to the labyrinthine bureaucracy involved in a fund administered by two directorates general, calls for proposals were issued only in 1994, 1996, and 2001, and the amounts allocated to projects fell well below the amount available. The ENSP calculates that since the creation of the grant, over €40 million that should have been allocated to public-information projects has effectively been lost. Moreover, by 2001, organizations that were allocated grants in

1994 and 1996 had yet to be paid—a further disincentive for those who might still be interested in applying.

Agricultural Subsidies

A major criticism of the EU has been that its agricultural policy—in particular, its policy on tobacco production—is diametrically opposed both to health promotion and to the work of the EACP. The payment of subsidies for tobacco production has been a long-running controversy.[67] In the early 1990s the EU spent about €1,000 million on subsidies to tobacco producers, but only about €1.5 million (0.15 percent of that amount) on smoking prevention.[68] These figures have changed little over the course of the decade: in 2000, €975 million (2.3 percent of the CAP and 1.09 percent of the total Commission budget) was spent on tobacco subsidies, and approximately €2 million on smoking prevention (excluding the 2 percent levy on the tobacco subsidies, which, as explained above, is rarely spent). From its inception the subsidy program had two quite distinct objectives: to encourage farmers to grow marketable varieties of tobacco, thus reducing imports, and to guarantee producers' income, thus expanding production in disadvantaged areas. In the face of sustained criticism, the subsidy was reformed in 1992 in order to limit production (by introducing a quota above which a subsidy would not be paid) and to end both export subsidies (which had been necessary in order to dispose of otherwise unmarketable high-tar, low-quality produce) and intervention subsidies (used to pay for unsold tobacco placed in storage). The reform also led to the creation of the Community Fund for Research and Information on Tobacco (described above).

Even after being reformed, the tobacco-subsidy program remained an expensive failure.[69] Soil and climate conditions in Europe mean that most EU-grown tobacco is of varieties for which there is little commercial market. Almost all tobacco produced is "sold" at minimal prices—often about 10 percent of the sum received in subsidies—to countries in central and eastern Europe and in North Africa that have no effective policy restrictions on tar levels. Thus, the policy has failed in its objective of replacing imports. It has had some small success in providing income for farmers. Only about 55 percent of the total subsidy is available for support of agricultural incomes, however; the remainder covers seeds, fertilizers, and so on. It would therefore cost considerably less simply to give farmers the money earmarked for income support, without requiring them to toil to produce a product that few want. It is, however, now clear that this situation is untenable and tobacco subsidies will be affected by current reforms of the CAP.

Legislative Action

The initial flurry in European tobacco-control activity has been discussed and documented above. The progress of the more recent legislation tells an interesting story of power struggles, industry interference, and legal uncertainty.

Advertising Ban

In 1989 a directive banning tobacco advertising on television, where the cross-border impact was undeniable, was passed as part of a much broader directive regulating transborder television services.[70] A comprehensive advertising and sponsorship ban was first proposed the same year but, following a lengthy and protracted process that led to its eventual passage in 1998, was legally challenged and then, in October 2000, finally annulled. Thus, as of 2001, Europe remains without a comprehensive advertising ban despite public support for such legislation.[71]

The comprehensive ban, proposed in 1989, was intended to standardize the EU as a single market for tobacco advertising. At that time, the scope of national advertising bans varied widely, with few countries having comprehensive bans. At the time of this writing, there is still much variation, although comprehensive advertising bans are in place in seven countries,[72] should shortly come into force in two others,[73] and are being considered in a few more. In 1990 the Parliament amended the initial proposal and, in February 1992, voted to impose the ban (with 150 votes in favor, 123 against, and 12 abstentions) despite massive lobbying by the tobacco and advertising industries. Progress then stalled in the Council of Ministers. As an internal market measure, the ban was subject to qualified majority voting, enabling a small number of countries to block it. With the blocking votes of Germany, the Netherlands, and the United Kingdom—the EU's largest producers and exporters—no qualified majority was possible in Council meetings from 1992 to 1996. (Greece and Denmark were somewhat more variable in their opposition to the proposed directive.) Germany, during its period of EU presidency in 1995, attempted to introduce a compromise bill,[74] widely believed at the time (and subsequently confirmed by industry documents) to have been developed by the industry. This bill stipulated that minimum advertising restrictions agreed upon by all EU members would be set forth in the directive, and that member states would then be free to introduce more stringent restrictions. As a consequence, the directive would have little impact in those countries with already weak tobacco-control policies. The bill failed to get adequate support.

The position of the United Kingdom changed with the election of a Labor government in 1997. Members of the previous Conservative government had strong financial links with the tobacco industry; for example, a former prime minister, Margaret Thatcher, received a large consultancy payment from Philip Morris,[75] and the outgoing finance minister (and previously health minister), Kenneth Clarke, became deputy chairman of British American Tobacco.[76] The Conservative government had argued in favor of a voluntary agreement between the government and the industry, despite extensive evidence that such an agreement would be ineffective. Indeed, it argued that despite the established track record in other countries, it was an advertising ban that would be ineffective.[77]

The new Labor government, however, was soon plunged into scandal when it was revealed that its agreement to an advertising ban was conditional on an exemption for Formula One motor racing. This revelation coincided with the acceptance of a large donation from a leading figure in Formula One racing.[78] The government's denial of a link provoked widespread public disbelief. Nevertheless, the United Kingdom's new position did make agreement on a ban possible (even though Germany, in particular, remained resolutely opposed).

In December 1997, the Council of Ministers finally agreed upon a common position in favor of the directive. In a tense debate, Greece, which had not declared its hand, held the key and, after being offered a variety of minor concessions, finally voted in favor of the directive. Germany and Austria remained opposed; Spain and Denmark abstained; but the minimum sixty-two out of eighty-seven votes was obtained. The directive passed by a qualified majority that would ban all forms of tobacco advertising and sponsorship within the EU. The abstention of Spain, which until that point had been in favor of the directive, caused some surprise, and many have suggested that Spain changed its position under German influence. In May 1998 the European Parliament, persuaded by the tobacco-control lobby (as described above), ratified the directive with no amendments, although almost all German members, with the exception of the Greens, voted against. In June the council approved the final directive.[79]

Soon afterward, however, Germany and four British tobacco companies mounted a challenge in the ECJ, arguing that the directive was illegal, violated several principles of treaty law, and was a misuse of the EU's legislative power. The challenge was mounted in September 1998 as Chancellor Helmut Kohl's term of office expired, and support for it continued under Chancellor Gerhard Schröder's new German government that took office in October—leading some to suggest that the friendly relationship between the German government and the tobacco industry looks set to continue.[80]

Since Article 129 of the EC Treaty expressly excludes the ability to take harmonizing measures for public health purposes, the directive was enacted as an internal market measure under Article 100a. The industry claimed that because the directive harmonized national laws when its principal aim was public health protection, the EU was not competent to act, and the directive was therefore a misuse of power. The advocate general rejected these claims but did rule in their favor on other points, finding two main grounds for annulment: legal basis and proportionality.[81] He concluded that the directive had exceeded its legal basis as an internal market measure. Instead of facilitating or removing barriers to trade, the directive prohibited it. Such a measure was disproportionate to what was needed to ensure the proper functioning of the internal market. He also noted that—partly due to the so-called safeguard clause that allows member states to introduce their own more stringent legislation—the directive neither harmonized national rules nor removed distortions of competition. The court upheld the challenge and annulled the directive, ruling that it had exceeded the legal basis on which it was adopted.[82]

A replacement directive was limited to measures that the Commission considered to be the minimum needed to achieve the proper functioning of the internal market. It was thus considerably weakened, confining itself to issues of cross-border advertising (in print media and on the radio and Internet) and sponsorship. Heeding the ECJ ruling, the new draft directive omitted the usual safeguard clause and the ban on indirect advertising, which was specifically mentioned by the advocate general as having an unproven impact on consumption.[83] The directive was scheduled for submission to the Commission in June 2001 and would need to be agreed upon by the Parliament and Council in co-decision.[84]

This rapid redrafting hid the concern felt over the ECJ ruling, which came as a surprise to many and had potentially major implications. Since lawyers of the EU's three main bodies, as well as those advising individual member states, scan all potential legislation, it is unusual for a directive with serious legal flaws to get as far as it did. The process followed by the advocate general and the court gives cause for concern because only those directly involved in prosecuting or defending the case are able to give evidence, and the decisions cannot be challenged. These issues are clearly important given that the advocate general concluded that there was no evidence for the impact of indirect advertising on tobacco consumption—even though experts, who were excluded from the proceedings, have compelling evidence of just that impact. Some have argued that if one follows the ruling to its logical limit, every consumer protection law passed could potentially be challenged and discarded. Furthermore, by omitting the usual safeguard clause from the new advertising directive, the EU may be entering a new era in terms of tobacco control and consumer protection. Until now, European legislation could facilitate tobacco control only by ensuring that member states with no tobacco-control legislation met a European minimum standard, while leaving those wishing to introduce more stringent measures free to do so. From now on, countries could, in theory, be challenged for going beyond the directive's minimum standard. Although other treaty clauses confer almost the same protection on member states as the safeguard clause, there are slight differences. Article 95(4) refers to the right to maintain existing legislation (not to *introduce* it), and Article 30 permits health protection measures that are not the subject of an existing directive as long as they are proportionate. Tobacco-control policies that ultimately aim to reduce cigarette sales are likely to conflict with policies that aim to enhance the internal market. Thus, while treaty provisions prevent the passage of harmonizing legislation for public health purposes, the EU will be faced with the problem that any measures needed to protect public health may be considered to be disproportionate to what is needed to protect the internal market. Treaty changes are, of course, possible (and there is a growing movement to have this matter considered at the next intergovernmental conference on treaty revision, scheduled for 2004) but would take years to come into force. Meanwhile, until the final form of the new Advertising Directive is determined and potential challenges to the Tobacco Products Directive (outlined below) are clarified, tobacco control in the EU looks to be facing a somewhat uncertain future. These recent, rather negative developments in European tobacco-control policy are reflected, some would argue, in the EU's negotiating stance on the Framework Convention on Tobacco Control, as will be explored later.

The position of Germany—which, of all member states, appears to be most pro-tobacco—raises many unanswered questions. In the case of the Advertising Directive, there were two possible reasons for Germany's legal challenge before the ECJ. The first was to prevent the EU from going beyond its authority. The second was to prevent implementation of the directive per se. The first is a legitimate concern and one undoubtedly shared by other member states (although no other states joined the ECJ challenge). This argument might have merit if successive German governments had not opposed EU tobacco directives. One possible explanation for Germany's steadfast opposition to effective action on tobacco is that the opposition is a reaction to the excesses of the past and to the Nazis' own strong opposition to smoking.[85] Also relevant is that libertarian views are more strongly held in Germany, and tobacco-control advocacy more poorly established there, than in some other member states. The relationship between the German government and the cigarette industry may also play a role. Tobacco-control advocates have denigrated that relationship as all too cozy, but tobacco industry journals continually refer to Germany in favorable terms as "a strong supporter of the tobacco industry."[86] Industry documents finally allow us to gain further insight. These show that industry scientists working for the Verband der Cigarettenindustrie (the German trade association for the tobacco industry) have had a uniquely close, long-term association with German government officials. Moreover, in the early 1980s, Professor Karl Überla, president of the Bundesgesundheitsamt (Federal Health Office) received research funds from the industry.[87] Other documents show that Germany was a constant and essential ally in the industry's carefully orchestrated attempt to prevent passage of the Advertising Directive.[88] The industry's contacts within Germany reached to the highest political level and were used both to try to have the Advertising Directive abandoned on the basis of the principle of subsidiarity[89] and, in 1995 (during Germany's EU presidency), to introduce the industry-sponsored directive mentioned above.[90] The industry suggested that the latter be "covertly suggested in the form of a draft directive to DG III of the Commission," the directorate general responsible for industry.[91] It appears that the German commissioner—Martin Bangemann, who was then head of Directorate General III and was previously minister of economy under Kohl (1984–88)—played a role in introducing this compromise legislation.

The industry was so confident of support within Germany that it focused its efforts on gaining the support of other member states in order to maintain the blocking minority in the Council of Ministers. A 1990 internal industry memorandum noted, "So far our efforts have concentrated on seeking support from the UK, Germany and the Netherlands. A separate program is being prepared for Denmark."[92] The industry's success in achieving Danish opposition offers a fascinating insight into its efforts to foster and support libertarian arguments. In a 1991 speech to Philip Morris executives, Bobby Kaplan, the corporation's manager of communication for corporate affairs, reported how they had created a coalition known (in English) as the Committee for Freedom of Commercial Expression, which included more than fifty prominent Danes. The coalition conducted media briefings, participated in debates, wrote articles, and undertook and publicized an opinion poll that showed more than 70 percent of Danes opposed the EEC Advertising Directive. The coalition managed to portray itself as distinct from Philip Morris, was viewed as a legitimate supporter of free speech, and was regularly consulted by the government. The industry saw it as a great success in the fight against the advertising ban, describing it as "instrumental in securing the commitment and public declaration of the Minister of Health to oppose an advertising ban."[93]

In the United Kingdom, Philip Morris helped maintain Britain's opposition to the Advertising Directive through its close relationship with Kenneth Clarke, who had been health minister and health secretary. In reply to correspondence on the topic of the directive from Philip Morris's director of corporate affairs, policies, and programs, Clarke wrote in 1992, "I will certainly do my best to ensure that our government maintains its opposition."[94] Interestingly, the industry had recognized the potential power of the British "anti-tobacco forces,"[95] which had at the time united in deciding to approach the issue of the advertising ban via Europe, recognizing that it would be impossible to obtain a U.K. advertising ban while the Conservative government was still in power.

Industry efforts to gain influence at the member-state level were carefully adjusted to meet the cultural norms and to maximize the use of industry contacts in each country. But in addition to these country-focused actions, Neuman and colleagues[96] show how the industry also acted at a European level by developing third-party allies—in particular in the advertising and media industries—to oppose the ban; for example, the industry supported the formation of media groups created solely to oppose the directive. The industry also engaged in contingency planning for litigation in case the ban was passed. In 1990, John Lepere, head of the CECCM, reported that the industry's German trade association was considering whether to challenge the implementation of the 1989 EC Labelling Directive in the German Constitutional Court. He reasoned that should the Labelling Directive be shown to conflict with the German Constitution, the lawsuit could later be used to challenge the main elements of any future EC advertising ban.[97] Philip Morris was also developing plans to challenge the ban at the supranational level through the ECJ and had anticipated Germany bringing such a case.[98]

Product Regulation and Labeling

In the late 1980s and early 1990s, the EU implemented a series of directives on labeling and tar yield that took as their basis the Common Market requirement that laws of member states should be harmonized in order to ensure free trade. The labeling directives required that all packs display tar and nicotine yields, and that they include a health warning covering no less than 4 percent of the most visible surface, and in a way that is clearly visible and not easily removable.[99] Despite initial industry opposition and the industry's subsequent attempts to overturn the legislation, these health warnings were ultimately to the industry's advantage; they provided the perfect legal protection against product liability lawsuits.

Over time, it became apparent that the directives had weaknesses that the industry had exploited. For example, although Directive 89/622 stipulated that health warnings should be clearly legible and printed on a contrasting background, a 1993 evaluation revealed that most cigarette packs in Europe used gold lettering for the warnings—which, being reflective, offered only minimum contrast.[100] In addition, manufacturers were using additives to increase the addictive effect of nicotine and to make cigarettes easier to smoke or more palatable to first-time users.[101] Consequently, especially in view of the growing body of evidence that larger health warnings are more effective, there were moves to strengthen the directive. In October 1996 the High Level Cancer Experts Committee proposed specific changes concerning cigarette labeling and content,[102] which led to the drafting of a new Tobacco Products Directive in November 1999. This recast the existing directives on labeling and tar yield (Directives 89/622/EEC, 92/41/EEC, and 90/239/EEC; see Table 9.2) and updated the provisions regulating tobacco manufacture and labeling. The principal features of the new, consolidated directive were: a reduction in maximum tar yield from 12 to 10 milligrams and the establishment for the first time of maximum nicotine and carbon monoxide yields; an increase in the size, and improvement in the specification, of health warnings; the disclosure of ingredients and additives, along with reasons for their use and evidence of their safety; and a ban on misleading product descriptions such as "light" or "mild." These features will apply to tobacco products marketed and manufactured in the EU, implying (although not clearly stating) that those intended for export are also affected.

The year 2000 saw intensive lobbying by both sides as the directive was batted between the European Parliament and the Council of Ministers. The industry and its trade union allies complained that the proposed directive would lead to job losses in EU manufacturing plants and attempted to cast doubt on the legal basis of the directive in light of the ECJ ruling on the Advertising Directive. The Parliament was nevertheless persuaded by the health lobby to strengthen the directive—for example, by increasing the size of the health warnings and twice made amendments to this effect. Twice the Council rejected most of these amendments, leading to conflict between members of the European Parliament and EU governments[103] and prompting a process of conciliation. Due in large part to the skilful negotiating of Jules Maaten, the Parliament rapporteur, a compromise directive was adopted on May 15, 2001, to go into effect on September 30, 2002. Although the product of a political compromise, the new Tobacco Products Directive[104] went well beyond the earlier directives.

In the Council, Germany, which had previously voted against the directive, abstained, as did Luxembourg. Both delegations made statements reserving their right to refer the matter to the ECJ,[105] thereby signaling their intention to do so. The British Tobacco Manufacturers Association announced plans to challenge the directive along similar lines to the challenge of the advertising ban.[106] Japan Tobacco International announced it was considering legal action on the basis that the directive infringed its intellectual property ("Mild Seven" is a registered trademark)[107] and violated World Trade Organization rules.[108]

In the passage of both this new directive and the Advertising Directive, it became clear that the European Parliament favored stronger tobacco-control measures than the Council of Ministers. This contrast raises important questions about the balance of power among, and the democratic accountability of, the EU's different political bodies. Some commentators have suggested that the Parliament's pro-tobacco control stance was, in part, simply a reflection of that body's attempt to exert its authority in its continuing power struggle with the Council of Ministers. It must be noted, however, that members of the Parliament, unlike health ministers, are not under the control of their national governments, whose other interests in tobacco may conflict with public health.

The Tobacco Products Directive offered many benefits, particularly with regard to additives and health warnings. The disclosure of additives was a major step forward bringing information on tobacco closer in line with the EC's approach to food safety. On the labeling issue, the final agreement was for greatly enlarged warnings covering 30 percent of the front surface and 40 percent of the back surface of each pack. The health lobby and environment committee had argued for 30 percent, consistent with new legislation in Poland—whose stance could otherwise be weakened on accession to the EU. The ban on misleading terms such as "light" and "ultralight" was particularly important since evidence suggests that the industry has used these terms to mislead customers. As British American Tobacco itself acknowledged as early as 1971: "Manufacturers are concentrating on the low [total particulate matter] tar and nicotine segment in order to create brands . . . which aim, in one way or another, to reassure the consumer that these brands are relatively more 'healthy' than orthodox blended cigarettes."[109]

The directive's standards for machine-measured levels of tar, nicotine, and carbon monoxide, which were to be indicated on the side of each pack, offered fewer benefits. These standards were those recommended in 1996 by the expert committee, but recent evidence and experience suggests that the use of such standards may be counterproductive.[110] Although tar is the major carcinogenic component of tobacco smoke—and reducing tar levels can therefore be reasonably assumed to reduce harm—machine-measured yields do not reflect smokers' actual tar exposure. Smokers compensate for reduced nicotine yields by inhaling more deeply and more often. In addition, smokers tend to block the ventilation holes designed by the industry to reduce machine (but not actual) yields. Thus, when smoking low-tar brands, smokers' tar exposure may be as high as when smoking conven-

rettes. There is also evidence that smokers mistakenly believe that (relative) health benefit can be obtained by shifting from high- to -tar brands, and may therefore transfer to low-tar brands rather than quitting.

Some might consider these somewhat outdated recommendations to reflect a failure by the expert committee. Indeed, concern about its role has been expressed among both industry and tobacco-control groups. The committee comprises "experts" nominated by member states—usually academic experts in cancer research, plus some civil servants. In their current role, the experts provide scientific expertise for the whole of the EACP and its action plans, but some have questioned the experts' expertise on tobacco control per se. The group meets on an ad hoc basis, advising the Commission when required. Despite some concern over the relevance of the expertise provided, there is little consultation on the expert recommendations or any other clear system within the Commission for obtaining public health or tobacco-control advice.

Environmental Tobacco Smoke

European countries have been slower than Australia and the United States in implementing measures to prevent exposure to environmental tobacco smoke (ETS).[111] Other authors have attributed this lack of action to the relatively small number of European studies on the impact of ETS[112] and also to the lesser threat of litigation.[113] Cultural attitudes toward restrictions on public smoking (as explored in other chapters) may also play a large role. Over time, however, and largely since the release of internal industry documents, it has become apparent that the ETS issue is the industry's *bête noire*. The tobacco transnationals have attempted not only to distort the scientific debate about the interpretation of secondhand-smoke studies,[114] thereby delaying pressure for action in this area, but have also sought to hinder legislative change.

As early as 1986, authoritative bodies in Europe,[115] along with those in the United States[116] and Australia,[117] concluded that involuntary smoking was a cause of disease, including lung cancer. Further evidence—primary epidemiological studies,[118] meta-analyses,[119] and other secondary reviews of the evidence,[120] and toxicological research—provides incontrovertible evidence of a causal association between exposure to ETS and lung cancer, heart disease, and other serious illnesses. Direct epidemiological evidence is corroborated by calculations of the expected level of risk (based on the degree of exposure in passive smokers[121] and risks in active smokers[122]) that match the risks seen in epidemiological studies. The WHO has estimated that in Europe as a whole (not just within EU countries), ETS will result in approximately 3,000 to 4,500 cases of cancer in adults per year, considerably more cases of cardiovascular disease (although numbers are difficult to estimate), and 300,000 to 550,000 episodes of lower respiratory illness in infants.[123]

Although the overall burden of disease due to ETS is high because of the number of people exposed, the increased risk to an individual from passive smoking is relatively small, especially when compared with the risk of active smoking. Such small risks can be difficult to detect in epidemiological studies, and there was consequently some genuine academic debate about the limitations of the early studies. The industry, which as early as 1978 identified the health effects of passive smoking as "the most dangerous development yet to the viability of the tobacco industry,"[124] was quick to fuel these debates and to create unwarranted controversy around the research on passive smoking.[125]

In the mid-1990s the industry arranged a series of advertisements in newspapers across Europe that compared the risk of lung cancer from passive smoking with a variety of other apparent risks from everyday activities such as eating biscuits or drinking milk, thereby attempting to confuse the public.[126] These advertisements asked readers to request a copy of a report reviewing the evidence linking passive smoking to lung cancer risk, and written by the "European Working Group on Environmental Tobacco Smoke and Lung Cancer," a group funded by the tobacco industry. Even this industry-funded report found an increased risk in its meta-analysis of the evidence, but it then attempted to discredit the findings by highlighting methodological issues that would lead to an *over*estimation of the risks. The report failed to mention, however, the methodological issues that, leading epidemiologists suggested, would lead to an *under*estimation of the risks.[127] Reports published in the medical literature continued to challenge the evidence[128] but were written by scientists who, it later became apparent, were funded by the tobacco industry.[129] Internal industry documents have revealed that, while publicly denying the evidence—criticizing the methodology of published research and funding its own research to refute the existing evidence[130]—the industry was privately more circumspect, admitting that "we are constrained because we can't say its safe."[131]

Perhaps the industry's most outrageous attempt to fuel controversy over ETS was its effort to undermine the largest European study—by IARC— on the risk of lung cancer in passive smokers.[132] Philip Morris Corporate Services in Brussels was concerned that the IARC study would become "Europe's EPA,"[133] a reference to the 1992 U.S. Environmental Protection Agency report that classed environmental tobacco smoke as a class A carcinogen and stimulated legislation in the United States for clean indoor air.[134] The industry waged a three-pronged attack, spending more than twice that spent by IARC on the original study.[135] First, the industry commissioned research, directed by firms of lawyers representing the industry, that would either contradict IARC's findings or confuse the picture.[136] Second, the industry arranged to selectively leak the IARC study, enabling the industry to present its own interpretation to the media at a time when the study was still under peer review, which prevented the authors from responding. The industry's interpretation—that passive smoking does not cause cancer—was readily accepted by leading broadsheets.[137] Another advantage of this approach was that, when the report was finally published, it was "old news." Third, the industry engaged in extensive lobbying of politicians to counteract the report's potential impact, and it even arranged to have the Commission sponsor a seminar that was organized by an industry consultant and covered the topic of good epidemiological practices and risk assessment.[138]

While the industry was attempting to confuse the evidence and shift the focus of the debate, there were ongoing developments on the legislative front. In 1989 the Council of Ministers, aware that the EU lacked the legal competence to legislate on smoking in public places (other than those that are also workplaces), issued a nonbinding resolution that invited member states to implement policies on smoking in public places,[139] using legislation or other methods.[140] In 1992 and 1996[141] the Commission reviewed the measures taken in member states and concluded that the resolution had led to action. In most member states, regulations were instituted shortly before or after the adoption of the resolution, but despite the Commission's conclusion, not all the changes could be directly attributed to the EU resolution. For example, the *loi Evin* in France, although implemented after 1989, was conceived in France independently of the EU resolution. Nevertheless, Austria, Finland, and Sweden put new regulations into effect prior to joining in 1995, and may have done so in order to implement the resolution. In any case, by 1996 the regulations in member states had become more homogeneous, both in approach and field of application,[142] with the United Kingdom remaining the exception in having taken no legal measures and in simply relying on a voluntary code of practice.

Although unable to act on smoking in public places, the EU did have the authority, under the rubric of health and safety at work, to legislate against smoking in the workplace. Directive 89/654/EEC, adopted in 1989, required that "in rest rooms and rest areas appropriate measures must be introduced for the protection of non-smokers against the discomfort caused by tobacco smoke." Its passage, coupled with the nonbinding resolution discussed above, raised alarm in the industry. Tentative plans were hatched, including: long-term preventive action through strategic alliance-building; communication of key industry messages to potential allies;[143] and efforts to counter nonsmoking events such as the WHO nonsmoking day (May 31).[144] The industry's key messages were the promotion of cooperation and tolerance between smokers and nonsmokers (to help maintain the social acceptability of smoking), and the use of ventilation as an alternative means of reducing exposure to ETS. The plans went so far as to provide industry-linked speakers to the top business and hotel schools in Europe—an effort to ensure that the future business leaders of Europe were well versed in industry arguments.

Action on secondhand smoke gradually progressed on a number of fronts. The French *loi Evin* was passed in 1991, and the following year saw the publication of the long-awaited U.S. EPA report, an International Civil Aviation Organization resolution urging its members to ban smoking on passenger airlines, and, within the EU, the publication of a BASP newsletter on workplace smoking and the passage of Directive 92/85/EEC on the health and safety at work of pregnant mothers, which obligated employers to reduce the risk of exposure to passive smoke. By 1993 British Airways had banned smoking on European flights lasting less than ninety minutes; changes were afoot in Belgium and Italy, and at the regional level in Germany and Spain; and public opinion was shifting against smoking. With these changes and a 1993 draft directive that aimed to protect transportation workers against the risks caused by tobacco smoke—and that had the potential to lead to the prohibition of smoking on public transportation[145]—the industry became increasingly alarmed. Its main concerns were that the EU would act to extend the resolution on smoking in public places to include the hospitality sector, and to further restrict workplace smoking.[146]

The CECCM established a working group on smoking in the workplace and public places.[147] The group kept abreast of issues in member states, prepared lobbying papers on ETS,[148] and drafted workplace-smoking policies that promoted freedom to smoke at work (which were distributed, in turn, to human resources teams throughout Europe). By 1993 the industry had developed a comprehensive plan. Wirz of Philip Morris began working on a long-term strategy "to delay EC action [on workplace smoking] and/or secure a reasonably worded compromise."[149] His strategy was based on building a European network of national information centers (as discussed above) to defend smokers' issues and maintain the social acceptability of smoking. His argument was that such a network could help to achieve a variety of goals:

- Turn the industry into a legitimate voice in the smoker/nonsmoker debate

- Create an environment hostile to antismoking extremists
- Disrupt antismoking alliances
- Avoid placing Philip Morris in the front lines of defense by using an industry cover
- Offer strong defense against EC-level threats[150]

Alliance building was an important part of Wirz's strategy. International allies included the European Trade Union Confederation, the International Federation of Advertising Agencies, the International Hotel Association, the Union of Industrial and Employers' Confederations of Europe, and the hospitality industry. His plans were further consolidated with a three-year action plan on smoking restrictions. In addition to mitigating the impact of the IARC study described above, the plan's objectives on workplace smoking were to "[p]romote voluntary workplace policies based on accommodation, [l]ock in model legislation where conditions are appropriate thereby preventing adverse legislation, [and] [d]elay EC action."[151]

The industry's overall lobbying strategy, as described above, involved mobilizing the unions and employers, targeted lobbying of European institutions and politicians, working with supportive governments, using smokers' rights groups and others to promote libertarian arguments, and working with the media in whatever way necessary to maintain the social acceptability of smoking (for example, by feeding them "US-sourced 'ETS excess stories' (dismissal from work over smoking, career discrimination due to smoking etc.)").[152] The use of libertarian groups—including specifically prosmoking ones such as FOREST, an industry-funded front group[153] that had been established to give the impression of grassroots activism—was particularly important. These groups argued that the right of people to smoke was as important as the right of nonsmokers to a smoke-free environment. They thereby attempted to shift the debate to one of civil liberties and smokers' rights, while public opinion surveys, even those conducted by the industry, showed that both smokers and nonsmokers in Europe were in favor of ETS legislation. A 1995 survey of EU citizens found that approximately 80 percent favored legislation to prohibit smoking in places open to the public, including public transportation. A similar percentage supported workplace bans.[154] Industry data showed not only that 79 percent supported bans and 60 percent, legislative restrictions, but that 86 percent believed ETS to be harmful.[155]

On the particular issue of workplace smoking, Philip Morris aimed to minimize EU action by identifying countries that had yet to implement the workplace directive and by attempting to have favorable legislation implemented there. The company's favored legislation was the 1993 royal decree enacted in Belgium, which stipulated that employers "establish conditions for tobacco use during work hours" and that these hours be based on "reciprocal needs of smokers and non-smokers . . . [and on] individual liberties, courtesy and tolerance."[156]

At the time of this writing, the EU has taken no further action on work-place smoking. The possibility of enacting legislation in this area has been considered but has received little support. One possible explanation, of course, is that the industry's concerted effort to undercut any such legisla-tive effort was successful, but there are a number of other, largely adminis-trative reasons that could also explain the lack of action. Workplace legislation would have to be enacted as a measure to promote health and safety at work, rather than as an internal market measure, and would therefore need to be drafted by the Commission's employment unit rather than the EACP. Considerable bureaucratic and communication hurdles would need to be overcome to work on a directive spanning the interests of two directorates general (Health and Consumer Protection, and Employment and Social Affairs). There is also a perception that opposition would be severe—not only from the industry, but also from trade unions, employers, and business representatives. In addition, of all the areas of tobacco-control legislation, restrictions on public or workplace smoking cause most controversy. Introducing legislation at a time when the popula-tion is not on board may backfire; witness the poor enforcement of the *loi Veil* in France. Developing legislation that is acceptable to all fifteen EU countries is therefore fraught with difficulty. As a result, many remain reluc-tant to legislate in this area, believing that regulation of smoking in the workplace would be better achieved at the country level. To what extent industry plans to subvert a potential workplace ban have influenced these attitudes and the perceived opposition of unions and employers is difficult to ascertain, but they must, almost certainly, have had some impact.

Price, Taxation, and Smuggling

In 1992 the EU adopted three directives on harmonization of tobacco taxa-tion, effective from January 1, 1993.[157] These directives relate to the three principle forms of taxation on cigarettes: value-added tax (VAT), fixed spe-cific excise duty (imposed as a fixed amount per 1,000 pieces or grams), and variable ad valorem excise duty (proportional to the final retail price). The ad valorem tax leads to price differentials between cheaper and more expensive brands that increase as the percentage level of the tax itself increases—the so-called multiplier effect. A system based largely on ad valorem tax therefore allows more affordable cigarettes to exist on the mar-ket, but has the advantage of automatically taking account of inflation.

By contrast, since specific duties, by adding a fixed price to every cigarette regardless of its baseline price, do not have this multiplier effect, they reduce price differentials and lead very cheap brands to be withdrawn from the market. These duties have to be increased regularly to allow for inflation.

The three directives introduced in October 1992 were a compromise reached between those in favor of ad valorem taxation and those in favor of specific taxation. The directives stipulate that each member state should apply an *overall* excise duty (specific and ad valorem combined) of at least 57 percent of the final retail selling price of the price category most in demand. In addition, the minimum specified VAT rate was set at 13.04 percent, meaning that the minimum overall level of taxation on cigarettes was required to be 70 percent. Countries were free to set the balance between ad valorem and specific taxation—on the condition that the latter falls in the range of 5 to 55 percent, as previously agreed in the *acquis communautaire*. As a result, while leading to price increases in a number of countries, these directives did not eliminate large price differentials. By the same token, very cheap cigarettes continued to be produced, distributed, and sold.

In 1995, a Commission review raised two major concerns: that the 57 percent rule had widened price differences between member states, which was not in the interest of the internal market, and that an increase in manufacturers' prices would lead to an increase in retail prices, which might result in the overall excise falling below the 57 percent minimum. It later became apparent that these concerns had been fueled by the tobacco industry's lobbying effort, which had succeeded in confusing the Commission.[158] Unable to agree on a way forward, the Commission held an excise conference in July 1995. One health organization and forty-two industry representatives attended. The industry journal *Tobacco International* described the meeting as a "triumph for the national industries." It noted that, while member states generally intervene or respond only after the Commission has formulated a proposal, the industry intervened earlier in this case: "while the Commission was in the process of formulating its proposals the industry could, and did, intervene—this time successfully."[159] As a result of the lobbying, and despite the reduction in price differences from 623 percent in January 1992 to 372 percent in September 1996,[160] the Commission revised the taxation directive in 1999. This change gave member states greater flexibility in setting taxes but did little to reduce the price differentials within Europe.[161]

The Commission expressed a desire to further harmonize minimum taxation levels in order to respond to public health concerns.[162] Member states have been strongly divided on this matter, however, making it unlikely that a unanimous decision could be reached. Denmark, Germany, Ireland, the Netherlands, and the United Kingdom—a group that included the tobacco-manufacturing countries of northern Europe—favored specific taxes, which tend to benefit the exchequer. Belgium, France, Greece, Italy, Luxembourg, and Spain—a group that included the tobacco-producing countries of southern Europe—favored ad valorem taxes, which protect the cultivation of their low-priced tobaccos.

The debate about price and taxation heightened awareness about cross-border shopping and about smuggling. Cross-border shopping is the buying of duty-paid tobacco products in a neighboring country for the buyer's own consumption, and is legal under the provisions of the single market. Customs officials have developed guidelines on reasonable quantities that an individual might be expected to consume. The industry has argued that with the removal of frontier controls in January 1993, price differentials would lead to extensive cross-border shopping by consumers, but those in the health lobby who have examined the data say there is as yet no evidence to suggest such an increase.[163]

The industry arguments about smuggling have been similar: that price differences create an incentive to smuggle cigarettes from low-tax countries in southern Europe to the higher-tax countries in the north, and that this problem can be addressed by reducing taxes. Such arguments were successfully used elsewhere—for example, in Canada and Sweden. In Canada, taxes were reduced in response to concerns about smuggling in the early 1990s. Predictably, the lower price for cigarettes led both to an increase in smoking rates among Canadians and to a decline in revenue collected.[164]

In reality, smuggling is more complex. A distinction must be made between bootlegging (the small-scale, illegal, cross-border trade of tobacco products that are not intended for personal use) and smuggling (the large-scale export and import of tobacco on which no duty has been paid). Bootlegging is related to price differentials but accounts for a smaller proportion of illegal tobacco sales than smuggling—which, contrary to industry claims, does not appear to be related to price differences. Smuggling is more prevalent in southern and eastern European countries, where cheap cigarettes predominate, than where prices are much higher.[165] Smuggling appears, instead, to be associated with the presence of organized crime, a culture of street selling, and complicity of the industry.[166] For example, accusations that British American Tobacco was doing business with Serbian businessmen in the Balkan underworld led to the resignation of a senior European politician from the company's board;[167] as a result, a plan to establish a cigarette factory in the Balkans was condemned by European customs investigators.[168] Smuggling has also been made easier by the European customs arrangements designed to promote international trade by road[169]—highlighting the potential conflict between trade liberalization and health.

Smuggling benefits the industry in a number of ways. It stimulates consumption through the sale of cheap cigarettes (the industry gains its normal profit regardless of whether cigarettes enter the legal or illegal market). It enables the industry to penetrate new markets and allows it to argue for a reduction in tobacco taxation in order to reduce the incentive to smuggle, as illustrated above.

It is estimated that about 7 percent of the western European and 13 percent of the eastern European market is contraband.[170] Joossens argues that the scale of tobacco smuggling is such that it is likely that the industry is at least complicit in the process. For example, exports from Britain to Andorra (which, although situated between France and Spain, is not an EU member) increased 117-fold, from 13 million cigarettes in 1993 to 1.52 billion in 1997.[171] It would be physically impossible for the small Andorran population to smoke this many cigarettes, especially since they do not favor British brands. Yet few of these cigarettes were legally re-exported, making it fairly obvious that they were illegally exported from Andorra back to the British market (the so-called boomerang trade).

Debate continues about whether the transnational tobacco companies are directly involved in the smuggling. Kenneth Clarke has admitted that British American Tobacco supplies cigarettes even though it knows that they will end up on the black market: "Where any government in unwilling to act or their efforts are unsuccessful, we act, completely within the law, on the basis that our brands will be available alongside those of our competitors in the smuggled as well as the legitimate market."[172]

Evidence from internal industry documents suggests that the industry's involvement is even more direct. In evidence submitted to the House of Commons Health Committee, Duncan Campbell of the Centre for Public Integrity has argued that smuggling has been British American Tobacco company policy since the late 1960s, evolving from an ad hoc activity into an organized and centrally managed one.[173]

There have been several official smuggling investigations in different parts of the world, as well as a series of court cases accusing the industry of smuggling cigarettes.[174] Senior tobacco industry executives or affiliates were convicted of smuggling-related offenses in Hong Kong[175] and Canada.[176] Following a two-year investigation by the EU's antifraud unit, the Commission brought action against two American tobacco companies in the U.S. courts in an attempt to recover billions of dollars of customs revenues lost through smuggling.[177] The case came to court in July 2001, but the

American judge ruled that the Commission had failed to make a convincing case that it (rather than the individual member states) had directly suffered injury as a result of the smuggling.[178] Nevertheless, positive aspects of the ruling encouraged the EU to file a new suit in August 2001—this time joined in the proceeding by ten member states (Belgium, Finland, France, Germany, Greece, Italy, Luxembourg, the Netherlands, Portugal, and Spain).

International action, including controls on cigarette transport, will be crucial in efforts to control smuggling.[179] Spain is one of the few countries to have successfully tackled this problem; its example shows that through concerted action at both national and international levels—involving collaboration with the European Anti-Fraud Office, and political pressure by the EU—smuggling can be reduced.

Preventive Action, the WHO, and the Framework Convention on Tobacco Control

Although legislation forms the mainstay of the EU's role in tobacco control, the EU also takes a preventive approach[180]—largely through its funding, albeit limited, for initiatives in tobacco control and in tobacco-control research, as described above. In addition, the EU undertakes surveys of member states, providing comparative data and disseminating evidence of best practices.[181] Its role in this sphere overlaps with that of WHO Europe, which has its own action plans for a "smoke-free Europe." The WHO–EU relationship is often a difficult one, owing to the conflicting interests of an organization focused purely on health and one focused largely on economic interests.

The Commission communicates separately with WHO Geneva, and Gro Harlem Brundtland's appointment as WHO director general brought intensified communication, with annual meetings and Commission representatives attending the World Health Assembly. The WHO has placed much emphasis on the Framework Convention on Tobacco Control. In October 1999 the Commission received a mandate from the Council of Ministers to conduct the negotiations for the framework convention on behalf of member states in fields where the Community had competence. Thus, member states gave up considerable powers as they would be unable to speak at the negotiations on any issue covered by EU law. As a result, the EU found itself agreeing on the lowest common denominator and allowing countries such as Austria, Germany, and Luxembourg, which take permissive stands on tobacco control, to impose a weak position on the rest of the EU.[182]

Discussion

The treaty provision (originating with the Single European Act) that European policies should promote a high level of health has been used to enact a series of legislative changes on tobacco. Although these enactments may, in retrospect, be seen as quite limited, in the late 1980s and early 1990s they were a major step forward and enabled the EU to achieve changes in the field of tobacco control that were unlikely to have been reached simply through action by individual national governments. They had an important impact on tobacco control, particularly in countries whose governments had inadequately addressed this matter. Thus, the impact in Greece, for example, was considerably greater than in France. These legislative changes will also have a major impact on future members (although only on those with weak tobacco-control policies)[183]—who, before joining, have to sign up to the *acquis* in its entirety. In addition, EU action has had an important, albeit indirect, impact of putting tobacco-control issues on member states' national agendas, thereby influencing national action. Many member states enacted national legislation under European influence—in some instances before European legislation on the same issue was finalized, and even when European legislative effort proved to be unsuccessful. For example, the advertising ban implemented in the Netherlands almost certainly arose as a consequence of European action on advertising.

The early progress in the field of tobacco control was followed by a sudden decline in activity in the mid-1990s, enabling analysis of the factors favoring and hindering control. Initial progress was certainly facilitated by some dynamic groupings of individuals, free from bureaucratic hindrances and having high-level political support within Europe. But these factors alone were not enough. The crucial issue seems to be that during this period, when the health lobby was reasonably well organized, the tobacco industry had yet to awaken to the potential impact of EU action—and thus little effective opposition was in place.

The early 1990s saw numerous changes that seem likely to have hindered progress. The 1992 Treaty of Maastricht introduced the principle of subsidiarity and led to the emergence of eight new public health programs which resulted, in turn, in a downscaling of activity on cancer. Other changes included the bureaucratic reorganization and restaffing of the EACP. There is no reason to think, however, that these developments had anything but a short-term impact, and the Maastricht Treaty also introduced co-decision, thereby increasing the power of the Parliament—which, given its stance favoring tobacco control, should have encouraged progress. It appears, instead—especially when examining the progress of specific pieces of legislation—that it was the more pervasive impact of the industry lobby, coupled with the obstructive actions of some member states, that most influenced the downturn in activity.

Andrew Hayes, the EU liaison officer of the UICC, has drawn an interesting comparison between the EU response to tobacco and another recent health threat, bovine spongiform encephalopathy (BSE).[184] He highlights that the fear of mad cow disease led to several years of frenzied activity within the EU, producing a range of initiatives designed to minimize risk and protect the health of the public—despite the fact that BSE caused less than one hundred deaths in total compared to a yearly total of 500,000 deaths from tobacco. He argues that tobacco has not led to the same degree of activity for a number of reasons, which are, in part, historical. For example, tobacco was entrenched in many different cultures before the relationship between smoking and health was elucidated in the 1950s. Public perceptions of risk from these two health threats are also quite different (arguably influenced by the tobacco industry's attempts to confuse those perceptions with regard to smoking). Nevertheless, Hayes suggests that lack of action on tobacco has resulted mainly from political factors: the vested interests of farmers, producers, advertisers, distributors, retailers, and governments. Peter Taylor reaches the same conclusion in his book *The Smoke Ring*, when comparing the political action taken against cholera in the end of the nineteenth century with that taken against the scourge of tobacco in the twentieth century.[185]

The evidence presented in this chapter supports the conclusions of Hayes and Taylor. It is apparent that the industry has played a key role in subverting European tobacco-control policy. The industry's tactics are complex and all-embracing, striking at all levels of European policy-making. Such activity is to be expected, but the industry has also engaged in more subversive, hidden tactics that have been profoundly influential with regard to the public perceptions of smoking and its risks, and of the necessary or appropriate public policy responses. These tactics include the use of front groups and other third parties to present industry arguments, to submit industry-drafted directives, and to distort scientific evidence.

There is one additional key difference between tobacco and other health threats with which it is often compared: addiction. Nicotine has been rated as one of the most highly addictive drugs available, on a par with heroin.[186] While the libertarian view stresses freedom to smoke and freedom from interference, the health lobby emphasizes that addiction compromises freedom by making it physically difficult to reverse choices made in teenage years. Libertarian arguments have long been expounded in the liberal press. It was always thought this arose in part through indirect industry influence—the media's dependence on tobacco advertising compromising its news and health coverage.[187] There is now, however, overwhelming evidence of the industry's more direct involvement in this debate, in attempts to promote the social acceptability of smoking and the inappropriateness of "paternalistic" state action and to present tobacco-control advocates as health fascists.[188] Industry documents indicate, for example, that the tobacco companies funded and, if necessary, created hospitality associations to speak on their behalf and prevent the growth of smoke-free environments.[189] They also funded and effectively directed many grassroots smoking-rights groups such as FOREST in the United Kingdom or Hen-Ry ("courteous smokers") in Scandanavia linking these organizations with well-respected figures such as Uffe Ellemann-Jensen, the then Danish foreign minister.[190] The industry cultivated media contacts—journalists, scientists and doctors who were prepared to toe the industry line,[191] offering the less experienced media training.[192] More recently Roger Scruton, writer, philosopher, and doyen of the libertarian right whose writings, including a scathing attack on the WHO's Framework Convention, were widely cited,[193] was recently revealed to be receiving over £50,000 a year from Japan Tobacco International to whom he had put proposals to place articles attacking efforts to restrict tobacco use in leading international newspapers.[194] Such revelations, alongside the less secretive industry funding of organizations such as the American Civil Liberties Union (ACLU),[195] suggest that the industry has so effectively hijacked and exploited the libertarian viewpoint that it is now necessary to question carefully the motives and fundings of anyone who presents such arguments in relation to smoking.

Difference and Diffusion: Cross-Cultural Perspectives on the Rise of Anti-Tobacco Policies

Allan M. Brandt

In the course of the last half-century, the harms of cigarette smoking have become a categorical part of our science. The fact that smoking *causes* serious disease and premature mortality has become a critical aspect of modern understandings of epidemiology, statistical inference, and medical science.[1] Although the process of demonstrating the harms of smoking was neither simple nor straightforward, by late in the twentieth century there was no longer any serious debate among physicians, public health officials, and scientists over whether smoking constitutes a health risk of enormous consequence. Despite this impressive consensus, however, there remains considerable disagreement both within and across nations about the most appropriate public policy response to these scientifically understood harms. In this respect, the cigarette serves as a remarkably sensitive device for reading a specific culture's beliefs and values concerning risk, autonomy, individuality, the role of the state, and the nature of harm reduction (to name a few). A comparative assessment of these meanings also reveals how policy and debates about policy relate to deeper cultural perceptions about smoking itself.

Any examination of law and regulation, on the one hand, and cultural belief and practice, on the other, shows that cultural beliefs are not directly determinative of policy.[2] In the case of tobacco, there is no question that powerful economic interests of both corporations and nations have in large measure determined the limits of public health policy. Nonetheless, the cigarette's historical and social position does shape the parameters of the policy debate and reveals the strengths and limitations of various interventions.[3]

The erosion of the image of cigarette smoking as a rational consumer choice of informed adults has been critical to the enactment of aggressive tobacco regulations. Because smoking came to be configured historically as an individual, voluntary behavior, it frequently tested the appropriate limits of state action, especially in liberal states. In these countries, antismoking forces have therefore centered their attention and activity on questioning the voluntary nature of smoking. As Ronald Bayer and James Colgrove's chapter in this volume so effectively demonstrates, the focus on "children and bystanders first"—an abiding concern in public health—powerfully undercuts the traditional notion of smoking as a voluntary behavior, especially in the 1980s and 1990s.[4] The heavy emphasis of anti-tobacco advocates like David Kessler of the U.S. Food and Drug Administration was on the tobacco industry's targeting of children, the impact of passive smoking, and the addictive properties of nicotine; each significantly challenges the image of smoking as a rational choice made by individuals.[5] Significantly, the widespread recognition that the industry had acted aggressively to promote underage smoking and enhance the addictive properties of its product has contributed to a sharp erosion in the historical assumption of agency.[6]

Some of the most telling examples of cultural perceptions of smoking and smokers come from a historical examination of policies regarding *public smoking*. Unlike advertising and packaging regulations, restrictions on public smoking reveal how the product and behavior actually fit into day-to-day life in society. Certainly, the putative harms of passive smoking have proven to be an important aspect of such contests, but attitudes and practices regarding smoking as a public behavior are not limited to perceptions of risk. Rather, concerns about manners and etiquette, sociability and nuisance have historically dictated the very social legitimacy or stigmatization of smoking. By focusing on public smoking, this chapter—in brief synopsis—traces changing attitudes and values in the United States concerning the cigarette; provides a brief cross-cultural assessment; investigates the diffusion of antismoking policies internationally through the example of airline bans; and briefly evaluates tensions in diffusion of cigarette marketing to the developing world.

Of Manners and Mores: Cigarette Etiquette in the United States

Cigarette smoking has been defined historically by its powerful and positive association with sociability. Therefore, as cigarette smoking became so phenomenally popular in the course of the twentieth century in the United

States, complex notions of mores and manners governed its use. Where and when was it appropriate to smoke? Should men and women smoke in mixed company? Changes in such practices often revealed the subtle, but powerful, shifting cultural norms and meanings of cigarette use. Since these meanings changed over the course of the last century, social roles and public regulations offer an important route to understanding how smoking is embedded in specific cultures.

Indeed, one of the central elements in the rise of cigarette use was the opening up of public spaces to smoking. In the early twentieth century, the U.S. tobacco industry worked assiduously through its advertising and marketing to change expectations, thereby making the public use of the cigarette appropriate. The tobacco industry effectively read and exploited ongoing social and cultural change: the rise of a consumer culture, standardization of products, and mass production. The cigarette came to be widely associated with modern mores. Such a change ultimately proved crucial to establishing the powerful associations of smoking with pleasure, sociability, and personal attraction that became so strong by midcentury. In this respect, it was critical that social conventions *against* public smoking be overturned.

Take, for example, the rise of smoking among U.S. women in the early twentieth century. As women started to smoke in the late nineteenth century, they typically did so privately or in small groups—and always indoors. The tobacco companies fought against such strictures of convention, realizing that for the cigarette to triumph as a consumer product, it must emerge "on the street." This was the precise goal of Edward Bernays's famous publicity stunt to get young women to smoke in public: he recruited debutantes to march in the 1929 New York City Easter parade brandishing cigarettes as their "torches of freedom."[7] In doing so, the industry matched the cigarette's desirability with ideas about the new woman. In that time of flappers and youth culture, cigarette smoking fit well with broader, appealing images of freedom and pleasure.[8]

Manners, as a highly articulated mechanism of social control and practice, offer an important opportunity to observe the meaning of a particular public behavior, and how social, political, and economic interests publicly shape those meanings.[9] Codes of behavior around the cigarette have varied significantly both historically and culturally, and thus provide us with a mechanism for dissecting the relationship of social meanings to practice, policy, and regulation. Manners, it seems worth noting, are one form of such regulation, though in the last decades of the twentieth century, they often gave way to more official and political modes of control. Moreover, even in the debates about whether public smoking should be left to the realm of manners and interpersonal negotiation or, instead, be more aggressively regulated, central aspects of the nature of tobacco use are revealed.

By the mid-twentieth century, before its risks were fully understood, smoking became an almost unquestionable practice for both men and women, and norms of etiquette reflected its position. Emily Post, the doyen of manners experts, turned her attention in 1940 to those who continued to object to smoking even though it had become such a common behavior: "those who do not smoke cannot live apart, and when they come in contact with smokers, it is scarcely fair that the few should be allowed to prohibit the many from the pursuit of their comforts and their pleasure."[10] While making exceptions for visitors to a sickroom or to a bride with a veil on, Post felt that smoking was unquestionably appropriate in almost all settings.

Post's view is striking given the radical transformation in attitudes and practices regarding the cigarette in the last two decades. By the 1980s and 1990s, smoking had become such an increasingly unacceptable behavior in public settings that etiquette recommendations came to directly contradict Post's earlier advice. One indicator of this change was the way that cigarette smoke came to be fundamentally redefined. In the 1940s and 1950s, it was not unusual to see cigarette smoke referred to as both fragrant and appealing; by the 1980s and 1990s, people spoke of the "stink" of smoke. Indeed, as the tide shifted to favor nonsmokers, the United States' syndicated etiquette adviser, Miss Manners, frequently encountered discourtesies among the victors. "Miss Manners is not a smoker herself, but she has noted that foul emissions from non-smokers are hazardous to the public welfare," she explained. "The idea that health-conscious righteousness justifies rudeness is a repulsive one."[11] Consider, too, the question "Do you mind if I smoke?" The very question is now a complete anachronism in the United States, a reminder of times gone by, when etiquette rather than regulation shaped public smoking behavior. Today, one could not even pose the question in "polite" company. This prohibition is just one of many markers of the remarkable transformation in U.S. smoking behaviors in the last two decades.

The tobacco industry was eager to maintain the discourse of manners, however, and to keep smoking in the realm of socially acceptable behavior. As regulation of workplace and public smoking loomed, the tobacco industry continued to insist that conflicts regarding smoking could and should be dealt with through the mechanisms of "mutual respect" and accommodation.[12] According to this perspective, any tensions engendered by smoking could be resolved by a polite tolerance of others' needs. Smokers and nonsmokers could negotiate the use of public space. Such tobacco industry rhetoric became well established by the mid-1980s. Internal tobacco industry documents made public through recent litigation reveal the extensive planning, thought, and money put into the industry's effort to keep smoking a legitimated activity.[13] In 1985 the president of the Tobacco Institute outlined the industry's strategy concerning environmental tobacco smoke, explaining that the industry would act "to redefine [the issue], to broaden it, to demonstrate ... that we are contributing to the solution rather than to the problem."[14] This strategy quickly took tangible form. During the first four months of 1986, tobacco public relations people met with representatives of 1,500 companies, fourteen chambers of commerce, the National Restaurant Association, and thirteen state restaurant groups, running seminars concerning workplace smoking policies.[15]

A 1988 Philip Morris memorandum planning international public relations efforts summarized the company's main rhetorical strategy, just as the company was attempting to implement it beyond U.S. borders:

> Ultimately, we must recognize that there is strong emotionalism in the opponent's message and that science and rationality will not necessarily prevail. Our message must have its emotional elements—e.g., individual rights, fairness, reasonableness, keeping government out of private industry, etc. Determining which message will be most successful in which countries will require research efforts.[16]

In one typical and telling example from 1993, Philip Morris's public relations firm outlined a "breathing space" campaign for the United Kingdom in a memorandum. With the themes of "tolerance" over "antismoking zealotry," they described the planned launch of the "Philip Morris Accommodation Programme," based on one of the same name in the United States. Hoping to announce the campaign at Planet Hollywood in London, with actor Michael Caine standing beside an industry spokesperson, the proposal stressed the need "for everyone to respect one another's rights" and to "actively seek ways to accommodate the interests of both smokers and nonsmokers."[17]

While the industry worked to maintain public "breathing space" for its customers, however, antismoking activists found that contesting public smoking was among its most powerful strategies. In the course of the last half of the twentieth century, smoking went from being widely perceived as a marker of social attraction, pleasure, and fun to a critical risk to one's own health, a harm imposed by smokers on "innocent bystanders," and a dirty and smelly social offense.

The Failure of Manners

As a result of these battles, by the mid-1980s Miss Manners found that the whole smoking issue had devolved into conflict and acrimony, much to her professional chagrin. Here was a context for which simple manners advice held little potential for negotiated settlement. "Miss Manners is hard put to say who is behaving worse: those who insist upon offending other people with their smoke or those who insist that only rudeness and humiliation toward smokers will clear the air," she explained.[18] Given the bitterness enveloping the cigarette, Miss Manners now hoped that the issue would be legally regulated, freeing her to focus on more truly substantive questions of etiquette. In 1985 Miss Manners threw up her hands, exclaiming, "The issue of smoking has inspired such widespread, unacceptable manners in both smokers and nonsmokers for so long that Miss Manners would be relieved to have regulation of smoking made a matter of law, as many people are suggesting. She is more than ready to turn her attention to more complicated problems."[19] The very fact that smoking had passed from a problem of manners to a regulatory issue was an impressive victory for antismoking advocates in the tobacco wars. "Society has changed on this issue," Miss Manners would later conclude, "and smoking is no longer considered to be a standard liberty."[20]

But while the nonsmoking U.S. public had generally come to disapprove strongly of smoking—and to believe that it was an infringement on their liberty—regulation did not come easily. Even as public sentiment in the United States became strongly antismoking, shifts in policy were slow and piecemeal. From the mid-1960s on, most federal regulatory initiatives were blocked or radically diluted as a result of the impressive influence of the tobacco industry in Congress.[21] Indeed, the cigarette is arguably the single most unregulated consumer product in twentieth-century U.S. history. At every instance of intensive regulatory activity concerning food and drugs, tobacco was excepted. And even in the last quarter-century, as the potential for regulatory intervention increased with the emergence of overwhelming scientific evidence of the cigarette's harms, tobacco was typically excluded from almost all consumer-protection legislation.[22]

The power of the tobacco lobby at the federal level largely explains why most cigarette regulatory actions have taken place at the local, grassroots level (where the industry possesses significantly less authority) or in the courts (where traditional forms of political and economic influence are constricted).[23] Even the tobacco industry, with all its clout, could not prevent numerous local regulations. By the mid-1990s, well over five hundred local communities and states had enacted restrictions on public smoking;

prior to this time, literally thousands of workplaces and industries had set their own regulations.[24]

From Harm to Nuisance: Bans on Outdoor Smoking

In the United States, where public smoking has become anathema, the regulation of cigarette use has far outstripped scientific concerns about risk to others. Now, smoking is often explicitly regulated *not* as a health risk, but as a nuisance. Indoor regulations have now expanded to the great outdoors. During the 1980s and 1990s, smokers—expelled from their offices—often found new camaraderie in entryways and on stoops. Now, smoking is increasingly coming under fire in these areas, too.

In May 1995, the selectmen in the town of Sharon, Massachusetts, voted to ban smoking on the beaches of Lake Massapoag. In addition, smoking was banned at all parks and ball fields. Although petitioners collected signatures to repeal the ordinance, residents supported the ban by a vote of 670–470 at a town meeting in October.[25] Palo Alto, California, enacted a ban on smoking within twenty feet of all public buildings in 1995. Under the ordinance, employee-only entries were exempt. Hal Lesser, a Palo Alto barber who opposed the restriction, invited smokers to use his doorway and stoop.[26] In both instances, there was clear resistance to the measures, but sentiment in support of them prevailed.

Increasingly, employers are limiting smoking to explicitly designated areas for outdoor smoking. At Pittsburgh's Four Gateway Center, signs outside the building declare "This Is a Smoke-Free Zone," and "NO Smoking Beyond This Point." One woman noted, "Not only do we have to go outside, we have to stand where they want us to stand."[27] Such regulations have been forcefully advocated by anti-tobacco activists like John Banzhaf, the executive director of Action on Smoking and Health.

Bans on outdoor smoking—not to mention increasingly aggressive limits in restaurants and bars—are viewed by many as the ultimate excess of a self-righteous anti-tobacco crusade. Certainly, the bans do reflect the ongoing move of cigarette use from licit to illicit; the isolation and shaming of smokers have been significant elements in the social transformation of the behavior. In this context, smoking is not so much a risk to others as a nuisance and a social offense. As anti-tobacco activist Joe Cherner recently wrote:

> Government must decide what to do when smoking pollution is merely a nuisance. Government constantly makes such decisions when one person's pleasure causes another person discomfort. For

example, government bans loud music in a person's apartment when it bothers the neighbors. Government bans eating on the subways, talking in the library, pets in a restaurant, noisy nightclubs in a residential neighborhood, noisy trucks after certain hours, pungent odors which bother neighbors, adult video/book stores in certain neighborhoods, and loitering in public places.[28]

How far anti-tobacco reformers will succeed in this "zero tolerance" approach remains unclear, but this activity is indicative of the "abolitionist" perspective that has come to characterize U.S. anti-tobacco policies.   ·

From a cultural perspective, such health crusades may well reflect moral absolutism and health paternalism, but they also create a social context for a variety of potentially successful policy initiatives. For example, there seems little doubt that the character of juries hearing tobacco liability litigation reflects changing attitudes about smoking—which makes such suits increasingly viable. In nations that continue to focus on "balancing" the rights of smokers and nonsmokers, opportunities for certain anti-tobacco policies may be considerably more restricted. Nonetheless, for regulations and bans to achieve important social legitimacy and compliance, they must be broadly consistent with local practices, meanings, and health customs.

The Cultural Configuration of Risk

The aggressive regulation of public smoking that has occurred in so many localities and venues across the United States in the last two decades, coupled with the shifting cultural norms that prompted these measures, serves as an important foil with which to compare and contrast other nations. The variability from country to country noted in this book reflects, in part, the striking disparities with which the risks of passive smoking are regarded. However, these national differences reflect cultural perceptions far more deeply held than particular debates about the relative risk of passive smoke. At least three questions are important to consider. How much disapproval does smoking garner? What are the restrictions in public places? And how compliant with regulatory initiatives is the public? Ultimately, such assessments are often made in an explicitly cross-cultural framework. National approaches to smoking regulations provide a useful means for defining cultural differences.

In tracing the process of the critical shifts in the meaning of smoking, there can be little doubt that key scientific data on the risks of passive smoke played a critical role. Central to the cross-cultural comparisons of national tobacco policies and social attitudes concerning smoking behavior and regulations are deeply embedded notions of risk, risk assessment, and risk perception. Although the harms of smoking are widely understood, both the precise nature of these risks and strategies for their control are highly variable. In the United States, for example, the risks of sidestream smoke have, to a remarkable degree, led to a radical reconfiguration of tobacco politics and policy. In other countries, these risks are more fundamentally measured against the perceived benefits of smoking, the role of the state as an appropriate protector of public health, and concerns about state intrusions on individual behavior. Thus, much of the cross-cultural dissonance can be traced to sharply different social and cultural expectations about appropriate approaches to harm reduction.

In U.S. culture, where there are high levels of individual moral expectation and responsibility, there are also fundamental questions about influence, control, and loss of agency. As a result, anti-tobacco advocates have typically focused on aspects of industry manipulation of smokers, imposition of harms to others, the involuntary aspects of addiction, and the insidious intent of the tobacco industry. In Europe, where 35 percent of the population smokes, countries have generally been slower to pass public smoking laws, and compliance with such regulation has sometimes lagged.[29] Clearly, many Europeans feel that U.S. policy is "extremist." As Italian professor Franco Ferrarotti explained, Americans "are going crazy over there. Once they tried to prohibit alcohol, which was maddening. Now they're going after tobacco."[30] Similarly, as Erik Albæk has shown in his case study of Denmark in this volume, the campaign against tobacco in the United States was seen by Danes as "too American."

A brief summary of national and cultural perspectives on smoking and its regulation reveals two important and largely alternative viewpoints that may be placed on a gradient. The first orientation, strongly represented by recent U.S. approaches described above, centers on the reduction and elimination of smoking as a serious risk to health. Canada and Australia have developed similarly aggressive campaigns, sometimes exceeding U.S. approaches to regulation. A landmark legal suit won in May 2001 by non-smoking pub worker Marlene Sharp, who contracted throat cancer, put Australia at the forefront of bans on public smoking.[31] In Melbourne, where new state legislation will make it legal to smoke only in outdoor sections of restaurants, one smoker described the new policy as "fair."[32] With 75 percent of Australians opposed to smoking in restaurants as of 1994, public attitudes did not stand in the way of these governmental regulations.[33]

In the United States, Australia, and Canada, for example, smoking has become a highly stigmatized behavior even though tobacco is a licit product. The risk of smoking has come to be perceived as situated within the domain of the *individual*. As a result, the *elimination* of risks came to rest upon the assertion of individual control. In fact, the use of cigarettes is doubly stigmatized. Not only have cigarettes come to be identified with individuals willfully disregarding their own health, but in their public (and familial) use, they have come to indicate a wanton disregard for others in the form of sidestream harms. Although this dual perspective has a basis in science and epidemiology, it is more fundamentally constructed in the intersection of science, culture, and advocacy. The cigarette has become the preeminent symbol of "needless" and "corrupt" risk; this approach to the cigarette focuses on strategies for its eradication (banished risk rather than reduced risk).[34]

In other cultures as diverse as France, Germany, Denmark, and Japan, the cigarette and its harms are configured in starkly different ways. These societies have decidedly different notions of risk, risk toleration, and the balance of risk/pleasure. In such views, risk may be irreducible, and there are complex trade-offs of social toleration and etiquette, pleasure, and personal liberty. Where, and precisely how, health comes to be configured in the assessment of behaviors deemed risky is also highly variable. In these societies, especially because there is a stronger norm of communal and environmental perspectives on maintaining public health, tobacco controls—so heavily focused on the control of individual behavior—do not easily resonate. Another consideration is that in these cultures there are sharply different notions of the appropriate role of the state in policing what are defined as "individual" behaviors, even when they pose risks to self and others. Moreover, in these societies, where anti-tobacco claims are perceived as but another example of U.S.-imposed cultural (and puritanical) imperialism, such claims are particularly suspect.[35] The United States' prohibitions on smoking and its hostility to the cigarette are widely understood as characteristic of a deep-seated risk aversiveness and of a moralism that leads to regulatory and legal excesses.

For critics in countries with more permissive attitudes toward smoking, U.S. tobacco policy simply became part of a larger set of symbolic meanings about U.S. intolerance, rudeness, and hostility to pleasure. "The American laws against smoking are totally intolerant," explained one French woman. "It is just like Monica and President Clinton . . . What I do personally isn't anyone's business. Smoking is simply a freedom of expression." A French flight attendant, commenting on a recent trip to the United States, explained, "It's like Americans have put their smokers in a cage."[36]

In some countries, such as those of Scandinavia, the rise of aggressive antismoking bans produced a backlash. Funded by tobacco interests, public organizations—like Hen-ry in Denmark and Smokepeace in Sweden (which was more sympathetic to state regulation)—worked to establish an accommodationist ethic in the wake of more stringent smoking bans. Hen-ry, a smokers' rights organization, enlisted Denmark's foreign minister, Uffe Ellemann-Jensen, to participate in an advertising campaign promoting "tolerance and consideration [as] the basis of living together."[37] Almost half of the Denmark population smokes, by far the greatest proportion in Europe, and women smoke as much as men.[38]

Other Scandinavian countries have criticized the Danes, especially the example set by their queen. Queen Margrethe, singled out for widespread criticism of her public chain-smoking, has been dubbed the "Ashtray Queen" by columnists. According to Hagge Geigert, a Swedish journalist, "The Queen smokes everywhere," with a special servant who apparently follows her around with an ashtray. [39] An article in the *Lancet* tied rising rates of female mortality in Denmark to the queen's public example:

> As a role model for women, the Queen's example could offer an expla-
> nation for the unusual mortality in Danish women . . . Although
> the negative effect of the Queen's behaviour could be expected to
> impact on both sexes, it is plausible to assume a greater impact on
> women . . . The question arises as to whether Queen Margrethe's
> behaviour could be a risk factor for population health in Denmark.[40]

Professor Hans Kesteloot, the author of the study, suggested that the queen should quit as an experiment to test his hypothesis (and her influence), but most Danes have met such suggestions with considerable indignation. In this instance the antismoking movement is perceived as an intrusive affront to the royal family. When asked how she was dealing with her smoking problem, the queen replied, "I have no problem."[41]

The queen's smoking touched off impressive cultural hostilities between Denmark and Sweden. Reacting to Swedish journalistic criticism of the queen, the Danes responded, "Keep on puffing, Margrethe." Others noted the "hypocrisy" of King Carl Gustaf of Sweden, who apparently will smoke only in private. "Is it a sign of responsibility for the Swedish king to slink off to the toilets to have a drag on the sly?" queried Ekstra Bladet, a Danish correspondent.[42] Such cross-cultural antagonisms—like French antipathy to U.S. anti-tobacco policy—perhaps reflect hostilities that are independent of tobacco policy. (Danes refer to their neighbor as "Prohibition Sweden" due to restrictive alcohol policies.)[43] But they do demonstrate how the cigarette has come to embody deeply held cultural values and perspectives; attitudes about the cigarette hold symbolic meanings that possess considerable social and political weight.

Another marker of cultural difference and policy effectiveness is compliance with regulations. Despite increasingly strong antismoking policies in France, they have been widely disregarded—unlike those in the United States. A British antismoking advocate observed, "France is a good example of where they made the mistake of introducing a law before they had public support."[44] From a policy perspective, the French experience with noncompliance to regulation strongly indicates—as it does with other countries— the significance both of the precise timing of public health campaigns, and of their more general "fit" with prevailing cultural norms and expectations.[45]

If we agree that social attitudes and values are a critical element of the successful regulation of smoking, especially in instances where compliance with regulations is largely voluntary and difficult to enforce, then it seems clear that the media plays a central role in shaping either support for, or resistance to, such measures. In the United States, the nonsmoker's entitlement to assert authority over the smoker is the result of a complex historical social process that connects science and risk, "social" epidemiology, and cultural meanings. This shift led to what some have recently called a "tipping point" in which there would be general widespread acceptance of, and compliance with, the public regulation of smoking.[46]

But tipping points are constituted by a range of social forces. It may well be that the tipping point in the United States was also a function of the large number of individuals who, in recent decades, had quit smoking. Not only did many of these individuals become new allies in the antismoking consensus, but the ratio of smokers to nonsmokers had fundamentally shifted. The fact that most U.S. physicians quit in the first decade following the 1964 surgeon general's report may have proven especially influential.[47] In the United States and other nations examined in this volume, the general shift to a sizable nonsmoking majority occurred most significantly on a socioeconomic gradient that is a function of the social and political influence of the educated middle class.

If regulation does not conform to cultural meanings and social mores, the result may well be—as it has been in France—the de-legitimization and ineffectiveness of anti-tobacco policy. In the United States, for instance, the scientific verification of harm to others (as limited as it may be) proved crucial to the radical redefinition of smoking. Once this tipping point was reached (circa 1990?), the significance of scientific arguments regarding harm were no longer quite so significant in pushing forward the process of stigmatizing smoking. Now, smoking as a *nuisance* could be utilized to promote and justify further regulation founded on no discernible health risks.

Even though some countries strongly resist abolitionist nonsmoking policies, they may still have independent reasons to take steps toward conformity in this regard. In a country like China, for example, where public smoking is so prevalent, government officials considered implementing bans in restaurants and public venues as they lobbied to have the

2008 Olympics in Beijing.[48] Nonsmoking appears to be the desirable international image for trade and commerce. U.S. anti-tobacco preferences have had notable implications for international business and travel. Hilda Klinkenberg, the president of Etiquette International, provides those who consult her with the following cautions: "Smoking is not only hazardous to your health, it can be hazardous to your career. Smoking is now considered a sign of weakness rather than a sign of sophistication. In fact, smoking has strong ethnic and class associations."[49] Similarly, Miriam Meijer advised travelers in her "Worldly Manners" column that, as a result of the United States' "complete cultural reversal" toward smoking, individuals should probably abstain if there was any doubt about the propriety of lighting up.[50]

The expectations of U.S. citizens that the world should follow their enlightened lead, however, may also encourage conflict. Letitia Baldrige, in her guide to executive manners, warns Americans to stop lecturing smokers. "It is never justifiable for us to give sermons to internationals on the fact that they should give up smoking," she writes. "Several business people from other countries have mentioned this objection with no small amount of passion."[51] For Americans, who have come to expect smoke-free environs, Ann Marie Sabath, in her *International Business Etiquette*, recommends new tolerance.[52]

Airlines: The Friendly Skies

Airlines have become both the actual and symbolic conduit connecting diverse states and cultures. Correspondingly, by the late twentieth century, international travel had become a fundamental aspect of many critical issues in public health. Although aggressive anti-tobacco regulations—especially the public bans on smoking—have often been associated in the last decade with U.S. repression and absolutism, we have nevertheless witnessed the diffusion of such regulations. In no instance have regulations been internationalized so successfully as in airline bans. Observing this process—and accounting for its success—may provide important models for the consideration of the implementation of more universal regulations in other settings. The airline smoking bans therefore provide a useful vehicle for assessing both cross-culturally significant support for regulation and persistent resistance. Further, travel literature on the diffusion of anti-smoking policies provides a window on changing attitudes, values, and accommodations concerning smoking. In the airline example, the significance of catering to the tourist and business-travel economy—as well as to other economic interests supporting control—has largely trumped particular national considerations and beliefs.

Airline bans are a useful test case for cross-cultural investigation because they have been a sensitive indicator of changing consumer expectations and demands in an industry that has strong national identity and interests, but—by its very nature—is in constant contact with other peoples and nations. Although regulatory processes vary from nation to nation in the airline industry, there has, over the last decade, been an impressive move toward total bans even in nations that are generally tolerant of public smoking in other venues. Nonetheless, as travelers fly in smoke-free plane cabins, it is also easy to forget the recent history of resistance to tobacco regulations in flight. This section, after a description of attitudes and policies concerning smoking on airlines in the United States as they initially developed, will explore the development of smoking bans internationally and the cultural significance of the diffusion of smoke-free flights.

Characteristic of the U.S. approach to smoking policy, organized consumer demand led the charge for antismoking policies on airlines. Calls for smoking bans on airlines date back to 1969, when consumer advocate Ralph Nader first asked the Federal Aviation Agency to eliminate smoking on flights. Along with this organized effort, many individual consumers also complained to airlines. In 1971 United Airlines became the first carrier to develop segregated seating for smokers and nonsmokers.[53] Two years later, the Civil Aeronautics Board (CAB) made nonsmoking sections a federal requirement. By 1982 GASP, the peripatetic antismoking advocacy group, had established a Non-smokers Travel Club for members eager to avoid exposure to smoke in their travels.[54]

But the airline industry and public commentators did not quickly jump on the smoke-free bandwagon. In a 1977 editorial criticizing a proposed federal regulation to limit the number of smoking seats on all planes, the *Washington Post* claimed, "The CAB should tell anti-smoking groups to back off. It's reasonable to make smokers sit in the back of the plane. But it isn't the airlines' business, or the government's, to decide how many passengers should be allowed to smoke."[55] With smoker's rights still holding sway, the country did not immediately embrace nonsmoking policies. Even though the federal government did mandate nonsmoking sections on all U.S. airlines, the airlines by no means accepted smoking bans. The airline industry also reacted against the idea of federal regulation of smoking on airlines, claiming that the industry should be free to assess how to accommodate passengers without outside interference. Airline executives worried about federal policies putting them at a competitive disadvantage internationally, about the logistics and costs of effectively separating smoking and nonsmoking sections, and about the extra work these policies would create for their in-flight personnel.[56]

The development of separate smoking sections on airplanes, however, did little to control smoke in the cabin environment. Smokers often selected nonsmoking seats, but would then congregate in the back of the plane to smoke. As one disgruntled passenger described in an outraged letter to the editor in 1983, "Why is smoking permitted at all on airplanes? There appears to be no effective way to section off the fuselage so that non-smokers can be adequately protected from drifting smoke . . . Health and safety benefits will far outweigh the inconvenience suffered by temporarily deprived smokers."[57] Passengers seated near the smoking section frequently filed complaints. One critic later suggested that "a smoking section on an airplane . . . is like having a peeing section in a swimming pool."[58] Airlines found no easy solution to the common accommodation of both smokers and nonsmokers. And to an impressive degree, nonsmokers increasingly felt entitled to demand smoke-free space.

In one particular context, airline restrictions and bans brought together rising concerns about cigarette use as *both* a nuisance and an occupational hazard. While it was sometimes difficult for nonsmoking passengers to justify their demands for a smoke-free flight on the basis of risks to health, such was not the case for flight attendants whose work required repeated exposure to smoke-filled cabins. Flight attendants became leading advocates for more aggressive regulation of smoking on flights. For them, exposure was anything but "passive;" it was required as part of their job. Joyce Hagen, a flight attendant, explained, "While we wait for someone to take the lead on this, we are breathing this carcinogen for hours at a time every time we fly."[59] In the United States, the flight attendants successfully sued "Big Tobacco" in *Broin v. Philip Morris,* a landmark case on secondhand smoke and liability. During the trial, Norma Broin, a nonsmoker who had contracted lung cancer in 1989 after fourteen years of exposure on flights, explained, "There was an incredible amount of dense, dense cigarette smoke."[60] Further indicating the public disdain for smoking and for the tobacco industry—especially in the instance of flight attendants who could not control their exposure—the case was eventually settled for the impressive sum of $349 million.

Despite flight attendants' attitudes and increased general-public sentiment that condemned smoking on flights, bans did not quickly follow. As late as 1984, the U.S. tobacco industry joined forces with the airline industry to help defeat a proposed CAB smoking ban on short flights. The CAB's chairman, Dan McKinnon, explained at the time, "Philosophically, I think nonsmokers have rights, but it comes into market conflict with practicalities and the realities of life."[61] Three years later, however, public sentiment and the antismoking lobby won out. Congress voted to ban smoking on all flights under two hours; and after two more years, it enacted a ban on all domestic flights. "People choose to smoke, but there is no choice about breathing," explained conservative Republican Senator Orrin Hatch of

Utah, a supporter of the legislation. Opposing airline bans, the industry sought to foment grassroots protest. "People who smoke cigarettes have a right to [do so]," noted Senator Jesse Helms of North Carolina (also a conservative Republican), "but they are going to have no choice."[62] Even so, more and more individual airlines instituted broader and broader smoking bans in the 1980s and 1990s.

Changes in smoking norms on the airlines had an important influence on the ground: airports also developed distinctive no-smoking policies. Through the 1990s, regulations on smoking in airports became increasingly restrictive. As airline bans became the norm, airports increasingly segregated those smokers seeking necessary nicotine hits prior to boarding flights. Nonetheless, experienced travelers would frequently comment on the variability of restrictions on smoking in public places within nations, as well as cross-nationally. U.S. travelers, for example, often observe the relative tolerance for smoking in Southern airports compared to other parts of the country.

Although smoking bans did not seamlessly emerge in the United States or anywhere else, they became more and more common across the world during the 1980s and 1990s. International political pressure was another factor in this trend. The World Health Organization and British Medical Association called for a total smoking ban on all passenger aircraft in 1990. This call was soon followed by a resolution from the International Civil Aviation Organization (ICAO)—a UN agency with over 180 member states—urging a ban. Charged with setting standards for safety, security, and efficiency of civil aviation, the ICAO attempted in 1993 to assert regulatory authority over all airlines. A number of nations and airlines, however, resisted that effort. Further, the ICAO lacks statutory authority over smoking policies. Nonetheless, the ICAO's regulatory efforts reflect the desire within airline regulatory agencies to establish uniform rules—including ones to ban smoking.

The smoking bans of the last thirty years have followed a discernible pattern across countries. Air Canada, the leader in the movement, provides a good example of this pattern. The airline announced a three-month test ban on smoking on forty-four of its domestic flights in 1986—the first Canadian airline to do so. By focusing on the flights of shorter duration, Air Canada attempted to assess the feasibility and popularity of the policy. In reaction to the announcement of the ban, Canada's three largest cigarette makers announced a boycott of the airline, with Michael Descoteaux, public relations director of Imperial Tobacco, proclaiming, "Air Canada says it wants the reaction of its customers, and we're saying in effect that if Air Canada is going to choose non-smokers for its customers, then we are going to choose to fly another airline."[63] Even with this strong reaction from the tobacco industry, Air Canada soon pushed forward with the ban, making it permanent on thirty-nine of the forty-four original test flights. By 1991, after a policy of progressive expansion, all of the airline's domestic and international flights were smoke free.

Air Canada quickly found substantial cost savings in smoking bans; in-flight smoking had typically required additional cleaning and maintenance costs. "We've saved $600,000 (Canadian) a year on cleaning and maintenance alone," noted Anna Karina Tabunar, a spokesperson for the airline, in 1993. "Smoke dirties air filters, carpets, seat covers," explained Tabunar. "And then there's the man-hours required to empty ash trays after every flight."[64] Although a number of concerns were consistently raised by critics as the airlines implemented new smoking bans, the bans generally went into effect with surprisingly few disruptions and broad consumer support.

The process of instituting smoking bans followed a similar pattern internationally, with the airline industry often finding bans to be in its interest. In some countries with entrenched smoking habits and strong popular opinion against the regulation of public smoking, however, the movement toward smoking bans was difficult. In August 1990, the German airline Lufthansa announced plans to ban smoking on all its domestic flights as of October 28, 1990.[65] By October, however, the airline dropped those plans, citing the potential for conflict between smokers and nonsmokers: "We feared trouble on board," said Lufthansa spokesman Peter Hoebel. "There was so much pressure in the last couple of days from the smokers' lobby that we thought there could be confrontations. Our stewards and stewardesses are not policemen." The longest domestic flight in Germany takes barely more than an hour. "You'd think that wouldn't be a great hardship," Hoebel said. "But there's a German mentality that does not like the idea of an airline telling them they can't do something."[66]

Lufthansa was not the only airline to retract smoking bans. In the early to mid-1990s, some airlines that had announced smoking bans were forced to reconsider as smokers sought other carriers. The tobacco industry pushed for such reconsideration. "The view that prohibition will be popular with the traveling public, attracting non-smokers and anti-smokers to the airline and increasing revenue, has been proved false," triumphantly noted FOREST (Freedom Organization for the Right to Enjoy Smoking) in its booklet *Travel in Tolerance.*[67]

Even so, by the late 1990s most European carriers had come into conformance with U.S. and Canadian practice, following a similar process that began with some airlines instituting test bans on short flights. Although bans were second-guessed and delayed, especially in countries such as Germany with strong sentiments against the regulation of public smoking, by 1995 even Lufthansa instituted smoking bans on domestic flights—and over the next few years moved toward a total ban. By April 1998, British Airways and Virgin Atlantic eliminated smoking sections on all planes and all routes, thereby joining Aer Lingus, Finnair, Icelandair, Lufthansa, and Scandinavian Airlines.

The widespread diffusion of airline bans on smoking, typically instituted by corporate rather than governmental policy, indicates the cross-national influence of anti-tobacco sentiment and advocacy. Such bans generally succeeded for a number of reasons. Once implemented by a few leading carriers, they proved popular. Even many smokers saw advantages in tolerating these limited intrusions. Planes were both cleaner and safer from fire risk—advantages shared by consumers and industry alike. Corporations reduced costs and potential worker liabilities. Finally, the consensus that arose around airline bans sustained high levels of compliance (aided by smoke detectors in lavatories).[68]

Japan and other Asian countries, Eastern European countries, and some developing countries mark the last bastion of airplane smoking, but they, too, have moved in the direction of smoking bans. Passenger routes and demand, however, continued to influence the persistence of smoking on some flights in spite of this growing consensus. Czech Airlines, Malev Hungarian Airlines, Swissair, and the Dutch national airline, KLM, have continued to permit smoking on flights to Africa, Asia, and Latin America, while flights to European destinations and North America are entirely nonsmoking. The national airlines of Greece and Russia—Olympia and Aeroflot, respectively—have fought this trend and continued to permit smoking on all flights.[69] The continued popularity of smoking in Japan required Japan Airlines and All Nippon Airways to continue to allow smoking on most flights, and KLM, in order to remain competitive, was forced in 1998 to reintroduce smoking on its Japan flights. "On the smoker-infested routes there are just too many nicotine addicts to alienate," explained a British travel journalist.[70] Even so, it's clear that nonsmoking flights have largely become the international norm. Tracing the presence or absence of smoking bans generates a "map" of relationships between regulated and unregulated nations, between the developed and developing world.

Ongoing attempts to accommodate smokers have ultimately failed. In 1995, Air France chief Christian Blanc, as part of a general effort to upgrade the luxury of Air France, promised to include elegant "smoking bars" on all longer flights. Although all seats on these flights would be nonsmoking, passengers would be invited to visit designated "salons."[71] These areas, the airline promised, would be fitted with special ventilation to expel the smoke. Ashtrays supplied with odor-absorbing crystals would automatically extinguish abandoned cigarettes. In late 2000, however, Air France implemented a total ban, succumbing to international diplomatic pressure to conform. The airline promised to provide nicotine-starved customers with a substitute, and in order "to help anxious smokers prepare for inflight duress," arranged to post a "physician specializing in smokers' disorders" at the airport in Paris.[72]

The recent history of airline bans suggests that smoking policy is determined by more than deep cultural traditions and national sociopolitical forces. Airline regulation of smoking occurred amidst wide international debate about smoking, risk, and policy. Even in those countries where smoking has remained highly prevalent, airline bans have often been implemented. In 1993 Cathay Pacific announced its intention to extend its in-flight smoking ban, which then existed on most flights between Asian countries, to its European routes. Even as Cathay implemented these bans, however, it continued to permit smoking on flights to and from Japan, due to passenger demand.[73]

Coda: The Double Meaning of Diffusion

This chapter has examined the diffusion of restrictions on public smoking—in particular, the bans on the use of cigarettes in the commercial airline industry. The historical account of the spread of these policies was deployed as an example of changing norms and values concerning tobacco, and their implication for local policies often not promulgated by state agencies or legislation. Yet it seems critical to point out an essential irony: while no-smoking policies have spread throughout the airline industry, cigarette smoking has sharply increased in the developing world. As anti-smoking regulations have been diffused, so, too, has the cigarette itself. As a result, we appear to be at the onset of a truly global pandemic of tobacco-related disease.

According to the World Health Organization, four million annual deaths are attributable to tobacco-related disease; half of these occur in the developing world. If current trends continue, this death toll is expected to mount to ten million by 2030. Seventy percent of all tobacco-related deaths will occur in the developing world. And by that time, if current trends continue, only 15 percent of total tobacco consumption will remain in developed nations. We are in the process of witnessing a shift—of truly seismic proportions—in tobacco consumption from richer to poorer nations; a shift with health implications of equal significance. The diffusion of effective anti-tobacco policies to the developing world dramatically lags behind the diffusion of smoking itself.[74]

Ironically, even as the United States has become so fundamentally hostile to smokers, cigarette smoking continues in other nations to be frequently associated with American modernity, style, and fashion. As one journalist explained

Even in countries where the American government is disliked, there is a reverence for American things . . . I came upon 17-year-old Daniel Fuqs, who was leaning against an iron fence . . . He was wearing Levi's and loosely laced Nikes, and smoking a Marlboro: "We like American cigarettes, American music, American clothing. The poorer Brazilian kids can't afford Nikes or Reeboks, so instead they buy baseball caps with the names of American teams. Anything to tie yourself to America. We resent American imperialism, but there is no other way."[75]

And the American advertising icons are everywhere. "The red-and-white Marlboro chevron is as familiar as Coca-Cola signs in nations with large numbers of smokers, like the Philippines, where the entire city of Manila smells like an all-night poker game."[76]

What is apparent to many observers is that there is a deep, unresolved moral contradiction in the simultaneity of U.S. antismoking campaigns and the nation's efforts to open up global markets to American tobacco. Thus, in the global village, Americanization, with its deep puritanical values, will demand no smoking on flights and in restaurants and hotels. The Hertz rental car counter in Tokyo will supply smoke-free cars, and smoke-free hotel rooms will be available at the Hilton in Jakarta. But despite these impressive diffusions of public bans and regulatory approaches to smoking, far more impressive is the continuing, unabated diffusion of cigarettes with their powerful associations to modernity and commerce. Any cross-cultural assessment of tobacco use and policy must recognize that even as international travel has extended the reach of no-smoking policies, the tobacco industry has even more impressively begun a process of recruiting new smokers to replace those who quit—or die—in Western developed democracies.

Tobacco Control in Comparative Perspective: Eight Nations in Search of an Explanation

Theodore R. Marmor and Evan S. Lieberman

Since the 1960s, governments in economically advanced democratic nations have significantly increased their regulatory control over tobacco. The prevalence of cigarette smoking, as the chapters in this book demonstrate, has diminished in these countries. Factors other than government policy—especially shifts in social norms—have influenced that decline, but those norms have themselves been directly and indirectly influenced by government policies. In short, tobacco consumption has become, in part, a political outcome. Governments have been sites of great conflict over the use of tobacco.

Reflecting on the experience of these eight nations, we are struck by important similarities and differences in the politics of tobacco control. Given the rich national histories presented in this volume, what value do we hope to add by our comparative analysis? Identifying the variation in government control policies is our starting point. Doing so requires us to clarify how we characterize the tobacco policies of particular countries and how we explain why they vary. Government policy is a relatively large and unwieldy subject of analysis, difficult to measure and to compare. In this respect, comparative tobacco-policy analysis is analogous to other forms of cross-national research on public policy, raising a number of long-standing debates within political science and sociology about the advantages and disadvantages of case study, structured comparison, and statistical methods.[1]

There are solid grounds for believing that the contemporary efforts of industrial democracies to control smoking reflect some common causes and, as a consequence, similar control policies. After all, the scientific evidence about the effects of smoking has substantiated long-standing, widespread health concerns about tobacco. Moreover, the international dissemination of scientific knowledge has undeniably helped to legitimate reform efforts across the nations whose experiences constitute the focus of this book. In addition, the chapters of this book show that by the end of the twentieth century, diverse modern democracies had come to use very similar instruments in the effort to discourage smoking in their populations. Available to the advanced industrialized democracies at least from the late 1950s, widely published information emerged in summary form in the U.S. surgeon general's report of 1964 (British and Canadian counterparts were published earlier). By the 1960s, elites in all the industrial democracies had substantial information about, and overwhelming scientific support for, claims that tobacco use harmed their citizens generally and was a major contributor to lung cancer and heart disease. Moreover, since health expenditures claimed a large share of the national budgets of all the countries considered in this book, the costs of treating tobacco-related diseases were (and are) plain to informed health policy actors. Concerns about the costs of smoking-related illness thus provided another common source of pressure to reduce tobacco consumption. Of course, state revenues from taxation on tobacco have provided a countervailing force—since budget officials gained revenues from the consumption of tobacco.[2]

Policymakers from this set of countries, these chapters demonstrate, have faced a relatively common and well-understood menu of possible control policies. In Australia, Canada, Denmark, France, Germany, Japan, the United Kingdom, and the United States, tobacco products are taxed above and beyond ordinary taxation on most goods. In every one of these countries, government policy makes some effort to limit tobacco-company advertising, to control tobacco sales and distribution, and to apply warning labels on cigarettes and other tobacco products in order to prevent or limit the use of tobacco. In all of these countries, paternalistic constraints on sales to nonadults have long been regarded as consistent with liberal democratic values. Moreover, certain public places came to be protected by every government as smoke-free zones. Airlines are now the most commonly restricted site, as Allan Brandt's chapter emphasizes. But the range of restricted sites varies from hospitals (common) to workplaces (increasingly common) to public parks (rare). The last two decades of the twentieth century, as these chapters illustrate, were years of convergence in the tobacco-control agendas not only of these eight nations but of all the industrial democracies.

The chapters of this book illustrate these similarities, and this convergence of policy calls for explanation. Indeed, one of the most important findings of this comparative study is the active and successful dissemination of evidence, argument, and program examples across the borders of quite different nations. Identifying the reasons for convergence in these respects is a task that we address in parts. Our central goal, however, is to address differences in the pace and paths taken in the tobacco-control efforts of the eight countries investigated.

It is much less clear exactly how to represent and interpret the magnitude of those comparative differences. Each of the eight countries, from the perspective of detailed policies and practices, employs what could be considered a unique configuration of tobacco controls. The "thick descriptions" of the individual country portraits well illustrate the varied approaches. They provide illuminating accounts of who did what to whom and when, with no two countries following precisely the same "script." So, for instance, it is obvious that Denmark came to rely on heavy tobacco taxes long before Canada and the United States, and did so less in order to control use than to increase tax revenues. Likewise, the modest French efforts to control where smoking is permitted show how much more vigorous such constraints now are in Australia, Canada, and the United States. When we turn to the intensity of implementation, the differences appear to be matters more of degree than of kind. Nonetheless, there is a serious problem in characterizing the level of implemented controls, and explaining why varied patterns of control may have emerged across the advanced, industrialized countries.

One way of thinking about such national differences is to raise the following hypothetical question. If a foreign visitor, innocent of the prevailing national norms and customs, were to travel to each of these countries and wanted to smoke, how would that person's experiences vary in terms of government prohibitions and controls? If we had a common measure of restriction, we would be better able to arrange the nations on a spectrum of tobacco-control intensity. With a more refined comparative measure of control, we would be able to more precisely analyze similarities and differences in the regulation of smoking in particular settings, whether bars, hospital waiting rooms, public parks, or public libraries. We have earnestly grappled, however, with how to understand the individual country portraits—accounts that embrace both idiosyncratic and common features. Crafting credible generalizations from the national portraits requires some simplification. With broad strokes, we seek to describe *tobacco-control regimes,* by which we mean the aggregated set of policies and practices that governments use to control tobacco.

Our further aim is to identify the extent to which these differences in tobacco-control regimes are predictable or unexpected from the perspective of well-known political, economic, and institutional features of these countries. For our purposes, the historical characterizations of tobacco control introduce more complexity than we can handle for our cross-national comparison. We therefore focus on explaining patterns of cross-national variation in tobacco-control regimes at the end of the twentieth century, and do not attempt to account for patterns of continuity and change within the respective country histories. Even this more modest task is neither straightforward nor easy. Detailed, "thick" descriptions of national control policies are not easily compared or explained.[3] Precisely because these country histories avoid simplistic characterizations of national policies, grouping countries into clusters that suggest explanatory patterns is a significant challenge. So, for example, legal traditions (common law versus civil code) do not seem to illuminate these policy histories. Nor does an easy division between Catholic and Protestant nations—and our sample was suitable for testing that hypothesis. Taking into account the structure and dynamics of states with unitary, rather than federal, political institutions proved a more promising approach, as Constance Nathanson has argued in a probing essay on comparative tobacco politics.[4] The respective tobacco-control regimes emerge as largely consistent with broader public attitudes about the importance of health and "well-being," but we have less confidence about whether such attitudes influence the development of control legislation, or if the direction of causation is reversed.

Variation in Tobacco-Control Regimes

We can begin to understand the range of variation in tobacco-control regimes by considering five logically possible outcomes:

Hands-off tobacco regimes. Governments in these countries have no policies restricting tobacco use or distribution, and any taxation associated with tobacco is indistinguishable from taxes on other products.

Low-control regimes. Such countries are defined by minimal efforts to control the use of tobacco. Policies to make the public aware of the dangers of smoking and to prevent minors from having easy access to cigarettes characterize such regimes. Tobacco taxes are low in these regimes.

Moderate-control regimes. These countries are defined by a significant set of tobacco-control policies across the broad spectrum of policy targets, including the promotion, distribution, and consumption of tobacco. What differentiates moderate- from high-control regimes is the degree of restrictiveness: the enforcement of some or all of the control policies may be more lax in the moderate regimes; taxation may not be particularly high; and restrictions on tobacco may be more measured.

High-control regimes. These countries are characterized by high levels of taxation on tobacco products and by across-the-board policies that tightly restrict the promotion and consumption of tobacco.

Prohibitionist regimes. Tobacco use is banned completely, and people are seriously punished for selling or consuming tobacco.

In practice, none of the countries investigated in this book is an example of either of the two extremes. The eight nations vary across the range of what we have described as low to high control. To classify the countries by degree of policy restraint, we distinguish sharply between taxation and other forms of tobacco control. One reason for doing so concerns the countervailing fiscal imperative of tobacco taxation. After all, for much of the history of tobacco use, governments regarded tobacco taxation exclusively as a means of generating revenue, not as an instrument of health promotion. It makes sense, then, to separate taxation levels from the other types of restrictions placed on the tobacco industry and cigarette consumers. The problem is not that taxation levels are less important in influencing smoking behavior. In fact, the scientific consensus is that the price elasticity of tobacco consumption is relatively high.[5] Rather, the problem is that taxation is a more complex policy matter than, for example, regulating where smoking is permitted. With taxation, finance and health ministries can agree on higher prices for opposite reasons: increasing revenues in the first instance and reducing smoking in the second. Whether this tax measure correlates well with regulatory restrictions is something to be discovered rather than assumed. And as we have discovered, there is room for doubt.

In the case of taxation, it is relatively easy to compare the tax that each country levied per pack of cigarettes during any given time period. We gathered data from the World Bank Economics of Tobacco Control Project, which reported cigarette taxes per pack for 1995 in U.S. dollars. In 1995, the average taxes for the eight countries were $2.43 per pack, and ranged from a low of $.58 per pack in the United States to a high of $4.38 per pack in Denmark.[6]

In examining the results in Figure 11.1, we found ourselves wondering whether in trying to control tobacco consumption, countries use tax and nontax policy instruments in tandem. As it turns out, there is clearly some correlation between these two components of tobacco-control regimes as we have defined them. But the connection is quite mixed, with Canada and the United States providing contradictory evidence. Tax competition under federalism may well be part of the explanation for the low level of tobacco taxation in the United States; the fear is that wide variations in tax levels among states would encourage smuggling. But Canada's federal regime provides evidence of high national levels of taxation along with significant variations in provincial taxes. The instability of the high-tax Canadian regime may well make the North American experience less problematic, but we are still left with the puzzle of the Australian federal example of very high tax levels as shown in Figure 11.1.

There is clearly a strong relationship between levels of tobacco taxation and overall levels of taxation in the countries studied. Although a cohort of eight countries is not a powerful sample for statistical analysis, the correlation coefficient estimating the relationship between tobacco taxes per pack and the ratio of central state taxation to gross domestic product is .67—implying that almost 50 percent of the variance in tobacco taxes can be explained by the country's tax regime. (If taxes from all levels of government are included, the statistical relationship is weaker.) Of course, there are several possible causal explanations for this correlation. One hypothesis is that in high-tax countries, it is easier to pass high taxes of any kind. A second is that levels of taxation reflect the size and authority of the state

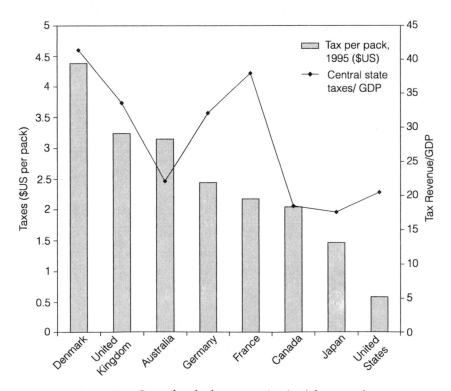

Figure 11.1 General and tobacco taxation in eight countries

within society, and that in countries with higher levels of taxation, we should expect higher levels of tobacco control, of which tobacco taxation is one component. Where substantial welfare states are involved, any substantial luxury tax that is legitimate commands attention.

Regarding nontax policies designed to restrict smoking, it was necessary to aggregate the instruments used to change smoking behavior and those used to limit the available options for where people may smoke. Given the difficulties of measuring such policies comparatively with any precision, we opted for a rough-and-ready three-point scale, ranging from low (1), to medium (2), to high (3). Applying this scale required that we categorize countries in terms of both the scope and the (apparent) intensity of their tobacco-control policies. (We could not confidently categorize the enforcement of those policies, for which reliable data are much harder to obtain.) That is to say, we considered both the sheer quantity of restrictions on tobacco use, as well as the degree to which they appear to have been implemented through voluntary agreements, legal guidelines, or bans on smoking in particular places.

Without a shared standard for measuring nontax policies for restricting smoking, we deployed two main sources of data and several alternative specifications for interpreting those data. First, we used the country chapters as the initial source of data. Based on our reading of those chapters, we initially scored each country on the three-point scale. Second, we surveyed the authors of those chapters and asked them to reduce their detailed characterizations of the contemporary tobacco-control regimes and provide us with answers using the same metric. We received responses from all of the authors and found that our readings were somewhat at odds with how the authors themselves characterized their respective national portraits. In the cases of Canada and Japan, there was agreement that the evidence pointed to cases of high and low control, respectively. Denmark, the United Kingdom, and the United States produced only small discrepancies, with all three countries scoring as high or medium-high for at least the contemporary period.[7] But in France and Germany, important differences in interpretation emerged. Both of us interpreted Germany as an instance of low control, while the author scored it as one of medium control. The two of us initially interpreted the chapter on France differently—one as involving high control, and the other, low control—while the author scored it as a case of high control. How strongly the antismoking policies were implemented and/or enforced proved to be the source of our different interpretations. Ultimately, we concluded that France was best classified as a case of "low-medium" control. Legal rules and their enforcement are separable dimensions of such restrictions. Simply knowing what the "law" is does not enable us to say which particular practices dominate.

Table 11.1 Comparing country scorings of national tobacco control

	Tobacco control scores			Tax/pack
	Readers	Author	American Cancer Society	World Bank
Australia	3 (3,3)	3	3	$3.15
Canada	3 (3,3)	3	3	$2.04
Denmark	2.5 (3,2)	2.5	3	$4.38
France	2 (3,1)	3	3	$2.17
Germany	1 (1,1)	2	2	$2.44
Japan	1 (1,1)	1	1	$1.46
United Kingdom	2.5 (3,2)	3	3	$3.24
United States	2.75 (2.5, 3)	3	2	$0.58

Sources: Country chapters, World Bank Economics of Tobacco Control Web site

Finally, we considered the very extensive American Cancer Society report on tobacco control around the world, which included country profiles of national policies.[8] In investigating four of the report's policy categories (advertising and sponsorship, sales and distribution restrictions, tobacco product regulations, and smoke-free indoor air restrictions), we developed a numerical index for the state of legislation in each area, assigning more weight to policies that involved outright bans, and less weight to policies encouraging voluntary cooperation. We then took a straight average of the scores of those four policy areas, each of which had been assigned a numerical score of 1 for low control, 2 for medium control, and 3 for high control, in order to arrive at an overall index of the extent of nontax tobacco control in each country.

The results of the above exercise largely confirmed the findings from the interpretations set forth in the country chapters—with modest, but not trivial, discrepancies. The American Cancer Society's data suggested, for example, that the United States had a less intensive control regime than what is reported in this book's country chapter. The society's score for Denmark was slightly higher, and its scores for France and Germany were a full point higher than ours (as were the scores by the respective authors). These differences illustrate the general problem in cross-national studies of identifying which phenomena are equivalent and therefore need to be similarly explained. With these qualifications in mind, we compare the eight cases in an exploratory mode.

In Figure 11.2, we plotted each of the eight countries by what we take to be their tax and nontax control policies during the late 1990s. We found several interesting patterns of convergence and divergence in the scoring of national policies. These patterns bring into clearer relief some of the more interesting puzzles apparent in the countries' distinctive trajectories of tobacco control. No country is a more obvious example of a low-control tobacco regime than Japan, where both tax and nontax control policies are slack. But that does not mean that Japan is free of antismoking influences. Indeed, there have been important changes in the world of Japanese smoking; for example, as Eric Feldman notes, the level of smoking has fallen substantially in recent decades, and the range of places where it is thought appropriate to smoke has become much more restricted. What is especially noteworthy, however, is that Japanese public policy does not appear to have been the main instrument of these changes.[9] The Japanese case study illustrates, moreover, the cross-national transfer of tobacco-control strategies; witness the recent efforts to use litigation as a means of circumventing the inaction of the executive and legislative branches of government.

We have classified as high-control regimes Australia, Canada, Denmark, and the United Kingdom. Although in Canada, taxes per pack are lower than in the other high-control cases,[10] and most of the intensity of Canada's tobacco control arose fairly late, in the mid-1980s, ultimately, Canada's

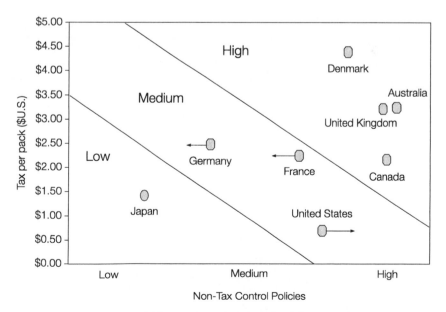

Figure 11.2 Tobacco control regimes in eight countries

extensive nontax controls during the period under investigation justify its classification as a case of high control.

In the middle of our grouping are France, Germany, and the United States, all of which are more difficult to classify. Both France and Germany have medium-level taxes between $2.00 and $3.00 per pack, and the United States has extremely low tobacco taxes (on average). Our interpretation of nontax control policies suggests that France and Germany may be closer to the low-control regimes and that the United States may be closer to the high-control regimes based on levels of implementation in practice. Nathanson's overall portrait of French law and practice supports our interpretation, by emphasizing the gap between strict legal controls and restrained enforcement, especially on the issue of where one might smoke in public. Likewise, Günter Frankenberg's detailed discussion of tobacco policy in Germany does not support an interpretation of vigorous control. Indeed, what is striking about both the French and German cases is the degree to which the enforcement of nontax tobacco controls remains relatively lenient. Moreover, in the United States there are wide differences in how particular states regulate and control tobacco. The interpretation of policy in these federal countries is, as a consequence, strongly mediated by how subnational variation is taken into account.

Discussion and Analysis

As noted earlier, we began our investigation with a variety of hypotheses about what might explain variations in tobacco-control policies. In practice, we have mostly sought to understand the shape of those policies and to suggest, more than provide, explanations. For example, in reflecting on our scores for the eight countries' tax and non-tax control policies, we ended up highlighting puzzles for which no easy answers are immediately apparent. Some aspects of the cross-national variation seem readily explainable from what we already know about these countries. Other aspects appear explainable only in terms of historically contingent political contexts or the countries' idiosyncratic configurations of the tobacco industry, political organization, and policy responses—that is, through the "thick" descriptive accounts set forth in each country's case study. In this section, we want to describe our admittedly tentative interpretation of some of the leading explanatory claims about tobacco control.

There is now a moderately large literature that purports to describe and explain tobacco politics and policies.[11] Our purpose here is not, however, to provide a definitive statement about the merits of different explanatory approaches, but simply to highlight what seem to be promising ways to make sense of the complex portraits presented in this book. In particular, we attempt to explore hypotheses elaborated within the country chapters, and we address three classes of explanatory approaches—policy diffusion, political culture, and political institutions.

The *policy diffusion* literature in comparative political analysis provides accounts that link national experience through the various means by which policy-reform ideas move across borders. This approach is undoubtedly helpful in making sense of the increased control of smoking that we observe in all the national portraits (if not all of the advanced industrialized nations). It is surely the case that cross-border diffusion helps to explain the similar menu of programmatic interventions in tobacco control. As is plain from the national case studies in this volume, the scientific information about tobacco's effects has been widely diffused. Moreover, there was also surely diffusion of information about tobacco-control modes. These approaches to control—whether tax increases, education campaigns, limits on where smoking could take place, or restrictions on advertising or sports sponsorship—were first diffused by networks of scientific and public health actors, and later by what amounted to internationally linked social movements and pressure groups.

Indeed, from a global perspective, the diffusion of these pressures has led to some degree of convergence in tobacco-control regimes. Smoking has been transformed from an accepted (and romanticized) habit in the middle of the twentieth century to a challenged, if not reviled, practice by the opening of the twenty-first century. Donley Studlar's work demonstrates the increased salience in contemporary control regimes of "denormalizing" smoking.[12] That has involved making smoking itself sinful, stupid, or both. And it also involve demonizing those who produce, sell, or use tobacco products. By contrast, the harm-reduction principle of traditional public health is perfectly consistent with educational campaigns, but not vilification. There is considerable evidence in this volume that by the beginning of the twenty-first century, the effort to turn tobacco smokers and producers into pariahs had become crucial elements in anti-tobacco movements.[13]

However, the diffusion argument is less useful for explaining patterns of variation. Typically, diffusion arguments suggest the importance of physical proximity as a basis for policy adoption, but the comparative portrait we present in Figure 11.1 contradicts this view: the neighboring pairs of Germany and Denmark and the United States and Canada appear more different than similar in the overall characterizations of tobacco control. Moreover, the clustering of the United Kingdom, Australia, and Canada as largely similar types of tobacco-control regimes, despite the fact that these countries are located at different corners of the globe, suggests the need to consider other approaches. Even in the face of European Union (EU) efforts to gain supranational control over tobacco use, the codification and implementation of policies have remained nationally distinct within Europe.

What is termed *political culture* in comparative politics is another plausible approach to explaining variation in the control measures adopted or rejected.[14] We reject the notion of a "smoking" culture as a determinant of tobacco-control regime-type, because smoking has been popular in all of the countries under examination in this volume, and norms and patterns of tobacco use have changed in response to new information and especially to changes in government policy. An alternative view of the possible influence of culture would relate more general norms and customs regarding the paternalistic nature of the state and authority, and the value of liberal individualism to the propensity of a given country to adopt more or less aggressive control measures.

A classic statement of how such cultural patterns can shape other types of political and economic outcomes is Max Weber's *Protestant Ethic*,[15] which is perhaps the most well-known example of how religious orientations can shape institutions and outcomes as profound as the functioning of modern capitalism. For the more focused problem considered here, one might imagine that the more Catholic the nation, the more accepting its political culture would be of alleged "sins" like smoking, and the less onerous would be the implemented forms of control. Alternatively, one could imagine higher levels of paternalism in Catholic approaches. Yet neither the country portraits in this book nor our own interpretations provide a solid basis for this way of explaining tobacco-control policies. For instance, the varying policies over time within each country argue against using religious or cultural orientations as a cross-national explanation. As Brandt has argued, basic cultural foundations change less rapidly than smoking habits. The United States, where prohibitionist zeal was vividly expressed in alcohol control, went from a nation that broadly celebrated smoking during the World War II era to one that, a few decades later, was home to some of the globe's most zealous critics of smoking behavior and of tobacco companies. Similarly, Canada's widespread acceptance of smoking as late as the early 1980s gave way to an equally zealous condemnation by both public authorities and anti-smoking figures a decade later.

A more promising approach to culture is contained in the investigation carried out by Ronald Inglehart and Marita Carballo of the World Values Survey.[16] Although their view of culture is not infinitely malleable, it explicitly allows for changing norms and values over time. Reporting results from their 1990–1991 surveys, they provide a mapping of countries in terms of the values emphasized by different societies—both in terms of the emphasis on "survival" versus "well-being,"[17] and "traditional authority" versus "secular-rational authority." Along these dimensions, the United States clusters with Canada as a "North American group," and Denmark with Germany as a "Northern Europe group." France clusters with "Catholic Europe," Japan with China and Korea (labeled by Inglehart and Carballo as the "Confucian countries"), and the United Kingdom straddles both the "Northern Europe group" and a larger cluster of "English-speaking countries," which includes Canada and the United States. Although the survey was not conducted in Australia, one would assume that it would cluster with this last group. This ordering of countries in terms of culture does a better job of predicting tobacco-control regimes than would a more narrow focus on religious orientations, particularly given the high degree of religious heterogeneity in many of the countries studied.

Most importantly, Denmark and Japan are described in Inglehart and Carballo's study as extreme cases in terms of the degree to which societies value "well-being" (Denmark) versus "survival" (Japan), and this maps perfectly onto our scoring of the tobacco regimes, as depicted in Figure 11.2. France and Germany appear as "intermediate" cases along the cultural continuum; they are intermediate cases of tobacco control. However, the cultural framework is less useful for explaining differences in tobacco-control regimes among the United Kingdom, the United States, and Canada, which are depicted as having highly similar cultures. Nonetheless, Inglehart and Carballo's view of culture provides a reasonable degree of explanatory power, as the basic emphasis on "well-being" within societies appears to correlate, if not perfectly, with the extent of tobacco control. We still cannot be sure, however, if tobacco and other forms of social control influence these cultural attitudes or if the reverse is true.

A third explanatory framework can be drawn from a literature on *political institutions,* which relates variations in institutional rules to cross-national differences in policy outcomes.[18] The notion here is that policy outcomes depend not merely on the underlying preferences of actors within society, but on how those preferences get aggregated and adjudicated. Among the economic interests with influential concerns are tobacco farmers, those media that are dependent on tobacco advertisements, the manufacturers and distributors of tobacco products, and most importantly, local and multinational tobacco companies. They compete with ministries of health, finance, and various political groups that may desire both tax and nontax controls. All of the countries studied in this book face all these constituency pressures (with the exception of tobacco farmers in countries where this crop is not a significant industry). What differs from country to country is the particular configuration of the institutional channels through which these interests seek expression.

In particular, many of the chapters suggest that the impact of a polity being organized along federal or unitary principles should be considered as an important explanatory principle. However, there are again conflicting views about how to interpret the influence of such institutional differences. One hypothesis is that unitary states, if they have the political will, have the institutional structure to implement control policies more quickly and effectively because they enjoy a more uniform sphere of influence. Holding reform pressures constant, it is plausible that unitary regimes would be able to implement more extensive controls earlier and more concertedly than nonunitary regimes. On the other hand, it appears quite plausible from the country chapters that the location and influence of reform pressures actually vary across countries according to institutional differences. In federal polities, political pressures for control are more likely to be pressed in those subnational units where they are most likely to meet success, providing greater opportunities for innovation. In unitary regimes, there is arguably only one key arena in which political conflict over tobacco control is likely to take place, and opponents of control can focus their power and influence at the national level. The implications for tobacco control appear to be important.

For example, Constance Nathanson argues that different types of actors will emerge as influential within different types of institutional settings. She has noted that where hierarchical and centralized political arrangements provide access for elites—especially scientific ones in the case of tobacco—a distinctive mode of tobacco-control policymaking emerges. The cases of unitary states in our sample—Denmark, France, Japan, and the United Kingdom—illustrate that claim. By contrast, the less centralized, federal states—Australia, Canada, the United States, and, to a lesser extent, Germany—illustrate the greater impact of outsiders, of nonscientific advocates willing to be more provocative in their challenge to smoking and the tobacco firms. The federal states included in this volume provide ample evidence of diffusion—of evidence, argument, and tactics—across the subnational units.

In all regimes, institutional arrangements shape the strategies of the actors, as the country portraits fully document. In every case, the tobacco industry spends substantial sums defending its interests; that is no surprise. But which groups take up the banner of tobacco control does vary considerably among the cases. In federal regimes with ideological heterogeneity, one would expect control advocates to shop for venues to pursue antismoking policy reforms. Elite accommodation of organized interests is more likely to be found in the unitary states. We would expect extreme political actors to be more powerful in federal systems, and indeed, with the exception of Germany, that is precisely what we found in the country portraits.[19]

This perspective makes sense of the commonality in the high level of nontax control policies that emerged by the end of the twentieth century in Australia, Canada, and the United States. We are not suggesting that federalism itself is the explanation. Indeed, it is surely true that federal regimes make national leadership over subnational units generally more difficult, as the case of Canada suggests. (Canada represents an instance where national institutions came to play a major role in advocating tobacco controls.) Instead, we believe that there is a crucial interaction of federalism, pressure-group strategies, and social movements in liberal regimes. That interaction makes it more likely that the most vigorous attacks on tobacco interests will arise first at the local level rather than at the level of national politics.[20]

Although most of the federal cases tend toward high-control, nontax policies, the unitary states are more varied in their approach to tobacco control. Again, Japan and Denmark represent the important extremes along the control continuum while simultaneously being cases of unitary states. Within our small sample, this suggests that the presence of federalism provides a more consistent influence on outcomes than does the absence of this institutional feature. Although we have not systematically compared the extent of tobacco control at the subnational level, the evidence available to us indicates that some of the most extreme forms of tobacco control are enacted within particular subnational units in the federal countries. For example, California and Minnesota are antismoking leaders, even while states such as Alabama and Georgia maintain more minimal controls. Similarly, British Columbia is far more restrictive than Alberta, and New South Wales than Queensland. We believe that federalism provides more opportunities for policy innovation, and in turn, that policy diffusion tends to be easier across subnational units than across countries (as discussed earlier in this chapter). In unitary states, antismoking radicals are less likely to be influential if they do not have a strong, national constituency. This may explain why the unitary states demonstrate very high- or very low-control regimes, whereas the federal polities tend toward medium and high control. In federal countries, just a few important pockets of tobacco-control advocacy can be successful in pushing for at least a modicum of legislation.

Germany is an exception to the claim that federalism will lead to more tobacco control. As it turns out, the potential impact of "competitive federalism" has been counterbalanced by resistance to aggressive health promotion policies. Günter Frankenberg's chapter on Germany identifies several factors that he hypothesizes as having contributed to relatively low levels of tobacco control, including the revenue imperative, skillful tobacco and media industries, the popularity of smoking, a limited group of enlightened experts, and the absence of a successful social movement, in the wake of resistance to state paternalism. Frankenburg argues that such resistance rests, in part, on the legacy of coercive, morally objectionable,

Nazi-era policies directed at improving the health of the German nation. Of the plausible explanations for German exceptionalism, only the last withstands comparative scrutiny. The first three are present in cases of both low- and high-control regimes, and the absence of experts seems to be more a product of potential political impact than lack of information, given the widespread availability of common scientific knowledge about the effects of smoking. This is not to say that the other factors he identifies do *not* matter. Rather it is that the task of explaining the German case requires that we identify why these forces were *more* powerful as checks on efforts to control tobacco than in the other countries.

While cross-national variation in the presence or absence of federalism helps to explain some of the important differences in tobacco-control regimes, clearly the relationship is not perfectly linear, nor does it trump all nationally specific political histories and legacies. If we had characterized countries in an alternative manner—for example, comparing countries in terms of the most extreme local examples of control, rather than using broad national portraits that incorporate "typical" subnational policies, the relationship between federalism and the extent of tobacco control might have appeared stronger. Other types of institutional variation, including the nature of political party systems, or the presence/absence of plebiscitary mechanisms for adopting policies could be explored in future research about the political determinants of tobacco policy.

Conclusions

Understanding the determinants of contemporary tobacco regimes requires that we understand the factors and pressures that simultaneously influenced convergence and divergence across countries. A mix of general-izable and historically contingent factors must be taken into account.

Our comparative analysis, though more modest in historical scope than what is presented in the single-country studies in the previous chapters, has attempted to provide a coherent synthesis of contemporary tobacco-control regimes in eight advanced, industrialized democracies. It prompted us to ask some general questions about the determinants of policy and practice. We do not pretend to provide any simple conclusions about why tobacco-control regimes vary across these countries—our analyses are admittedly rudimentary. However, we have attempted to demonstrate some of the analytic value added by an expressly comparative approach, in which the possibilities for reaching general conclusions are far greater than in single-country studies.

One of the lessons from this collective exercise is simple, but important. In comparative policy analysis, the twin problems of conceptualization and measurement are, to say the least, challenging. State authority comes in many forms, and it is not always easy to describe the differences as simply "more" or "less." We believe that our attempts to simplify—when combined with this book's country chapters—constitute a contribution that gains analytical insights without loss of historical specificity and context.

Our overall conclusion is that certain factors predictably constrain the development of tobacco-control regimes, and political institutions provide an important starting point for explaining patterns of cross-national variation, even if they do not determine the control policies of a given country or the role of the state in tobacco more generally. More general cultural orientations toward "well-being" do appear to be associated with the extent of control policies, but the exact direction of causality cannot be inferred from our analysis. Because these countries are all wealthy democracies, levels of income and political regime type cannot be said to explain differences among these countries, but such factors would likely be influential in a broader comparative study.

Although we do not take a normative approach in this investigation of tobacco control, we believe that this restricted comparative analysis shall be useful to others trying to understand the national histories of tobacco control in order to design and to reform policy. Simply put, it is not possible to draw lessons about tobacco reform from other countries without a baseline understanding of how countries compare, particularly in the contemporary era. The complexity of national context and national histories is important, as the chapters in this book reveal. But given the welter of experience, there is value to simplification as well.

Conclusion:
Lessons from the Comparative
Study of Tobacco Control

The case studies in this volume,[1] as well as the cross-national chapters, underscore the rich differences among liberal democracies in their understandings of public health, their conceptions of freedom of expression, and their tolerance of risk-taking behaviors that may also impose harms on others. Despite the universal recognition of the toxicity of cigarette smoking, and a shared tool box of possible policy interventions, these case studies reveal the emergence by the end of the twentieth century of a complex array of tobacco-control strategies in eight industrialized democracies.

As we considered the underlying political, legal, economic, and sociocultural features of the nations brought together in this project, and sought to identify and understand both similarities and differences in their tobacco-control regimes, we identified four particularly important themes. They did not so much inform the national case studies as emerge from them. Hence they serve both as conclusions to this comparative study and as a starting point that could orient others who may press the comparison in new and revealing directions.

The four themes are:

- Science and evidence have played a critical but not determinative role in influencing anti-tobacco advocacy and policy. In the face of uncertainties and ambiguities, ideological and political factors have been central.
- The identification of vulnerable third parties held to be in need of protection has been a crucial justification for anti-tobacco policy and advocacy.

- Public policy alone does not explain the extent to which the demography of smoking has changed. Broad cultural and social changes have also been important.
- Over the past five decades, smoking has been transformed from a behavior that knew no social bounds. A social gradient has now emerged. Class differentiates smokers and nonsmokers.

Science and Evidence Influence but Do Not Determine Tobacco-Control Policy

The contemporary campaign to regulate tobacco began with innovative epidemiological studies in the 1950s that were supplemented and consolidated during the following decade. From the outset, the evidence presented by cancer epidemiologists and public health advocates was debated by the scientific community and challenged by industry.[2] A series of studies by Richard Doll in Great Britain and American Ernst Wynder, among others, demonstrated a compelling connection between smoking and lung cancer. Those studies clearly showed a correlation between smoking and disease; what was less clear, at least to some, was whether the data justified conclusions about the *causal* relationship between tobacco consumption and cancer.[3] Equally vexing was the question of what types of policy interventions, if any, were justified. Those committed to the protection of public health, whether governments or private parties, embraced the data, however limited, as supporting (sometimes necessitating) the implementation of innovative policy. Others, particularly but not exclusively those tied to some part of the tobacco industry, emphasized the data's limitations and demanded policy restraint.

These conflicting approaches still characterize controversies over smoking policy. The tobacco industry continues to be particularly attentive to the uncertainties and ambiguities of the science surrounding tobacco and health, exploiting them even when the data are compelling. Using its considerable financial power, the industry funds research and disseminates allegedly scientific findings aimed at delegitimizing respectable scientific inquiry and creating uncertainty about even the most compelling evidence. In part out of necessity, public health and anti-tobacco activists, albeit on a smaller scale, also invoke ambiguous or incomplete data to press their claims, at times over-interpreting, on other occasions ignoring or minimizing, the significance of inconvenient findings. They do so because of their focus on the gravity of tobacco's dangers and their desire to marshal broad-based support against the tobacco industry.

In the United Kingdom, few immediate policy consequences resulted from Doll's work. The British tobacco industry, with its long-standing ties to the government, funded research through the Medical Research Council that took issue with some of his findings. Scientific conflict was not the only barrier to reshaping public health policy in light of the newly discovered link between smoking and cancer; the government was ambivalent about the policy implications of this knowledge, because it threatened to undermine a crucial source of state revenue.[4] A different set of concerns can be found in France, where the emerging scientific consensus that smoking was a cause of lung cancer made hardly a ripple. Not only were the important U.K. and U.S. studies in the 1950s unnoticed; the French managed substantially to ignore the two most important scientific reports on the health consequences of smoking—the 1962 U.K. Royal College of Physicians (RCP) study, and the 1964 U.S. surgeon general's report.

Canada also provides an interesting example of the disjuncture between science and policy. In 1961, a year before the RCP issued its internationally influential report on smoking and cancer, and three years before the surgeon general's report ignited the contemporary U.S. anti-tobacco movement, the Canadian Medical Association concluded that smoking caused lung cancer. The association's views, however authoritative, did not have a discernable influence on the creation of tobacco-control policy. Instead, it took ten years for federal legislation to be introduced that was aimed at limiting smoking, and the legislation was ultimately rejected in favor of voluntary industry self-regulation.

Resistance has been striking in Germany and Japan, where what are now almost universally regarded as scientific facts continue to be disputed. In Germany, for example, industry fought the mandated European Community cigarette packet warning, which read: "The EC Health Ministers: Giving up smoking reduces the risk of serious disease." The German Minister of Health asked the EC to change the warning to include the word "may" (before "reduce"), and when the EC refused, the government brought the case to the German Federal Constitutional Court. Politicians, some legal scholars, and (predictably) the tobacco industry also criticized the directive, arguing that it merely restated the views of American cancer experts, whose ideas were allegedly based on questionable data and unreliable studies. Likewise, in Japan, the small number of epidemiologists, an inadequate budget, and the influence of finance officials on tobacco policy limit the capacity of the Ministry of Health, Labor, and Welfare to monitor and act on scientific studies of smoking and health.

In national battles over tobacco advertising, decisions were made to impose partial restrictions (for example, prohibitions on advertising in some media, but not in others) or bans before there was evidence about how such measures might affect tobacco consumption.[5] Of eleven studies conducted in the United States, Australia, and the United Kingdom between 1972 and 1986, seven showed that limitations on advertising had no effect on smoking, three found a small but ambiguous positive effect, and only one indicated a less ambiguous positive effect. A 1975 study, based on data from eleven OECD countries, found that advertising bans had no impact on tobacco consumption.[6] Assumptions about the role of advertising in consumer culture, sprinkled with a common-sense notion that if advertising didn't sell more products manufacturers would not bother to advertise, informed the early advertising limitations. Those who opposed restrictions—primarily the tobacco industry and the media that benefited from advertising revenue—argued that advertising served only to lure smokers from one brand to another. Even as international evidence began to mount that partial restrictions on advertising had little if any impact on consumption, many nations remained wedded to such measures, perhaps because they were more politically acceptable than total advertising bans.

In Australia, for example, the industry began voluntarily regulating advertising on television in the 1960s. The Danish government was even more aggressive. An expert committee of the Ministry of Interior in 1964 proposed a draft bill that banned all forms of tobacco advertising—there has never been advertising on broadcast media—but the bill failed, and the nation turned to industry self-regulation. Antismoking groups in Germany have, since the 1970s, pressed for a total advertising ban, but there, too, the industry has managed to maintain voluntary advertising limits. The British government moved in 1967 to ban and/or limit various forms of promotion and advertising, but Labor's concern about its working-class constituency, not industry influence, thwarted its effort. It seems that at least some parties to the British debate recognized that although the evidence on the impact of advertising bans was ambiguous, banning advertisements was an important symbol of the growing social unacceptability of smoking. Such symbolism was also meaningful to the Institute of Medicine in the United States as it sought to address this issue.[7]

Using evidence about the harms of environmental tobacco smoke (ETS) to justify restrictions on smoking in public settings was also controversial. Evidence came initially from studies of the nonsmoking spouses of smokers, particularly a 1981 Japanese paper by Takeshi Hirayama, "Non-Smoking Wives of Heavy Smokers Have a Higher Risk of Lung Cancer: A Study from Japan," published in the British Medical Journal.[8] A critical question was raised by this study—did these findings have any traction when removed from the domestic environment and applied to other settings? It was one thing to apply the conclusions from Hirayama's work on smoking and nonsmoking spouses to other similarly enclosed environments, like small workplaces or airplanes. It was a greater stretch to assert their relevance to large interior locations or open-air spaces like train platforms and sports stadiums. While public health advocates pressed for an expansive interpretation of the available science, the tobacco industry rejected the data's relevance even to settings where both logic and evidence suggested the likely presence of danger.

Interestingly, many countries had begun to debate policies aimed at protecting nonsmokers even before the publication of Hirayama's study. In Japan, for example, a lawsuit alleging harm to nonsmokers, and demanding smoke-free train cars, was filed more than a year before Hirayama's data were available. Canadian Minister of Health Marc Lalonde, in 1974, oversaw the publication of "A New Perspective on the Health of Canadians," which concluded that smoking was an environmental problem that caused harm to passive smokers. Action on Smoking and Health (ASH) and other anti-tobacco groups in the United Kingdom were arguing by the late 1970s that nonsmokers needed protection from passive smoking. In the United States, anti-tobacco activists and some public health officials began to press for restrictions early in the 1970s despite the fact that Claude L'Enfant of the National Heart, Lung and Blood Institute described the evidence at the time as merely anecdotal. In each of these cases, assertions and policy pronouncements about the negative health consequences of ETS, although ultimately verified for some settings, were made well in advance of the necessary scientific support.

Even after the evidence of ETS harms began to emerge, the data were contested on scientific and ideological grounds. In Germany, for example, the German Association of Cigarette Manufacturers first tried to suppress information on ETS, then tried to dismiss it, and finally countered it with its own research. A U.K. group called Freedom for the Right to Enjoy Smoking Tobacco (FOREST) was still claiming in 1991 that there was no causal link between ETS and lung cancer, and a statistician funded by the British tobacco industry flatly rejected the emerging international scientific consensus about the harms of passive smoking.[9] More ideologically, the debate over ETS in France reflected the left's hostility to the issue of passive smoking, rooted in its concern about the state's intrusion into matters of personal behavior and its consequent privileging of the interests of nonsmokers. Demonstrating the complex interplay of science, ideology, and advocacy, the editor of an influential antismoking journal, *Tobacco Control*, disappointed some in the tobacco-control community by arguing that the ETS data do not support outdoor smoking restrictions.[10]

The uses and misuses of data have also powerfully shaped debate over tobacco taxation. Most nations had imposed some form of a tobacco tax many decades (sometimes centuries) before a connection was established between smoking and health. They did so because taxing the sale of an increasingly popular consumer good was an important source of government revenue. As data emerged about the connection between cigarettes and cancer, taxation took on a new dimension. Rather than treating a tax as a simple mechanism to raise revenue, public health actors pressed governments to consider tobacco taxes as a public health measure that, by increasing the cost of smoking, would decrease its prevalance and contain its health consequences. Even as early as the 1970s, for example, U.K. anti-tobacco groups saw tobacco taxation as a tool to reduce smoking, despite the absence (at that point) of evidence establishing a clear relationship between smoking rates and the cost of tobacco.

In addition, some public health advocates justified increasing the tax on tobacco products by arguing that smokers imposed financial costs on society because they were disproportionately afflicted by cancer, heart disease, and other illnesses that were costly to treat. The U.K. government in 1992 committed itself to increasing tobacco taxes to pay for the cost of treating smoking-related disease, based only on a general estimate by the National Health Service of those costs. Assertions about the burdens associated with tobacco-related morbidity were prone to a variety of fiscal and moral objections. Most significantly, the estimations opened a contentious debate about whether the costs of caring for those with tobacco-related disease were balanced by the cost savings that resulted from the mortality of smokers. Policy makers in both the United States and Germany explicitly debated the long-term fiscal costs and "benefits" of smoking. Nevertheless, the landmark American legal settlement between the states and the tobacco industry was in important ways predicated on the presumed costs imposed by smoking on Medicaid systems.[11]

Some find the very terms of this debate objectionable, particularly the implication that if smoking is good for the public coffer it should be encouraged. They argue that tobacco tax policy should focus on whether higher taxes will discourage smoking and therefore limit disease and death, not on a ghoulish calculus that compares morbidity-associated costs and mortality-associated savings.[12] In the end, the vulnerability of tobacco products to increasingly burdensome taxes reflects the shifting social standing of smoking and smokers more than it does a fine-tuned analysis of the fiscal impacts associated with cigarette use.

Tobacco Control Advocacy and Policy Have Focused on Vulnerable Parties

In the United States, where individualism is a central cultural and political value, John Stuart Mill's famous dictum in *On Liberty* resonates: "The sole purpose of which power can be rightfully exercised over any member of a civilized community against his will is to prevent harm to others. His own good, either physical or moral is not sufficient warrant."[13] As a consequence, tobacco policy was (even after the surgeon general's 1964 report) founded on interventions compatible with a nonpaternalistic ethos. Protecting innocent, vulnerable third parties, particularly children and non-smoking bystanders, informed the efforts of the tobacco-control movement. In every important area of tobacco policy—the zoning of social space, advertising, even taxation—protecting nonsmokers was the resonant rhetorical and political strategy, not the emphasis on limiting the choices of smokers themselves.

The United States was not alone in confronting the specter of paternalism. In Australia, for example, Prime Minister John Howard rejected a set of proposed tobacco regulations by declaring, "There does come a time when you cannot protect people against themselves and perhaps the state shouldn't." The theme was seized by industry as well. Faced with the threat of greater public health restrictions in Australia, Philip Morris released a cigarette brand called Freedom; on the side of the packet was emblazoned a quotation from Mill.

Strikingly, both in nations with strong traditions of individualism and those where public health powers make it easier to trump the claims of individuals, the need to protect innocents served as a foundation for tobacco policy. Even in Japan, for example, where there is a strong bureaucratic state, tobacco control increasingly is being justified by the invocation of third-party harms that strain credulity. A 2002 ordinance that prohibits smoking on some streets in central Tokyo, for example, and imposes fines on noncompliant smokers was not endorsed for its potentially salutary impact on smokers' health. Instead, the official justification was that it was necessary to limit outdoor smoking in order to cut back on cigarette litter, and because those who walk and smoke often hold their cigarettes beside their hips, making the burning embers a hazard to the eyes of children.

It was the threat of environmental tobacco smoke (ETS) to nonsmokers that caused the most bitter controversy over the way efforts to protect the rights of the vulnerable could serve as warrant for limitations on the preferences of smokers. Banning smoking in international air travel—first by nations with strong commitments to tobacco-control measures and then globally—provides a signal example of how the protection of nonsmokers fundamentally altered the behavior of smokers. The culture of both leisure and business travel was transformed; smokers who previously were able to light up at any hour now had to endure long periods of abstinence, while nonsmoking passengers and flight attendants enjoyed a smoke-free flight. The debate over smoke-free workplaces and public spaces was also rooted in third-party harms. In Germany, for example, the labor courts imposed restrictions on smokers because nonsmoking workers had a right to a smoke-free environment. But in France and Denmark, the extension and enforcement of restrictions in the name of nonsmokers' rights have faced deeply embedded resistance. French opposition politicians have termed attempts to impose limitations on public smoking "health fascism," an interference with one of life's "little pleasures." In Denmark, with long-standing limitations on advertising and high tobacco taxes, a commitment to voluntarism and individual choice blocked the creation of smoke-free zones that had long been accepted in other nations.

In the context of the battles over ETS, the specter of American moralism has been invoked in several nations. Many Danes describe efforts to severely limit smoking in particular settings as "too American," and in Germany some opponents of zoning measures believe that they are reflective of "a fundamentalist American approach." Ironically, the characterization of tobacco policy as involving a clash between liberty and paternalism, and the emphasis on individual choice, has also been viewed as an undesirable American export.

In the end, where efforts to impose exacting measures were made, the needs or rights of non-smokers and children have played an important role. However, as we shall note below, as smoking rates have declined and have become more concentrated among the lower classes, and as the denormal-ization of tobacco use has become an explicit goal of policy, measures that are explicitly paternalistic have been more readily embraced.

Public Policy Alone Does Not Explain the Changing Patterns of Smoking

Writing about the role of law in American tobacco policy, Robert Kagan and Jerome Skolnick noted:

> Like surfers, legislators and corporate officials who wish to change everyday social norms must wait for signs of a rising wave of cultural support, catching it at just the right time. Legislate too soon and they will be swamped by the swells of public resistance. Legislate too late and they will be irrelevant. Legislate at the right moment and an emerging cultural norm still tentatively struggling for authority . . . acquires much greater social force.[14]

The studies in this volume bear out Kagan and Skolnick's suggestion that changes in smoking-related behavior may have a complex and unpredict-able connection to changes in tobacco-control policy.

Table C.1. Percent cigarette smoking among men and women, 1963–2001

Country	Male Early period (1963–1965)	Male Late period (2000–2001)	Male % change	Female Early period (1963–1965)	Female Late period (2000–2001)	Female % change
Australia	58%	21%	−64	28%	18%	−36
Canada	61%	24%	−61	38%	20%	−48
Denmark	71%	32%	−55	41%	29%	−29
France	72%	33%	−54	33%	21%	−36
Germany	61%	39%	−36	24%	31%	−28
Japan	83%	47%	−43	16%	12%	−27
United Kingdom	68%	28%	−59	43%	26%	−40
United States	52%	26%	−50	34%	21%	−38

Sources: **Australia**: A. Nicolaides-Bouman, N. Wald, B. Forey, and P. Lee, eds., *International Smoking Statistics: A Collection of Historical Data from 22 Economically Developed Countries*, (London: Wolfson Institute of Preventive Medicine, 1993); 7–8; Australian Institute of Health and Welfare, *2001 National Drug Strategy Household Survey: State and Territory Supplement*, (Canberra, Australia: 2002). **Canada**: *A Critical Review of Canadian Survey Data on Tobacco Use, Attitudes and Knowledge, 1965–1986*, Tobacco Programs Unit, Health and Welfare Canada, 1988; Health Canada Tobacco Control Programme. (2002). Canadian Tobacco Use Monitoring Survey (CTUMS) February–December 2001. Available at: <http://www.hc-sc.gc.ca/hecs-sesc/tobacco/research/index.html>. **Denmark**: P. E. Nielsen et al., "Ændring i danskernes rygevaner 1958–1976," *Ugeskrift for læger* 140: 2528–2532 (1978); P. E. Nielsen et al., "Ændringer i danskernes rygevaner 1970–1987," *Ugeskrift for læger* 150: 2229–2233 (1988); WHO Health for All Database, reported in World Health Organization (2002); European Country Profiles on Tobacco Control (Copenhagen: WHO Regional Office for Europe, 2001). **France**: Nicolaides-Bouman et al., International Smoking Statistics, pp. 139–141; *Enquêtes permanentes sur les conditions de vie, 2000—indicateurs sociaux*, INSEE, 2000, reported in World Health Organization (2002); European Country Profiles on Tobacco Control, (Copenhagen: WHO Regional Office for Europe, 2001). **Germany**: Nicolaides-Bouman et al., *International Smoking Statistics* pp. 165–170; Population survey on the consumption of psychoactive substances in the German adult population, reported in World Health Organization (2002); European Country Profiles on Tobacco Control (Copenhagen: WHO Regional Office for Europe, 2001). **Japan**: Nicolaides-Bouman et al., *International Smoking Statistics* pp. 258–260, Ministry of Health, Labor and Welfare (2002). Kokumin-eiyou no Genjo: Heisei 12-nen Kokumineiyou chosa kekka [Results of National Nutrition Survey, 2000], reported in the WHO Global NCD Infobase. **United Kingdom**: Nicolaides-Bouman et al., *International Smoking Statistics* pp. 425–430; Department of Health—United Kingdom (2001); General Household Survey—Great Britain. Available at <http://www.statistics.gov.uk/lib2001>, reported in the WHO Global NCD Infobase. **United States**: CDC, Office on Smoking and Health, from the Current Population Survey, 1955 and the National Health Interview Surveys, 1965–1994; Centers for Disease Control and Prevention, Cigarette Smoking Among Adults—United States, 2000, MMWR 2002; 51 (29): 642–645.

   In some nations, changes in the patterns and prevalence of tobacco consumption have occurred in the absence of a restrictive legal and political regime of tobacco control. In others, explicit regulations have had little apparent impact. In still others, the implementation of tobacco-control policies appears to have reshaped certain smoking practices but left others untouched. Crafting appropriate policy is an important step in changing smoking-related norms and in influencing the emergence of new social regimes, but such efforts are rarely sufficient to bring about fundamental change in the social patterns of starting, continuing, or ceasing to smoke.

   On one all-important dimension, the nations we have examined share a common feature; with just one exception, smoking prevalence and per-capita cigarette consumption among men has dropped sharply in the past three decades. Only in Japan has prevalence decreased but per-capita cigarette consumption increased; even there, between 1980 and 2000, consumption has declined. Despite variations in the data among countries, the trend is clear. Women, who came later to smoking and who smoked less than men in the 1960s, have not experienced the same dramatic decline in smoking rates. In Germany, possibly because of the effects of unification, the proportion of women smokers has increased (although, revealing the perils of data, the chapter on Germany in this volume suggests that there was in fact a decline). What remains difficult to discern is the relationship between national policies and individual preferences, between legal regimes and social realities. Whether (and when) tobacco-control policy will stimulate changes in smoking behavior, how much of a difference policy will make, and what types of policy tools are most effective should be questions of critical importance to the tobacco-control community.

Table C.2. Per-capita cigarette consumption (measured in cigarette sticks) by country

Country	1970	1980	1990	1995	2000	change
Australia	3,011	3,279	2,689	2,184	1,568	−47.9
Canada	3,301	3,549	2,030	1,998	1,777	−46.2
Denmark	1,937	1,972	1,860	1,913	1,856	−4.2
France	1,850	2,236	2,168	2,055	1,594	−13.8
Germany	2,333	2,423	2,234	2,297	1,843	−21.0
Japan	2,810	3,450	3,037	2,905	3,023	7.6
United Kingdom	2,987	2,636	2,170	1,901	1,374	−54.0
United States	3,681	3,544	2,755	2,480	2,082	−43.4

   Information provided by personal communication from Omar Shafey, Ph.D., American Cancer Society, International Tobacco Surveillance Unit.

Those nations we have identified as having the most vigorous tobacco-control policies have witnessed steep declines in smoking rates. On the other hand, countries with weak antismoking strategies have experienced a similarly dramatic decline. In Japan, for example, smoking rates have fallen considerably (almost 1 percent per year among men for the past thirty-five years), but there are few concrete laws or regulations aimed at the public health consequences of tobacco consumption.[15] Restrictions on tobacco advertising are voluntary; cigarette vending machines are proliferating; tobacco taxes are considered from the perspective of revenue, not health; separating smokers from nonsmokers by designating smoke-free areas remains informal and ad hoc; and one of the few tobacco-control laws, the prohibition on youth smoking, is honored in the breach. Nonetheless, tobacco-related behavior in Japan is changing. An ever-expanding variety of spaces have been designated smoke-free, and the advertising of tobacco products has decreased, limited by time, place, and content restrictions *voluntarily* adopted by the Tobacco Institute of Japan.

Denmark's preference for voluntary over legal controls presents a particularly interesting set of issues. There, the consequences of the tobacco tax defy expectations. Danish tax represents a higher proportion of the price of cigarettes than in most other nations, but Danes smoke at higher rates than most other populations. As taxes fell after Denmark's level of taxation was brought into line with EU policy, tobacco consumption and the total num-

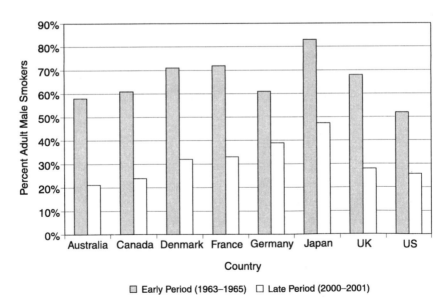

Figure C.1 Smoking prevalence among men in eight nations, 1963 and 2001

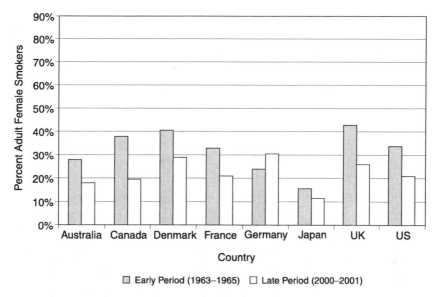

Figure C.2 Smoking prevalence among women in eight nations, 1963 and 2001

ber of smokers in Denmark also dropped. Similarly, tobacco advertising was never allowed on Denmark's broadcast media (which is free from all advertising), and was voluntarily restricted in other areas, but that does not seem to have suppressed the Danish urge to smoke. These and other aspects of the Danish story make it difficult to credit policy implementation with causing the overall drop in the number of smokers, and tobacco consumption, in the 1990s.

Finally, the case of France demonstrates that formal legal regimes may have little to do with either (real) policy or social regimes. There, two laws—the *loi Veil* and the *loi Evin* —were implemented with legal sanctions, not merely informal agreements. But neither of them has been rigorously enforced, and neither has brought about the changes that appear to be envisioned by their legal provisions. Such hortatory legal pronouncements, which superficially require enforcement but are commonly understood to be only aspirational, are an accepted feature of French political culture, not a unique aspect of French tobacco control.

A Social Gradient Based on Education and Income Characterizes Tobacco Consumption

Four decades ago cigarette smoking was democratic. The rich smoked alongside the destitute; presidents, professors, and prisoners puffed with impunity; Ivy League graduates and high school dropouts shared at least one thing, their affection for cigarettes. The only significant social distinction that divided smokers was the uniformly greater likelihood that smokers were male. A very different picture has now emerged. In every country we studied, a social gradient, steeper in some nations than in others, characterizes tobacco consumption. Those with more education and higher incomes smoke with decreasing frequency. Those at the bottom of the social ladder continue to smoke.

By 1974 the gradient in the United States was already clear; 52 percent of men with no high school diploma smoked, but that was true for only 28 percent of those who had graduated from college. By 2000 the rate of smoking had declined among men with less than a high school education (to 36 percent), while smokers accounted for only 11 percent of those with a bachelor's degree or more. A similar pattern was found among women. While 36 percent of less educated women smoked in 1970, 25 percent of those with university degrees smoked. Sixteen years later, 27 percent of women with less than a high school education smoked, but only 10 percent of those who had a university education were smokers.

In Denmark, data for the period 1970–2001 reveal a similar pattern. In 1970, 73 percent of the highest stratum of male workers and 75 percent of unskilled laborers smoked. By 2001, the rate of smoking among the former had declined to 21 percent, while 49 percent of unskilled workers continued to smoke. A similar gulf exists in Canada, despite its aggressive anti-tobacco campaign (in 2001, 26 percent of those with less than a secondary education smoked, as compared to 13 percent of those who had a college degree[16]), and in Germany, with its less forceful tobacco-control efforts (48 percent of those with elementary education smoked, as compared to 27 percent of university graduates). Commenting on the international evidence of a social gradient, two analysts noted that "the association between smoking and social disadvantage is so close that in most cases one can identify disadvantaged groups by simply observing their smoking prevalence."[17]

Evidence for the existence of a social gradient in the 1990s is presented in Table C.3. It expresses the gradient in terms of the odds that the least educated men and women will smoke as compared to those with the highest education. Although there are marked differences among the nations, and while the rank ordering in terms of women and men differ, there is no nation in our study where disparities based on education do not exist.

The transformation of smoking prevalence represents both an enormous achievement and a great failure. To have so dramatically affected the consumption of cigarettes among the middle and upper classes will ultimately save millions of lives. But the more modest decreases among the lower social classes suggest the limits of public health policy. It also highlights the subtlety of normative change. By the end of the twentieth century, as smoking was increasingly beyond the bounds of middle-class culture, smoke itself went from an aroma to a stink. Smokers, who at first felt obligated to ask "May I smoke?" came to understand that they had to withdraw from social contexts when they wanted to smoke. Some went so far as to hide the fact that they still were smokers. Where "manners" and etiquette continued to shape social relations around smoking behavior, they became increasingly restrictive. In Japan, for example, with its high prevalence of male smokers, the emphasis on good smoking manners has gradually (but incompletely) redefined the meaning of acceptable smoking behavior.

In the most extreme cases, smokers became social pariahs, and smoking became a sign of weakness, a moral failing if not a pathological condition.

In Germany, the image of the smoker as a handsome, successful executive was increasingly displaced by one that depicted smokers as asocial, irresponsible, and self-destructive. In the United States, there was some discussion of treating smoking by parents as a form of child abuse.[18] A 2002 issue of the high-toned *New Yorker* magazine sported a cover depicting smokers peering through the bars of a cage, a disappearing breed in a zoo, captive to its own poor judgment.[19] Even in Denmark, which viewed itself as immune to the lures of moral crusades, there were signs that the aura around tobacco had been tainted.

For public health advocates who sought to prevent adolescents from smoking and who viewed it as imperative to get smokers to break their deadly addiction, the process of denormalization and the attendant stigmatization were increasingly considered powerful allies. Where antismoking educational campaigns, advertising restrictions, and other explicit policy interventions had not, at least individually, reconfigured the moral meaning of smoking, their accumulated weight was used to recast the social meaning of cigarettes and smokers. Ironically, in the context of AIDS, and in efforts to propound a harm-reduction strategy for drug use and drug users, the public health community argued that stigmatization would deepen the fissure between health advocates and those they sought to protect.

Table C.3. Comparison of smoking rates of men and women with low and high educational attainment (high = reference category)

Men		Women	
Great Britain	2.3	Great Britain	2.5
France	2.3	West Germany	1.5
West Germany	1.6	France	1.4
Denmark	1.3	Denmark	1.3

Source: AEJM. Cavelaars et al., "Educational Differences in Smoking: International Comparison," *British Medical Journal* 320: 1102 (2000).

Stigmatization was also viewed as morally suspect, imposing unfair burdens on the most vulnerable. As smoking is increasingly linked to lower socioeconomic status, these concerns will require an explicit response.

That it is the poorest who continue to smoke not only raises profound questions about stigmatization, but also poses other ethical problems for anti-tobacco efforts. The burden of taxes on cigarettes, for example, will increasingly fall on the least well off. While some will give up smoking because of the cost, individuals who do not will be compelled to spend an ever-greater proportion of their relatively limited incomes on tobacco.[20] For those whose central concern is the rights of the least advantaged, therefore, the social gradient of smoking provokes a heightened sense of scrutiny over the direction of public policy. Burt Neuborne, former legal director of the American Civil Liberties Union, discussing ETS, has noted:

> Assertions about the third-party costs of controversial behavior should . . . be viewed skeptically when they are advanced as the last phase in the evolution of a prohibition, . . . not because they cannot be true, . . . Particular care must be paid to the scientific foundation underlying the claims of third-party harm, especially where the target behavior is one that is engaged in disproportionately by weak actors in the society.[21]

Concern about the social-class gradient of smoking within the economically advanced nations addressed in this book highlights the chasm between those countries and the world's poorest nations, where smoking rates have been relatively untouched by effective public health measures. Tragically, an international social gradient now characterizes the global epidemiology of smoking. A World Bank report vividly underscores this point.[22] While per-capita smoking rates have been declining in the world's high-income counties, they have risen precipitously in many low- and middle-income nations. By the mid-1990s, approximately 60 percent of men in East Asia and the Pacific regions smoked, as did close to 45 percent of men in the Middle East and North Africa and 40 percent of men in Latin America and the Caribbean. The extent to which concern about tobacco-related morbidity and mortality has failed to take hold in the poorest nations is underscored by the fact that while about 30 percent of men in the wealthiest nations were former smokers, that was true of only 10 percent of Vietnamese, 5 percent of Indian, and 2 percent of Chinese men. The health consequences of this smoking ethos are all too easy to predict. According to a World Bank estimate, by the year 2030, 70 percent of tobacco-related deaths will be in low- and middle-income countries; in China alone, 100 million men are expected to die as a result of smoking. The politics and economics of this transformation, fueled at least in part by trade liberalization and the search for markets to replace those lost in the wealthiest nations, must be the subject for another study.

We began this project with the assumption that a fuller appreciation of the nature of U.S. tobacco policy required a comparative analysis—one that would locate the American experience with tobacco control within a broad context of other democratic nations. Our expectation was not that we would identify a simple set of tobacco-related policies or practices for import or export. Instead, we sought to understand whether and how the central political and ideological commitments of the nations in this volume had shaped and limited what could be done both to affect the behaviors of hundreds of millions of smokers and to confront the industries that have long profited from the sale of cigarettes. In the end, we came to appreciate the power of the international community of public health advocates and anti-tobacco activists that has begun to change the cultural and ideological contexts within which tobacco policy is made in all economically advanced democracies. It is that community of scientists, physicians, government officials, lawyers, and lay people—in conflict with multinational tobacco corporations—that will continue to shape and reshape the landscape of tobacco policy in the coming decades.

Notes

Introduction

1. Robert Goodin, *No Smoking: The Ethical Issues* (Chicago: University of Chicago Press, 1989), 30–31.
2. Jacob Sullum, *For Your Own Good: The Anti-Smoking Crusade and the Tyranny of Public Health* (New York: Free Press, 1998), 12–13.
3. Kenneth Warner, John Slade, and David T. Sweanor, "The Emerging Market for Long Term Nicotine Maintenance," *Journal of the American Medical Association* 278: 1089 (1997). In the 1980s and 1990s, some public health advocates and others committed to harm reduction began to press for liberalization of the regime surrounding drugs, even suggesting that tolerance for drug use would produce public health benefits unobtainable through repressive measures. At a minimum, the harm reduction philosophy embraces policies and programs "aimed at reducing drug-related harms without requiring abstention from drug use." Diane Riley et al., "Harm Reduction: Concepts and Practice. A Policy Discussion Paper," *Substance Use and Misuse* 34: 9–24 (1999). In the context of tobacco control, especially in the United States, discussion of the possible relevance of harm reduction, less toxic tobacco products, and "safer cigarettes" often has been rejected.
4. Robert Kagan and David Vogel, "The Politics of Smoking Regulation: Canada, France, and the United States," in *Smoking Policy: Law, Politics, & Culture,* eds. Robert L. Rabin and Stephen D. Sugarman (New York: Oxford University Press, 1993), 22.
5. "How Do You Sleep at Night, Mr. Blair?" *The Lancet* 362: 1865 (2003).
6. Cass Sunstein, "Sober Lemmings," *The New Republic,* April 14, 2003. As Sunstein notes, "It is hardly unproblematic to try to manipulate people, even if the manipulation can be made to work and even if it is in the service of desirable ends."

1. Children and Bystanders First

1. U.S. Department of Health and Human Services, *Reducing Tobacco Use: A Report of the Surgeon General* (Washington, DC: U.S. Government Printing Office, 2000), 296.
2. Ibid., 307–308.
3. Ibid., 38.
4. Cited in U.S. Department of Health, Education and Welfare, *Smoking and Health: Report of the Advisory Committee to the Surgeon General of the Public Health Service* (Washington, DC: U.S. Government Printing Office, 1964), 8.
5. Ibid.
6. Ibid., 30–31.
7. Kenneth Michael Friedman, *Public Policy and the Smoking-Health Controversy: A Comparative Study* (Lexington, MA: Lexington Books, 1975), 1–2.
8. Hazel Gaudet Erskine, "The Polls: Smoking," *Public Opinion Quarterly* 30 (1): 150 (1966).
9. Robert McAuliffe, "The FTC and the Effectiveness of Cigarette Advertising Regulations," *Journal of Public Policy and Marketing* 7: 52 (1988).
10. Thomas Whiteside, "Annals of Advertising: Cutting Down," *New Yorker,* December 19, 1970, 42–95.
11. Friedman, *Public Policy and the Smoking-Health Controversy,* 44.
12. *Banzhaf v. Federal Communications Commission,* 405 F.2d 1082 (D.C. Cir. 1968).
13. Federal Trade Commission, *Report to Congress for 1998 Pursuant to the Federal Cigarette Labeling and Advertising Act* (Washington, DC: FTC, 2000), 20.
14. Whiteside, "Annals of Advertising," 46.
15. Cited in *Banzhaf v. FCC,* 405 F.2d at 1086.
16. Whiteside, "Annals of Advertising," 56.
17. *Banzhaf v. FCC,* 405 F.2d at 1103.
18. Kenneth E. Warner, "Clearing the Airwaves: The Cigarette Ad Ban Revisited," *Policy Analysis* 5: 439 (1979).
19. Federal Communications Commission, *Notice of Proposed Rulemaking: In the Matter of Amendment of Part 73 of the Federal Communications Commission Rules with Regard to the Advertisement of Cigarettes,* 16 F.C.C.2d 284, 287 (1969).
20. Whiteside, "Annals of Advertising," 66.
21. Federal Trade Commission, *Report to Congress for 1998,* 20.
22. *Capital Broadcasting Co. v. Mitchell,* 333 F.Supp. 582 (D.D.C. 1971), 583.
23. Ibid., 587.
24. Federal Trade Commission, *Report to Congress for 1998,* 21.
25. Warner, "Clearing the Airwaves," 442.
26. Ibid., 446.

27. Federal Trade Commission, *Cigarette Report for 2000* (Washington, DC: FTC, 2002), 10.

28. Lawrence H. Tribe, "Communication and Expression," in *American Constitutional Law,* 2d ed. (Mineola, NY: Foundation Press, 1988), 893.

29. *Posadas de Puerto Rico Associates v. Tourism Company of Puerto Rico,* 478 U.S. 328 (1986).

30. Board of Trustees, American Medical Association, "Media Advertising for Tobacco Products,"*Journal of the American Medical Association* 255: 1033 (1986).

31. Kenneth E. Warner, Virginia L. Ernster, John H. Holbrook, et al., "Promotion of Tobacco Products: Issues and Policy Options," *Journal of Health Politics, Policy and Law* 11 (3): 388 (1986).

32. John K. Iglehart, "The Campaign against Smoking Gains Momentum," *New England Journal of Medicine* 314: 1059–1064 (1986).

33. Kenneth E. Warner, "Cigarette Advertising and Media Coverage of Smoking and Health," *New England Journal of Medicine* 312 (6): 384–388 (1985).

34. Ibid., 388.

35. Vincent Blasi and Henry P. Monaghan, "The First Amendment and Cigarette Advertising," *Journal of the American Medical Association* 256 (4): 502–509 (1986).

36. Burt Neuborne, Statement, *Hearings before the Subcommittee on Health and the Environment of the Committee on Energy and Commerce,* House of Representatives, 99th Cong., 2d sess., August 1, 1986, Serial No. 99–167 (Washington, D.C.: U.S. Government Printing Office, 1986).

37. Warner, Ernster, Holbrook, et al., "Promotion of Tobacco Products."

38. Ibid., 371.

39. Ibid., 373.

40. Ibid., 377.

41. Ibid., 383.

42. Jeffrey A. Berman, "Constitutional Realism: Legislative Bans on Tobacco Advertisements and the First Amendment," *University of Illinois Law Review* 1986: 1193–1231.

43. Michael Schudson, "Symbols and Smokers: Advertising, Health Messages and Public Policy," in *Smoking Policy: Law, Politics, & Culture,* eds. Robert L. Rabin and Stephen D. Sugarman (New York: Oxford University Press, 1993), 211.

44. U.S. Department of Health and Human Services, *Preventing Tobacco Use among Young People: A Report of the Surgeon General* (Atlanta, GA: DHHS, 1994), at <http://www.cdc.gov/tobacco/sgryth2.htm>.

45. Barbara S. Lynch and Richard J. Bonnie, eds., *Growing Up Tobacco Free: Preventing Nicotine Addiction in Children and Youths* (Washington, D.C.: National Academy Press, 1994), Institute of Medicine, Committee on Preventing Nicotine Addiction in Children and Youths, Division of Biobehavioral Sciences and Mental Disorders.

46. Ibid., 5.

47. Ibid., 131.
48. David A. Kessler, "Nicotine Addiction in Young People," *New England Journal of Medicine* 333: 186–189 (1995).
49. Food and Drug Administration, "Regulations Restricting the Sale and Distribution of Cigarettes and Smokeless Tobacco to Protect Children and Adolescents; Final Rule," *Federal Register* 61(168), 44,395 (August 28, 1996).
50. Food and Drug Administration, *Executive Summary, The Regulations Restricting the Sale and Distribution of Cigarettes and Smokeless Tobacco to Protect Children and Adolescents* (1996), at <http://www.fda.gov/opacom/campaigns/tobacco/execrule.html>.
51. "Free Speech Flaps," *Wall Street Journal*, June 24, 1996.
52. "Smoking Out Tobacco," *Washington Post*, August 25, 1996.
53. "Cigarettes and Free Speech," *New York Times*, December 20, 1997.
54. Martin Redish, Testimony, *Cigarette Advertising and the First Amendment to the Constitution: Hearing before the Committee on the Judiciary*, United States Senate, 105th Cong., 2d sess., February 10, 1988, Serial No. 105–541 (Washington, D.C.: U.S. Government Printing Office, 1988), 27–38.
55. Master Settlement Agreement, November 23, 1998, at <http://www.naag.org/tobaccopublic/library>.
56. *Lorillard Tobacco Co. v. Reilly*, 533 U.S. 525 (2001).
57. Jesse L. Steinfeld, "Women and Children Last? Attitudes toward Cigarette Smoking and Nonsmokers' Rights, 1971," *New York State Journal of Medicine* 83 (13): 1257–1258 (1983).
58. U.S. Department of Health and Human Services, *Reducing Tobacco Use*.
59. Constance A. Nathanson, "Social Movement as Catalysts for Policy Change: The Case of Smoking and Guns," *Journal of Health Politics, Policy and Law* 24 (3): 448 (1999).
60. Gerald Markle and Ronald Troyer, "Smoke Gets in Your Eyes: Cigarette Smoking as Deviant Behavior," *Social Problems* 26: 618 (1979).
61. Roger W. Schmidt, "The U.S. Experience in Nonsmokers' Rights," *American Lung Association Bulletin* 1975 (December): 11–15.
62. U.S. Department of Health and Human Services, *Reducing Tobacco Use*, 198.
63. Gary L. Huber, "Smoking and Nonsmokers—What Is the Issue?" *New England Journal of Medicine* 292: 858–859 (1975).
64. Claude L'Enfant and Barbara Marzetta Liu, "(Passive) Smokers versus (Voluntary) Smokers," *New England Journal of Medicine* 302: 742–743 (1980).
65. Roper Organization, *A Study of Public Attitudes toward Cigarette Smoking and the Tobacco Industry in 1978*, vol. 1 (New York: Roper Organization, 1978).
66. James White and Herman Froeb, "Small-Airways Dysfunction in Nonsmokers Chronically Exposed to Tobacco Smoke," *New England Journal of Medicine* 302: 720–723 (1980).
67. L'Enfant and Liu, "(Passive) Smokers versus (Voluntary) Smokers."
68. Dmitrios Trichopoulos, Anna Kalandidi, Loukas Sparros, and Brian MacMa-

hon, "Lung Cancer and Passive Smoking," *International Journal of Cancer* 27: 1–4 (1981).

69. Takeshi Hirayama, "Non-smoking Wives of Heavy Smokers Have a Higher Risk of Lung Cancer: A Study from Japan," *British Medical Journal* 282: 183–85 (1981).

70. "Smoking Your Wife to Death," *New York Times,* January 21, 1981.

71. Committee on Indoor Pollutants, *Indoor Pollutants* (Washington, D.C.: National Academy Press, 1981), 8.

72. American Lung Association, "Summary of Results of the April 1983 Survey by the Gallup Organization, *Survey of Attitudes toward Smoking,* " News Release, September 20, 1983; Institute for Social Research, *Poll of Michigan Residents regarding Law Limiting Smoking in Public* (Ann Arbor, MI: University of Michigan, 1984); Mervin D. Field, "California Poll: Majority Would Restrict Smoking," *Sacramento Bee,* March 1, 1984.

73. Joseph A. Califano Jr., Testimony, *Hearings before the Subcommittee on Civil Service, Post Office, and General Services of the Committee on Governmental Affairs,* United States Senate, 99th Cong., 2d sess., September 30, 1985, Serial No. 99–704 (Washington, D.C.: U.S. Government Printing Office, 1986).

74. U.S. Department of Health and Human Services, *The Health Consequences of Involuntary Smoking.* (Washington, D.C.: U.S. Department of Health and Human Services, 1986.)

75. Ibid.

76. Ross Brownson, Michael P. Eriksen, Ronald M. Davis, and Kenneth E. Warner, "Environmental Tobacco Smoke: Health Effects and Policies to Reduce Exposure," *Annual Review of Public Health* 18: 172 (1997).

77. Deborah Barnes and Lisa A. Bero, "Industry-Funded Research and Conflict of Interest: An Analysis of Research Sponsored by the Tobacco Industry through the Center for Indoor Air Research," *Journal of Health Politics, Policy and Law* 21: 515–542 (1996).

78. M. Teresa Cardador, Ann R. Hazan, and Stanton P. Glantz, "Tobacco Industry Smokers' Rights Publications: A Content Analysis," *American Journal of Public Health* 85: 1212–1217 (1995).

79. Cited in U.S. Department of Health and Human Services, *State and Local Legislative Action to Reduce Tobacco Use* (Bethesda, MD: DHHS, 2000), 52.

80. Joan Hamilton et al., "'No Smoking' Sweeps America," *Business Week,* July 27, 1987.

81. Stanton A. Glantz, "Achieving a Smokefree Society," *Circulation* 76: 750 (1987).

82. Ibid., 746.

83. Robert L. Rabin, "Some Thoughts on Smoking Regulation," *Stanford Law Review* 43: 487 (1991).

84. Environmental Protection Agency, *Respiratory Health Effects of Passive Smoking: Lung Cancer and Other Disorders* (Washington, D.C.: Department of Health and Human Services, 1992).

85. "No Right to Cause Death," *New York Times*, January 10, 1993.
86. "No Smoking," *Wall Street Journal*, June 7, 1994.
87. U.S. Department of Health and Human Services, *Reducing Tobacco Use*, 201.
88. American Lung Association, *Annual Report 1999* (New York: American Lung Association, 2000), Appendix A.
89. Allan Brandt, "Blow Some My Way: Passive Smoking, Risk and American Culture," in *Ashes to Ashes: The History of Smoking and Health*, eds. Stephen Lock, Lois Reynolds, and E. M. Tansey (Amsterdam: Rodopi, 1998).
90. Stanton A. Glantz and William W. Parmley, "Passive Smoking and Heart Disease: Epidemiology, Physiology and Biochemistry," *Circulation* 83: 1–12 (1991).
91. Ibid., 10.
92. Jian He et al., "Passive Smoking and the Risk of Coronary Heart Disease—A Meta-Analysis of Epidemiologic Studies," *New England Journal of Medicine* 340: 920–926 (1999).
93. John C. Bailar, "Passive Smoking, Coronary Heart Disease, and Meta-Analysis," *New England Journal of Medicine* 340: 958–959 (1999).
94. Stanton A. Glantz and William W. Parmley, "Even a Little Second-Hand Smoke Is Dangerous," *Journal of the American Medical Association* 286: 462–463 (2001); Ryo Otsuka et al., "Acute Effects of Passive Smoking on the Coronary Circulation in Healthy Young Adults," *Journal of the American Medical Association* 286: 436–441 (2001).
95. Bruce Samuels and Stanton A. Glantz, "The Politics of Local Tobacco Control," *Journal of the American Medical Association* 266: 2111 (1991).
96. Michelle Bloch and Donald Shopland, "Outdoor Smoking Bans: More Than Meets the Eye," *Tobacco Control* 9: 99 (2000).
97. James Repace, "Banning Outdoor Smoking Is Scientifically Justifiable," *Tobacco Control* 9: 98 (2000).
98. Simon Chapman, "Banning Smoking Outdoors Is Seldom Ethically Justifiable," *Tobacco Control* 9: 95–97 (2000).
99. Ross C. Brownson et al., "Environmental and Policy Interventions to Control Tobacco Use and Prevent Cardiovascular Disease," *Health Education Quarterly* 22: 485 (1995).
100. Friedman, *Public Policy and the Smoking-Health Controversy*.
101. U.S. Department of Health and Human Services, *Reducing Tobacco Use*, 345–346.
102. Friedman, *Public Policy and the Smoking-Health Controversy*, 18.
103. Kenneth Warner, "State Legislation on Smoking and Health: A Comparison of Two Policies," *Policy Sciences* 13: 143 (1981).
104. Eugene Lewit and Douglas Coate, "The Potential for Using Excise Taxes to Reduce Smoking," *Journal of Health Economics* 1: 142 (1982).
105. Kenneth E. Warner, "Cigarette Taxation: Doing Good by Doing Well," *Journal of Public Health Policy* 5: 312–319 (1984).

106. Ibid., 314.
107. Ibid., 317.
108. Ibid., 314.
109. Ibid., 315.
110. Ibid.
111. "Make Smokers Pay the Price," *New York Times,* July 30, 1986.
112. Kirk Victor, "Strange Alliances," *National Journal,* August 15, 1987.
113. Toni Locy, "Tobacco Firms Pay $4.5 Million to Fight Tax," *Boston Globe,* September 5, 1999.
114. Betsy Lehman, "Raising the Cost of Risky Behavior," *Boston Globe,* October 12, 1992.
115. Don Aucoin, "Cigarette Tax Is Hailed, Hit at Debate," *Boston Globe,* October 23, 1992.
116. Frank Phillips, "Tobacco Industry Ads Tout Tolerance," *Boston Globe,* October 24, 1992.
117. Jack Nicholl, "Perspective on Smoking; Bans Alone Won't Win the War," *Los Angeles Times,* June 25, 1993.
118. U.S. Department of Health and Human Services, *Reducing Tobacco Use,* 341–345.
119. Ibid., 345.
120. David Cay Johnston, "Anti-tobacco Groups Push for Higher Cigarette Taxes," *New York Times,* April 3, 1997.
121. Frank Chaloupka and Henry Wechsler, *Price, Tobacco Control and Smoking among Young Adults* (National Bureau of Economic Research Working Paper No. 5012, 1995), 22–23.
122. "Response to Increases in Cigarette Prices by Race/Ethnicity, Income, and Age Groups—United States, 1976–1993," *Morbidity and Mortality Weekly Report* 47: 606 (1998).
123. Ibid., 608.
124. Kenneth E. Warner, "The Economics of Tobacco: Myths and Realities," *Tobacco Control* 9: 78–89 (2000).
125. Thomas A. Hodgson, "Cigarette Smoking and Lifetime Medical Expenditures," *Milbank Quarterly* 70 (1): 110 (1992).
126. Ibid., 111.
127. John Shoven, Jeffrey Sundberg, and John Bunker, "The Social Security Cost of Smoking," in *The Economics of Aging,* ed. David A. Wise (Chicago: University of Chicago Press, 1989), 244.
128. Willard Manning, Emmett Keeler, Joseph Newhouse, Elizabeth Sloss, and Jeffrey Wasserman, "The Taxes of Sin: Do Smokers and Drinkers Pay Their Way?" *Journal of the American Medical Association* 261: 1604 (1989).
129. W. Kip Viscusi, "Cigarette Taxation and the Social Consequences of Smoking," *Tax Policy and the Economy,* 75.
130. Warner, "The Economics of Tobacco: Myths and Realities."

131. Gary L. Schwartz, "Tobacco, Liability, and Viscusi," *Cumberland Law Review* 29: 555 (1998/99).

132. Ibid., 567.

133. U.S. Department of Health and Human Services, *Reducing Tobacco Use,* 346.

134. "Tobacco Use—1900–1999," *Morbidity and Mortality Weekly Report* 48: 986–993 (1999).

135. Federal Trade Commission, *Report to Congress for 1998.*

136. National Center for Health Statistics, *Health, United States, 2002* (Hyattsville, MD: NCHS, 2002).

137. Richard Kluger, *Ashes to Ashes: America's Hundred-Year Cigarette War, the Public Health, and the Unabashed Triumph of Philip Morris* (New York: Alfred A. Knopf, 1996).

138. Tobacco Control Resource Center, Northeastern University School of Law, *The Multistate Master Settlement and the Future of State and Local Tobacco Control: An Analysis of Selected Topics and Provisions of the Multistate Master Settlement Agreement of November 23, 1998* (1999).

139. *Food and Drug Administration v. Brown & Williamson Tobacco Corp.,* 529 U.S. 120 (2000), *affirming* 153 F.3d 155 (4th Cir. 1998).

140. Michael Cooper, "Mayor Signs Law to Ban Smoking Soon at Most Bars," *New York Times,* December 31, 2002.

141. California Department of Health Services, *A Model for Change: The California Experience in Tobacco Control* (Sacramento, CA: California Department of Health Services, 1998), 4.

142. Michael Cooper, "Cigarettes Up to $7 a Pack with New Tax," *New York Times,* July 1, 2002.

143. Tobacco Use and Dependence Clinical Practice Guideline Panel, Staff, and Consortium Representatives, "A Clinical Practice Guideline for Treating Tobacco Use and Dependence: A US Public Health Service Report," *Journal of the American Medical Association* 283: 3244–3254 (2000).

144. John R. Hughes, Michael G. Goldstein, Richard D. Hurt, and Saul Shiffman, "Recent Advances in the Pharmacotherapy of Smoking," *Journal of the American Medical Association* 281: 72–76 (1999).

2. The Limits of Tolerance

Support for the research and writing of this paper was provided by an Abe Fellowship from the Japan Foundation's Center for Global Partnership; the Robert Wood Johnson Foundation's Substance Abuse Policy Research Program; the Japanese Society for the Promotion of Science; and the University of Pennsylvania Law School. The insightful comments of two anonymous reviewers are greatly appreciated. I have greatly benefited from conversations and written comments about the material in this chapter from Glen S. Fukushima, John Haley, Robert Leflar, Mark Levin, Kristin Madison, Mark Ramseyer, Kim Lane Scheppele, Frank Upham, Hozumi Tadao, Isayama Yoshio, Masakatsu Akedo, Minowa Masumi, Mochizuki-Kobayashi Yumiko, Ohashi Muneo, Ono Katsushi, Sone Tomofumi, and Watanabe Bungaku. Kurumisawa Yoshiki and Miyazawa Setsuo provided me with a comfortable and intellectually stimulating atmosphere at Waseda University's Faculty of Law. Yuko Tsutsui offered expert research assistance.

1. As discussed below, I do not intend to imply that policy makers have balanced fiscal and physical health, and decided to value profits more highly than lives. No such weighing takes place. Tobacco regulators in MOF, trained in economics rather than epidemiology, think about the business aspects of tobacco and have no interest in, or incentive to think about, public health. Institutional histories and processes, not individual choices, explain why tobacco is managed as a matter of public finance rather than public health. For a related discussion, see Mark Levin, "Smoke around the Rising Sun: An American Look at Tobacco Regulation in Japan," *Stanford Journal of Law and Policy* 8 (1): 99 (1997), who argues that tobacco regulation is an example of "the sacrifice of public health for the benefit of fiscal and economic interests."

2. See, for example, Hanai Kiroku, "Weak Tobacco Pact Reflects Japan's Lukewarm Attitude," *Japan Times,* Editorial, March 25, 2003.

3. See, for example, Kip Viscusi, *Smoke-Filled Rooms: A Postmortem on the Tobacco Deal* (Chicago: University of Chicago Press, 2002).

4. Confidential interviews with senior MOF officials, 2001.

5. Aurelia George Mulgan, *The Politics of Agriculture in Japan* (New York: Routledge, 2000).

6. Comments of Japan Tobacco Inc., in "Investigation of Japan's Practice with Respect to the Manufacture, Importation and Sale of Tobacco Products," Chairman, Section 301 Committee, Office of the United States Trade Representative, Docket No. 301–350, p. 38, on file with author. Similarly, the amount of land devoted to tobacco cultivation has been shrinking, from over 85,000 hectares in 1965, to 47,801 in 1985 and 23,991 in 2000. Because of more efficient farming techniques, however, there has been a much smaller proportional drop in production. Data provided by Zenkoku Tabako Kōsaku Kumiai (Tobacco Growers Association), Tokyo, Japan.

7. Kaori Iida and Robert N. Proctor, "Learning from Philip Morris: Japan Tobacco's Campaign to Distort the Nature and Magnitude of Tobacco Health Harms as Revealed in Internal Documents from the American Tobacco Industry," unpublished manuscript, on file with author.

8. See, for example, Jennifer Robertson, *Takarazuka: Sexual Politics and Popular Culture in Modern Japan* (Berkeley, CA: University of California Press, 1998); Ian Buruma, *Behind the Mask: On Sexual Demons, Sacred Mothers, Transvestites, Gangsters, and other Japanese Cultural Heroes* (New York: Pantheon Books, 1984).

9. For a discussion of the denormalization of smoking in the United States, see Robert A. Kagan and Jerome H. Skolnick, "Banning Smoking: Compliance Without Enforcement," in *Smoking Policy: Law, Politics, and Culture*, eds. Robert L. Rabin and Stephen D. Sugarman *(New York: Oxford University Press*, 1993), 69–94.

10. See infra pp. 58–64.

11. Daniel H. Foote, "The Benevolent Paternalism of Japanese Criminal Justice," *California Law Review*, vol. 80 (1992).

12. Dorrine Kondo, *Crafting Selves: Power, Gender, and Discourses of Identity in a Japanese Workplace* (Chicago: University of Chicago Press, 1990); Frank K. Upham, "Weak Legal Consciousness as Invented Tradition," in *Mirror of Modernity: Invented Traditions of Modern Japan*, ed. Steven Vlastos (Berkeley, CA: University of California Press, 1998), 48–64.

13. Japan Tobacco Foundation, *Tobacco & Salt Museum* (Tokyo: Benrido Ltd., 1988), 24–25.

14. Ibid.

15. Nihon Tabako Sangyo Kabushiki Gaisha (Japan Tobacco Inc., or JT), "Heisei 11 Nen Zenkoku Tabako Kitsuensharitsu Chōsa" (National survey of smoking prevalence, 1999), News Release No. 19, October 22, 1999.

16. Ibid.

17. JT, News Release, November 10, 2003. These statistics are similar to the conclusions of the Koseirodosho (Ministry of Health, Labor and Welfare, or MHLW). In 1999, the ministry surveyed 12,858 people and determined that smoking prevalence was 52.8 percent among men and 13.4 percent among women. See MHLW, Kitsuen to Kenkō Mondai ni Kansuru Jittai Chōsa Hōkokusho (Report of a survey on the actual conditions of the smoking and health problem) (Tokyo, March 2000), 18. Interestingly, MHLW smoking data has for the past decade identified substantially fewer smokers than has JT data. For example, according to JT, in 1991, 61.2 percent of men and 14.2 percent of women smoked, whereas according to MHLW the figures were 50.6 percent and 9.7 percent, respectively. See Tobacco Problems Information Center (Tokyo) (TOPIC), "Smoking in Japan—2000 Profile," March 2000, 8.

18. The steady decline in the percentage of male smokers in Japan may seem to suggest that Japanese anti-tobacco policy is having an impact. There is no policy or set of policies, however, that could plausibly account for the steady fall in smoking rates. The most likely reason for the decline is that as the link between smoking and cancer has become publicly known, an increasing number of people have been unwilling to take the health risk associated with tobacco consumption. In addition, there has been a subtle shift in the social acceptability of smoking, from uncritical acceptance to the grudging creation of no-smoking areas, and this gentle social sanction may be causing a smaller percentage of people to smoke.

19. "Smoking on the Rise among Young Japanese Women," Kyodo News Service,

November 11, 1987. The data, presented by Dr. Saito Rieko, were based on several small surveys conducted around Tokyo; the findings were not robust.

20. "Survey: Smoking Up among Youth, Women, Survey Indicates," Kyodo News Service, May 6, 1989.

21. MHLW, *Report of a Survey on the Actual Conditions of the Smoking and Health Problem,* 18–19.

22. Sone Tomofumi, "Exposure of Japanese School Children to Smoking-Related Environmental Factors," *Journal of Epidemiology* 10 (3): 183 (2000). It should also be noted that Japanese health professionals are heavy smokers. Results of a survey published in May 2000, which investigated smoking prevalence of all members of Fukui Prefecture's medication association, found that 27.8 percent of men were smokers, as were 5.2 percent of women. See Kawahara Kazuo et al., "Study of Smoking Behavior of Medical Doctors in Fukui, Japan and Their Antismoking Measures," *Journal of Epidemiology* 10 (3): 157 (2000). These results are similar to the preliminary findings of a study by National Institute of Public Health (Japan) epidemiologist Minowa Masumi, indicating that 26.1 percent of male medical professionals smoke, as do 6.6 percent of the females. See Minowa Masumi et al., "Nihon Ishikaiin Kitsuen Chōsa" (Survey of smoking among members of the Japan Medical Association, 2000) (preliminary findings, on file with author). Similarly, Kobayashi Yumiko, formerly of Japan's National Cancer Center, conducted a survey in 1993 that compared smoking rates between two groups—4,500 nurses and women generally. She found that nurses working at general hospitals and medical centers were 1.2 times more likely to smoke than women generally. See "More Young Women Light Up despite Decline in Smoking," *Daily Yomiuri,* July 28, 1994.

23. Kaori Honjo and Ichiro Kawachi, "Effects of Market Liberalization on Smoking in Japan," *Tobacco Control* 9: 193–200, figure 2 (2000).

24. Ibid., figure 3.

25. MHLW, *Report of a Survey on the Actual Conditions of the Smoking and Health Problem,* 20.

26. JT, <http://www.jtnet.ad.jp/WWW/JT/JTI/keiei/97/3–2.html>.

27. TOPIC, "Smoking in Japan," 8.

28. <http://www5.who.int/tobacco/repository/tld104/Japan.pdf>

29. Some researchers claim that lung cancer rates in Japan are still quite low, at least when compared to per-capita tobacco consumption, and they seek to explain this biologically. One group of researchers, from Aichi Cancer Center, recently argued that the consumption of fish, particularly sushi, may explain low lung cancer rates in Japan. See Toshiro Takezaki et al., "Dietary Factors and Lung Cancer Risk in Japanese: With Special Reference to Fish Consumption and Adenocarcinomas," *British Journal of Cancer* 84: 1199–1206 (2001).

30. Tominaga Suketami and Oshima Akira, eds., *Cancer Mortality and Morbidity Statistics: Japan and the World—1999* (Tokyo: Japan Scientific Societies Press, 1999), 14 (Japanese Cancer Association, Gann Monograph on Cancer Research No. 47).

31. Ibid., 10.

32. Ibid.

33. Currently, approximately 2 percent, down from 18 percent. The Japanese government is not alone in valuing high tobacco-tax revenues. In 1999, 6 percent of German tax revenues came from tobacco, as did 13 percent of those in China. See "Governments Can Be Addicted to Cigarettes," *Wall Street Journal*, October 2, 2000.

34. Section 301 of Trade Act of 1974, 19 U.S.C. §2411 (1994).

35. Andrea J. Hageman, "US Tobacco Exports: The Dichotomy between Trade and Health Policies," *Minnesota Journal of Global Trade* 1: 178 (1992).

36. *Federal Register* 44(63), 37,609 (March 30, 1979).

37. *Federal Register* 44(218), 64,938 (November 8, 1979). Eventually, the CAA and ATM complaints were consolidated by the U.S. Trade Representative, and a General Agreement on Tariffs and Trade (GATT) panel was formed. Before the case reached a conclusion, however, there was an agreement, tariffs were reduced, and other import restrictions were liberalized. See Hageman, "US Tobacco Exports," 185.

38. Hageman, "US Tobacco Exports," 185, citing *The Life and Selected Writings of Thomas Jefferson,* eds. Adrienne Koch and William Peden (New York: Random House Modern Library, 1944), 369.

39. Japan Tobacco Foundation, *Tobacco & Salt Museum.*

40. Peter Schmeisser, in "When Health and Trade Policies Clash," *National Journal,* April 16, 1988, implies that foreign pressure was the only important cause.

41. Sato Hajime, Araki Shunichi, and Yokoyama Kazuhito, "Influence of Monopoly Privatization and Market Liberalization on Smoking Prevalence in Japan: Trends of Smoking Prevalence in Japan in 1975–1995," *Addiction* 95 (7): 1080 (2000).

42. See JT, *1999 Annual Report* (for the year ending March 31, 1999), 15.

43. Japan Tobacco Inc. Law (Nippon Tabako Sangyo Kabushiki Gaisha), No. 69 of August 10, 1984.

44. The Japan Tobacco Inc. Law created JT as a joint-stock company with 2 million shares. Until 1994 the government held all the shares. In October of that year, MOF sold 394,276 shares to the public, and in June 1996, it sold 272,390 more. In total, therefore, 666,666 shares were sold, and the government continues to hold 1,333,334 shares, or 66.7 percent. See JT, *1999 Annual Report,* 4.

45. Aurelia George Mulgan, *The Politics of Agriculture in Japan* (New York: Routledge, 2000).

46. Tobacco Enterprise Law, No. 68 of August 10, 1984 (enforced from April 1, 1985, abolishing the Tobacco Monopoly Law, No. 111 of 1949, and Tobacco Products Fixed Price Law, No. 122 of 1965).

47. One consequence of this high tariff was that U.S. cigarettes, such as Lark, cost ¥290, while domestic brands, such as Mild Seven, cost ¥180. See Honjo and Kawachi, "Effects of Market Liberalization," 194.

48. *Executory Order and Reasons for a Tobacco Manufacturing Monopoly* (Tabako seizō sembai seido riyūoyobi shikō junjo), quoted in *Tabako Sembai-shi* (A history of the tobacco monopoly), 6th ed., vol. 1 (Tokyo: Nihon Tabako Sangyō (K. K. Shashi Hensan-shitsu, 1991), 7, cited in Levin, "Smoke around the Rising Sun."

49. Gale Eisenstodt and Hiroko Katayama, "A Trade Threat That Worked," *Forbes*, April 3, 1989.

50. *Federal Register* 10, 37,609 (September 16, 1985). For data on the trade deficit, see <http://www.mnsfld.edu/depts/lib/trade-data.txt>.

51. Ibid.

52. Ibid.

53. Clayton Yeutter, "Memorandum for Minister Makoto Utsumi," February 19, 1986 (on file with author).

54. Japan's market was not the only one that U.S. negotiators sought to open. After the Japanese market was cracked in 1986, Taiwan's opened in 1987, South Korea's in 1988, and Thailand's soon after. See Ted T. L. Chen and Alvin E. Winder, "The Opium Wars Revisited as US Forces Tobacco Exports in Asia," *American Journal of Public Health* 80 (6): 659 (1990).

55. The organization representing U.S. tobacco leaf exporters opposed the action, since American tobacco leaf was imported in large quantities by Japan to blend with domestically grown tobacco.

56. One of the Japanese negotiators complained to me that because there is nothing in Japan like the U.S. Trade Representative, the Japanese side was at a distinct disadvantage. Author's confidential interviews with Japanese corporate/government officials, summer 2000.

57. Peter Schmeisser, "Pushing Cigarettes Overseas," *New York Times Magazine*, July 10, 1988.

58. "U.S. Settles Tobacco Dispute with Japan; No Deal Reached with Brazil on Informatics," *International Trade Reporter* 3: 1215–1216 (1986).

59. Ibid.

60. Ibid.

61. JT, *1999 Annual Report*.

62. Statistics and Information Department, Ministry of Agriculture, Forestry and Fisheries, *Abstract of Statistics on Agriculture Forestry and Fisheries in Japan 1999*, 54.

63. Sato, Araki, and Yokoyama, "Influence of Monopoly Privatization and Market Liberalization," 1084.

64. Alvin E. Winder, Ted T. L. Chen, William C. Mfuko, "Influence of American Tobacco Imports on Smoking Rates among Women and Youth in Asia," *International Quarterly of Community Health Education* 14 (4): 345–359 (1993–1994).

65. Chen and Winder, "The Opium Wars Revisited," 660.

66. Some critics argue that U.S. trade policy should not contradict its health policy, and that it is immoral to maintain a strict set of antismoking measures

at home while promoting the sale of tobacco products abroad. See, for example, "US Tobacco Exports," 196, where Hageman praises the Cigarette Export Reform Act, which would assign officials from the Department of Health and Human Services to committees contemplating action under Section 301 of the Trade Act. See also Jonathan Wike, "The Marlboro Man in Asia: U.S. Tobacco and Human Rights," *Vanderbilt Journal of Transnational Law* 29: 329–361 (1996); Chen and Winder, "The Opium Wars Revisited."

67. Honjo and Kawachi, "Effects of Market Liberalization," 198.

68. Isayama Yoshio, *Gendai Tabako Sensō* (The contemporary tobacco war) (Tokyo: Iwanami Shinsho, 1999), chap. 1.

69. Sato, Araki, and Yokoyama, "Influence of Monopoly Privatization and Market Liberalization," 1085.

70. <http://www.cdc.gov/tobacco/sgr/sgr_2000/factsheets/ factsheets_taxation.htm>, visited May 3, 2003.

71. Ibid.

72. Author's confidential interviews with Japanese corporate/government officials, summer 2000.

73. "Japan Tobacco Inc. Strongly Opposes the Liberal Democratic Party Tobacco Excise Tax Initiative," *Business Wire,* December 8, 1999.

74. Ibid.

75. TOPIC, "Smoking in Japan."

76. Centers for Disease Control and Prevention, "Responses to Increases in Cigarette Prices by Race/Ethnicity, Income, and Age Groups, US 1976–93," *Morbidity and Mortality Weekly Report* 47: 605–628 (July 31, 1998); Kenneth E. Warner, "Cigarette Taxation: Doing Good by Doing Well," *Journal of Public Health Policy* (September 1984): 312–319.

77. Gary D. Allinson, *Japan's Postwar History* (Ithaca, NY: Cornell University Press, 1997), 164–165.

78. Statistics Bureau, Management and Coordination Agency, *Annual Report on the Family Income and Expenditure Survey—1998* (in Japanese) (Tokyo: Management and Coordination Agency, 1998), 152–155.

79. Tobacco Enterprise Law, Article 40.

80. For a detailed discussion of the history of tobacco advertising in the United States, see Richard Kluger, *Ashes to Ashes: America's Hundred-Year War, the Public Health, and the Unabashed Triumph of Philip Morris* (New York: Vintage Books, 1997).

81. See, for example, Donald MacIntyre, "No Warning," *Time Asia,* October 9, 2000, who notes that in September 2000 JT gave out 15 million cigarettes on Respect for the Aged Day. JT has been making these "contributions to society" since 1965.

82. TOPIC, "Smoking in Japan," citing MHLW, Tobacco Action Plan Study Committee, Report of March 29, 1995, p. 7.

83. Henry Saffer and Frank Chaloupka, "The Effect of Tobacco Advertising Bans on Tobacco Consumption," *Journal of Health Economics* 19: 1117 (2000).

84. Sato, Araki, and Yokoyama, "Influence of Monopoly Privatization and Market Liberalization," 1084.

85. TOPIC, "Smoking in Japan–2003," August 1, 2003, 4–5.

86. JT, *1999 Annual Report.*

87. According to JT Corporate Profile (Tokyo: JT, n.d.), in 1996 the National Federation of Tobacco Retailers of Japan issued restrictions on night sales of cigarettes from vending machines.

88. Mark Levin, "Japan: Streets Unsafe as Machines Prey on Children," *Tobacco Control* 9: 132–133 (2000).

89. Hirayama Takeshi, "Non-Smoking Wives of Heavy Smokers Have a Higher Risk of Lung Cancer: A Study from Japan," *British Medical Journal* 282: 183–185 (1981); see also Hirayama Takeshi, "Cancer Mortality in Nonsmoking Women with Smoking Husbands Based on a Large-Scale Cohort Study in Japan," *Prev Med* 6: 680–690 (Nov. 13, 1984).

90. One of the most innovative attempts in Japan to reduce tobacco consumption and limit the impact of ETS is the recent development by Triumph International Ltd. of its so-called "non-smoking manifesto bra" and panties. Both are said to release fragrances that discourage the desire to smoke, and are covered with anti-smoking logos. Neither is yet commercially available. See "Japanese Company Invents Nonsmoking Bra," *Billings Gazette*, November 5, 2003.

91. Isayama, *The Contemporary Tobacco War,* chap. 3.

92. "Anti-smoking Campaign Meets Stiff Resistance," Jiji Press Ticker Service, April 21, 1988.

93. "Smoking Faces Ban on Japanese Flights," United Press International, May 14, 1998; "JAL, ANA to Ban Smoking on All International Flights," Kyodo News Service, September 9, 1998.

94. "Airlines to Press Ban on Smoking," *Asahi Evening News,* February 9, 2000.

95. Ibid.

96. "Warnings Alone Are Not Enough," *Japan Times,* March 21, 1999.

97. JT, *Environmental Report 1999,* 16.

98. Stephen Sugarman has argued that Japan's weak warning on cigarette packs makes JT vulnerable to product liability suits because the warning misleadingly implies that moderate smoking is not dangerous. See Stephen D. Sugarman, "Tobacco Litigation and the Anti-smoking Movement in the U.S. and Japan," 7 (as revised, March 15, 1999), at <http://www.law.berkeley.edu/faculty/sugarmans/WASEDA.htm>.

99. "Over 60 percent of Japanese Men Smoke, Report Says," Kyodo News Service, May 28, 1993.

100. "Survey: Smoking Up among Youth, Women, Survey Indicates," Kyodo News Service, May 6, 1989.

101. See Nishida Eiichi, "Kitsuen o Meguru Kenri Ishiki" (Rights consciousness and smoking), in *Tabako Byō Soshō no Hōshakaigaku: Gendai no Hō to Saiban no Kaidoku ni Mukete* (The legal sociology of litigation over tobacco-related

illness: Deciphering the contemporary laws and trials), ed. Tanase Takao (Kyoto: Sekai Shisōsha, 2000).

102. "Warnings Alone Are Not Enough."

103. Asako Murakami, "Secondhand Smoke Has More Fuming, Hotline Finds," *Japan Times*, June 6, 1999.

104. Antismoking activity in Japan goes back at least to 1886, when the Japan Women's Temperance Union (JWTU) was founded. In the late nineteenth century, minors had easy access to tobacco, and smoking was often permitted in schools. Nemoto Shō, a prominent Christian politician, returned to Japan after studying in the United States and began to press for a law that would limit tobacco use among children. He mobilized politicians and laypersons, and successfully sponsored Japan's 1900 legislation that prohibits minors from smoking. Author's interview with Matsumoto Shigeko and Kawatani Yoshiko, JWTU, June 8, 2000. Part of Nemoto's legacy is the surprising number of Christians involved in Japan's contemporary antismoking movement. I say "surprising" because less than 10 percent of Japan's population are Christian, and they are not terribly active in the political arena. My unsystematic questioning nevertheless revealed that a large number of Christians are involved in the current antismoking movement. The Japan Association against Tobacco (formerly Japan Action on Smoking and Health), for example—an umbrella organization of seventy-one antismoking groups with 70,000 members—is run by a Seventh Day Adventist. Other antismoking groups include Nihon Kin-en Yūaikai (smoking cessation friendship group), the biggest group of its kind in Japan, with 45,000 members; Tabako Mondai Shutoken Kyōgikai (metropolitan conference on the tobacco problem), a support group for the lawsuit against JT and the government; Tabako Mondai Jyōhō Senta (tobacco problem information center); Tabako Soshō o Sasaeru Kai (tobacco litigation support group); Bun-en Shakai o Mezasu Kai (group for the separation of smokers and nonsmokers); and the Japan Medical-Dental Association for Tobacco Control.

105. A detailed account of the movement can be found in Isayama Yoshio, *Ken-en-Ken o Kangaeru* (Thinking about the right to hate smoke) (Tokyo: Iwanami Shinsho, 1983). The descriptive details I provide in this section are drawn from Isayama's book.

106. Ibid.

107. Ibid. The full opinion of the Tokyo District Court can be found at 630 *Hanrei Taimuzu* 234–258 (May 15, 1987).

108. Isayama, *Thinking about the Right to Hate Smoke.*

109. See, for example, Hasegawa Kōchi, "Gendaigata Soshō Shakai Undōronteki Kōsatsu" (A social-movement inquiry into contemporary litigation), *Hōritsu Jihō* 61 (12): 65–71 (1989).

110. Article 13 provides: "All of the people shall be respected as individuals. Their right to life, liberty, and the pursuit of happiness shall, to the extent that it does not interfere with the public welfare, be the supreme consideration in legisla-

tion and in order governmental affairs." Article 25 provides: "All people shall have the right to maintain the minimum standards of wholesome and cultured living. In all spheres of life, the state shall use its endeavors for the promotion and extension of social welfare and security, and of public health."

111. See Isayama, *Thinking about the Right to Hate Smoke,* chap. 3.

112. *Jyunin gendo* functions as a balancing test that weighs the value of a particular act against the harm it causes. Courts have used this standard in a variety of environmental cases as a way of comparing the social benefits of certain actions with their attendant harms to individual rights. If courts find that the harms are within "tolerable limits," then they will neither enjoin nor penalize the actions.

113. Isayama, *Thinking about the Right to Hate Smoke,* chap. 3.

114. Some of the more interesting cases are the following. In 1991, the Nagoya District Court rejected the request of a teacher who wanted to limit smoking to a particular room in the school. The Tokyo District Court rejected a similar case at almost the same time, denying relief to a researcher at the Tokyo Institute of Hygiene who wanted smoking limited to a single, well-ventilated smoking room. A case brought by a local government official to the Yamaguchi District Court, and later appealed to the Hiroshima High Court and the Supreme Court in 1998, sought to ban smoking in the local government office, and asked for financial compensation. The plaintiff's claim was denied. In a 1996 case against the state before the Nagoya High Court, five office workers in Aichi Prefecture claimed to be suffering from ETS and sought a ban on the production and importation of tobacco. The case was dismissed *(kyakka)* on the grounds that the issue was inappropriate for a legal claim. In an ETS-based suit against JT, four office workers in the same prefecture demanded a ban on the production and sale of tobacco, and ¥1 million each. The Nagoya District Court rejected *(kikyaku)* the case in November 1998. A group of teachers brought a case against Prime Minister (and former Minister of Health and Welfare) Hashimoto Ryutaro, a heavy smoker and longtime ally of big tobacco. They insisted that as a matter of public education, he should be prohibited from smoking. In February 1998, Nagoya District Court Judge Inada Tatsuki found that Hashimoto's smoking was not unconstitutional. In September of that same year, Nagoya High Court Judge Teramoto Eiichi upheld the lower-court ruling, stating that "smoking is a question of individual preference."

The first case against a foreign tobacco manufacturer was brought to the Nagoya courts in March 1998—a claim against Philip Morris on behalf of twenty teachers, public servants, and other antismoking activists. The plaintiffs demanded that Philip Morris stop selling its products in Japan (the company had a 13 percent share of the Japanese market in 1998). In addition, they expressed concern about passive smoking, complained that Philip Morris took advantage of Japan's lax tobacco-control laws by substituting the Japanese for the American warning on cigarette packs, and asserted that the company sold its products despite knowing about tobacco's dangers. Each plaintiff requested ¥100,000. This case is currently pending.

115. Nagoya District Court, Case No. 4181, p. 59 (March 15, 1999).

116. Nagoya District Court, Case No. 1180, p. 48 (November 13, 1998).

117. Ibid., 39.

118. Nagoya District Court, Case No. 4181, pp. 36, 39.

119. Given the limited fact-finding abilities of Japanese courts, it may be that plaintiffs' attorneys have failed to provide the judges in these cases with the relevant medical literature.

120. Nicotine dependence is classified as a disease in the United States in the *Diagnostic and Statistical Manual III,* and internationally by the World Health Organization's *International Statistical Classification of Diseases, Tenth Revision.* Yet in 1998 Judge Nakamura cited both of these sources and still concluded that nicotine dependence is not generally thought of as a disease. His conclusions echo the claims of an MOF Smoking and Health Subcommittee in a 1991 report, which minimized the seriousness of tobacco dependence and carefully avoided calling it a disease.

121. Nagoya District Court, Case No. 4181, p. 40.

122. Nagoya District Court, Case No. 778, p. 37 (February 26, 1998); Nagoya High Court, Case No. 199, p. 52 (September 30, 1998).

123. See Nishida, "Rights Consciousness and Smoking."

124. Author's interviews with anti-tobacco attorneys in Japan, 2000–2001.

125. JT was a party of the U.S. Master Settlement Agreement. In JT's *1999 Annual Report,* 10, the company writes that it participated in the settlement because it could not otherwise continue to be profitable in the United States. "We see the settlement as reflecting the unique nature of legal, political and cultural issues in the United States." According to the company, three points were confirmed in the settlement: settling helps to avoid the further expense of continuing litigation; manufacturers denied allegations of unlawful conduct; and the settlement is effective only in the United States.

126. Three have lung cancer; three, emphysema; one, throat cancer. Four plaintiffs have died since the start of the litigation, so there are currently three living plaintiffs.

127. Plaintiffs propose the following warnings: "tobacco (cigarettes) causes cancer," "smoking might kill you," "tobacco causes heart attacks and heart disease," "smoking by pregnant women may result in fetal injury," "tobacco is very addictive," "smoking cessation reduces serious damage to your health," and "your smoke harms the health of others around you."

128. JT, *1999 Annual Report,* 14.

129. Tokyo District Court, Case No. 10379, October 21, 2003.

130. Nagoya District Court, Case No. 4181, p. 40 (emphasis added).

131. That is not exactly how things worked out in the United States, but the logic of shifting wealth from the evil tobacco industry to suffering individuals had a certain ring of plausibility.

132. See statistics in Committee to Establish a Plan for *"Healthy Japan 21," Healthy Japan 21 Report.* See also note 132 and its accompanying text.

133. See the MHLW's 1987 and 1993 white papers on smoking and health.

134. In *Thinking about the Right to Hate Smoke,* Isayama states that from 1994 to 1997, MHLW's smoking-related budget was only ¥7.8 million per year.

135. See note 132 and accompanying text.

136. Chang-Ran Kim, "Japan Unveils Plan to Reduce Cigarette Consumption," *Wall Street Journal Interactive Edition,* August 12, 1999.

137. Quoted in "Industry Opposition Thwarts Ministry Plan to Cut Smoking," *Daily Yomiuri,* January 26, 2000.

138. "Now the Japanese Are Really Smokin'," *Independent Online,* May 10, 2000 (article no. 42430 at <http://www.globalink.org> (access restricted)).

139. Ibid.

140. In "Smoking, Sake, and Suicide: Japan Plans a Healthier Future," *Lancet* 354 (9181) (September 4, 1999), Sarah Ramsay states: "An intra-ministerial confrontation now looms between finance and health bureaucrats over the new proposals. In the past, this would have been a no-contest, but the Finance Ministry has been weakened by scandals and recession, while the influence of the Health Ministry is set to grow along with the rapid aging of Japan's population." She overestimates the changes in the balance of bureaucratic power, for a weakened MOF remains far more powerful than a strengthened MHLW.

141. The MHLW's *21 Seiki ni Okeru Kokumin Kenkō Zukuri Undō* (Kenkō Nihon 21) (Movement to improve the health of citizens in the twenty-first century: *Healthy Japan 21*) (March 2000), is the final report, based on the report of the Kenkō Nihon 21 Kikaku Kentō Kai (Committee to establish a plan for *"Healthy Japan 21"*, *Kenkō Nihon 21 Keikaku Sakutei Kentō Kai, 21 Seiki ni Okeru Kokumin Kenkō Zukuri Undō (Kenkō Nihon 21 ni Tsuite): Hōkokushō* (February 2000) [hereinafter *Healthy Japan 21 Report*].

142. Committee to Establish a Plan for *"Healthy Japan 21," Healthy Japan 21 Report,* 4–8.

143. Ibid., 4–3 to 4–5.

144. Ibid., 4–3. Hoizumi Tadao, a prominent Japanese attorney, points out in *Kabushiki Kaisha Kinyobi* (Corporate Weekly Friday, Tokyo), April 21, 2000, that even if the targets had survived, there was nothing in the plan to make them attainable, which makes one wonder if MHLW took them seriously.

145. Sato Noriko, "Antismokers Say Antismoking Measures Halfhearted in Japan," Kyodo News International, July 28, 1998. For the committee, see note 132 and accompanying text.

146. "Passive Smoking Law Clears the Air, No Butts About It," *Asahi Shimbun,* May 2, 2003, <www.asahi.com/english/national/k2003050200392.html>.

147. Ibid.

3. Rights and Public Health in the Balance

1. Robert A. Kagan and David Vogel, "The Politics of Smoking Regulation: Canada, France, the United States," in *Smoking Policy: Law, Politics, and Culture*, (eds. Robert L. Rabin and Stephen D. Sugarman (New York: Oxford University Press, 1993), 24.

2. Rob Cunningham, *Smoke & Mirrors: The Canadian Tobacco War* ((Ottawa: International Development Research Center, 1996), 189, 194.

3. Ibid., 191.

4. Quoted in Cunningham, *Smoke & Mirrors*, 49.

5. According to Cunningham, *Smoke & Mirrors*, 189, Canada ranked first in the world in per-capita consumption of cigarettes from 1980 to 1982.

6. Kagan and Vogel, "The Politics of Smoking Regulation," 28.

7. Health Canada, *Canadian Tobacco Use Monitoring Survey (CTUMS)*, 2000 (available at <http://www.hc-sc.gc.ca/hecs-sesc/tobacco/research/ctums/ctums_ annual_2000.html>). Note that in 1993 Health and Welfare Canada became Health Canada.

8. Statistics Canada, *Canadian Statistics—Percentage of Smokers in the Population* (2002) (available at <http://www.statcan.ca/english/Pgdb/People/Health/health07b.htm>).

9. *Tobacco Act*, S.C. 1997, c. 13, §4.

10. The Court identified these deficiencies in *RJR-MacDonald Inc. v. Canada (Attorney-General)*, [1995] 3 S.C.R. 199 (available at http://www.lexum.umontreal.ca/csc=scc/en/pub/1995/vol3/html/1995scr30199.html). We elaborate on this decision in the next section.

11. The TPCA simply banned all tobacco advertising. The Tobacco Act defines "lifestyle advertising" as "advertising that associates a product with, or evokes a positive or negative emotion about or image of, a way of life such as one that includes glamour, recreation, excitement, vitality, risk or daring." Brand-preference advertising is "advertising that promotes a tobacco product by means of its brand characteristics." Tobacco Act, §22(4).

12. Tobacco Act, §15(3).

13. Ibid., §17(a).

14. *J.T.I. MacDonald Corp. v. Canada*, No. 500–05–031299–975, Quebec Superior Court, December 13, 2002.

15. Non-Smokers' Health Act, R.S.C. 1985, c. 15 (4th Supp.). The legislation was introduced as a private members' bill in 1986, was passed by Parliament in 1988, and came into force in 1989.

16. Ibid., §3(1).

17. Michael J. Stewart, "The Effect on Tobacco Consumption of Advertising Bans in OECD Countries," *International Journal of Advertising* 12: 155–180 (1993); N. E. Collishaw et al., "Monitoring the Effectiveness of Canada's Health-Oriented Tobacco Policies" (Health Canada, 1990).

18. Joy Townsend, "Price and Consumption of Tobacco," *British Medical Bulletin* 52: 32–142 (1996).

19. For an overview of tobacco litigation in Canada, see Margaret Drent, "Backgrounder 41: Recent Developments in Tobacco Litigation" (Ontario Legislative Library, 2000) (available at <http://www.ontla.on.ca/library/b41tx.htm>).

20. *JTI-MacDonald v. Attorney-General of British Columbia,* (Docket Nos. C985777, C985780, C985781, para. 222 (S. Ct. B.C., March 12, 2000) (available at <http://www.courts.gov.bc.ca/ jdb-txt/sc/00/03/s00–0312.htm>).

21. Available at <http://www.ncth.ca/NCTHweb.nsf>.

22. John Stuart Mill, *On Liberty* (Indianapolis: Bobbs-Merrill, 1956), 100.

23. *R. v. Butler,* [1992] 1 S.C.R. 452, 492.

24. Kagan and Vogel, "The Politics of Smoking Regulation," 28–29.

25. The tobacco industry has had close ties to policy makers in Canada. For example, Paul Martin (the former minister of finance) and Bernard Roy (the former principal secretary to Prime Minister Brian Mulroney) have been directors of major tobacco companies, and the industry's lobbying arm was led by Norman Spector, Mulroney's former chief of staff. See Cunningham, *Smoke & Mirrors,* 21, 155.

26. See <http://www.tobaccofacts.org> (a Web site sponsored by the British Columbia Ministry of Health).

27. Government of Canada, Cabinet Minutes 41 (May 11, 1967), p. 7 (cited in Cunningham, *Smoke & Mirrors,* 52).

28. Cunningham, *Smoke & Mirrors,* 60, 180. Canada is the sixth largest producer of flue-cured tobacco in the world.

29. Marc Lalonde, *A New Perspective on the Health of Canadians* (Ottawa: Health and Welfare Canada, 1974).

30. Malcolm Taylor, *Insuring National Health Care: The Canadian Experience* (Chapel Hill, N.C.: University of North Carolina Press, 1990), 201–202.

31. Jake Epp, *Achieving Health for All: A Framework for Health Promotion* (Ottawa: Health and Welfare Canada, 1986).

32. Since then, Canada has been lauded in the international community for its commitment to the public health aspects of reducing tobacco consumption. In 1997, Canada hosted the first WHO meeting to prepare an international framework convention on tobacco control and has pledged support to the Framework Convention on Tobacco Control, (a multilateral initiative passed by the WHO member states in 1999.

33. Cunningham, *Smoke & Mirrors,* 68–69, 186.

34. A. Paul Pross and Iain S. Stewart, "Breaking the Habit: Attentive Publics and Tobacco Regulation," in *How Ottawa Spends, 1994–95: Making Change,* ed. Susan D. Phillips (Ottawa: Carleton University Press, 1994), 134–135. Canadian World Cup champion skiers Ken Read and Steve Podborski refused to accept their awards in the "Export 'A' Cup" in 1983, and the Canadian Ski Association's Medical Committee also protested the sponsorship.

35. Cunningham, *Smoke & Mirrors,* 70–77.

36. By November 1987, a Gallup poll found that 61.5 percent of respondents in Canada supported bans on tobacco advertising. Pross and Stewart, "Breaking the Habit," 140.

37. See "Tobacco Timeline," available at <http://www.tobaccofacts.org/tru-timeline-05 .html> (accessed March 4, 2002).

38. The warnings were:
    - Cigarettes are addictive
    - Smoking can kill you
    - Tobacco smoke can harm your children
    - Cigarettes cause fatal lung disease
    - Smoking during pregnancy can harm your baby
    - Tobacco smoke causes fatal lung disease in non-smokers
    - Cigarettes cause strokes and heart disease

39. Charlotte Gray, "Tobacco Wars: The Bloody Battle between Good Health and Good Politics," *Canadian Medical Association Journal* 156: 238 (1997).

40. Cunningham, *Smoke & Mirrors,* 125. On February 28, 2003, the Royal Canadian Mounted Police charged eight tobacco company executives with fraud and conspiracy following a four-year investigation into tobacco smuggling operations. Peter Cheney and Victor Malarek, "Top Tobacco Executives Charged with Sending Cigarettes to Smugglers," *Globe and Mail,* March 1, 2003, p. A1.

41. Vivian H. Hamilton, Carey Levinton, Yvan St-Pierre, and Franque Grimard, "The Effect of Tobacco Tax Cuts on Cigarette Smoking in Canada," *Canadian Medical Association Journal* 156: 188 (1997).

42. Ibid., 189–190.

43. *RJR-MacDonald v. Canada (Attorney-General),* [1995] 3 S.C.R. 199 (available at <http://www.lexum.umontreal.ca/csc-scc/en/pub/1995/vol3/html/1995scr3_0199.html>).

44. Interveners are analogous to amici curiae before the U.S. Supreme Court. There were no interveners in support of the tobacco companies' position. Quebec intervened to challenge the law's constitutionality on federalism grounds.

45. See Christopher P. Manfredi, *Judicial Power and the Charter: Canada and the Paradox of Liberal Constitutionalism,* 2d ed. (Toronto: Oxford University Press, 2001), 60–68.

46. Ibid., 38–42.

47. In rejecting the act's restrictions on promotion, Justices Major, McLachlin, and Sopinka refused to find even a rational connection between them and the legislative objective of preventing the harmful effects of tobacco consumption.

48. *RJR-MacDonald v. Canada (Attorney-General),* para. 75.

49. Ibid., para. 118.

50. Ibid., para. 136.

51. In an effort to blunt the impact of this concession to the tobacco companies, the regulations require the warnings to be larger and more graphic.

52. *Vriend v. Alberta,* [1998] 1 S.C.R. 493.

53. Ibid., 565.

54. The principal source for the dialogue metaphor was Peter W. Hogg and Allison A. Bushell, "The *Charter* Dialogue between Courts and Legislatures," *Osgoode Hall Law Journal* 35: 75–124 (1997).

55. *R. v. Mills,* [1999] 3 S.C.R. 668, para. 58.

56. Donley T. Studlar, "Tobacco Control and Loss Imposition: Canada and the United States" (paper presented at the biannual meeting of the Association of Canadian Studies in the United States, Pittsburgh, PA, November 1999).

4. The Politics of Tobacco Control in Australia

1. David Rees Davies, "3 Year Plan," Bates Nos. 2504106548–50 (November 30, 1993). Simon Chapman and Melanie Wakefield provide similar quotations from industry documents in "Tobacco Control Advocacy in Australia: Reflections on 30 Years of Progress," *Health Education and Behaviour* 29: 274–289 (2001). The Bates documents cited in this chapter are available online at <http://www.pmdocs.com>.

2. Margaret Winstanley, Stephen Woodward, and Noni Walker, *Tobacco in Australia: Facts and Issues* (Melbourne: QuitVictoria, 1995), at <http://www.quit.org.au/quit/FandI/welcome.htm>; Australian Institute of Health and Welfare, *Statistics on Drug Use in Australia 2000* (Canberra: AIHW, 2001), 2. Tobacco consumption among Aboriginals and Torres Strait Islanders is almost double the national rate. Maggie Brady, "Historical and Cultural Roots of Tobacco Use among Aboriginal and Torres Strait Islander People," *Australian and New Zealand Journal of Public Health* 26: 120–124 (2002).

3. Chapman and Wakefield, "Tobacco Control Advocacy in Australia."

4. Australian Institute of Health and Welfare, *Statistics on Drug Use in Australia 2000,* p. 4.

5. Two substantial histories of Australian tobacco use and policy—Robin Walker, *Under Fire: A History of Tobacco Smoking in Australia* (Melbourne: Melbourne University Press, 1984), and Ian Tyrrell, *Deadly Enemies: Tobacco and Its Opponents in Australia* (Sydney: University of New South Wales Press, 1999)—provide the basis for analysis of the period up to 1980.

6. Tyrrell, *Deadly Enemies,* 22.

7. Walker, *Under Fire,* 75–85.

8. Tyrrell, *Deadly Enemies,* 164; Walker, *Under Fire,* 84.

9. Winstanley, Woodward, and Walker, *Tobacco in Australia.*

10. Tyrrell, *Deadly Enemies,* 172.

11. Walker, *Under Fire,* 88.

12. Ibid., 104.

13. Ibid., 112.

14. Heath Kelly, John Mengler, and Bruce Armstrong, "Smoking and Lung Cancer: The History of the Evidence That Smoking Causes Lung Cancer: Contemporary Criticisms and Legal Implications," *Journal of Law and Medicine* 2: 147–162 (1994).

15. Walker, *Under Fire*, 90–91, 110–111.

16. Nigel Gray, "Forty Years of Plotting for Public Health," *Medical Journal of Australia* 167: 587–589 (1997).

17. Walker, *Under Fire*, (109.

18. James Killen, *Killen: Inside Australian Politics* (North Ryde: Methuen Hayes, 1985), 256–257.

19. A declaration of interest: the author in more innocent times held the WD & HO Wills chair of administrative studies at the University of Papua New Guinea from 1974 to 1976.

20. Margaret H. Winstanley and Stephen Woodward, "Tobacco in Australia: An Overview," *Journal of Drug Issues* 22: 733–742 (1992).

21. Action on Smoking and Health (U.K.), *Danger! PR in the Playground: Tobacco Industry Initiatives on Youth Smoking* (London: ASH, 2000), at <http://www.ash.org.uk/html/advspo/html/playground.html>.

22. H. Cullman, "Smoking and Health Strategy—Some Recent Developments in Australia," Bates Nos. 2024978017–48, p. 18 (January 1978).

23. Walker, *Under Fire*, 98–99.

24. Simon Chapman, "A David and Goliath Story: Tobacco Advertising and Self-Regulation in Australia," *British Medical Journal* 281: 1187–1190 (1980).

25. Cullman, "Smoking and Health Strategy," 4.

26. Ibid., 10.

27. Ibid., 22.

28. Walker, *Under Fire*, 110.

29. Ibid., 88.

30. Cullman, "Smoking and Health Strategy," 14–15.

31. Media Council of Australia, *Voluntary Advertising Code for Cigarettes in Australia*(Australian Advertising Industry Council, 1979).

32. Chapman, "A David and Goliath Story."

33. Simon Chapman, "Civil Disobedience and Tobacco Control: The Case of BUGA UP," *Tobacco Control* 5: 179–185 (1996).

34. Simon Chapman, *The Lung Goodbye* (n.p., 1986); Simon Chapman and Deborah Lupton, *The Fight for Public Health: Principles and Practice of Media Advocacy* (London: BMJ, 1994).

35. See James Jupp, "Political Culture: The 'Bourgeois' and 'Proletarian' Variations," in *The Sydney-Melbourne Book*, ed. Jim Davidson (Sydney: Allen and Unwin, 1986); Leanne Wells, "The Australian National Tobacco Strategy," *Development Bulletin* 54: 33–38 (1986).

36. G. Egger et al., "Results of Large Scale Media Anti-Smoking Campaign in Australia: North Coast Quit for Life Campaign," *British Medical Journal* 287: 125–128 (1983).

37. John P. Pierce, "Australia's Leadership Role in the Evolution of Tobacco Programs in the United States," *Health Promotion Journal of Australia* 7: 11–17 (1997).

38. John Ballard, "The Constitution of AIDS in Australia: Taking 'Government at a Distance' Seriously," in *Governing Australia: Studies in Contemporary Rationalities of Government*, eds. Mitchell Dean and Barry Hindess (Cambridge, U.K.; New York: Cambridge University Press, 1998).

39. A. W. Musk, Ruth Shean, and Stephen Woodward, "Legislation for Smoking Control in Western Australia," *British Medical Journal* 290: 1562–1565 (1985).

40. William M. Castleden, David J. Nourish, and Stephen D. Woodward, "Changes in Tobacco Advertising in Western Australian Newspapers in Response to Proposed Government Legislation," *Medical Journal of Australia* 142: 305–308 (1985).

41. Simon Chapman and Christopher Reynolds, "Regulating Tobacco: The South Australian Tobacco Products Control Act 1986," *Community Health Studies* 11 (Supp.): 9–15 (1987).

42. Gray, "Forty Years of Plotting for Public Health."

43. Margaret Winstanley, *Overview of the Lobbying for the Victorian Tobacco Act (1987)* (Melbourne: Anti-Cancer Council of Victoria, 1993).

44. Lyn Roberts and Jean Leahy, *Case Study of the 1988 South Australian Lobbying Campaign for the Introduction of the Tobacco Products Control Act Amendment Act 1988* (Adelaide: Action on Smoking and Health, 1989).

45. Chapman and Lupton, *The Fight for Public Health*, 113–126.

46. Margaret Winstanley, *Lobbying for the Australian Smoking and Tobacco Products Advertisements (Prohibition) Act 1989* (Melbourne: Anti-Cancer Council of Victoria, 1993).

47. Philip Morris (Australia) Ltd., "Corporate Affairs Plan," Bates Nos. 2023240608–27 (1992).

48. David Collins and Helen Lapsley, *The Social Costs of Drug Abuse in Australia in 1988 and 1992* (Canberra: Commonwealth Department of Human Services and Health, 1996) (National Drug Strategy Monograph No. 30), at <http://www.health.gov.au/pubhlth/publicat/document/mono30.pdf>.

49. Roland Everingham and Stephen Woodward, *Tobacco Litigation: The Case against Passive Smoking, AFCO v TIA* (Sydney: Legal Books, 1991).

50. Simon Chapman et al., "Why the Tobacco Industry Fears the Passive Smoking Issue," *International Journal of Health Sciences* 20: 417–427 (1990).

51. Robyn Richmond, "A Survey of Policies and Programs for Tobacco, Alcohol and Other Drugs in Australia's Top 600 Companies," in *Conference on Alcohol and Drugs in the Workplace: Reducing the Costs: Melbourne, 18–19 April 1991* (Canberra: Australian Government Publishing Service, 1991).

52. Donna Staunton, "National Health and Medical Research Council's Review of Its 1986 Publication Entitled 'The Effects of Passive Smoking on Health,'" Bates Nos. 2504088601–06 (April 7, 1994).

53. Konrad Jamrozik, Simon Chapman, and Alistair Woodward, "How the NHMRC Got Its Fingers Burnt," *Medical Journal of Australia* 167: 371–374 (1997).

54. David Hill and Kate Hassard, "Australia's National Tobacco Campaign: Strong Medicine for a Big Problem," *Development Bulletin* 54: 39–42 (2001).

55. Commonwealth Department of Health and Aged Care, *National Tobacco Strategy 1999 to 2002–3: A Framework for National Action* (2000), at <http://www.health.gov.au/pubhlth/publicat/document/metadata/tobaccostrat.hrm>.

56. Wells, "The Australian National Tobacco Strategy."

57. National Public Health Partnership, *National Response to Passive Smoking in Enclosed Public Places and Workplaces: A Background Paper* (Melbourne: NPHP, 2000), at <http://www.dhs.vic.gov.au/nphp/legtools/smoking/passive/>.

58. PricewaterhouseCoopers, *The Current Economic and Policy Environment for the Australian Tobacco Industry* (2000), 8, at <http://www.bata.com.au/industud.asp>.

59. Australian Institute of Health and Welfare, *Statistics on Drug Use in Australia 2000,* 2.

60. PricewaterhouseCoopers, *The Current Economic and Policy Environment,* 9.

61. Michelle Scollo and Simon Chapman, "The US Tobacco Settlement: Should Australia Follow Suit" *Australia and New Zealand Journal of Public Health* 21: 559–561 (1997).

62. Neil Francey and Simon Chapman, "'Operation Berkshire': The International Tobacco Companies' Conspiracy," *British Medical Journal* 321: 371–374 (2000).

63. *McCabe v. British American Tobacco,* [2002] VSC 73 (Sup. Ct. Australia), at <http://www.ash.org.uk/html/conduct/pdfs/mccabejudgement.pdf>.

64. See Hugh Collins, "Political Ideology in Australia: The Distinctiveness of a Benthamite Society," *Daedalus* 1985 (winter): 147–169; Brian Galligan, "No Bill of Rights for Australia," *Papers on Parliament,* No. 4 (Canberra: Senate, 1989).

65. Alice Tay, "Human Rights and Wrongs" (Mitchell Oration, Human Rights and Equal Opportunity Commission, Adelaide, October 30, 1998), at <http://www.hreoc.gov.au/about_the_commission/speeches_president/human_rights_and_wrongs.html>.

66. See <http://www.forest-on-smoking.org.uk/News/nananny01.htm>.

67. Quoted in "The Last of the Great Tobacco Wars" (August 10, 1997), at <http://www.abc.net.au/rn/talks/bbing/stories/s10584.htm>.

68. Bruce Stannard, "Smokers' Last Rights," *Bulletin* (Australia) (October 1, 1991), 26–31.

69. *Sydney Morning Herald,* November 20, 1991, quoted in Chapman and Lupton, *The Fight for Public Health.*

70. On file with author.
71. E.g., Alan Moran, "The 'R' Files: The Sot Weed Offensive," *IPA Review* 50 (February 1998), at <http://www.ipa.org.au/pubs.htm>.
72. Simon Chapman, "Banning Smoking Outdoors Is Seldom Publicly Justified," *Tobacco Control* 9: 95–97 (2000).
73. Pierce, "Australia's Leadership Role in the Evolution of Tobacco Programs."
74. British Medical Association, *Smoking Out the Barons: The Campaign against the Tobacco Industry* (Chichester, England: John Wiley & Sons, 1986), 50–52.
75. Action on Smoking and Health (U.K.), letter to minister for public health, July 3, 2001 (on file with author).

5. Militants, Manufacturers, and Governments

1. Hilary Graham, "Women's Smoking and Family Health," *Social Science and Medicine* 25: 47–56 (1987).
2. Jordan Goodman, *Tobacco in History: The Cultures of Dependence* (London: Routledge, 1993).
3. Matthew Hilton, *Smoking in British Popular Culture, 1800–2000* (Manchester, U.K.: Manchester University Press, 2000); Charles Webster, "Tobacco Smoking Addiction: A Challenge to the National Health Service," *British Journal of Addiction* 79 (1): 8–16 (1984); Charles Webster, *The Health Services since the War*, vol. 1, *Problems of Health Care: The National Health Service before 1957* (London: HMSO, 1988); Charles Webster, *The Health Services since the War*, vol. 2, *Government and Health Care: The British National Health Service 1958–1979* (London: Stationery Office, 1996).
4. Peter Taylor, *The Smoke Ring* (London: Bodley Head, 1984); Melvyn Read, *The Politics of Tobacco* (Aldershot, U.K.: Avebury, 1996).
5. Office of National Statistics, Social Survey Division, *Living in Britain: Results from the 1998 General Household Survey* (London: Stationery Office, 2000), 19.
6. Ibid., 116.
7. Nicholas Wald and Ans Nicolaides-Bouman, *UK Smoking Statistics*, 2d ed. (Oxford, U.K.: Oxford University Press, 1991).
8. Martin Jarvis, "Cigarette Smoking in Young Adults: Are Women Overtaking Men?" (unpublished, 1999).
9. Taylor, *The Smoke Ring*.
10. Read, *The Politics of Tobacco*.
11. Bernard W. E. Alford, *W. D& H. O. Wills and the Development of the U.K. Tobacco Industry, 1786–1965* (London: Methuen, 1973); Howard Cox, *The Global Cigarette: Origins and Evolution of British American Tobacco, 1880–1945* (Oxford, U.K.: Oxford University Press, 2000).
12. Hilton, *Smoking in British Popular Culture*; Paolo Palladino, "Discourses of Smoking, Health, and the Just Society: Yesterday, Today, and the Return of the

Same?" *Social History of Medicine* 14 (2): 313–335 (2001); Webster, "Tobacco Smoking Addiction." The appearance of "discoveries" in quotation marks reflects the author's views concerning the social construction of scientific knowledge. See Virginia Berridge and J. Stanton, "Science and Policy: Historical Insights," *Social Science and Medicine* 49 (9): 1133–1138 (1999) (introduction to special issue entitled "Science Speaks to Policy").

13. Richard Doll, "Journal Interview 29. Conversation with Sir Richard Doll," *British Journal of Addiction* 86: 365–377 (1991); Richard Doll, "The First Reports on Smoking and Lung Cancer," in *Ashes to Ashes: The History of Smoking and Health,* eds. Stephen Lock, Lois Reynolds, and E. M. Tansey (Amsterdam: Rodopi, 1998).

14. Richard Doll and Austin Bradford Hill, "Smoking and Carcinoma of the Lung: Preliminary Report," *British Medical Journal* 1950 (2): 746.

15. Virginia Berridge, "Science and Policy: The Case of Postwar British Smoking Policy," in *Ashes to Ashes*

16. Allan Brandt, "The Cigarette, Risk, and American Culture," *Daedalus* 119 (4): 155–176 (1990); John Burnham, "American Physicians and Tobacco Use: Two Surgeons General, 1929 and 1964," *Bulletin of the History of Medicine* 63: 1–31 (1989).

17. Webster, "Tobacco Smoking Addiction."

18. Wald and Nicolaides-Bouman, *UK Smoking Statistics.*

19. Ministry of Health papers, MH55/1011, quoted in Rodney Lowe, *The Welfare State in Britain since 1945,* 2d ed. (Basingstoke, U.K.: Macmillan, 1998), 377.

20. Ministry of Health papers, MH55/1011, quoted in Virginia Berridge, "The Early Policy Response to Smoking in the UK" (unpublished).

21. Berridge, "The Early Policy Response to Smoking in the UK."

22. Berridge, "Science and Policy."

23. Webster, *Problems of Health Care;* Richard Crossman, *The Diaries of a Cabinet Minister,* vol. 3, *Secretary of State for Social Services, 1968–70* (London: Hamish Hamilton and Jonathan Cape, 1977).

24. Crossman, *Secretary of State for Social Services,* 147.

25. Matthew Hilton, "'Tabs', 'Fags' and the 'Boy Labour Problem' in Late Victorian and Edwardian Britain," *Journal of Social History* 28 (3): 587–607 (1995); John Welshman, "Images of Youth: The Issue of Juvenile Smoking, 1880–1914," *Addiction* 91 (9): 1379–1386 (1996).

26. Unlike the 1908 act, the 1933 act did not include provisions for the removal of park keepers. The 1986 Protection of Children (Tobacco) Act amended the earlier act, making it an offense to sell tobacco (and not only smoking tobacco, as in the earlier act) to anyone under sixteen years of age even if the tobacco was for someone else's use. In 1991 came the Children and Young Persons (Protection from Tobacco) Act, which increased penalties, prohibited sales of unpackaged cigarettes (for example, sales of one or two cigarettes to children), required the publication of warning statements in retail premises and on vending machines, and made provision with respect to enforcement action by

local authorities relating to tobacco offenses. The wording of the notice was to be, "It is illegal to sell tobacco products to anyone under the age of 16." Vending machines had to carry the sign, "This machine is only for the use of people aged 16 and over." For both outlets, not displaying the signs was an offense. It became the duty of every local authority to undertake an appropriate enforcement program—one that included prosecuting offenders, investigating complaints, and taking other (unspecified) measures. The white paper on tobacco, *Smoking Kills*, (which was published by the government in 1998, talks of the development of a new enforcement protocol, for use by local authorities in carrying out their duty under the 1991 act. "Best practice" (the best way of doing this) is being disseminated and will incorporate the local authority "best value" approach (a new monitoring system in local government to ensure high standards of service delivery).

27. Webster, *Government and Health Care.*

28. Action on Smoking and Health (U.K.), *Key Dates in the History of Anti-tobacco Campaigning* (2002), at <http://www.ash.org.uk/html/schools/keydates.html>.

29. The system of health-warning development, as part of a joint agreement between government and industry, continued until 1992. A European Community directive resulted in new health warnings that were introduced in the Tobacco Products Labelling (Safety) Regulations 1991 (under the Consumer Protection Act 1987) and that required the warning "Tobacco seriously damages health" to appear on the front of the pack. A second health warning must now appear on the back of the pack, chosen in rotation from the following: "Smoking kills," "Smoking causes cancer," "Smoking causes heart disease," "Smoking causes fatal diseases," "Smoking when pregnant harms your baby," and "Protect children: don't make them breathe your smoke." Each warning must cover 6 percent of the respective pack face. One side of the cigarette pack also must list the brand's tar and nicotine levels. Additional health warnings were added to hand-rolling tobacco, cigars, and pipe tobacco under the terms of the Tobacco Products Labelling (Safety) Amendment Regulations 1993. In November 1999, the European Commission issued a new draft directive to replace existing laws on health warnings and the tar yields of cigarettes. The main provisions are as follows: to set a maximum upper limit of tar, nicotine, and carbon monoxide for cigarettes sold in the European Union; to replace the current health warnings with larger ones occupying 25 percent of the front surface of the pack; to require tobacco companies to disclose the ingredients of cigarettes to governments; and to ban words such as "light" or "mild" as part of a name unless authorized by member states.

30. Virginia Berridge, "Passive Smoking and Its Pre-history in Britain: Policy Speaks to Science?" *Social Science and Medicine* 49 (9): 1183–1195 (1999).

31. Webster, *Government and Health Care,* 665–668.

32. Michael Daube, "The Politics of Smoking: Thoughts on the Labour Record," *Community Medicine* 1: 306–314 (1979).

33. Expenditure Committee, *First Report from the 1976–77 Session: Preventive Medicine,* vol. 1, (London: HMSO Expenditure Committee, 1977).
34. As quoted in Berridge, "Passive Smoking and Its Pre-history in Britain," 1187.
35. Read, *The Politics of Tobacco.*
36. Taylor, *The Smoke Ring.*
37. Peter Froggatt, "Determinants of Policy on Smoking and Health," *International Journal of Epidemiology* 18 (1): 1–9 (1989).
38. Berridge, "Passive Smoking and Its Pre-history in Britain"; Allan Brandt, "Blow Some My Way: Passive Smoking, Risk and American Culture," in *Ashes to Ashes.*
39. Berridge, "Passive Smoking and Its Pre-history in Britain."
40. FOREST (Freedom Organisation for the Right to Enjoy Smoking Tobacco), *Information Sheet No.1 : A Response to Passive Smoking* (London: FOREST, 1991).
41. SCOTH (Scientific Committee on Tobacco and Health), *Report of the Scientific Committee on Tobacco and Health* (London: Stationery Office, 1998). In 2003, the Greater London Authority undertook an online questionnaire to gauge public opinion about ETS. www.thebigsmokedebate.com accessed December 16, 2003.
42. "How Do You Sleep At Night, Mr. Blair?" *The Lancet* 362:1865 (2003).
43. Interview by author, July 4, 1996.
44. The first agreement, in 1971, established the health warning on cigarette packs and required posters, newspapers, and magazine advertisements to mention that packs carried such a warning. In 1974 another agreement was drawn up, providing for the inclusion of warnings in newspaper and magazine advertisements, on posters and cinema advertisements, and in promotional leaflets, consumer catalogs, and circular letters. The pace quickened in the latter half of the 1970s. In 1975 it was agreed that tar yields would be printed on packs and in advertising, and the Code of Advertising Practice was taken out of the hands of the industry, to be monitored by the Advertising Standards Authority (ASA). Imperial Tobacco, which then controlled two-thirds of the U.K. market, agreed unilaterally to remove brand names and logos from racing cars taking part in U.K. races. The industry also agreed to withdraw advertising associated with the showing of "U" certificate films (that is, certified under the British film-censorship system as suitable for the whole family) and to stop advertising through the distribution of free samples. In 1976 the ASA implemented a new code of advertising practice governing cigarettes. The long-standing Marlboro cowboy and Rothmans pilot campaigns were immediately withdrawn as a result. In 1977 a new voluntary agreement stipulated slightly strengthened health warnings on cigarette packs and in advertisements; advertising of high-tar brands was to be stopped immediately, and of middle- to high-tar brands by 1978; no new brands in these categories were to be introduced; a new, stronger code of advertising practice was to be introduced; and a code of practice for sponsorship was to be discussed with the minister

for sport. The following year, 1978, saw the Independent Broadcasting Authority (IBA) publish its Code of Advertising Standards, which regulated commercial television and radio broadcasting. Cigarettes and cigarette tobacco were deemed to be "unacceptable products" that were not to be advertised on commercial radio.

Increasingly, sports sponsorship and indirect advertising led to public discussion. For example, the State Express sports-sponsorship scheme caused concern in the media; under this widely advertised scheme, prizes sponsored by the tobacco industry were awarded to sportsmen and sportswomen in various areas. There were increasing calls for a total ban on tobacco advertising, including a House of Commons Early Day Motion, tabled by Conservative Sir George Young and signed by 54 MPs in May 1978. In 1980 a short-lived agreement cut expenditures for poster advertising by 30 percent and introduced restrictions on placing posters near schools.

Because of concerns about sports sponsorship, separate voluntary agreements have been drawn up for tobacco advertising and for sports sponsorship since the early 1980s. The 1982 agreement limited the prize money offered in sporting events to £6 million, and advertisements for sponsored events had to carry a health warning. The 1983 agreement sought to reduce expenditures on advertising, increased the space for government health warnings in press and poster advertising, prohibited advertising on video for sale or hire, and imposed restrictions on content (for example, with respect to the use of celebrities and other public personalities). A further voluntary agreement in 1986 introduced new warning phrases and also a specifically female-oriented curb on advertising. Tobacco advertising in women's magazines with at least 200,000 readers, of whom at least a third were aged sixteen to twenty-four, were banned, and so was advertising for brands with a tar level of 18 mg and above. The industry agreed to spend £1 million a year in publicity to make it clear that children under sixteen must not be sold cigarettes. This agreement also set up a committee, the Committee for Monitoring Agreements on Tobacco Advertising and Sponsorship (COMATAS), to monitor the agreement. The committee comprised representatives from the DHSS, the Scottish Office, the Welsh Office, the Department of the Environment, the Tobacco Advisory Council, the main tobacco companies (one each), and the Imported Products Advisory Council. The joint secretaries were from the DHSS and the Tobacco Advisory Council, and the committee's work was funded jointly by government and industry. The committee was also responsible for the agreement on sports sponsorship that was reached that same year. That agreement introduced, for the first time, a ceiling on advertising and promotional expenditures for such events. There was also to be a wider use of health warnings at sports events. The agreement on advertising was revised in 1991 and again in 1994; the one on sports sponsorship was revised in 1996.

45. Tobacco Advisory Council, "The Case for Tobacco Advertising," Wellcome Library, ASH Archive No. SA/ASH K1/1/7 (1985).

46. House of Commons Health Committee, *The Tobacco Industry and the Health Risks of Smoking,* vol. 1, *Report and Proceedings of the Committee* (London: Stationery Office, 1992); Simon Chapman, *Cigarette Advertising and Smoking: A Review of the Evidence* (London: British Medical Association, 1985).

47. C. Smee, *Effect of Tobacco Advertising on Tobacco Consumption: A Discussion Document Reviewing the Evidence* (London: Department of Health, 1992); Hugh High, *Does Advertising Increase Smoking?* (London: Institute of Economic Affairs, 1999).

48. High, *Does Advertising Increase Smoking?* 118.

49. Berridge, "Science and Policy."

50. In *Smoking Kills,* the Department of Health argued for working with business and others to achieve change. The department had examined the case for an outright ban or for legal restrictions, as tried in other countries. These approaches, the department argued, had proved difficult to implement. Instead, the strategy chosen was to work with business, building on best practices that would provide adequate choices for both smokers and non-smokers. The government announced a Public Places Charter, agreed upon by the hospitality industry, that contained principles to be worked out in detail, along with targets to be achieved within an established time frame. The charter starts from the assumption that nonsmoking is the general norm, and sets forth principles to which the signatories commit themselves. These principles include: a written policy on smoking available to customers and staff; implementation through nonsmoking areas, air cleaning, and ventilation; communication to customers through signage; implementation and monitoring through independent research; and recognition that smoking policies are a management responsibility to be reflected in general work practices.

51. As quoted in Berridge, "Passive Smoking and Its Pre-history in Britain," 1192.

52. Children under fourteen years of age are barred from pubs and other areas where drinks are sold unless the establishment has a special certificate allowing such children to be present.

53. My own institution, the London School of Hygiene and Tropical Medicine, has a large sign on its steps stating that smoking is not permitted on them.

54. This code is intended to define the kind of smoking policies that employers would need to implement in order to comply with existing health and safety legislation. The content would be based on existing guidance from the Health and Safety Executive. Employers would be required to introduce smoking policies that give priority to the needs of nonsmoking employees, and to take special care for people who have a health condition that may be worsened by tobacco smoke. Such "approved codes of practice" have a special status under the 1974 Health and Safety at Work Act. When employers are prosecuted for breaching health and safety law, and it is proven they did not follow the code in place, the employers would need to show they had complied with the law in some other way, or the court would find them at fault. In practice, the new

code will, if and when adopted, put the burden of proof on employers, making the code stronger than existing voluntary guidance.

55. Cheryl Swann and Peter Froggatt, *The Tobacco Products Research Trust, 1982–1996*(London: RSM Press, 1996).

56. Nicholas Wald and Peter Froggatt, eds., *Nicotine, Smoking and the Low Tar Programme* (Oxford, U.K.: Oxford University Press, 1989).

57. Martin Raw, Patti White, and Ann McNeill, *Clearing the Air: A Guide for Action on Tobacco* (London: WHO-Euro/BMA, 1990).

58. Berridge, "Passive Smoking and Its Pre-history in Britain."

59. 505 U.S. 504 (1992).

60. Wald and Nicolaides-Bouman, *UK Smoking Statistics.*

61. Joy Townsend, "Price and Consumption of Tobacco," *British Medical Bulletin* 52 (1): 132–142 (1996); Geoffrey Hardman and Alan Maynard, "Consumption and Taxation Trends," in *Preventing Alcohol and Tobacco Problems,* vol. 1, *The Addiction Market,* eds. Alan Maynard and Philip Tether (Aldershot, U.K.: Avebury, 1990).

62. Daube, "The Politics of Smoking," 309.

63. Joy Townsend, "Smoking and Class," *New Society* 0 (March): 709–710 (1978).

64. Alan Marsh and Stephen McKay, *Poor Smokers* (London: Policy Studies Institute, 1994).

65. Virginia Berridge, "Two Histories of Addiction: Opium and Nicotine," *Human Psychopharmacology* 12: S45–S52 (1997).

66. Berridge, "Passive Smoking and Its Pre-history in Britain."

67. Virginia Berridge and Penny Starns, "Nicotine Replacement Therapy: Policy and Industrial History" (forthcoming).

68. See Gilmore and McKee's chapter on the European Union.

69. William McAllister, *Drug Diplomacy in the Twentieth Century* (London: Routledge, 2000).

70. See Chapter 10, "Difference and Diffusion."

71. David Pollock, *Denial and Delay: The Political History of Smoking and Health, 1951–1964* (London: Action on Smoking and Health, 1999); Stanton A. Glantz et al., *The Cigarette Papers* (Berkeley, CA: University of California Press, 1996) (available at <http://www.library.ucsf.edu/tobacco/cigpapers/>). Court settlements and whistleblowers from within the tobacco industry have given access to quantities of archival material. Other archival material waits to be fully exploited, and there is currently an effort to make the tobacco industry documents deposited in an archive in Guildford, England, more accessible for research. Further research is thus in prospect. Some evidence already in play relates to the British industry and indicates the distinctiveness of the British case during the early years. British manufacturers were initially (from the 1950s to the 1970s) concerned about risk reduction and safety rather than legal actions. See Virginia Berridge, "Why Have Attitudes to Industry Funding of Research Changed?" *Addiction* 92 (8): 965–968 (1997) (article in series entitled "What I Would Most Like to Know").

72. I am aware, of course, that this stance is the matter of considerable discussion among historians.

6. Liberté, Egalité, Fumée

1. Jordan Goodman, *Tobacco in History: The Cultures of Dependence* (London: Routledge, 1993).
2. Ibid.; Didier Nourrisson, "Tabagisme et antitabagisme en France au XIXe siècle," *Histoire économie et société* 2 (4): 535–547 (1988).
3. Goodman, *Tobacco in History*, 47.
4. Jordan Goodman, "Webs of Drug Dependence: Towards a Political History of Tobacco," in *Ashes to Ashes: The History of Smoking and Health*, (eds. Stephen Lock, Lois Reynolds, and E. M. Tansey (Amsterdam: Rodopi, 1998).
5. Cited in Nourrisson, "Tabagisme et antitabagisme," 536. All translations from the French are by the author.
6. Ibid., 538. I do not have current, precise data on the percentage of imported tobacco in French-manufactured cigarettes. It continues to be substantial, however, ranging from one-third to over one-half in the (relatively) new *Gauloises Blondes*.
7. By way of comparison, sales in 2000 amounted to 92,000 tons, down from a peak of 104,000 tons in 1991—but still substantial by comparison with 1914.
8. Nourrisson, "Tabagisme et antitabagisme."
9. Sales prior to World War II were in the form of cut tobacco intended for pipe smoking, although possibly also used for rolled cigarettes. Goodman, *Tobacco in History*, 91.
10. Nourrisson, "Tabagisme et antitabagisme."
11. Nicolaides-Bouman and colleagues argue that smoking is substantially under-reported in prevalence surveys; they estimate the range of underreporting in France from 10 to 30 percent. See Ans Nicolaides-Bouman, Nicholas Wald, Barbara Forey, and Peter Lee, eds., *International Smoking Statistics* (Oxford, U.K.: Oxford University Press, 1993). Sales data have the additional advantage that they are reported in a form that can be compared over relatively long time periods.
12. The quality of the French survey data is difficult to evaluate. They are reported in the French equivalent of the Morbidity and Mortality Weekly Report (MMWR), the *Bulletin épidemiologique hebdomadaire*. However, the sampling method is not clearly stated, and the definition of "smoker" does not distinguish between daily and occasional smokers. See François Baudier et al., "La consummation de tabac en France: Évolution récentes dans la population adulte," *Bulletin épidemiologique hebdomadaire* (April 28, 1998), 17. Keeping these limitations in mind, there are other interesting differences in the pattern of smoking between France and the United States. The prevalence of smoking

among French respondents aged eighteen to twenty-four (52 percent) is high relative to the same age group in the United States and to older age groups in France (perhaps due to the inclusion of occasional smokers). Gender differences in smoking are diminishing, as they are in the United States, due to a plateau in men and a slight increase among women. Finally, social class differences in smoking appear to be substantially less marked, particularly among women and the young, than they are in the United States. See M. Anguis and D. Dubeaux, "Les fumeurs face aux recentes hausses du prix du tabac," *INSEE Premiere,* No. 551 (1997); Gary D. King et al., "Smoking Behavior among French and American Women," *Preventive Medicine* 27 (4): 520–529 (1998); Jean Y. Nau, "La cigarette, un moyen d'acceder au statut d'adulte et de s'affirmer," *Le Monde* (Paris), October 13, 1999.

13. Catherine Hill, "Avis des personnalités, organisations et administrations auditionnés," in Commissariat général du plan, *La loi relative à la lutte contre le tabagisme et l'alcoolisme: Rapport d'évaluation* (Paris: La Documentation française, 2000), 393–394. (For further information on this document, see note 20). The two principal French authorities on smoking-related mortality in France are the epidemiologist Catherine Hill (Institut Gustave Roussy, Villejuif) and the demographer Alfred Nizard (l'Institut national d'études démographiques). I rely on their estimates.

14. Alfred Nizard, "La mortalité par tumeur en France au tournant des années quatre- vingt-dix," *Population* 3: 665–698 (1997).

15. David G. Hoel et al., "Trends in Cancer Mortality in 15 Industrialized Countries, 1969–1986," *Journal of the National Cancer Institute* 84 (5): 313–320 (1992).

16. Jacob M. Price, "Tobacco Use and Tobacco Taxation: A Battle of Interests in Early Modern Europe," in *Consuming Habits: Drugs in History and Anthropology,* eds. Jordan Goodman and Paul E.S.A. Lovejoy (London: Routledge, 1995), 167.

17. Roger Price, *A Concise History of France* (Cambridge, U.K.: Cambridge University Press, 1991), 296.

18. Accompanying the move toward light-tobacco cultivation has been a sharp drop in the area planted and the number of growers. In 1971 there were close to 42,000 tobacco growers in France; by the year 2000 the number had dropped to under 6,000. The level of production has declined much less, however, no doubt due to increased agricultural efficiencies. It is worth noting that among French consumers of French cigarettes, the dark outsells the light by more than two to one. Consumers who prefer *blonde* buy American. Centre de documentation et information sur le tabac (CDIT), *Tabac news,* vol. 22 (July 2001).

19. The details of the arrangement between SEITA and Tabacelera are complex, and the long-term economic prospects of Altadis, unknown. Both questions are beyond the scope of this chapter. Among the merger's attractions for

SEITA must have been Tabacelera's dominant position in the cigar market (including ownership of a cigar factory in the United States) and its much stronger position internationally.

20. CDIT, *Tabac news;* Commissariat général du plan, *La loi: Rapport d'évaluation.* French tobacco legislation (described in a later section) called for evaluations of the law's operation to be prepared by the government and presented to Parliament in 1993 and 1995. Those evaluations were not undertaken. However, a full-scale evaluation was initiated in 1997 and completed in October 1999. In the course of this evaluation, testimony was received from a wide range of interested parties, existing research was reviewed, and additional research was commissioned. This evaluation, authored by the Commissariat général du plan, Conseil national de l'évaluation, was published in 2000 under the title *La loi relative à la lutte contre le tabagisme et l'alcoolisme: Rapport d'évaluation.* It is an authoritative source for current French perspectives on tobacco control in France.

21. CDIT, *Tabac news.*

22. The following account draws on a large number of published and unpublished documents, as well as on extended interviews that I conducted in 1995 with three of the five physicians primarily responsible for the passage of the second major piece of tobacco legislation, the *loi Evin* of 1991. The three physicians are Maurice Tubiana, Albert Hirsch, and Gérard Dubois. Professor Tubiana also played a major role in the initiation of the first major piece of tobacco legislation, the *loi Veil* of 1976.

23. The official title of the *loi Veil* is *Loi no 76–616 du 9 Juillet 1976 relative à la lutte contre le tabagisme (Journal Officiel,* July 10, 1976, p. 4148).

24. Auto-racing sponsorship (for example, of Formula One and other races) is a perennial and continuing bone of contention, in England as well as France.

25. *Loi Veil,* Titre II, Dispositions diverses, Article 16.

26. French usage here may be confusing. The smoking prohibition does not refer to "public places" in the sense of public spaces such as parks, or public buildings such as courthouses (although the latter would be included). It refers to places *open to the general public*—for example, hospitals, railroad stations, and so on. But the language of the Veil law *décret* appeared to narrow that definition to a limited number of specified places.

27. The sensitivity of the price issue was reflected in the 1976 parliamentary debate on the Veil law. Simone Veil noted that the government had rejected an increase in tobacco prices, observing that a massive increase in prices would amount to "shocking" discrimination based on wealth. In his response, a member noted the "illogic" of condemning tobacco while at the same time selling cigarettes at "dumping" prices and distributing an even cheaper monthly cigarette ration to members of the military. See *Journal Officiel* (June 12, 1976), pp. 4077–4078.

28. A striking example is the enormous gap between French narcotic drug laws and the reality of French practices when confronted with drug users. In the

course of the past twenty years, this gap has been noted by no less than three commissions responsible for evaluating the management of the drug problem. All three insisted that the law cannot be changed because of its symbolic importance as a statement of official norms. See Constance A. Nathanson, "Disease Prevention as Social Change: The State, Society, and Public Health in the U.S., Canada, Britain, and France" (unpublished).

29. The official title of the *loi Evin* is *Loi no 91–32 du 10 janvier 1991 relative à la lutte contre le tabagisme et l'alcoolisme* (*Journal Officiel,* January 12, 1991, p. 615).

30. *Cinq sages* was a label initially applied to these five doctors by the media. It may be translated as "five wise men," but *sage* also means "well behaved;" a good child is *sage*. Thus, the term has a perhaps intentional double meaning when used in the context of alcohol and tobacco control.

31. Some indication of Got's stature is that he was invited by the government to do the first overall report on AIDS in France, just after the French blood scandal broke. See Claude Got, *Rapport sur le SIDA* (Paris: Flammarion, 1989). He has also published a wide-ranging book on the current state of public health in France. See Claude Got, *La Santé* (Paris: Flammarion, 1992). Got had a brief stint as a civil servant in the minister of health's office in the early 1980s. Based outside of Paris and in "public health" rather than one of the medical specialties, Dubois ranks considerably below Got on the French scale of medical prestige. (Dubois received his public health training in the early 1970s at the Johns Hopkins School of Hygiene and Public Health.)

32. A further discovery was that "the most powerful lobby wasn't the alcohol lobby, that was the advertising one, and politicians needed money to be elected and needed the advertising world to be elected too." Gérard Dubois, interview by author, tape recording, Paris, May 1995. Dubois argues (in agreement with the other *sages* (whom I interviewed) that government inaction on the public health issues presented by tobacco and alcohol (including, at the time of the alcohol brouhaha, support for alcohol advertising by the then health minister, Michelle Barzach) is attributable far more to the economic power of "the advertising world" than to the alcohol and tobacco lobbies. Dubois, interview.

33. Albert Hirsch, interview by author, tape recording, Paris, May 1995.

34. Ibid.

35. The report had almost nothing to say about what was essentially nonimplementation of the Veil law's provisions on smoking in places open to the public. I return to the question of passive smoking at a later point.

36. Albert Hirsch et al., *Lutter contre le tabagisme* (Paris: La Documentation française, 1987), 10.

37. See Albert Hirsch and Serge Karsenty, *Le prix de la fumée* (Paris: Editions Odile Jacob, 1992).

38. Hirsch, interview.

39. Ibid.

40. Consistent with the diverse public health backgrounds of the *cinq sages* and with their strategy of using smoking as a "way in" to the regulation of less tractable negative health behaviors, their questions dealt with alcohol and speeding—not just tobacco.
41. Dubois, interview.
42. Quoted in Claude Evin, "Garantir à chaque individu un access à des soins de qualité," in *Santé publique et libertés individuelles,* ed. Emile Malet (Paris: Passages tirer profit, 1993), 139.
43. The problem for public health created by *le poids historique* (the historical weight) of alcohol (meaning wine) is a recurring theme in written discussions and in my interviews of how the Evin law evolved; the influence of this "weight" is clear from the transcripts of parliamentary debate on the law. Regulation of alcohol advertising presented far more of a problem than regulation of tobacco advertising, and, indeed, the provisions on alcohol advertising were never implemented by ministerial decree (the normal procedure for giving effect to acts of Parliament).
44. *Loi Evin,* Article 3.
45. Ibid.
46. *Loi Evin,* Titre I, Dispositions relative à la lutte contre le tabagisme, Article 16 (emphasis added).
47. *Journal Officiel* (June 26, 1990), p. 2902.
48. Jean Y. Nau, "Neuf ans aprés sa promulgation, la loi evin est mal appliquée," *Le Monde* (Paris), June 1, 2000. The *jour sans tabac* was itself a requirement of the Evin law.
49. Commissariat général du plan, *La loi: Rapport d'évaluation.*
50. This is, of course, immediately obvious to any visitor from the United States. My own experience in interviewing physicians and other professionals was that, with the exception of anti-tobacco advocates, everyone smoked.
51. In September 1999, for example, the French railroad was required by a court (cour d'appel de Lyon) to pay 10,000 francs in fines (about U.S.$2,000 at 5 francs to the dollar) to CNCT and the Ligue contre la fumée du tabac en public (see note 72) for inadequate protection of nonsmokers in the station at Lyons. As noted below, CNCT has a long history of success in litigation against violations of advertising bans, dating back to the early 1980s.
52. For a detailed account of the background to this provision and of its effects in litigation, see Constance A. Nathanson, "Associational Standing in France and the United States with Special Reference to Tobacco Litigation" (1996, unpublished). Briefly, the provision gave the force of law to existing judicial practice. The CNCT's standing to bring suit for violations of France's laws against tobacco advertising had been recognized by the Cour de cassation (France's highest court) in 1984 and again in 1986. See Cour de cassation (Cass. crim.), February 7, 1984, *Bull. crim.,* No. 41, p. 110; Cour de cassation (Cass. crim.), April 29, 1986, *Bull. crim.,* No. 146, p. 373. CNCT brought its first suit, against Reynolds-France, in the late 1970s and has been reasonably successful. My

figures concerning the number of suits and the recoveries associated with them are incomplete, limited to the period 1991–1994.

53. Cited in Nau, "Neuf ans."

54. Hirsch, interview; see also CNCT, *Les prix des cigarettes en France* (Paris: CNCT, 1994).

55. Unwillingness to publicly acknowledge European influence does not, of course, mean that that influence is not present. Nevertheless, among the arguments advanced by politicians against the Evin law has been that France is out of step with (that is, more draconian than) its European partners (see, for example, "La rentrée parlementaire réveille les lobbies anti-Evin," *CB News* (Paris), No. 407, September 10, 1995).

56. Virtually all of the innovative tobacco litigation in France—including CNCT's suits alleging violation of the Evin law, the one French lawsuit on behalf of a victim of smoking, and this most recent lawsuit—have been initiated by the same lawyer, Francis Caballero.

57. Jean-Francis Pecresse, "Santé: Pour la premiere fois . . . ," *Les Echos* (Paris), February 16, 1999. As of this writing, both the lawsuit on behalf of a cancer victim—Richard Gourlain—and the CPAM–St. Nazaire lawsuit are still in the courts. The tribunal de grande instance de Montargis (Loiret) awarded a partial victory to Gourlain in December 1999, currently under appeal by both parties. The tribunal de grande instance de Saint-Nazaire has accepted (deemed *recevable*) the CPAM suit; the case is under examination by a three-judge panel.

58. The reluctance I describe does not apply to alcohol, the sale of which is now restricted to persons seventeen and over. I can only speculate on the reasons for this difference.

59. Hirsch and Karsenty, *Le prix de la fumée,* 179.

60. Ibid., 178.

61. This and subsequent statements about the French "climate" for public health are based on interviews and observation, as well as written documents, in the arenas of both tobacco control and HIV/AIDS.

62. There is a school of public health in France, at Rennes. This school was discounted by my physician informants (one with public health training obtained in the United States) as a low-level vocational school for administrators. While I cannot independently judge the accuracy of this depiction, it was highly consistent across informants (several of whom have made the same point in writing). See also Bruno Jobert, "Mobilisation politique et système de santé en France," in *Les politiques de santé en France et en Allemagne,* eds. Bruno Jobert and Monika Steffen (Paris: Observatoire européen de la protection sociale, 1994).

63. The idea and meaning of the *clinique* is elaborated at some length in Michel Foucault, *The Birth of the Clinic* (New York: Vintage Books, 1963).

64. Serge Karsenty, personal communication.

65. See, e.g., Malet, *Santé publique et libertés individuelles.*

66. There is a dual problem here: although French scientists are reluctant to address the issue of smoking and health in their own research, there is also considerable unwillingness to accept the results of research from other countries as applicable to France.

67. This same individual pointed out to me that the *fer de lance*—the leaders—in the cause of smoking and health in France were not epidemiologists, but specialists in cancer and heart disease. His point was that the status associated with these latter specialties was a necessary condition for attention to be paid.

68. An additional element of the "outsider" strategy was the use of public opinion polls to demonstrate widespread support for the proposed advertising bans and regulation of smoking in spaces open to the public. Support was, indeed, very high (as noted in the previous section). However, the relative influence of this support on ministers and legislators is unclear. Opinion polls taken in France have been consistent over at least the past fifteen years in showing widespread belief in the harm caused by smoking and equally strong verbal approval of regulation. Consistent with my observation of British doctors' "insider" approach, public opinion polls were never an important part of their anti-tobacco strategy.

69. Hirsch, interview.

70. In much of their rhetoric, the doctors also included traffic accidents—considered as largely due to alcohol abuse. Traffic accidents were not, however, a direct target of the Evin law.

71. Hirsch and Karsenty, *Le prix de la fumée,* 188–189.

72. There is, in addition to CNCT, a second advocacy group, the *Ligue contre la fumée du tabac en public—Les Droits des non-fumeurs (LCFTP-DNF)* (League against the Smoking of Tobacco in Public—The Rights of Non-smokers), founded in 1985. Both groups are extremely small, and there is substantial overlap in officers and membership. In the mid-1990s the *cinq sages* moved to form a coalition, l'Alliance pour la santé, headed by Maurice Tubiana. This coalition included CNCT, LCTP-DNF, the Ligue nationale contre le cancer, the Comité français d'éducation à la santé, and several other health associations. How effective this alliance has been is uncertain. The following account of "grassroots" activity in France focuses on CNCT, by far the most publicly visible "lay" combatant in France's tobacco wars.

73. I document this statement more fully below.

74. CNCT long predated the emergence of the *cinq sages.* Unlike the British ASH (Action on Smoking and Health), it was not created by antismoking physicians to be their lobbying arm. It assumed that role on its own.

75. Commissariat général du plan, *La loi: Rapport d'évaluation.*

76. Michel Augendre, "Je gene moi?" *Vie naturelle,* September 1981; A. Dufour, "Centenaire du comité national contre le tabagisme," *Tabac et santé,* No. 29 (1978).

77. The director, Phillippe Boucher, had gained much of his experience in the United States and was married to an American. Boucher was forced to resign

as director of CNCT in late 1997, accused of misappropriating government funds to his own use. Although a type of figure familiar to Americans—a militant activist dedicated to a single cause—Boucher was an anomaly in France and to the French (a fact of which he himself was fully aware—"they think I am crazy"). Philip Boucher, interview by author, Paris, May 1995. CNCT's marginal status (for example, "fanatics," "bizarre") was made clear to me on many occasions by individuals—even those generally sympathetic to the antismoking cause—who were outside the immediate confines of CNCT. In addition to Boucher, the new leadership included Jean Tostain, founder of the LCTP-DNF. Tostain, a former parachutist and veteran of the Algerian war, was militant on behalf of nonsmokers, to the point where even CNCT tried to keep him under wraps.

78. The exact amount of that income is difficult to determine. In 1995 CNCT's stated income was 17,736,000 francs, or about U.S.$3,547,200. Close to half of that amount, however, represented not actual cash, but the value of time and space donated by various media in lieu of fines, space, and time that CNCT was not always able to use. Subtracting these media "donations" leaves a total of about U.S.$1,750,000 in actual revenue. Stated expenses totaled U.S.$1,775,646 (again leaving out the "donations"). From 1991 through 1998, CNCT's newsletter, *Tabac et santé,* reflected the group's constant concern with the inadequacy of its resources for the task at hand.

79. A recent report gives a somewhat more modest accounting: 132 suits initiated through 1999, and a total recovery of approximately U.S.$1 million. Yael Attal, *La gazette du palais* (March 23, 2000), cited in Nau, "Neuf ans."

80. Michel Burton, "Justiciers ou rapaces?" *Revue des tabacs* 408: 3, 25–27 (1995). SEITA's comments to the commission to evaluate the Evin law, however, reflected its awareness of the substantial difference between France and the United States with regard to the impact of the anti-tobacco movement: "En terme de réglementation, nous connaissons en France une législation très stricte qui n'a rien de comparable avec celle des États-Unis où règne un climat passionel, entretenu par les antitabacs." Commissariat général du plan, *La loi: Rapport d'évaluation,* 532.

81. Burton, "Justiciers ou rapaces?" 3.

82. My comparative research in several other Western countries suggests that it is by no means unusual for governments to quietly support a level of health militancy by nongovernmental organizations that these governments do not wish to be perceived as engaging in themselves.

83. That CNCT had been burned is reflected in Hirsch's statement to the commission evaluating the Evin law: "C'est au Parquet, et non plus aux associations, à faire respecter l'interdiction de la publicité et des promotions en faveur du tabac." Commissariat général du plan, *La loi: Rapport d'évaluation,* 371. Industry representatives' submissions to the commission uniformly suggested that CNCT's primary interest was in feathering its own nest. See, e.g., ibid., 533. As noted above, however, CNCT continues very much in the busi-

ness of litigation, albeit with a shift in focus from advertising violations to passive smoking.

84. Alain Ehrenberg, *L'individu incertain* (Paris: Calmann-Lévy, 1995), 80.

85. The quote is from an interview with Luc Bihl, one of the lawyers for CNCT and a smoker, conducted by a member of the CNCT staff. "Entretien avec Luc Bihl realisé par Lise Mingasson le 15 avril 1995," *Tabac et santé*, No. 135 (1995). This interpretation of the meaning of cigarettes and smoking is by no means unique to Bihl, however. I suggested this characterization of the contrast between French attitudes about illegal drugs and the "legal drug" tobacco, to a meeting of French demographers, including at least one highly respected expert on French smoking practices, Alfred Nizard. These scholars confirmed my interpretation.

86. As these observations may suggest, French public health authorities have difficulty with the notion of "risk groups" and consequently with the idea of public health programs targeted at these groups. This aversion surfaces in a wide variety of public health settings other than smoking.

87. A poll conducted in 1994 showed that a majority of the French public believes that the *loi Evin* is not respected, except in public transportation. *Le Monde* (Paris), February 26, 1994. The exact proportions for different public settings were as follows: not respected in cafés, 78 percent; in workplaces, 61 percent; in restaurants, 58 percent. The 1999 evaluation of the law's operation indicates that little has changed.

88. Norbert Bensaïd, "Les illusions de la mobilization, ou comment informer les citoyens," in *Santé publique et libertés individuelles,* ed. Malet, 53. This difference in perspective is conditioned in part, of course, by the fact that France has a system of national health insurance that provides health care coverage to virtually all its citizens. The state's responsibility for *individual* medical care in the case of illness is taken for granted.

89. Among the notable aspects of this debate is its elevated philosophical tone. Both sides draw on central themes in French political thought: on the one hand, the necessity for individuals to resist the encroachment of an oppressive, authoritarian state; on the other, the state's responsibilities to act on behalf of the common good, to protect its citizens, and to erase—or at least address—social inequalities. The contradictory nature of these ideas—the state as oppressive authority versus the state as benevolent parent—should be self-evident. Steven Lukes has a highly relevant discussion of the problematic nature of the concept of *individualisme* in French social and political thought. See Steven Lukes, *Individualism* (Oxford, U.K.: Basil Blackwell, 1973).

90. Maurice Tubiana, "Tabagisme passif: Rapport et voeu de l'Académie nationale de médecine," *Bulletin de l'Académie nationale de médecine* 181 (4): 10 (1997).

91. The quote is from an essay by a young woman fired from her job for complaining about environmental tobacco smoke. It was reprinted in *Tabac et santé*, No. 137 (1997).

92. Ibid.

93. *Le Figaro*, March 25, 2003. http://web.lexis-nexis.com/universe.

7. Between Paternalism and Voluntarism

1. It is crucial to note that Germany was first united in 1871. For the previous epoch, it is more precise to refer to "German territories" rather than "Germany." Concerning the social history of smoking, see Henner Hess, *Rauchen: Geschichte, Geschäfte, Gefahren* (Frankfurt N.Y.: Campus, 1987), chap. 1.

2. For a thorough analysis of the medicopharmacological discourse, see Martina C. Enke, *Über die Bedeutung des Tabaks in der europäischen Medizin vom 16. bis zum 20. Jahrhundert* (Berlin: Verlag für wissenschaftliche Forschung, 1998).

3. All translations are by the author. For an elaborated historical narrative, see Thomas Hengartner and Christoph M. Merki, eds., *Genussmittel: Ein kulturgeschichtliches Handbuch* (Frankfurt, New York: Campus, 1999); Hess, *Rauchen;* Wolfgang Schivelbusch, *Das Paradies, der Geschmack und die Vernunft* (Frankfurt, New York: Campus, 1983).

4. For further references, see Egon C. Corti, *Die trockene Trunkenheit: Geschichte des Rauchens* (Frankfurt: Insel, 1986).

5. It is interesting to note that at that time, and following the example of St. Peter's in Rome, smoking was permitted even in many churches.

6. For example, the Prussian General Land Law of 1794 (Part II, Title 20, §1550).

7. See Corti, *Die trockene Trunkenheit,* 290.

8. See Christoph M. Merki, "Die nationalsozialistische Tabakpolitik," *Vierteljahresschrift für Zeitgeschichte* 46 (1): 19–42 (1998); Robert N. Proctor, *The Nazi War on Cancer* (Princeton, N.J.: Princeton University Press, 1999), chap. 6.

9. See Proctor, *The Nazi War on Cancer.*

10. Ibid., 230.

11. Henner Hess, "The Other Prohibition: The Cigarette Crisis in Post-war Germany," *Crime, Law & Social Change* 25: 43–61 (1996).

12. Ibid., 44–45.

13. Ibid., 47–51.

14. Nichtraucherschutzprogramm des Bundes und der Länder (1978).

15. "Der Aufstand der Nichtraucher," *Der Spiegel,* No. 19, 1981.

16. For a history of the tobacco industry, see Karl Bormann, "Die deutsche Zigarettenindustrie" (Dissertation, University of Leipzig, 1910); Rainer Bransemann, "Tabak und Volkswirtschaft" (Dissertation, University of Köln, 1971); Egon C. Corti, *Die Geschichte des Rauchens* (Frankfurt: Insel, 1986); Dieter Roos, *Nicht nur blauer Dunst: Über Tabak, Zigarren und Pfeifen* (Kleve: Verlag für Kultur und Technik, 1999); Eckhard Thomale, "Standorte der deutschen Zigarettenindustrie 1860–1990," *Geographie und Schule* 12: 16–31 (1990); Ines

Vetter, "Die Entwicklung der Dresdner Zigarettenindustrie bis 1933," *Dresdner Hefte* 18: 72–77 (2000).

17. In 1862, workers produced manually a maximum of 1,500 to 1,700 cigarettes during a ten-hour workday.

18. The number of cigarette producers increased from thirty-three in 1877, to fifty-eight in 1887, to 189 in 1900. See Michael Weisser, *Cigaretten-Reclame: Über die Kunst blauen Dunst zu verkaufen* (Münster: Coppenrath Verlag, 1980).

19. The first Russian-owned cigarette factory in Dresden employed six rollers and one cutter. See Irene Reintzsch, *Zur Geschichte der Dresdner Zigarettenindustrie* (Leipzig: Verlagsbüro Reintzsch, 1993).

20. Proctor, *The Nazi War on Cancer*, 176–178.

21. *Frankfurter Allgemeine Zeitung*, May 25, 2000.

22. Statistisches Bundesamt, ed., *Wirtschaft und Statistik* (1996); Deutsche Tabakwaren-Industrie, ed., *Deutsche Tabakzeitung*, No. 17, April 28, 2000; Deutsche Hauptstelle gegen die Suchtgefahren e.V., ed., *Jahrbuch Sucht 2000* (Geesthacht: Neuland, 1999); "Population Survey on the Consumption of Psychoactive Substances in the German Adult Population," *Sucht: Zeitschrift für Wissenschaft und Praxis* 44 (1): 52–56 (1998); Bundesverband Deutscher Tabakwaren-Großhändler und Automatenaufsteller, ed., *Der deutsche Tabakwarenmarkt* (1999); Bundeszentrale für gesundheitliche Aufklärung, ed., *Die Drogenaffinität Jugendlicher in der Bundesrepublik Deutschland 1997* (Köln: Bundeszentrale für gesundheitliche Aufklärung, 1998); Bundeszentrale für gesundheitliche Aufklärung, ed., *Dokumentation der abgeschlossenen Studien: Auszug: Rauchen, Drogen und Rauschmittel* (Köln: Bundeszentrale für gesundheitliche Aufklärung, 1999).

23. The available data differ from study to study primarily according to the age groups included (over ten years, over fifteen years, fifteen to forty-six years, and so on). Comparability of the data is also rendered difficult, if not impossible, because of the differences in survey designs. See *Jahrbuch Sucht 2000*; (Nicole D. Rademacher, "Das Tabakwerbeverbot im nationalen und internationalen Vergleich," *Zeitschrift für Rechtspolitik* 34 (2): 64–67 (2001).

24. Bundesministerium für Gesundheit, ed., *Drogen- und Suchtbericht 1999* (2000), 14.

25. Eike von Hippel, "Zum Kampf gegen die Tabak-Epidemie," *Zeitschrift für Rechtspolitik* 28 (4): 137–140 (1995); Ruth Roemer, *Legislative Action to Combat the World Tobacco Epidemic*, 2d ed. (Geneva: World Health Organization, 1993), 118–127.

26. Within the age group ranging from fifteen to forty years, more than 60 percent identified themselves as smokers, compared with 45.8 percent of the gainfully employed persons in the same age group.

27. The figures concerning tobacco consumption are taken from *Jahrbuch Sucht 2000*, chap. 2.2.

28. See Gilmore and McKee's chapter on the European Union.

29. *Frankfurter Allgemeine Zeitung*, May 25, 2000.

30. Hess, *Rauchen*, 137.

31. Richard Peto et al., *Mortality from Smoking in Developed Countries 1950–2000* (Oxford, U.K.: Oxford University Press, 1994).

32. See Burkard Junge, *Passivrauchen: Wie gefährlich ist es wirklich?* (Berlin: Max Planck-Institut, 1996).

33. *Die Welt*, March 22, 1997.

34. Rolf Coeppicus, "Entlasten Raucher die Krankenkassen?" *Zeitschrift für Rechtspolitik* 31 (7): 251–252 (1998).

35. Jan J. Barendregt, *Münchner Medizinische Wochenschrift* 140 (8): 24–36 (1998) (for the Netherlands).

36. Coeppicus, "Entlasten Raucher die Krankenkassen?" 251.

37. Hess, *Rauchen*, 85–95.

38. For example, Allgemeine Ortskrankenkasse, *Krankheitsartenstatistik 1997* (containing data concerning the type and duration of diseases).

39. *Frankfurter Allgemeine Zeitung*, August 27, 1997.

40. *Jahrbuch Sucht 2000*, 47; Bundeszentrale für gesundheitliche Aufklärung, ed., *Aktionsgrundlagen 1990: Teilband Rauchen* (Köln: Neuland Verlag, 1992); Statistisches Bundesamt, *Gesundheitsbericht für Deutschland* (Stuttgart: Metzler-Poeschel, 1998), chap. 4; Burckhard Junge, "Tabak—Zahlen und Fakten zum Konsum," in *Jahrbuch Sucht 2000*, 19–42.

41. A 1999 survey conducted by the International Research Associates (London), quoted in *Jahrbuch Sucht 2000*, 49.

42. Deutsche Tabakwaren-Industrie, ed., *Deutsche Tabakzeitung*, No. 17, April 28, 2000.

43. These figures reflect only the official, custom-controlled imports.

44. *Jahrbuch Sucht 2000*, 9.

45. Hess, *Rauchen*, 98.

46. See Ute Frevert, *Krankheit als politisches Problem 1770–1880* (Göttingen: Vandenhoeck & Ruprecht, 1984); Wolfram Lamping and Ingo Tamm, "Die Grundlegung der Krankenversicherung in Deutschland und England: Analyse ihrer Genese, Funktion und politischen Ausgestaltung," in *Krankheit und Gemeinwohl*, (ed. Bernhard Blanke (Opladen: Leske & Budrich, 1994); Alfons Fischer, *Geschichte des deutschen Gesundheitswesens*, vol. 1 (Berlin: Kommissionsverlag F. A. Hebrig, 1933).

47. Public health insurance (as well as other forms of social insurance, such as accident, old-age, and disability insurance) is referred to in Germany as "legal," thereby distinguishing such insurance programs, for which membership is established by law, from voluntary insurance arrangements.

48. Wolfgang Eckart, "Die Vision vom 'gesunden Volkskörper,'" in *"Hauptsache gesund!" Gesundheitsaufklärung zwischen Disziplinierung und Emanzipation*, eds. Susanne Roeßiger and Heidrun Merk (Marburg: Jonas Verlag, 1998).

49. Norbert Frei, *Medizin und Gesundheitspolitik in der NS-Zeit* (München: Oldenbourg Verlag,1991), 7–19.

50. See Proctor, *The Nazi War on Cancer.*

51. See Günter Frankenberg, "Germany: The Uneasy Triumph of Pragmatism," in *AIDS in the Industrialized Democracies: Passions, Politics, and Policies,* eds. David L. Kirp and Ronald Bayer (New Brunswick, NJ: Rutgers University Press, 1992), 99–133.

52. See Joachim Heilmann, "Verfassungsmäßigkeit eines Nichtraucherschutzgesetzes," *Zeitschrift für Rechtspolitik* 30 (7): 268–270 (1997); von Hippel, "Zum Kampf gegen die Tabak-Epidemie"; Dieter Suhr, "Die Freiheit vom staatlichen Eingriff als Freiheit zum privaten Eingriff?" *Juristenzeitung* 35 (5/6): 166–174 (1980); Rüdiger Zuck, "Bundeskompetenz für einen gesetzlichen Nichtraucherschutz nach französischem Vorbild," *Die öffentliche Verwaltung* 193 (21): 936–947 (1993); and the decision of the Federal High Court on Administrative Law (BVerwG), in *Bayerische Verwaltungsblätter* 34 (22): 692–693 (1988).

53. In 1976 the European Parliament held that initiatives of the European Community against tobacco abuse were necessary; see report in Jürgen Grunwald et al., "Europa-Report," *Europäische Zeitschrift für Wirtschaftsrecht* 1 (1): 2–7 (1990).

54. See Article 152 of the EC Treaty.

55. See the following decisions of the Federal Constitutional Court (BVerfG): BVerfGE 56: 73–80 (1981); BVerfGE 39: 61 (1982); and BVerfGE 88: 251 (1993). See also Georg Hermes, *Das Grundrecht auf Schutz von Leben und Gesundheit* (Heidelberg: Müller, 1987).

56. Sondergutachten der Bundesregierung "Luftverunreinigungen in Innenräumen," Bundesrats-Drucksache No. 876/92, November 24, 1992.

57. Cf. Winfried Brohm, "Rechtsstaatliche Vorgaben für informelles Verwaltungshandeln," *Deutsches Verwaltungsblatt* 109 (3): 133–147 (1994).

58. See Hanspeter Beißer, *Wettbewerbsbeschränkungen im Dienste der Gesundheit* (Weinheim: VCH, 1987).

59. Cf. Axel Heim, "Das Tabakwerbeverbot," in *Werbung und Werbeverbote im Lichte des europäischen Gemeinschaftsrechts,* ed. Jürgen Schwarze (Baden-Baden: Nomos, 1999), 60–65.

60. Ibid.

61. *Frankfurter Allgemeine Sonntagszeitung,* April 22, 2001.

62. For example, Heim, "Das Tabakwerbeverbot."

63. See Michael James Stewart, "The Effect on Tobacco Consumption of Advertising Bans in OECD Countries," *International Journal of Advertising* 12 (2): 155–180 (1993); Peter Leeflang and Jan Reuyl, "Effects of Tobacco Advertising on Tobacco Consumption," *International Business Review* 4 (1): 39–54; Reinhold Bergler, *Zigarettenkonsum im Jugendalter: Bedingungen der Entwicklung gesundheitlichen Fehlverhaltens* (Köln: Deutscher Instituts-Verlag, 1992); Reinhold Bergler, *Ursachen gesundheitlichen Fehlverhaltens im Jugendalter* (Köln: Deutscher Instituts-Verlag, 1995).

64. Bundestags-Drucksache No. 12/2487, April 28, 1992.

65. BVerfGE 95: 187 (Federal Constitutional Court, 1997).

66. Council Directive 89/622/EEC, 1989 O.J. (L 351) 1; see Klaus Zapka, "Gesund-heitspolitik durch Harmonisierung?" *Recht der internationalen Wirtschaft* 36 (10), 814–820 (1990).

67. See Grunwald et al., "Europa-Report."

68. See Gerhard Schricker, "Werbeverbote in der EG," *Gewerblicher Rechtsschutz/Urheberrecht* 3: 85–92 (1991).

69. Council Directives 89/622/EEC (concerning the labeling of tobacco products) and 90/239/EEC, 1990 O.J. (L 137) 36 (concerning maximum tar yields of cigarettes); (German) Ordinances concerning the Labeling of Tobacco Prod-ucts and the Maximum Content of Tar of 1991 and 1994.

70. Council Directive 89/622/EEC.

71. See BVerfGE 95: 181 (Federal Constitutional Court, 1997).

72. For references, see Zapka, "Gesundheitspolitik durch Harmonisierung?" 815; see also Office of the Surgeon General, *Reducing the Health Consequences of Smoking: 25 Years of Progress: A Report of the Surgeon General: Executive Summary* (Washington, D.C.: U.S. Government Printing Office, 1989), 38–71.

73. *Frankfurter Allgemeine Zeitung,* November 24, 1996.

74. See Norbert Hirschhorn, "Shameful Science: Four Decades of the German Tobacco Industry's Hidden Research on Smoking and Health," *Tobacco Control* 9: 242–247 (2000).

75. Ibid.

76. Concerning the anti-tobacco campaign of the World Health Organization, see *Frankfurter Rundschau,* May 31, 2000.

77. See *Jahrbuch Sucht 2000,* 22.

78. *Die Welt,* January 6, 1994.

79. Eike von Hippel, "Ersatz von Tabakschäden," *Zeitschrift für Rechtspolitik* 31 (1): 6–7 (1998).

80. von Hippel, "Zum Kampf gegen Tabak-Epidemie," 138.

81. Suhr, "Die Freiheit vom staatlichen Eingriff als Freiheit zum privaten Ein-griff?"; Benedikt Buchner and Friedrich J. Wiebel, "Die Fehlerhaftigkeit des Produkts Zigarette," *Versicherungsrecht* 51 (1): 29–34 (2000).

82. Klaus Zapka, *Passivrauchen und Recht* (Berlin: Duncker & Humblot, 1993), 48; Joseph H. Kaiser, "Raucher- und Nichtraucher-Kontroversen in der Verwaltung," *Die Öffentliche Verwaltung* 31 (20): 757–758 (1978).

83. Since 1998, Lufthansa has offered only nonsmoking flights.

84. See sections 5 and 32 of the Arbeitsstättenverordnung and sections 5, 15 I, and 17 I of the Arbeitsschutzgesetzes.

85. Neue Juristische Wochenschrift 52 (30): 2203–2206 (Federal Labor Court (BAG), 1999).

86. Bundestags-Drucksache No. 13/6166, November 18, 1996; see also Heilmann, "Verfassungsmäßigkeit eines Nichtraucherschutzgesetzes."

87. See *Neue Juristische Wochenschrift*52 (30): 2203–2206 (Federal Labor Court, 1999); BVerfGE 95: 173–185 (Federal Constitutional Court, 1997).

88. Bundestags-Drucksache No. 14/3231, June 29, 2000.
89. *Neue Juristische Wochenschrift* 49 (45): 3028–3030 (Federal Labor Court, 1996). See also section 618 of the Civil Code (BGB); the decision of the Federal Administrative Court (BVerwG) prohibiting smoking in exam rooms in *Bayerische Verwaltungsblätter* 34 (22): 692 (1988), and the previous decision by the Higher Administrative Court of Bavaria (BayVGH), *Bayerische Verwaltungsblätter* 22 (1): 30 (1976), holding that the right of nonsmokers not to be disturbed prevails over the right of smokers to exercise their freedom, and that the state as the organizer of the particular examination involved in the dispute has a duty to protect nonsmokers.
90. See Wilhelm J. Zimmermann, *Die Tabaksteuer* (Frankfurt: Lang Verlag, 1987); Klaus Tipke, *Steuerrecht*, (14th ed. (Köln: O. Schmidt, 1994), §§3, 4, 15.
91. See Council Directives 72/464/EEC, 1972 O.J. (L 303) 1, and 79/32/EEC, 1979 O.J. (L 10) 8. Council Directive 92/12/EC, 1992 O.J. (L 76) 1 finally laid down the general system of excise taxes.
92. Ibid.; Zentralverband der deutschen Werbewirtschaft, ed., *Tabak Werbung Fakten ohne Filter* (Bonn: Verlag edition ZAW, 1999), 29.
93. The most important sources being the value-added tax (DM 129 billion), the income tax (DM 108 billion), the mineral oil tax (DM 66 billion), and the solidarity surcharge (DM 26 billion). See also *Frankfurter Allgemeine Zeitung* (May 25, 2000), 30.
94. Federal Statistical Office, ed., *Fachserie 14: Finanzen und Steuern*, as cited in *Jahrbuch Sucht 2000*, 29.
95. See von Hippel, "Ersatz von Tabakschäden," 6.
96. See Coeppicus, "Entlasten Raucher die Krankenkassen?"
97. Eike von Hippel, *Verbraucherschutz*, 3rd ed. (Tübingen: Mohr, 1986).
98. Buchner and Wiebel, "Die Fehlerhaftigkeit des Produkts Zigarette."
99. According to the principles of liability, causation of damage would imply more than the repetition of a long-standing practice (for example, the sale of tobacco products).
100. See Hess, *Rauchen*, 135.

8. Holy Smoke, No More?

The author wishes to thank Peter Th. Madsen of the Tobacco Manufacturers Association of Denmark, and Henrik Frøkjær and Florence Longunoc of the House of Prince, for their help in furnishing industry documents; Thomas Svane Christensen, Jakob Jensen, and Maja Kieffer for research assistance; and Helle Blomquist, HRH Crown Prince Frederik, Jens Blom-Hansen, Peter Munk Christiansen, Peter Kragh Jespersen, Asbjørn Sonne Nørgaard, Lise Togeby, Signild Valgårda, and Martynas Vilkelis for their critical comments on earlier drafts.

1. See Peter A. Hall and Rosemary C. R. Taylor, "Political Science and the Three New Institutionalisms," *Political Studies* 44: 936–957 (1996); Asbjørn Sonne Nørgaard, *The Politics of Institutional Choice* (Århus: Politica, 1997).

2. *Jyllands-Posten,* August 23, 2000; *Politiken,* August 23, 2000. It was further revealed that the former chairman of Hen-ry—a well-known Danish physician—had received a fixed monthly allowance from Philip Morris for a number of years. *Jyllands-Posten,* January 2, 2000; *Politiken,* August 23, 2000.

3. Niels Gustav Bardenfleth and Peter Th. Madsen, *Tobaksindustrien 1875–2000* (Copenhagen: Tobaksindustrien, 2000).

4. *Statistisk Årbog* 1929.

5. Bardenfleth and Madsen, *Tobaksindustrien 1875–2000,* 88–89; *Statistisk tiårsoversigt* 2000.

6. James Q. Wilson, "The Politics of Regulation," in *The Politics of Regulation,* ed. James Q. Wilson (New York: Basic Books, 1980).

7. Erik Albæk, "Political Ethics and Public Policy: Homosexuals Between Moral Dilemmas and Political Considerations in Danish Parliamentary Debates," *Scandinavian Political Studies* 26: 245–267 (2003).

8. *Passive Smoking or the Pollution of Non-smokers by Smokers* (Eurobarometer survey, 1993), at <http://europa.eu.int/comm/public_opinion/archives/special.htm>.

9. *Politiken,* February 26, 2001.

10. Hugo Keseloot, "Queen Margrethe II and Mortality in Danish Women," *Lancet* 357: 871–872 (2001). The article was widely mentioned and discussed in the Danish media, and Danish epidemiologists questioned its scientific validity. See Rune Jacobsen et al., "Queen Margrethe II and Mortality in Denmark," *Lancet* 358: 75 (2001).

11. World Health Organization, "Denmark," in *Tobacco or Health: A Global Status Report: Country Profiles by Region, 1997,* at <http://www.cdc.gov/tobacco/who/whofirst.htm>.

12. Ibid.

13. Ronald Inglehart, Miguel Basanez, and Alejandro Moreno, *Human Values and Beliefs* (Ann Arbor: University of Michigan Press, 1998).

14. Lise Togeby, "The Political Implications of the Increasing Number of Women in the Labour Force," *Comparative Political Studies* 27 (2): 211–240 (1994); see also Constance A. Nathanson, "Mortality and the Position of Women in Developed Countries," in *Mortality in Developed Countries: From Description to Explanation,* eds. Alan D. Lopez, Graziella Caselli, and Tapani Valkonen (Oxford, U.K.: Clarendon Press, 1995).

15. Jan Andreasen, "Rygning—den store dræber," *Ugeskrift for læger* 161: 6688 (1999).

16. World Health Organization, "Denmark," in *Tobacco or Health: A Global Status Report: Country Profiles by Region, 1997,* at <http://www.cdc.gov/tobacco/who/whofirst.htm>.

17. Sundhedsstyrelsen et al., *Tobak i sundhedsplanlægningen* (Copenhagen: Sundhedsstyrelsen, 1995), 12.

18. Susanne Reindahl Rasmussen and Jes Søgaaard, "Tobaksrygningens samfundsøkonomiske omkostninger," *Ugeskrift for læger* 162 (23): 3329–3333 (2000);

Skatteministeriet, *Rapport om Grænsehandel* (Copenhagen: Skatteministeriet, 2000), 266.

19. Jørn Henrik Petersen, *Den danske alderdomsforsørgelseslovgivnings udvikling*, vol. 1 (Odense: Odense Universitetsforlag, 1985), 32.

20. Ibid., 95–107.

21. *Statistisk Årbog* 1903, pp. 160–161.

22. Helge Smith, "Tobaksbeskatning: Udviklingen i Danmark," in Kristof Glamann, *75-foreningen: 1875–1950* (Copenhagen: Cigar- og Tobaksfabrikanternes forening af 20. juni 1875, 1950), 251.

23. *Rigsdagstidende* 1911–12, Tillæg B, 1007. The translations from the Danish are by the author.

24. Smith, "Tobaksbeskatning," 250.

25. Kristof Glamann, *75-foreningen: 1875–1950*, 221–241; Smith, "Tobaksbeskatning," 249–250.

26. *Rigsdagstidende* 1918–19, Tillæg C, 27–42.

27. Beretning fra Tobakskommissionens Underudvalg angaaende Revisionen af Tobaksafgiftsloven af 21. December 1918 m.m., *Rigsdagstidende* 1921–22, Tillæg A, 3497–3520.

28. *Rigsdagstidende* 1921–22, Tillæg C, 397–426.

29. Smith, "Tobaksbeskatning," 254–255.

30. Ibid.

31. Peter Gundelach, *Sociale bevægelser og samfundsændringer* (Århus: Politica, 1988), 159.

32. Sidsel Eriksen (associate professor and specialist in the history of alcohol consumption and control policies in Denmark, Department of History, University of Copenhagen), interview by author, November 30, 2000.

33. This refusal to take health issues into account was quite different from what happened with regard to tax policies on alcohol—which were debated during the same period. Despite a steady decrease in alcohol consumption since the 1850s, the temperance movements sharply increased their membership from 55,000 in 1895, to 137,000 in 1905, to 200,000 in 1917, making them one of the major social movements of the time. Apparently, increased urbanization had rendered drinking more visible and thereby intensified the understanding of alcohol consumption as a social problem. The movements were instrumental in making the harmful health and social effects of alcohol consumption highly visible on the public agenda. A question to the finance minister in 1880 resulted in an 1882 report on intemperance problems in Denmark. Although the Parliament did not base the 1891 beer duty on health or social concerns, it was seen as a major victory for the temperance movements. In 1903 a temperance commission was established, whose mandate closely followed the view of the temperance movements, and another commission was established in 1912. In 1917 the government temporarily prohibited sale of distilled spirits and wine during the month of March; the war had caused such a shortage of

grain and potatoes that prices might have spiraled out of control. Recognizing an opportunity to turn the government's temporary prohibition into a permanent arrangement, the temperance movements organized a petition in support of prohibition. About half of all voters actually signed the petition, which was quite an achievement for the temperance movements, but the effort fell short. The government opted, instead, for a solution with fiscal benefits for the state: state monopolization of the production of distilled spirits; rationing; and dramatically increased taxes. The excise duty on a bottle of *snaps* (distilled spirits) increased from 99 øre to 11 *kroner*—that is, by an astonishing 1,111.11 percent. After the level of alcohol consumption plummeted and reached a record low, the temperance movements lost their popular appeal in national politics, and their membership decreased sharply. See Gundelach, *Sociale bevægelser og samfundsændringer*, 152–170.

34. Bo Rothstein, *Vad bör staten göra? Om välfärdsstatens moraliska och politiska logik* (Stockholm: SNS Förlag, 1994); Nørgaard, *The Politics of Institutional Choice*.
35. *Folketingets Forhandlinger* 1928–29, col. 758.
36. Ibid., col. 1038.
37. Christian Lemvigh Poulsen, "Tobakspolitik i Danmark?" (M.A. thesis, Århus: Institut for Statskundskab, Aarhus Universitet, 2001), cover.
38. Ibid., 101–102.
39. Skatteministeriet, *Rapport om Grænsehandel*, 243.
40. *Statistisk Årbog* 1914, p. 177; 1921, pp. 185–186; 1951, pp. 258–260.
41. *Statistisk tiårsoversigt* 2001.
42. *Børsens Nyhedsmagasin*, November 5–11, 2001.
43. Skatteministeriet, *Rapport om Grænsehandel*, 43.
44. *Mandag Morgen*, March 3, 2000.
45. Skatteministeriet, *Rapport om Grænsehandel*, chap. 7.
46. *Betænkning om foranstaltninger til nedsættelse af cigaretforbruget afgivet af det af Indenrigsministeriet under 29. maj 1963 nedsatte udvalg*, Betænkning No. 357, pp. 33–35 (1964).
47. Figure 8.1 presents only overall cigarette consumption in Denmark. Studies indicate, however, that price affects cigarette consumption among young people, in particular—and therefore in the long term may have a positive effect on overall consumption. See Frank J. Chaloupka et al., "Advice to Governments: Tobacco Taxes, Control Policies, and Tobacco Use" (paper presented at the 126th Annual Meeting and Exposition of the American Public Health Association, Washington, D.C., November 1998), 19.
48. Skatteministeriet, *Rapport om Grænsehandel*, chap. 7. It should be noted that historically the high price of cigarettes in Denmark has given rise to only limited illegal import. For forty-five years Gallup has asked a representative sample of one thousand Danes almost every other week: "Did you smoke yesterday?" If yes, "How much did you smoke yesterday?" The respondents'

answers account for 95 percent of the cigarette consumption registered by the Danish tax authorities. See Niels Søren Hansen, *Rygningens sociologi* (n.p.: Tobaksskaderådet, 1995), 9.

49. *Folketingets Forhandlinger* 1925–26, cols. 1117–1129.

50. *Kulturministeriets bekendtgørelse nr. 416 af 18. juni 1987 om indholdet af reklameindslag, der bringes på TV2.*

51. *Betænkning om foranstaltninger til nedsættelse af cigaretforbruget afgivet af det af Indenrigsministeriet under 29. maj 1963 nedsatte udvalg*, 7.

52. As part of the campaign, there was a live radio broadcast of a lung cancer operation. The press wrote the next day that the "sound of knives cutting into bones, the bubbling blood, the wheezing sound of air entering the breast cavity accompanied by the neutral comments of the surgeons made a deep impression." *Politiken*, February 10, 1961.

53. *Betænkning om foranstaltninger til nedsættelse af cigaretforbruget afgivet af det af Indenrigsministeriet under 29. maj 1963 nedsatte udvalg*, 9.

54. Ibid., 35.

55. Abraham Rosenberg, *Ryg mindre—lev længere* (Copenhagen: Schønberg, 1954).

56. *Betænkning om foranstaltninger til nedsættelse af cigaretforbruget afgivet af det af Indenrigsministeriet under 29. maj 1963 nedsatte udvalg*, 17–18.

57. The expert was a professor of sales and marketing at the Copenhagen Business School. In 1952 he had published his doctoral thesis on the demand pattern for cigarettes from1920 to 1950. See Max Kjær-Hansen, *Cigaretforbruget 1920–50* (Copenhagen: Einar Harcks Forlag, 1952).

58. *Betænkning om foranstaltninger til nedsættelse af cigaretforbruget afgivet af det af Indenrigsministeriet under 29. maj 1963 nedsatte udvalg*, 18.

59. The latter restriction had just that year been introduced in trams and buses in the cities of Copenhagen and Frederiksberg.

60. *Betænkning om foranstaltninger til nedsættelse af cigaretforbruget afgivet af det af Indenrigsministeriet under 29. maj 1963 nedsatte udvalg*, 16.

61. Ibid., 15.

62. *Regler for reklamering* (Copenhagen: Cigar- og Tobaksfabrikanternes Forening af 20. Juni 1875, April 1972).

63. Arbetsgruppen tillsatt med anledning af Nordiska rådets rekommendation nr 12/1972, angående förbud mot tobaksreklam, *Nordiska tobaksarbetsgruppens betänkande* (Nordisk Utredningsserie 1975: 24), 9.

64. Ibid.

65. *Regler for markedsføring af tobaksvarer* (Copenhagen: Cigar- og Tobaksfabrikanternes Forening af 20. Juni 1875, 1980); *Aftale mellem Tobaksindustrien og Indenrigsministeriet: Regler for markedsføring af tobaksvarer* (Copenhagen: Cigar- og Tobaksfabrikanternes Forening af 20. Juni 1875, March 11, 1986); *Aftale mellem Tobaksindustrien og Sundhedsministeriet om markedsføring af tobaksvarer* (Copenhagen: Cigar- og Tobaksfabrikanternes Forening af 20. Juni 1875, November 6, 1991).

66. Forslag til folketingsbeslutning om forbud mod markedsføring og reklamering for tobak og spiritus (B 67), *Folketingstidende* 1987–88, Tillæg A, 2625.

67. Forslag til lov om sikring af røgfri miljøer og mærkning m.v. af tobaksvarer (L 58), *Folketingstidende* (1987–88, Tillæg A, 1233–36; Forslag om mærkning sikring af røgfri miljøer og mærkning af tobaksvarer m.v. (L 63), *Folketingstidende* 1987–88, Tillæg A, 1367–1370.

68. See Chapter 9 on the European Union.

69. For similar reasons Denmark objected to a convention—the European Convention on Transfrontier Television—adopted by the European Council in May 1989 prohibiting hidden advertising (Article 13(3)) and tobacco advertising (Article 15). Due to widespread skepticism in the Danish population and the Danish Parliament toward increased EU integration, Danish governments have had to object on several occasions to EU policy proposals on grounds of principle, even though the government and, indeed, the parliamentary opposition may substantially have agreed with the proposals.

70. With its pending veto, the Danish government had placed itself in an awkward position: it could not bring other member states before the European Court of Justice for noncompliance and, at the same time, consistently claim that the directive was contrary to the terms of the EC Treaty. Tobaksskaderådet, *Tobaksreklamer og sponsorering: En redegørelse fra Tobaksskaderådet* (1990).

71. See Act No. 426 (June 13, 1990), the Ministry of Health's Departmental Order No. 1213 (December 23, 1992), and Act No. 1086 (December 23, 1992).

72. *Lov nr. 492 af 7. juni 2001 om forbud mod tobaksreklame m.v*

73. Tobaksskaderådet, *Tobaksreklamer og sponsorering*, 21.

74. *Politiken*, June 25, 1996.

75. Tobaksskaderådet, *Tobaksreklamer og sponsorering*, 19, 26–28.

76. Lov om et forebyggelsesråd (L 203), *Folketingstidende* (1978–79, Tillæg A, 3379.

77. *Folketingstidende* 1986–87, Tillæg B, 2191–2198; *Folketingets Forhandlinger* 1986–87, cols. 12613–12620. In 2001 the Parliament decided to further promote public health in Denmark by merging a number of public health councils, including the Council on Smoking and Health, into a National Council of Public Health and a Center for Public Health under the National Board of Health. *Lov nr. 141 af 5. marts 2001 om ændring af lov om sundhedsvæsenets centralstyrelse m.v. med flere love og om ophævelse af lov om et forebyggelsespolitisk råd og et tobaksskaderåd (Oprettelse af et nationalt råd for folkesundhed samt styrkelse af Sundhedsstyrelsens opgaver vedrørende kvalitetsudvikling, evaluering m.v. inden for sundhedsvæsenet).*

78. Poulsen, *Tobakspolitik i Danmark?* 80–81.

79. Ibid., 75.

80. *Udviklingen i det årlige salg af cigaretter fordelt efter kondensatniveauet, 1990/ 1991–1999/2000* (Skandinavisk Tobakskompani, on file with author).

81. *Aftale mellem Tobaksindustrien og Sundhedsministeriet om indberetning af tilsætningsstoffer i cigaretter m.v.* (March 30, 2000).

82. Forslag til folketingsbeslutning om, at tilsætningsstoffer og aromastoffer til tobak, der øger rygningens omfang, ikke længere kan tillades (B 154), *Folketingstidende* 1999–2000, Tillæg A, 7949.

83. Bjarke Thorssteinsson (chief of Public Health Section, Ministry of Health), interview by author, November 30, 2000.

84. One of the few exceptions was the Danish Hemophilia Society. In the late 1980s and early 1990s, the society mobilized media, popular, and political support by exploiting a number of judicial inquiries regarding the entry of HIV into the blood supply. Although the courts dismissed the society's substantive claims, Danish politicians gave in to growing pressure on several successive occasions and raised the level of *ex gratie* compensation to HIV-infected hemophiliacs and transfusion recipients—who, in the end, received the highest medical-injury compensation in Danish history. See Erik Albæk, "The Never-Ending Story? The Political and Legal Controversies over HIV and the Blood Supply in Denmark," in *Blood Feuds: AIDS, Blood, and the Politics of Medical Disaster,* eds. Eric A. Feldman and Ron Bayer (New York and Oxford, U.K.: Oxford University Press, 1999).

85. *Ansøgning om fri process* (application for free legal aid prepared by Anker Laden-Andersen, attorney-at-law, on behalf of the client, October 18, 2000).

86. Folketingsbeslutning om sikring af røgfri miljøer (B 116), *Folketingstidende* 1985–86, Tillæg C, 914.

87. *Folketingets Forhandlinger* 1985–86, col. 9394.

88. Ibid., col. 1850.

89. Ibid., col. 12004.

90. *Folketingets Forhandlinger* 1986–87, col. 5799.

91. Ibid., col. 13291.

92. Ibid., col. 5780.

93. *Berlingske Tidende,* January 22, 1987.

94. *Sundhedsministeriets cirkulære om sikring af røgfri miljøer i statslige lokaler, transportmidler o.lign. af 23. marts 1988.*

95. *Socialministeriets cirkulære nr. 203 af 26. oktober 1990 om dagtilbud for børn og unge efter bistandslovens § 64; Arbejdsministeriets bekendtgørelse nr. 1163 af 16. december 1992 om faste arbejdspladsers indretning.*

96. Samarbejdsnævnet, *Rygning på arbejdspladserne* (Copenhagen: DA og LO, 1989).

97. Benny Jensen (consultant, Central Organization of Industrial Employees in Denmark), interview by author, November 29, 2000.

98. *Opmandskendelse i faglig voldgift: Grafisk Arbejdsgiverforening for Avery Etiketsystemer A/S mod Grafisk Forbund, Dansk Metalarbejderforbund og Handels- og Kontorfunktionærernes Forbund i Danmark* (1995).

99. Peter Bjerregaard and Knud Juel, *Middellevetid og dødelighed: En analyse af dødeligheden i Danmark og nogle europæiske lande 1950–1990* (Copenhagen: Sundhedsministeriet, 1993) (first report from the Life Expectancy Committee of the Ministry of Health).

100. Ibid.; Sundhedsministeriets Middellevetidsudvalg, *Levetiden i Danmark* (Copenhagen: Sundhedsministeriet, 1994) (second report from the Life Expectancy Committee of the Ministry of Health); Bjarne Hjort Andersen, *Tværnationale sammenligninger af ændringer i levekårene i lyset af udviklingen i middellevealderen* (Copenhagen: Sundhedsministeriet, 1994) (fourth report); Henning Hansen, Niels Kristian Rasmussen, and Jytte Poulsen, *Livsstil og sundhedsvaner i Danmark: Status, forskelle og udviklinger* (Copenhagen: Sundhedsministeriet, 1994) (fifth report).

101. Jørgen Falk (executive consultant, Council on Smoking and Health), interview by author, February 5, 2001.

102. *Lov nr. 436 af 14. juni 1995 om røgfri miljøer i offentlige lokaler, transportmidler og lignende.*

103. Only four years later, in 1999, members of the nonsocialist opposition parties, along with a member from the governing Social Democratic Party, moved a motion requesting the government to present a bill to establish uniform rules for smoke-free environments for institutions and means of transportation, both at the central and local levels of government. They also sought to prohibit all smoking in hospitals and in institutions for children and teenagers. *Forslag nr. 107 af 25. marts 1999 til folketingsbeslutning om ensartede regler for røgfri miljøer inden for stat, amtskommuner og kommuner samt Hovedstadens Sygehusfællesskab.* The movers stated that the reason for the motion was that the 1995 act had simply proved ineffective. The motion lapsed, however, because it was still before the Parliament at the end of its session.

104. Peder Sass (member of Parliament, Social Democrats), interview by author, February 5, 2001. Sass is a firm nonsmoker, but also the chairman of Ungdomsringen, an association of Danish youth clubs and recreation centers.

105. *Forslag nr. 45 af 11. oktober 2000 til lov om ændring af lov om røgfri miljøer i offentlige lokaler, transportmidler og lignende.*

106. Jørgen Falk, interview.

107. Erik Albæk, "Political Ethics and Public Policy: Homosexuals between Moral Dilemmas and Political Considerations in Danish Parliamentary Debates," *Scandinavian Political Studies* 26: 245–267 (2003).

108. *Jyllands-Posten* (in the autumn of 2000).

109. Such utilitarian arguments are not considered legitimate, however, when it comes to other substances. Politicians have not been willing to liberalize the availability of other substances—not even marijuana for medical purposes. Denmark's strictness with regard to other substances is not in line with its usual liberal stance (in contrast, for instance, to the Netherlands and Switzerland). It seems as if politicians have actually gone quite moralistic on this issue.

110. Productschap voor gedestilleerde dranken, *World Drink Trends 2002* (n.p.: NTC Publications, 2001); Swedish Council for Information on Alcohol and Other Drugs, *The 1999 ESPAD Report* (2000).

111. Hansen, *Rygningens sociologi,* 15–21.

112. Lau Laursen and Knud-Erik Sabroe, *Alkoholbrug og alkoholpolitik* (Århus: Aarhus Universitetsforlag, 1996), 33–34, 96–97.

113. Wilson, "The Politics of Regulation." Contrary to Wilson, the argument here is that the institutional organization of policy, rather than the nature of policy per se, may shape politics. Cf. Nørgaard, *The Politics of Institutional Choice,* 52–54.

114. Bardenfleth and Madsen, *Tobaksindustrien 1875–2000,* 82–83.

9. Tobacco-Control Policy in the European Union

1. Gerard Wirz, [European Network of Information Centres with Brussels as a Central Point], Bates Nos. 2028395314–27, executive summary (June 23, 1993). All Bates documents cited in this chapter are available online at <http://www.pmdocs.com>.

2. This quote is taken from a Web site, <http://goeurope.about.com/travel/goeurope/library/weekly/aa990624.htm>, that provides advice for travelers to Europe.

3. *World Tobacco Trends 1998* (Henley-on-Thames, U.K. : NTC Publications, 1998).

4. Food and Agriculture Organization, FAOSTAT, at <http://apps.fao.org/page/collections?subset= (agriculture> (under "Agricultural Production/Crops Primary").

5. Luk Joossens, "Tobacco," in *Priorities for Public Health Action in the European Union,* eds. Oliver Weil, Martin McKee, Marc Brodin, and Daniel Oberlé (Paris: Société française de santé publique, 1999).

6. World Health Organization, *European Health for All Database,* (at <http://www.who.dk/hfadb>).

7. Marlo Ann Corrao, Emmanuel Guindon, Namita Sharma, and Dorna F. Shokoohi, eds., *Tobacco Control Country Profiles* (Atlanta: American Cancer Society, 2000).

8. Hilary Graham, "Smoking Prevalence among Women in the European Community 1950–1990." Social Science and Medicine 43(2): 243–254 (1996).

9. Joossens, "Tobacco."

10. Adriënne Cavelaars, Anton Kunst, José Geurts, Roberta Crialesi, Liv Grötvedt, Uwe Helmert, "Educational Differences in Smoking: International Comparison," *British Medical Journal* 320: 1102–1107 (2000).

11. Richard Peto, Alan D. Lopez, Jilian Boreham, Michael Thun, and Heath Clark Jr., *Mortality from Smoking in Developed Countries* (Oxford, U.K.: Oxford University Press, 1994).

12. Commission Report to the European Parliament, the Council, the Economic and Social Committee, and the Committee for the Regions: Progress Achieved in Relation to Public Health Protection from the Harmful Effects of Tobacco Consumption, COM (99) 407 final. European Commission documents are available online at <http://europa.eu.int>.

13. See, for example, the low proportion of female deaths from tobacco in Greece, Portugal, and Spain in Table 9.1.

14. European Commission, "European Survey: Strong Support for Anti-smoking Measures," *Prevention: Progress in Community Public Health* 2: 14–15 (1997).

15. Peter Boyle et al., "Characteristics of Smokers' Attitudes towards Stopping," *European Journal of Public Health* 10 (3S): 5–14 (2000).

16. One appointed by each member state except for France, Germany, Italy, Spain, and the United Kingdom, each of which appoints two.

17. Prior to the 2000 Prodi reorganization, responsibility in this area lay with Directorate General V—Employment, Industrial Relations and Social Affairs.

18. European Commission, *The Community Budget: The Facts and Figures* (Luxembourg: Office for Official Publications of the European Communities, 2000).

19. Council Directive 83/477/EEC of 19 September 1983 on the Protection of Workers from the Risks Related to Exposure to Asbestos at Work, 1983 O.J. (L 263) 25.

20. Although it was not made public for many years, Mitterrand had at that time only recently been diagnosed with prostate cancer.

21. Some observers have suggested that his interest stemmed, in part, from his son's having cancer.

22. Resolution of the Council and the Representatives of the Governments of the Member States, Meeting within the Council, of 7 July 1986, on a Programme of Action of the European Communities against Cancer, COM (86) 717, 1986 O.J. (C 184) 19.

23. Centre d'Information sur le Tabac, "Argumentation Used by the EEC in Its Struggle against Tobacco," Bates nos. 2501348648–65 (1992).

24. Most were introduced under the Single Market Programme (mainly Article 100a (now Article 95), which requires qualified majority voting). The directives on taxation of cigarettes were an exception; these directives do not fall under the responsibility of the public health sector, but under Article 99, which requires unanimity.

25. France, for example, has excellent tobacco-control legislation on public smoking, but enforcement is lax, thus undermining its impact.

26. Decision of the Council and the Representatives of the Governments of the Member States Meeting within the Council, on 17 May 1990 Adopting a 1990 to 1994 Action Plan in the Context of the "Europe against Cancer" Programme, 1990 O.J. (L 137) 31.

27. Decision No. 646/96/EC of the European Parliament and of the Council of 29 March 1996 Adopting an Action Plan to Combat Cancer within the Framework for Action in the Field of Public Health (1996 to 2000), 1996 O.J. (L 095) 9.

28. Doc. CAN-16-2000 (draft), Action Plan to Combat Cancer within the Framework for Action in the Field of Public Health: Annual Work Programme for 2001 Indicating Priorities for Action.

29. Luk Joossens, "Successes and Failures of Tobacco Control in the European Union" (paper presented at Fifth WHO Seminar for a Tobacco-Free Europe, Warsaw, October 1995).

30. Letter from W. Hunter to H. C. Jones (director general), December 16, 1994, cited in Leonard Doyle, "Brussels Stubs Out Cash for Anti-smoking Group," *Guardian,* November 29, 1995.

31. Ivo Ilic Gabara, "Why the EU's Tobacco Policy Is Up in Smoke," *Wall Street Journal Europe,* October 10, 1996.

32. Rory Watson, "European Antismoking Group Loses Grant," *British Medical Journal* 311: 10 (1995).

33. Philip Morris, "The Activist Movement," Bates nos. 2025599925–37 (November 1993).

34. Philip Morris, "List of Leading Activists," Bates nos. 2400121052–53 (1992).

35. John Lepere, "BASP Publication—'Give Children a Chance,'" Bates No. 2501342094 (April 30, 1991); Gerard Wirz, "BASP Brochure on Smoke-Free Workplaces," Bates nos. 2028391404–07 (June 3, 1992).

36. In one thirteen-page document on the international activist movement, they dedicate almost an entire page to BASP's activities, considerably more than given to other organizations. See Philip Morris, "The Activist Movement."

37. "We shall make a concerted effort to counter the pressure of the antis, particularly BASP." Philip Morris Corporate Affairs Europe, "Smoking Restrictions 3-Year Plan 1994–1996," Bates nos. 2025497291–303 (December 1993).

38. Ernst Heynig, "The European Community in 1976," Bates nos. 2024266495–97 (January 1977).

39. Douglas Herbison, "Monthly Report (Tobacco Highlights for the Month of January 1992)," Bates nos. 2021573313–48 (February 1992).

40. David Bushong (Gold and Liebengood, Washington, D.C.), "Philip Morris' EC Capability" [memorandum to David Greenberg], Bates nos. 2045756540–47 (April 17, 1991).

41. Each member state maintains an embassy in Brussels whose purpose is to manage the country's dealings within the EU. These permanent national representations exert considerable influence at both the European and national levels.

42. The Committee of Permanent Representatives comprises the member states' Brussels-based ambassadors. Their most important task is to prepare for the Council of Ministers meetings.

43. Trevor King (assistant general secretary, Infotab), [Letter to J. Lepere, CECCM chairman], Bates No. 2501361972 (January 23, 1990).

44. See CECCM, "CECCM Working Group on Smoking at the Workplace and in Public Places" [June 1992], Bates nos. 2501356767–71, section 6.

45. Philip Morris Corporate Affairs Europe, "Smoking Restrictions 3-Year Plan."

46. Daniel Martin and Dyson Bell Martin, "Why Philip Morris Needs the United Kingdom" [memorandum to Gerard Wirz], Bates nos. 2501207805–09 (June 9, 1992).

47. Philip Morris Corporate Affairs Europe, "Smoking Restrictions 3-Year Plan."
48. CECCM, "CECCM Working Group on Smoking at the Workplace and in Public Places" [June 1992].
49. Philip Morris Corporate Affairs Europe, "Smoking Restrictions 3-Year Plan."
50. Wirz, [European Network of Information Centres].
51. A former *Financial Times* foreign correspondent and European affairs columnist for the *International Herald Tribune*.
52. See, for example, the conference proceedings for "Beyond Maastricht: The Issues at Stake in the 1996 IGC." The conference was held at the Sorbonne in Paris on January 31, 1995. Giles Merritt shared a platform with Guido Brunner (previously EC commissioner for energy, research, and technology in Brussels, and German ambassador to Spain), Neelie Kroes (Dutch minister of transport and public works), and Sergio Arzeni (senior economist at OECD, Paris).
53. Bushong, "Philip Morris' EC Capability."
54. These organizations included think tanks such as the Centre for the New Europe in Belgium, and Institut Euro 92 in France. See R. E. Marden, "Policy Groups—Europe" [memorandum to Helene Lyberopoulos and Matthew Winokur], Bates nos. 2025496759 & 2025496760–73 (August 1, 1994).
55. Philip Morris Corporate Affairs Europe, "Smoking Restrictions 3-Year Plan."
56. Martin and Martin, "Why Philip Morris Needs the United Kingdom."
57. Gerard Wirz, "Summary of October 11 Meeting," Bates nos. 2501453677–81 (October 15, 1990); Wirz, [European Network of Information Centres].
58. Philip Morris Corporate Affairs Europe, "Smoking Restrictions 3-Year Plan."
59. Freedom for the Right to Enjoy Smoking Tobacco (FOREST), "Defending Smokers' Rights," Bates No. 2501021528 (1993).
60. In a 1993 document, Philip Morris planned to continue its support to groups in France, Greece, Italy, the Netherlands, and Spain, and to increase assistance to those in Denmark and the United Kingdom. See Philip Morris Corporate Affairs Europe, "Smoking Restrictions 3-Year Plan." A recent report in the *Guardian* suggested that 96 percent of the funding for the U.K.-based group, FOREST, came from the cigarette industry. James Meikle, "Cigarette Firm Stops Cash for Pro-smoking Group," *Guardian,* June 28, 2001.
61. See Laura Girod, "Field Meeting Brussels—Notes," Bates nos. 2501344091–96 (April 13, 1994). The document makes reference to a meeting between Associazione Fumatori, the Italian smokers' rights group, and Philip Morris—when plans for the III Smokepeace Conference, which the Associazione had agreed to organize, were discussed—and states that the "organisation of the event is starting now after the meeting."
62. FOREST, "Defending Smokers' Rights."
63. Philip Morris Corporate Affairs Europe, "Smoking Restrictions 3-Year Plan."
64. Wirz, "Summary of October 11 Meeting"; Wirz, [European Network of Information Centres].

65. Philip Morris Corporate Affairs Europe, "ETS 3-Year Plan: 1994–1996," Bates No. 2024187135 (October 1993).

66. Philip Morris, "The Activist Movement."

67. Luk Joossens and Martin Raw, "Tobacco and the European Common Agricultural Policy," *British Journal of Addiction* 86: 1191–1202 (1991).

68. Luk Joossens and Martin Raw, "Are Tobacco Subsidies a Misuse of Public Funds?" *British Medical Journal* 312: 832–835 (1996).

69. Joy Townsend, "Tobacco and the European Common Agricultural Policy," *British Medical Journal* 303: 1008–1009 (1991).

70. Council Directive 89/552/EEC of 3 October 1989 on the Coordination of Certain Provisions Laid Down by Law, Regulation or Administrative Action in Member States Concerning the Pursuit of Television Broadcasting Activities, 1989 O.J. (L 298) 23.

71. A 1995 survey of 18,500 EU citizens in all fifteen member states found that in each country, between 44 percent and 77 percent favored legislation banning all direct and indirect tobacco advertising. European Commission, "European Survey: Strong Support for Anti-smoking Measures."

72. Belgium (1997), Finland (1976), France (1991), Ireland (latest decree 2000, with further changes being planned to cover indirect advertising and sponsorship), Italy (1991), Portugal (latest decree 1998), and Sweden (1993, with further legislation being planned on indirect advertising).

73. Denmark and the Netherlands.

74. "Opposition to Total Ad Ban," *World Tobacco for Russia and Eastern Europe* 2: 89 (1995).

75. James Rupert and Glenn Frankel, "In Ex-Soviet Markets, US Brands Took On Role of Capitalist Liberator," *Washington Post*, November 19, 1996.

76. Ewen MacAskill, "Tories Attack Old Ally in Onslaught on Tobacco Firm," *Guardian*, July 20, 1999.

77. House of Commons Health Committee, *The European Community and Health Policy: Health Committee Third Report* (London: HMSO, 1992).

78. John Warden, "UK Adheres to Formula One Exemption," *British Medical Journal* 315: 1397–1402 (1997).

79. Directive 98/43/EC of the European Parliament and of the Council of 6 July 1998 on the Approximation of the Laws, Regulations and Administrative Provisions of the Member States Relating to the Advertising and Sponsorship of Tobacco Products, 1998 O.J. (L 213) 9.

80. Luk Joossens, "The Future of the Tobacco Control Movement in the 21st Century" (paper presented at Second European Conference on Tobacco and Health, Las Palmas de Gran Canaria, February 26, 1999).

81. Rory Watson, "Legality of European Ban on Tobacco Advertising Questioned," *British Medical Journal* 320: 1691 (2000); Opinion of Advocate General Fennelly, Case C-376/98, *Federal Republic of Germany v. European Parliament and Council of the European Union* (Eur. Ct. Justice, 2000); Judgment, Case

C-74/99, *Queen v. Secretary of State for Health* (Eur. Ct. Justice, 2000). The cases and materials of the European Court of Justice are available online at <http://curia.eu.int>.

82. Judgment, Case C-376/98, *Federal Republic of Germany v. European Parliament and Council of the European Union* (Eur. Ct. Justice, 2000).

83. Opinion of Advocate General Fennelly, Case C-376/98; Judgment, Case C-74/99; see F. Kling, "Ban on Tobacco Advertising Not Legal," *Tobacco Journal International* 4: 58 (2000).

84. Rory Watson, "EU to Phase Out Tobacco Advertising despite Ruling," *British Medical Journal* 321: 915 (2000).

85. George Davey Smith and Matthias Egger, "Smoking and Health Promotion in Nazi Germany," Journal of Epidemiology and Community Health 50: 109–110 (1996).

86. "European Union: Vote on Controls," *Tobacco Journal International* 4: 4 (2000).

87. Norbert Hirschhorn, "Shameful Science: Four Decades of the German Tobacco Industry's Hidden Research on Smoking and Health," *Tobacco Control* 9: 242–247 (2000).

88. Mark Neuman, Asaf Bitton, and Stanton Glantz, "Tobacco Industry Strategies for Influencing European Community Tobacco Advertising Legislation," *Lancet* 359: 1323–1330 (2002).

89. A 1992–93 speech recommends "work[ing] with Chancellor Kohl to put ad ban directive on commission subisidiary list." Philip Morris, "Marketing Freedoms," Bates nos. 2501021740–46 (n.d.).

90. See text accompanying note 86.

91. John Lepere, [Letter to W. Dembach], Bates nos. 2501362375–76 (April 23, 1992).

92. John Dollisson, "EEC Advertising Directive," Bates nos. 2024671385–88 (January 26, 1990).

93. Bobby Kaplan, "Speech by Bobby Kaplan, Manager of Communications—PMI-CA, International Marketing Training Conference," Bates nos. 2500120186–202 (August 12, 1991).

94. Kenneth Clarke, [Letter to Ian Sargeant], Bates No. 2501015055 (May 1, 1992).

95. Martin and Martin, "Why Philip Morris Needs the United Kingdom."

96. See Neuman, Bitton, and Glantz, "Tobacco Industry Strategies."

97. John Lepere, "Proposed Court Proceedings before the German Constitutional Court," Bates nos. 2501473712–13 (August 30, 1990).

98. See Neuman, Bitton, and Glantz, "Tobacco Industry Strategies"; Philip Morris, "Marketing Freedoms."

99. Countries were free to have health warnings of a larger size; for example, warnings in the United Kingdom took up 6 percent of the pack face. See Council Directive 89/622/EEC of 13 November 1989 on the Approximation of the Laws, Regulations and Administrative Provisions of the Member States Concerning the Labelling of Tobacco Products and the Prohibition of the

Marketing of Certain Types of Tobacco for Oral Use, 1989 O.J. (L 359) 1; Council Directive 92/41/EEC of 15 May 1992 Amending Directive 89/622/ EEC on the Approximation of the Laws, Regulations and Administrative Provisions of the Member States concerning the Labelling of Tobacco Products and the Prohibition of the Marketing of Certain Types of Tobacco for Oral Use, 1992 O.J. (L 158) 30.

100. C. Naett and C. Howie, *The Labelling of Tobacco Products in the European Union* (1993) (report undertaken by the European Bureau for Action on Smoking Prevention at the request of the European Commission); R. Watson, "Europe Gets Tougher on Tobacco," *British Medical Journal* 309: 1037–1038 (1994).

101. Clive Bates, Gregory Connolly, and Martin Jarvis, *Tobacco Additives: Cigarette Engineering and Nicotine Addiction* (London: Action on Smoking and Health, 1999).

102. High Level Cancer Experts Committee, "Recommendations on Tobacco" (presented at "Europe against Cancer" program, consensus conference on tobacco, Helsinki, October 2, 1996).

103. Rory Watson, "MEPS Back Tougher Health Warnings on Cigarette Packets," *British Medical Journal* 322: 7 (2001).

104. Directive 2001/37/EC of the European Parliament and of the Council of 5 June 2001 on the Approximation of the Laws, Regulations and Administrative Provisions of the Member States concerning the Manufacture, Presentation and Sale of Tobacco Products—Commission Statement, 2001 O.J. (L 194) 26.

105. Council of the European Union, Interinstitutional File 99/0244 (COD) 8129/01 ADD 2 (statement by the German delegation, Brussels, May 14, 2001); Council of the European Union, Interinstitutional File 99/0244 (COD) 8129/01 ADD 3 (statement by the Luxembourg delegation, Brussels, May 14, 2001).

106. Andrew Clark, "Tobacco Trade Launches Tar Wars," *Guardian,* September 6, 2001.

107. AFX Europe, "Japan Tobacco Considering Taking Legal Action after EU Tobacco Decision," May 17, 2001, at <http://globalarchive.ft.com/globalarchive/article.html?id= (010517011312> (access restricted).

108. "European Union: Shutting Brands Out," *Tobacco Journal International* 4: 4 (2000).

109. P. L. Short (British American Tobacco Company), "A New Product," October 21, 1971, as quoted in *Tobacco Explained: The Truth about the Tobacco Industry in Its Own Words* (London: Action on Smoking and Health, 1998), at <http://www.ash.org.uk/html/conduct/html/tobexpld0.html>.

110. Clive Bates et al., "The Future of Tobacco Product Regulation and Labelling in Europe: Implications for the Forthcoming European Union Directive," *Tobacco Control* 8: 225–235 (1999).

111. Simon Chapman et al., "Bans on Smoking in Public Become More Commonplace," *British Medical Journal* 316: 727–730 (1998).

112. Paul Boffetta et al., "Multicenter Case-Control Study of Exposure to Environmental Tobacco Smoke and Lung Cancer in Europe," *Journal of the National Cancer Institute* 90: 1440–1450 (1998).

113. Richard A. Daynard, Clive Bates, and Neil Francey, "Tobacco Litigation Worldwide," *British Medical Journal* 320: 111–113 (2000); Simon Chapman, "Smoking in Public Places," *British Medical Journal* 312: 1051–1052 (1996).

114. "Resisting Smoke and Spin," *Lancet* 355: 1197 (2000).

115. International Agency for Research on Cancer, *IARC Monographs on the Evaluation of the Carcinogenic Risk of Chemicals to Humans: Tobacco Smoking* (vol. 38) (Lyon, France: World Health Organization, 1986); U.K. Department of Health and Social Security, *Fourth Report of the Independent Scientific Committee on Smoking and Health* (London: HMSO, 1988).

116. U.S. Department of Health and Human Services, *The Health Consequences of Involuntary Smoking: A Report of the Surgeon General* (Washington, D.C.: DHHS, 1986).

117. Australian National Health and Medical Research Council, *Effects of Passive Smoking on Health* (Canberra: Australia Government Publishing Service, 1987).

118. Boffetta et al., "Multicenter Case-Control Study."

119. Allan K. Hackshaw, Malcolm R. Law, and Nicholas J. Wald, "The Accumulated Evidence on Lung Cancer and Environmental Tobacco Smoke," *British Medical Journal* 315: 980–988 (1997); M. R. Law, Joan K. Morris, and N. J. Wald, "Environmental Tobacco Smoke Exposure and Ischaemic Heart Disease: An Evaluation of the Evidence," *British Medical Journal* 315: 973–980 (1997); U.K. Department of Health, *Scientific Committee on Tobacco and Health Report of the Scientific Committee on Tobacco and Health* (London: Stationery Office, 1998).

120. National Cancer Institute, *Health Effects of Exposure to Environmental Tobacco Smoke: The Report of the California Environmental Protection Agency* (Smoking and Tobacco Control Monograph 10) (Bethesda, MD: National Cancer Institute, 1999).

121. Ibid.

122. William J. Blot and Joseph K. Mclaughlin, "Passive Smoking and Lung Cancer Risk: What Is the Story Now?" *Journal of the National Cancer Institute* 90: 1416–17 (1998).

123. World Health Organization, *Air Quality Guidelines for Europe,* 2d ed. (WHO Regional Publications, European Series No. 91) (Copenhagen: WHO Regional Office for Europe, 2000).

124. Roper Organization. *A Study of Public Attitudes toward Cigarette Smoking and the Tobacco Industry in 1978,* vol. 1 (New York: Roper Organization, 1978).

125. "Project Down Under Conference Notes," Bates nos. 2021502102–3434 (June 24, 1987).

126. George Davey Smith and Andrew N. Phillips, "Passive Smoking and Health: Should We Believe Philip Morris's 'Experts'?" *British Medical Journal* 313:

929–933 (1996); Cyrilli Colin and Herve Maisonneuve, "Misleading Information on Environmental Tobacco Smoke in the French Lay Press," *International Journal of Epidemiology* 26: 240–241 (1997).

127. Smith and Phillips, "Passive Smoking and Health."

128. Peter N. Lee, "Difficulties in Assessing the Relationship between Passive Smoking and Lung Cancer," *Statistical Methods in Medical Research* 7: 137–163 (1998).

129. Work by the WHO, for example, has revealed that Peter N. Lee acted as a tobacco company consultant and was closely involved in the attempts to undermine the IARC study. See, for example, the Committee of Experts report on tobacco industry documents, *Tobacco Company Strategies to Undermine Tobacco Control Activities at the World Health Organization,* at <http://www.who.int/genevahearings/inquiry.html> (published by WHO in July 2000; see especially pages 197–198 and 205–206).

130. Deborah E. Barnes et al., "Environmental Tobacco Smoke: The Brown and Williamson Documents," *JAMA* 274: 248–253 (1995).

131. "Project Down Under Conference Notes."

132. Boffetta et al., "Multicenter Case-Control Study."

133. Eliza Ong and Stanton A. Glantz, "Tobacco Industry Efforts Subverting International Agency for Research on Cancer's Second-Hand Smoke Study," *Lancet* 355: 1253–1259 (2000).

134. Environmental Protection Agency, *Respiratory Health Effects of Passive Smoking: Lung Cancer and Other Disorders* (Washington, D.C.: EPA, 1992).

135. Ong and Glantz, "Tobacco Industry Efforts."

136. Deborah E. Barnes and Lisa A. Bero, "Industry-Funded Research and Conflict of Interest: An Analysis of Research Sponsored by the Tobacco Industry through the Center for Indoor Air Research," *Journal of Health Politics, Policy and Law* 21: 515–542 (1996).

137. Simon Chapman, "The Hot Air on Passive Smoking," *British Medical Journal* 316: 945 (1998).

138. Ong and Glantz, "Tobacco Industry Efforts."

139. These public places included hospitals, schools, entertainment facilities, sports facilities, railway stations, airports, and public transportation, but excluded the hospitality sector (hotels, restaurants, and cafés).

140. Resolution of the Council and the Ministers for Health of the Member States, Meeting within the Council of 18 July 1989 on Banning Smoking in Places Open to the Public, 1989 O.J. (C 189) 1.

141. Commission of the European Communities, Report from the Commission to the Council, the European Parliament, the Economic and Social Committee and the Committee of the Regions on the Response to the Resolution of the Council and the Ministers for Health and the Member States Meeting within the Council on Banning Smoking in Places Open to the Public, COMMA (96) 573 final (November 14, 1996).

142. Ibid.

Loan Receipt
Liverpool John Moores University
Library Services

Borrower Name: Fallon,Colette
Borrower ID: *********9119

Smoking :
31111010013546
Due Date: 02/10/2015 23:59

Tobacco :
31111013591126
Due Date: 02/10/2015 23:59

Unfiltered :
31111011285457
Due Date: 12/06/2015 23:59

Total Items: 3
05/06/2015 13:21

Please keep your receipt in case of
dispute.

Smokers
— cluster
headaches.

143. Allies included all pan-European associations, particularly in the hospitality industry, potentially interested in workplace smoking.
144. Wirz, "Summary of October 11 meeting."
145. Philip Morris Corporate Affairs Europe, "Smoking Restrictions 3-Year Plan."
146. Wirz, [European Network of Information Centres].
147. CECCM, "CECCM Working Group on Smoking at the Workplace and in Public Places" [June 1992]; CECCM, "CECCM Working Group on Smoking at the Workplace and in Public Places" [July 1992], Bates nos. 2501356762–66.
148. See, for example, the CECCM paper, "Environmental Tobacco Smoke: A Summary of the Scientific Literature," Bates nos. 2501356777–79 (July 30, 1992), which states that "the key to a comfortable indoor environment is adequate ventilation," and that "the most likely conclusion [from the available scientific evidence] is that ETS has not been proven to cause disease in nonsmokers."
149. Wirz, [European Network of Information Centres].
150. Ibid.
151. Philip Morris Corporate Affairs Europe, "Smoking Restrictions 3-Year Plan."
152. Ibid.
153. A recent report in the *Guardian* (suggested that 96 percent of FOREST's funding came from the cigarette industry. Meikle, "Cigarette Firm Stops Cash for Pro-smoking Group."
154. European Commission, "European Survey: Strong Support for Anti-smoking Measures."
155. Philip Morris Corporate Affairs Europe, "Smoking Restrictions 3-Year Plan."
156. Ibid.
157. Council Directive 92/79/EEC of 19 October 1992 on the Approximation of Taxes on Cigarettes, 1992 O.J. (L 316) 8.
158. Luk Joossens, *Comments on the Commission Report COM (95) 285 Final on the Approximation of Taxes on Cigarettes* (Brussels: International Union Against Cancer, 1996).
159. Robert Garran, "Setback for RYO: EU Tobacco Tax Harmonisation," *Tobacco International,* December 1995, 43–45.
160. In April 2001, the price differential was just under 400 percent, the cost of a pack of twenty varying from a maximum of 433 U.K. pence in the United Kingdom to a minimum of 110 U.K. pence in Spain. See <http://www.the-tma.org.uk/statistics/eu_facts_figures_98.htm>.
161. Council Directive 1999/81/EC of 29 July 1999 Amending Directive 92/79/EEC on the Approximation of Taxes on Cigarettes, Directive 92/80/EEC on the Approximation of Taxes on Manufactured Tobacco Other Than Cigarettes, and Directive 95/59/EC on Taxes Other Than Turnover Taxes Which Affect the Consumption of Manufactured Tobacco, 1999 O.J. (L 211) 47.
162. Commission Report to the European Parliament, the Council, the Economic and Social Committee, and the Committee of the Regions: Progress Achieved in Relation to Public Health Protection from the Harmful Effects of Tobacco Consumption.

163. Luk Joossens and Martin Raw, "Smuggling and Cross Border Shopping of Tobacco in Europe," *British Medical Journal* 310: 1393–1397 (1995).

164. Luk Joossens and Martin Raw, "How Can Cigarette Smuggling Be Reduced?" *British Medical Journal* 321: 947–950 (2000); Joossens and Raw, "Smuggling and Cross Border Shopping."

165. Luk Joossens and Martin Raw, "Cigarette Smuggling in Europe: Who Really Benefits?" *Tobacco Control* 7: 66–71 (1998).

166. Luk Joossens, *Smuggling and Cross-border Shopping of Tobacco Products in the European Union: A Report for the Health Education Authority* (December 1999).

167. Anthony Barnett and Pazit Ravina, "Clarke Tobacco Firm Linked to Serb 'Smuggler,'" *Observer,* July 15, 2001; Nicholas Forster and Sead Husic, "Investigators Probe Montenegro's Role at Centre of Illegal Cigarette Trade," *Financial Times,* August 10, 2001.

168. Nicholas Forster, Sead Husic, and Stefan Wagstyl, "EU Hits at BAT Plan for Serbia Plant," *Financial Times,* August 13, 2001.

169. Joossens and Raw, "Smuggling and Cross Border Shopping."

170. Luk Joossens and Martin Raw, "How Can Cigarette Smuggling Be Reduced?"

171. Ibid.

172. Kevin Maguire, "Clarke Admits BAT link to Smuggling: BAT Exposé: Special Report," *Guardian,* February 3, 2000.

173. House of Commons, Health Committee Session 1999–2000, Inquiry into the Tobacco Industry and the Health Risks of Smoking, *Note of Evidence by Duncan Campbell in Respect of Planning, Organisation and Management of Cigarette Smuggling by British American Tobacco PLC and Related Issues.*

174. Christopher Dickey and Rod Nordland, "Big Tobacco's Next Legal War," *Newsweek,* July 31, 2000.

175. Centre for Public Integrity. Tobacco Companies Linked to Criminal Organizations in Cigarette Smuggling: China, March 2001. Available at: http://www.publici.org/story_OZ_030301.htm

176. Associated Press, "Former B&W Executive Convicted of Cigarette Smuggling," October 16, 1997; Dow Jones Newswires, "RJR Affiliate to Pay $15M for Acting as Smuggling Front," December 22, 1998.

177. Ian Black and Jane Martinson, "Tobacco Firms Sued over EU Smuggling," *Guardian,* November 7, 2000; "European Union: Plans to Sue," *Tobacco Journal International* 5: 3 (2000).

178. Andrew Osborn, "EU Cigarette Tax Claim Fails," *Guardian,* July 19, 2001.

179. Joossens and Raw, "How Can Cigarette Smuggling Be Reduced?"

180. John F. Ryan, "Tobacco Control Issues in the European Union," *Eurohealth* 6: 5–8 (2000).

181. See European Commission, Communication to the Council and the European Parliament on the Present and Proposed Community Role in Combating Tobacco Consumption, COM (96) 609 final; Commission Report to the European Parliament, the Council, the Economic and Social Committee, and the

Committee for the Regions: Progress Achieved in Relation to Public Health Protection from the Harmful Effects of Tobacco Consumption.

182. Anna Gilmore and Jeff Collin, "A Wake Up Call for Global Tobacco Control: Will Leading Nations Thwart the World's First Health Treaty?" *British Medical Journal* 325: 846–847 (2002).

183. Anna Gilmore and Witold Zatonski, "Free Trade v. the Protection of Health: How Will EU Accession Influence Tobacco Control in Poland" *Eurohealth* 8: 31–33 (2002).

184. Andrew Hayes, "A Health Lobby Response to the Draft EU Directive on Tobacco Content Regulation," *Eurohealth* 6: 9–10 (2000).

185. Peter Taylor, *The Smoke Ring: The Politics of Tobacco* (London: Bodley Head, 1984).

186. Tobacco Advisory Group of the Royal College of Physicians, *Nicotine Addiction in Britain* (London: Royal College of Physicians, 2000).

187. Lynn MacFadyn et al.,"'They Look Like My Kind of People'—Perceptions of Smoking Images in Youth Magazines." *Social Science and Medicine* 56: 491–499 (2000); and Julian Brookes, "Tobacco and Rupe," *Mother Jones,* August 25, 1998, available at <http://www.motherjones.com/sideshow/murdoch.html>.

188. Joanna E. Cohen et al., "Political Ideology and Tobacco Control," *Tobacco Control* 9: 263–267 (2000).

189. Jackie V. Dearlove, Stalla A. Bialous, and Stanton A. Glantz, "Tobacco Industry Manipulation of the Hospitality Industry to Maintain Smoking in Public Places," *Tobacco Control* 11: 94–104 (2002).

190. Donald Harris, "Memo on Public Relations Effort Being Conducted by Hen-Ry," March 2, 1989, Philip Morris, Bates nos. 2023270361–2; Philip Morris, "Communication—Smokers' Organizations," in *Infotopics: Summaries of Public Information*, vol. 6 no. 8 (August 28, 1987), pp. 39; Philip Morris, Bates nos. 506648064–8103; Tore Dineson, "Interim Report on the Hen-ry Promotion Campaign," March 8, 1989; Philip Morris, Bates nos. 2023270359–60; Stig Carlson, "World Congress of Smokers' Rights Groups (SRGs), 1982," June 28, 1981, Philip Morris, Bates nos. 2500041706–9.

191. Philip Morris, "Europe: Recommended Media, Journalists and News Distribution Systems" [undated], Philip Morris, Bates nos. 2021181754–777.

192. For example, Dr. Tage Voss identified as one of Philip Morris's "key writers/journalists" in Denmark was trained by Burson-Marstellar, Philip Morris' public relations advisors, as part of the Hen-ry campaign.

193. Annabel Ferriman, "Vilified for Attacking Tobacco," *British Medical Journal* 320: 1482 (2000).

194. Nicholas Timmins and Frances Williams, "Writer Failed to Declare Tobacco Interest," *Financial Times*, January 24 2002; and Alexander Stille, "Advocating Tobacco, on the Payroll of Tobacco." *New York Times*, March 23, 2002.

195. David Moyer, Chapter 32: Political Issues. In *The Tobacco Reference Guide*. UICC, available on-line at <http://www.globalink.org/tobacco/trg/Chapter32/ Chapter32POLITICSPage71.html>.

10. Difference and Diffusion

1. See Allan M. Brandt, "The Cigarette, Risk, and American Culture," *Daedalus* 119 (4): 155–176 (1990). The 1964 surgeon general's report, *Smoking and Health* (Washington, D.C.: U.S. Government Printing Office, 1964), was the watershed for acknowledging the harms of cigarette smoking.

2. For a historical discussion that illustrates well the complicated relationship of cultural beliefs and policy, see James T. Patterson, *Brown v. Board of Education:A Civil Rights Milestone and Its Troubled Legacy* (New York: Oxford University Press, 2001).

3. See Robert L. Rabin and Stephen D. Sugarman, eds., *Smoking Policy: Law, Politics, and Culture* (New York: Oxford University Press, 1993).

4. See Chapter 1 on the United States.

5. See David Kessler, *A Question of Intent: A Great American Battle with a Deadly Industry* (New York: Public Affairs, 2001). On addiction, see U.S. Department of Health and Human Services, *The Health Consequences of Smoking: Nicotine Addiction: A Report of the Surgeon General* (Washington, D.C.: U.S. Government Printing Office, 1988); on passive smoking, see U.S. Department of Health and Human Services, *The Health Consequences of Involuntary Smoking: A Report of the Surgeon General* (Washington, D.C.: U.S. Government Printing Office, 1986).

6. Industry intent came to be understood following the widespread disclosure of industry documents resulting from the discovery process in tobacco-liability litigation.

7. See Allan M. Brandt, "Recruiting Women Smokers: The Engineering of Consent," *Journal of the American Medical Women's Association* 51 (1 & 2): 63–66 (1996).

8. See Paula S. Fass, *The Damned and the Beautiful: American Youth in the 1920s* (New York: Oxford University Press, 1977).

9. See John F. Kasson, *Rudeness and Civility: Manners in Nineteenth-Century Urban America* (New York: Hill and Wang, 1990); Norbert Elias, *History of Manners,* trans. Edmund Jephcott (New York: Urizen Books, 1978).

10. Emily Post, "The Etiquette of Smoking," *Good Housekeeping* 111: 37 (1940).

11. Judith Martin (pseud. Miss Manners), "Non-smoker's Behavior Was Publicly Offensive," *Toronto Star,* August 23, 1991.

12. This approach was supported, for example, in R. J. Reynolds advertisements.

13. See Monique E. Muggli et al., "The Smoke You Don't See: Uncovering Tobacco Industry Scientific Strategies Aimed against Environmental Tobacco Smoke Policies," *American Journal of Public Health* 91: 1419–1423 (2001).

14. William Kloepfer Jr., "Report on Public Smoking Issue, Executive Committee," Bates Nos. TIMN0013710–23 (April 10, 1985). The Bates documents cited in this chapter are available online at <http://tobaccodocuments.org>.

15. Susan Stunz, Jeff Ross, and Lisa Osborne, "Corporate Contacts Re Workplace Smoking," Bates Nos. 85544385–435 (April 15, 1986).

16. Burson-Marsteller, "Philip Morris International Public Relations Proposal," Bates Nos. 2028375325–44, p. 4 (October 5, 1988).

17. Burson-Marsteller, "Breathing Space: PM Recommended Action," Bates Nos. 2046532684–90 (September 1993).

18. Judith Martin (pseud. Miss Manners), "Where There's Smoke, There's Ire," *Washington Post,* December 1, 1985.

19. Ibid.

20. Judith Martin (pseud. Miss Manners), "Wait until Course Is Over before Trying to Date Prof," *Toronto Star,* March 17, 1989.

21. A. Lee Fritschler, *Smoking and Politics: Policy Making and the Federal Bureaucracy* (Englewood Cliffs, NJ: Prentice Hall, 1989).

22. Allan M. Brandt, "Tobacco," in *Encyclopedia of the United States Congress,* eds. Donald C. Bacon, Roger H. Davidson, and Morton Keller (New York: Simon & Schuster, 1995).

23. Constance A. Nathanson, "Social Movements as Catalysts for Policy Change: The Case of Smoking and Guns," *Journal of Health Politics, Policy and Law* 24 (3): 421–488 (1999).

24. Rabin and Sugarman, *Smoking Policy;* Howard M. Leichter, *Free to Be Foolish: Politics and Health Promotion in the United States and Great Britain* (Princeton, NJ: Princeton University Press, 1991); Nancy Rigotti, *Implementation and Impact of a City's Regulation of Smoking in Public Places and the Workplace: The Experience of Cambridge, Massachusetts* (Cambridge, MA: Institute for the Study of Smoking Behavior and Policy, John F. Kennedy School of Government, Harvard University, 1988).

25. Matt Bai, "Sharon Votes to Keep Smoking Ban," *Boston Globe,* October 31, 1995.

26. "Outdoor Smoking Limits Take Effect in Palo Alto," *San Francisco Chronicle,* October 28, 1995.

27. L. A. Johnson, "Clearing the Air; Some Workplaces Now Restrict Outdoor Smoking Areas, Much to Smokers' Chagrin," *Pittsburgh Post-Gazette,* March 14, 2001.

28. Joe Cherner, "Smokefree Parks and Beaches," May 20, 2001 (distributed through JoeCherner-Announce list at <http://www.smokescreen.org>).

29. Daniel Rubin, "Europe Still a Smoker's Haven as Pressure Stepped Up," *Houston Chronicle,* June 30, 2001.

30. Andrew Selsky, "Europe Ignores Smoking Rules," *Toronto Star,* (January 4, 1997.

31. Patrick Barkham, "Stubbing Out Public Smoking," *Guardian Unlimited,* (May 7, 2001.

32. Sally Finlay, "Chilly Times for Cafes as Smoking 'Uncool,'" *Age,* April 26, 2001, at <http://www.theage.com.au/news/2001/04/26/FFXUBR81YLC.html>; see also Ballard's chapter on Australia.

33. Gene Borio, "Australia: Smoking Poll," *Tobacco News,* July 23, 1994, at <http://www.tobacco.org/News/94.07.23_tob_news.html>.

34. Charles Rosenberg, "Banishing Risk: Continuity and Change in the Moral Management of Disease," in *Morality and Health,* eds. Allan M. Brandt and Paul Rozin (New York: Routledge, 1997). On the United States, see Bayer and Colgrove's chapter; on Canada, see Manfredi and Maioni's chapter.

35. See, in this volume, Albæk's chapter on Denmark, Nathanson's chapter on France, Frankenberg's chapter on Germany, and Feldman's chapter on Japan.

36. Vivienne Walt, "Oblivious to Laws, French Puff On in Public," *USA Today,* August 10, 2000.

37. Arthur Max, "Scandinavian Smokers Huff and Puff as Legal Restrictions Get Tougher to Swallow," *Los Angeles Times,* February 11, 1990.

38. Dick Polman, "Where Smoking Unabashedly Is a Way of Life," *Philadelphia Inquirer,* September 25, 1994.

39. "Huff and Puffs," *Financial Times,* January 1, 1997.

40. Hugo Kestsloot, "Queen Margrethe II and Mortality in Danish Women," *Lancet* 357: 871–872 (2001).

41. Caroline Davies, "Denmark's Ashtray Queen Denies Being Femme Fatale: Margrethe May Be a Deadly Role Model for Women," *Daily Telegraph,* March 21, 2001.

42. "Huff and Puffs."

43. See Albæk's chapter on Denmark.

44. Linus Gregoriadis, "Smokers in the Front Line as the World Takes Steps to Stub Out Cigarettes," *Independent,* May 28, 1998.

45. See Robert A. Kagan and Jerome H. Skolnick, "Banning Smoking: Compliance without Enforcement," in Rabin and Sugarman's *Smoking Policy* for a good discussion of the relationship between compliance, regulation, and the social norm.

46. See Malcolm Gladwell, *The Tipping Point: How Little Things Can Make a Big Difference* Boston: Little, Brown, 2000).

47. Lawrence Garfinkel, "Cigarette Smoking Habits among Physicians and Other Health Professions, 1959–1972," *Ca: A Cancer Journal for Clinicians* 26 (6): 373–375 (1976).

48. Bruce Finley, "A Question of Liberty: To Some, Holding 2008 Olympics in Beijing Will Right Wrongs; To Others, It Is Just Wrong," *Denver Post,* May 6, 2001; No Kwai-yan, "Sydney Model for Outdoor Ban," *South China Morning Post,* May 24, 2001.

49. Hilda Klinkenberg, "Tips for Smokers" (available at the Etiquette International Web site, <http://www.etiquetteintl.com/smoking.htm>).

50. Miriam Meijer, "Worldly Manners" (WorldTravelCenter.com's Travel Health Newsletter, October 2000, at <http://www.worldtravelcenter.com/jetstream/newsweather/newsletter/Oct00/manners.htm>).

51. Letitia Baldridge, *Letitia Baldridge's New Complete Guide to Executive Manners* (New York: Rawson Associates, 1993), 249.

52. Ann Marie Sabath, *International Business Etiquette, Europe: What You Need to Know to Conduct Business Abroad with Charm and Savvy* (Franklin Lakes, NJ: Career Press, 1999).

53. See Nicholas D. Kristof, "'No Smoking' in Translation," *New York Times,* June 30, 1996.

54. Morris D. Rosenberg, "Fearless Traveler: Speaking of the Fair," *Washington Post,* August 15, 1982.

55. "Smoke Gets in the Skies" (editorial), *Washington Post,* June 17, 1977.

56. James Ott, "Carriers Strongly Oppose CAB Smoking Restrictions," *Aviation Week and Space Technology,* August 20, 1979.

57. Norman A. Adler, "Airliners Devoid of Unpolluted Air," *New York Times,* July 1, 1983.

58. Mitchell Smyth, "Hey, Weed Addicts! Here's Your Smoking Salon in the Sky," *Toronto Star,* September 30, 1995.

59. Scott Thurston, "Support Growing for Smoking Ban on Overseas Flights: Attendants Stepping to Forefront of Battle," *Atlanta Journal-Constitution,* March 12, 1994.

60. Mike Williams, "Flight Attendant Testifies in Lawsuit; Burden of Proof; Woman Says Smoke on Planes Was 'Dense' before In-Flight Ban in 1990," *Atlanta Journal-Constitution,* August 12, 1997; see also John Schwartz, "Secondhand Smoke Trial Ends in Deal; Tobacco Firms' Settlement Includes $300 Million for Research Foundation," *Washington Post,* October 11, 1997.

61. Douglas B. Feaver, "Smoking on Airliners Off, Then On," *Washington Post,* June 1, 1984; and Irvin Molotsky, "No-Smoking Rule Is On and Off Again," *New York Times,* June 1, 1984.

62. "Senator Weighs Ban of Flight Smoking," *New York Times,* September 14, 1989.

63. Jim Emmerson, "Air Canada Bans Smoking on 44 flights," *Toronto Star,* April 4, 1986; Bernard Simon, "Air Canada Curbs Smoking," *Financial Times* (London), April 5, 1986; "Tobacco Firms Boycott Airline over Its Ban on Smoking," *Toronto Star,* April 24, 1986.

64. Gene Sloan, "Smoking Bans Take Wing over International Skies," *USA Today,* September 3, 1993.

65. "Lufthansa Will Ban Smoking," *Wall Street Journal,* August 23, 1990.

66. Marc Fisher, "In Germany, Smokers on Cloud 9," *Washington Post,* October 23, 1990.

67. "Smoky Flights on a Comeback," *USA Today,* August 4, 1994. FOREST is a prosmoking lobbying group funded by the tobacco industry.

68. As smoking bans became widely enacted, there had been some concern about the risks of noncompliance, irritable passengers, and so-called rogue smokers, but these problems proved to be uncommon.

69. See Alisto DaRosa, "European Airlines Are Clearing the Air," *San Diego Tribune,* March 15, 1998; "Travel Advisory: Smoke-Free Zones at 35,000 Feet," *New York Times,* March 15, 1998.

70. Sue Bryant, "Special Report Business Travel: More Ciggy Smoke Trails in the Sky Are Stubbed," *Daily Telegraph*, April 17, 1998; Yumi Kuramitsu, "Airlines Serving Japan Continue to Offer Smoking Seats," *Daily Yomiuri*, December 6, 1995.
71. "Air France Strives to Tap Growing Asian Traffic," *Jakarta Post*, December 1, 1997; "Business Travel Today," *USA Today*, September 13, 1996.
72. "Air France Breaks the Smoking Habit," *Los Angeles Times*, August 27, 2000.
73. Barry Porter, "Smoking Ban Pervades Asian Routes," *South China Post*, May 13, 1993.
74. World Health Organization, *The World Health Report 1999: Making a Difference* (Geneva: WHO, 1999), 67.
75. William Ecenbarger, "We Are the World: The Americanization of Everywhere," *Plain Dealer*, August 15, 1993.
76. Ibid.

11. Tobacco Control in Comparative Perspective

The authors gratefully acknowledge the careful attention and comments from Ron Bayer and Eric Feldman, who have commented extensively on several drafts. We thank the various authors of the chapters in this volume for providing the basis for much of our analysis, and for responding to our repeated queries. Thanks also to members of the Robert Wood Johnson Health Policy Seminar at Yale University for their probing comments and questions. This work was supported in part by an Investigation Award in Health Policy Research from the Robert Wood Johnson Foundation, but the views expressed are those of the authors alone.

1. See, for example, Donald T. Campbell, "'Degrees of Freedom' and the Case Study," *Comparative Political Studies* 8(2): 178–193 (1975); Gary King, Robert Keohane, and Sidney Verba, *Designing Social Inquiry: Scientific Inference in Qualitative Research* (Princeton, NJ: Princeton University Press, 1994); Charles C. Ragin, *The Comparative Method: Moving Beyond Qualitative and Quantitative Strategies* (Berkeley, CA: University of California Press, 1989); and Robert W. Jackman, "Cross-National Statistical Research and the Study of Comparative Politics," *American Journal of Political Science* 29: 161–182 (1985).
2. Frank J. Chaloupka, Melanie Wakefield, and Christina Czart, "Taxing Tobacco: The Impact of Tobacco Taxes on Cigarette Smoking and Other Tobacco Use," in *Regulating Tobacco*, eds. Robert L. Rabin and Stephen D. Sugarman (New York: Oxford University Press, 2001).
3. Our original aim was to offer explanations for the different patterns of control policies across the eight cases. We anticipated accounting for this variation on three dimensions. One was the *timing* of policy action—the dates of which

differed widely in the country studies. A second dimension was variation in the extensiveness of policy interventions. We thought of that as the *scope* of tobacco control. Those controls range in principle from outright bans on smoking in all public places, to financial penalties to the smoker and restrictions on advertising to the young (and others), to limited educational campaigns about the dangers of smoking. A third potential dimension was the *intensity* of policy implementation. By that we understood the policies in practice, which would most reliably indicate the character of each tobacco-control regime. Unfortunately, this aim was impossible to satisfy in practice. The elements of policy action were conceptualized differently, and the documentation of implemented policies was not consistently available across all the cases. The different country narratives stimulated the quest for a better understanding of how tobacco-control policies varied cross-nationally from a more static perspective at the end of the twentieth century. For a discussion of the costs, benefits, and limits of cross-national policy research, see Theodore R. Marmor, Amy Bridges, and Wayne Hoffman, "Comparative Politics and Health Policies: Notes on Benefits, Costs, and Limits," in *Comparing Public Policies: New Concepts and Methods,* ed. Douglas E. Ashford (Beverly Hills, CA: Sage Publications, 1978). For an informed discussion of the problem of comparability in what is to be explained in, and learned from, comparative policy analysis, see Rudolf Klein, "Learning from Others: Shall the Last Be the First?" (paper presented at the Four Country Conference on Health Care Reforms in the United States, Canada, Germany and the Netherlands, Amsterdam, February 1995); also appeared in *Journal of Health Politics, Policy and Law* 22(5): 1267–1278 (1997).

4. See Constance A. Nathanson, "Tobacco Politics: Nation-States and Collective Action" (unpublished).

5. Chaloupka, Wakefield, and Czart, "Taxing Tobacco: The Impact of Tobacco Taxes on Cigarette Smoking and Other Tobacco Use."

6. Using alternative measures of taxation, such as tax as the proportion of cigarette price in 2000, *The Tobacco Atlas* provides essentially the same rank orderings, and the two measures are highly correlated (Pearson's $r = .84$). See Judith Mackay, Michael P. Eriksen, and the World Health Organization, *The Tobacco Atlas* (Geneva: World Health Organization, 2000). We prefer the nominal, per-pack measure because it is not influenced by the relative cost of consumer goods in each country. The persistence of the relative tax burdens across countries during the last decade of the twentieth century suggests that while within-country changes may seem dramatic from the vantage point of a single nation, a comparative perspective highlights the need to distinguish between variations of degree and of kind. We are focused on the latter.

7. Had we tried to describe these three countries over time, however, they would not have constituted a consistent set of countries with medium-high controls.

8. Marlo A. Corrao, G. Emmanuel Guindon, Namita Sharma, Dorna F. Shokoohi, eds., *Tobacco Control Country Profiles, American Cancer Society,* Atlanta,

2000, available at <http:// www5.who.int/tobacco/page.cfm?sid= (57>, accessed April 29, 2003. The report, *Tobacco Consumption 1970–1994 in the Member States of the EU, in Norway & Iceland,* available at <http:// www.globalink.org/tobacco/docs/misc-docs/tobacco.pdf>, attempts a similar type of classification scheme for the European countries based on similar data, but from an earlier (1994) report.

9. Eric A. Feldman, "The Landscape of Japanese Tobacco Policy: Three Perspectives," *American Journal of Comparative Law* 48: 679–706 (2001). More recently, Japanese legal restrictions have increased on *where* smoking is permitted in major cities, with substantial fines for smoking on the crowded streets of Tokyo, for example. The general rationale for this change is the traditional liberal argument about externalities and protection of children. The particular grounds are fascinating: cigarettes smoked outdoors in Japan are commonly held at one's side—a level that endangers both little children and the clothing of walkers.

10. We are attempting to make broad characterizations, in order to distinguish general, cross-national differences. Clearly, there remain important limits to the ideal-type scores we have provided. For example, no visitor to Denmark would regard the constraints on the location of smoking as being as restrictive as those in Australia (especially New South Wales) or Canada (especially British Columbia). The chapter portraits of Australia, Canada, and Denmark support these distinctions, but they do not fit with the American Cancer Society's rankings.

11. See, for example, Rabin and Sugarman, *Regulating Tobacco;* Donley Studlar, *Tobacco Control: Comparative Politics in the United States and Canada* (Peterborough, Ontario: Broadview Press, 2001); Carrick Mollenkamp et al., *The People vs. Big Tobacco: How the States Took On the Cigarette Giants* (Princeton, NJ: Bloomberg Press, 1998); David Phelps et al., *Smoked: The Inside Story of the Minnesota Tobacco Trial* (Minneapolis: MSP Communications, 1998); Cassandra Tate, *Cigarette Wars: The Triumph of the "Little White Slaver"* (New York: Oxford University Press, 1999); Mike Males, *Smoked: Why Joe Camel Is Still Smiling* (Monroe, ME: Common Courage Press, 1999); Stanton A. Glantz and Ethel Balbach, *Tobacco War: Inside the California Experience* (Berkeley: University of California Press, 2000); Dan Zegart, *Civil Warriors: The Legal Siege on the Tobacco Industry* (New York: Delacorte Press, 2000); David A. Kessler, *A Question of Intent: A Great American Battle with a Deadly Industry* (New York: Public Affairs Press, 2001); and Tara Parker-Pope, *Cigarettes: Anatomy of an Industry from Seed to Smoke* (New York: New Press, 2001).

12. Studlar, *Tobacco Control: Comparative Politics in the United States and Canada.*

13. The distinction between the politics of harm reduction and the politics of "denormalization" is, we believe, an important one for further understanding of tobacco control. A number of the political analyses of tobacco regulation have used this distinction in one form or another, but not for a comparative

study of the kind that has been attempted in this book. Kagan and Nelson, for example, have contrasted interest-group understandings with those emphasizing entrepreneurial politics; that dichotomy highlights the standard distinction between reducing the harm to others, on the one hand, and the social movement features of political entrepreneurs who, with moral fervor, rebuke both tobacco firms and inconsiderate smokers, on the other. In combination with an emphasis on the dispersed nature of the American polity, Kagan and Nelson use this distinction to make sense of the nation's low tobacco taxation and its typically zealous control of where tobacco can be used. But since the authors do not engage in any comparative analysis, they cannot distinguish the general from the idiosyncratic in the American case. Robert A. Kagan and William P. Nelson, "The Politics of Tobacco Regulation in the United States," in *Regulating Tobacco,* eds. Rabin and Sugarman. The emphasis on social movements and moralistic appeals is one of the themes of Nathanson's essay on tobacco politics, and most of the political analyses in this book have focused on the moralism of contemporary tobacco reformers and on how such attitudes have influenced the controls that have come into prominence. Without that emphasis, it would be impossible to understand why a California community actually proposed banning smoking in public parks. No understanding of the harm principle could justify that option, though aesthetic objections might justify suggesting keeping some physical distance between smokers and nonsmokers.

14. For an important debate about the merits of culture as an explanatory variable in comparative politics and political science more generally, see David Laitin and Aaron Wildavsky, "Political Culture and Political Preferences," *American Political Science Review* 82 (2): 589–597 (1988).

15. Max Weber, *The Protestant Ethic and the Spirit of Capitalism* (London: Harper Collins Academic, 1991).

16. Ronald Inglehart and Marita Carballo, "Does Latin America Exist? (And Is There a Confucian Culture?): A Global Analysis of Cross-Cultural Differences," *PS: Political Science and Politics* (March 1997): 34–47.

17. Essentially, this dimension distinguishes societies in terms of the emphasis on basic economic needs (survival) as compared with more subjective notions of well-being that incorporate many non-economic goods.

18. See, for example, Sven Steinmo, *Taxation and Democracy* (New Haven, CT: Yale University Press, 1993); Sven Steinmo, Kathleen Thelen, and Frank Longstreth, eds. *Structuring Politics: Historical Institutionalism in Comparative Analysis* (New York: Cambridge University Press, 1995); Markus M. L. Crepaz, "Inclusion Versus Exclusion: Political Institutions and Welfare Expenditures," *Comparative Politics* 31 (1): 61–80; and Ellen M. Immergut. *Health Politics: Interests and Institutions in Western Europe, Cambridge Studies in Comparative Politics* (Cambridge: Cambridge University Press, 1992).

19. See also Constance A. Nathanson, "Tobacco Politics: Nation-States and Collective Action."

20. Few scholars have regarded Australia, Canada, and the United States as similar in the appeal of moralistic politics or in the spread of prohibitionist constraints on personal habits. Indeed, appeals to the frontier feature—including claims of libertarian strains from Alberta to Texas to Queensland—would be more common. But the data reported in this book support the characterization of these three federal regimes as the most restrictive on the use of tobacco—particularly the use of tobacco in public places.

Conclusion

Elizabeth Robilotti provided invaluable assistance in organizing the comparative data on smoking behavior included in the tables and charts in this chapter.

1. Unless otherwise indicated, all references to nations included in this volume are to the relevant chapters.
2. See generally, Sir Richard Doll, "Tobacco: A Medical History," *Journal of Urban Health: Bulletin of the New York Academy of Medicine,* 76 (3): 289–313 (1999).
3. Ibid.
4. In 1950, 16 percent of the government's central revenue came from the sale of tobacco.
5. Michael Schudson, "Symbols and Smokers: Advertising, Health Messages, and Public Policy," in *Smoking Policy: Law, Politics, and Culture,* eds. Robert L. Rabin and Stephen D. Sugarman (New York: Oxford University Press, 1993).
6. Henry Saffer and Frank Chaloupka, "The Effect of Tobacco Advertising Bans on Tobacco Consumption," *Journal of Health Economics* (19: 1117–1137 (2000).
7. Barbara S. Lynch and Richard J. Bonnie, eds., *Growing Up Tobacco Free: Preventing Nicotine Addiction in Children and Youths* (Washington, DC: National Academy Press, 1994) (Institute of Medicine, Committee on Preventing Nicotine Addiction in Children and Youths, Division of Biobehavioral Sciences and Mental Disorders).
8. Hirayama Takeshi, "Non-Smoking Wives of Heavy Smokers Have a Higher Risk of Lung Cancer: A Study from Japan," *British Medical Journal* 282: 183–85 (1981).
9. Even Sir Richard Peto emphasized that smokers themselves were at greatest risk, perhaps an indication of how substantially some tobacco-control advocates were overplaying the ETS data.
10. Simon Chapman, "Banning Smoking Outdoors Is Seldom Ethically Justifiable," *Tobacco Control* 9: 95–97 (2000).
11. Kip Viscusi, *Smoke-Filled Rooms: A Postmortem on the Tobacco Deal* (Chicago: University of Chicago Press, 2002).
12. Kenneth E. Warner, "The Economics of Tobacco: Myths and Realities," *Tobacco Control* 9: 78–89 (2000).
13. John Stuart Mill, *On Liberty* (Cambridge, U.K.: Cambridge University Press, 1989), 13.

14. Robert A. Kagan and Jerome H. Skolnick, "Banning Smoking: Compliance without Enforcement," in *Smoking Policy: Law, Politics, & Culture,* eds. Robert L. Rabin and Stephen D. Sugarman (New York: Oxford University Press, 1993), 85.

15. "The Landscape of Japanese Tobacco Policy: Three Perspectives," *American Journal of Comparative Law* 49(679), 2001.

16. Canadian Tobacco Use Monitoring Survey, Annual 2001.

17. Mohammad Siahpush and Ron Borland, "Socio-demographic Variations in Smoking Status Among Australians Aged > or = 18: Multivariate Results from the 1995 National Health Survey," *Australia New Zealand Journal of Public Health* 25: 438–442 (2001).

18. Carlos Clark, "An Argument for Considering Parental Smoking in Child Abuse and Neglect Proceedings," *The Journal of Contemporary Health Law and Policy* 19: 225–246 (2002).

19. *The New Yorker,* September 23, 2002.

20. Dahlia Remler, "Poor Smokers, Poor Quitters and Cigarette Tax Regressivity." *American Journal of Public Health* (in press).

21. Burt Neuborne, "Prohibitions and Third-Party Costs: A Suggested Analysis," in Robert D. Tollison (ed.) *Clearing the Air: Perspectives on Environmental Tobacco Smoke* (Lexington, MA: Lexington Books, 1988), 95-96.

22. Prabhat Jha and Frank J. Chaloupka, *Curbing the Epidemic: Governments and the Economics of Tobacco Control* (Washington, DC: World Bank, 1999).

Contributors

During the course of this project, the editors and authors have all received support from the Robert Wood Johnson Foundation's Substance Abuse Policy Research Program. Because of widespread concern about conflicts of interest, we adapted the form used by the *BMJ* (*British Medical Journal*) for declaring competing interests. Every author filled out and submitted the form to the editors. The results are included in each author's biographical statement.

Erik Albæk is professor of public administration at the Department of Economics, Politics and Public Administration, Aalborg University, Denmark, and since 2001 has served as chairman of the Danish Social Science Research Council. His research includes comparative public policy and the utilization of social science research in public policy making. He is currently researching the role of experts in public policy making. He declared no competing interests.

John Ballard is currently a visiting fellow in the graduate school of the Australian National University, having previously been a political scientist at universities in the United States, Nigeria, Papua New Guinea, and Australia. Following earlier research on policymaking during decolonization, he has published widely on public health policy in Australia, especially on HIV and blood. He declared no competing interests.

Ronald Bayer is a professor at the Center for the History and Ethics of Public Health, Mailman School of Public Health, Columbia University. He is the author of *AIDS Doctors: Voices from the Epidemic; Private Acts, Social Consequences: AIDS and the Politics of Public Health;* co-editor, with David Kirp, of *AIDS in the Industrialized Democracies: Passions, Politics, and Policies;* and co-editor, with Eric Feldman, of *Blood Feuds: AIDS, Blood, and the Politics of Medical Disaster.* Bayer's research has examined ethical and policy issues in public health. He is currently involved in a study of the history of public health surveillance. He has received funding from the American Legacy Foundation.

Virginia Berridge is a professor of history at the London School of Hygiene and Tropical Medicine, University of London. She heads a group of historians who research the contemporary history of health and the relationship between science and policy. She is currently researching a study of postwar smoking policy and the changing ideology of public health. Her most recent publication is *Poor Health. Social Inequality Before and After the Black Report.* She declared no competing interests.

Allan M. Brandt is the Kass Professor of the History of Medicine at Harvard Medical School, where he directs the Program in the History of Medicine and the Division of Medical Ethics. He holds a joint appointment in the Department of the History of Science at Harvard University, where he is currently chair. His work focuses on social and ethical aspects of health, disease, and medical practices in the twentieth-century United States. He is the author of *No Magic Bullet: A Social History of Venereal Disease in the United States since 1880;* and the editor of *Morality and Health.* He is currently completing a book on the social and cultural history of cigarette smoking in the United States. He has served as an expert witness for the Department of Justice in *U.S. v. Philip Morris.* His work on the chapter was supported in part by a grant from the Flight Attendants Medical Research Institute.

James Colgrove is a staff associate and doctoral candidate at the Center for the History and Ethics of Public Health, Mailman School of Public Health, Columbia University. His research has examined alcohol and drug policy, harm reduction, and the uses of persuasion and coercion in public health. He is working on a book about the development of vaccination policy in the United States. He declared no competing interests.

Eric A. Feldman is an assistant professor of law at the University of Pennsylvania Law School, a senior fellow at the University of Pennsylvania's Center for Bioethics, and a trustee of the Law and Society Association. He is the author of *The Ritual of Rights in Japan: Law, Society, and Health Policy* and the co-editor, with Ronald Bayer, of *Blood Feuds: AIDS, Blood, and the*

Politics of Medical Disaster. His current research involves the comparative study of law, policy, and public health in the United States and Japan. He declared no competing interests.

Günter Frankenberg teaches public law, philosophy of law, and comparative law at the J. W. Goethe-University in Frankfurt. He has written about public health, sociology, welfare regulation, and more recently the impact of globalization. His books include *Die demokratische Frage (The Democratic Question)* and *Die Verfassung der Republik (The Constitution of the Republic)*. Among his many articles are "Germany: The Uneasy Triumph of Pragmatism," in *AIDS in the Industrialized Democracies*, and "Why Care? The Trouble With Social Rights," *Cardozo Law Review*. He declared no competing interests.

Anna Gilmore, a public health clinician with expertise in tobacco control, is a clinical research fellow in the European Centre on Health of Societies in Transition at the London School of Hygiene and Tropical Medicine, where she heads the Centre's tobacco-control work. Her current research focuses on the wider determinants of health, in particular the impact of trade policies and macroeconomic change on public health. She is currently working on a study funded by the U.S. National Institutes of Health called "Globalisation, the Tobacco Industry and Policy Influence," based on an analysis of internal tobacco industry documents. She has received funds from the European Union and the World Health Organization. She is currently a board member of ASH-UK but was not in this position at the time of writing the chapter.

Evan S. Lieberman is assistant professor of politics at Princeton University, where he teaches classes in comparative politics and research methods. He is the author of *Race and Regionalism in the Politics of Taxation in Brazil and South Africa*. His research has considered the relationship between political institutions, identities, and public policies in comparative perspective. His current research investigates the politics of HIV/AIDS policies in the developing countries. He declared no competing interests.

Antonia Maioni is director of the McGill Institute for the Study of Canada, associate professor of Political Science, and William Dawson Scholar at McGill University. She is also an adjunct professor in the Department of Health Administration at the University of Montreal. She is the author of *Parting at the Crossroads: The Emergence of Health Insurance in the United States and Canada*. Her current research focuses on health care reform in Canada, with a particular emphasis on federal-provincial relations, public opinion, and law and health policy. She declared no competing interests.

Christopher P. Manfredi is professor and chair of the Department of Political Science at McGill University, specializing in Canadian public law and comparative legal systems. He is the author of *Judicial Power and the Charter: Canada and the Paradox of Liberal Constitutionalism*, 2d ed., and *The Supreme Court and Juvenile Justice*. He is currently completing a book on feminist activism in the Supreme Court of Canada. He declared no competing interests.

Theodore R. Marmor is professor of public policy and management at the Yale School of Management, where he specializes in the modern welfare state with an emphasis on medical care and health issues. A consultant to government agencies and foundations since the mid-1960s, he frequently testifies before the Congress about medical care reform, Social Security, and welfare issues. He has been published in a wide range of scholarly journals, leading newspapers, and magazines. His most recent book is the second edition of *The Politics of Medicare*. He has served as an expert witness for the defense in two cases: one brought by a union health fund against the tobacco industry in Ohio and another brought by Empire Blue Cross of New York.

Martin McKee is professor of European public health at the London School of Hygiene and Tropical Medicine and director of the School's European Centre on Health of Societies in Transition. He manages a major research program on health and health policy in central and eastern Europe and the former Soviet Union. His recent books include *EU Law and the Social Character of Health Care* and *International Co-operation and Health*. He has received funds from the European Union and the World Health Organization.

Constance A. Nathanson, a sociologist, is currently professor of clinical sociomedical sciences in the Mailman School of Public Health at Columbia University. Her primary research interests are in two areas: international comparative research on the social and political determinants of public health policies; and determinants of differential mortality by gender and socioeconomic status. She is the author of *Dangerous Passage: The Social Control of Sexuality in Women's Adolescence*. She is completing a book on the comparative politics of public health in the United States, the United Kingdom, Canada, and France. She declared no competing interests.

Index